AFRICA IN WORLD POLITICS

AFRICA IN WORLD POLITICS

edited by
John W. Harbeson
CITY UNIVERSITY OF NEW YORK
and Donald Rothchild
UNIVERSITY OF CALIFORNIA-DAVIS

Westview Press
BOULDER • SAN FRANCISCO • OXFORD

Published in 1991 in the United States of America by Westview Press, Inc., 5500 Central Avenue, Boulder, Colorado 80301, and in the United Kingdom by Westview Press, 36 Lonsdale Road, Summertown, Oxford OX2 7EW

Library of Congress Cataloging-in-Publication Data
Africa in world politics / edited by John W. Harbeson and Donald Rothchild.
p. cm.
Contains papers originally presented at the African Studies Association Meeting in San Francisco in 1989.
Includes index.
ISBN 0-8133-0972-7. ISBN 0-8133-0973-5 (pbk.).
1. Africa—Politics and government—1960—Congresses. 2. World politics—1985-1995—Congresses. I. Harbeson, John W. (John Willis), 1938- . II. Rothchild, Donald S. III. African Studies Association. Meeting (1989 : San Francisco, Calif.)
DT30.5.A3544 1991
960.32—dc20 91-21588
CIP

Printed and bound in the United States of America

The paper used in this publication meets the requirements of the American National Standard for Permanence of Paper for Printed Library Materials Z39.48-1984.

10 9 8 7 6 5 4 3 2 1

CONTENTS

TABLES AND FIGURES

Tables

Figures

ACKNOWLEDGMENTS

We appreciate the encouragement and support of Westview Press editor Barbara Ellington in the planning and development of this book. Special thanks to Pamela Evans and Caroline Hartzell for their editorial assistance in preparing the book for publication. Many of the chapters were first presented by the authors as papers at the African Studies Association meetings in San Francisco in 1989. From those sessions, we were encouraged to believe this book might fill a critical niche in the fields of African studies and international relations. We all hope it will succeed in doing so.

John W. Harbeson
Croton-on-Hudson, New York

Donald Rothchild
Davis, California

1

AFRICA IN POST-COLD WAR INTERNATIONAL POLITICS: CHANGING AGENDAS

JOHN W. HARBESON
AND DONALD ROTHCHILD

The end of the cold war is ushering in a new and as yet uncharted world order. The bipolar world system is losing its hold, and the great powers no longer hold the same sway over the countries of the Third World that they once did. The consequences of this remain unclear at this time. If old security ties with the European powers—particularly France—remain important, a more fluid international relationship portending fundamental changes in the structure of international politics is also apparent. These events will likely have a powerful influence on the agendas of strong and weak countries alike. African states, which have existed on the periphery of world politics since their independence, may become even more peripheral than before. At the same time, an emerging post-cold war order may become both the cause and the result of shifting foreign policy agendas of the major as well as the middle and minor powers. Ironically, as this process unfolds, Africa's concerns may be elevated to a level of importance out of line with its peripheral status in the current world order.

This introductory chapter will start by exploring the outline of these changing foreign policy agendas and their implications for post-cold war international politics. It will then briefly trace the evolution of Africa's participation in world politics, seeking thereby to place the emerging post-cold war relationships in a broader context. Finally, it will identify some of the new issues and opportunities that are likely to emerge as a consequence of this restructuring of Africa's participation in the emerging world order.

Certainly, current trends in international politics point to some significant shifts in the way Africa will interact with the industrialized countries in the years ahead. On the one hand, as John Ravenhill notes in this volume, trade relationships between the Western European countries and their former colonies are in decline. According to one estimate, sub-Saharan Africa accounts for less than 2 percent of current international trade.[1] Such a process of delinkage and marginalization alters the position of the African states in the world arena in important ways, influencing their foreign policy priorities and strategies. How they establish and implement their choices and with what success will prove important determinants of whether changing global agendas will result in intensifying or modifying Africa's peripheral economic and political status and in what ways.

On the other hand, as both cause and effect of the emerging post–cold war international order, the foreign policy agendas of the Western countries may shift in such a manner as to give Africa enhanced standing in world affairs. As bilateral Western-African relations decline in importance in the years ahead, there is no indication that—for the moment, at least—such multilateral donors as the World Bank and the International Monetary Fund (IMF) have shifted away from their efforts to overcome the current developmental stalemate. Paradoxically, at the very time that Western Europe and the United States are disengaging in terms of their bilateral economic relations (see Jeffrey Herbst's chapter in this volume), there has been increased multilateral and bilateral insistence that African countries pattern their economies after those of the major Western powers. The tendency of African governments to transform their economies along market lines may pick up as the Soviet Union and the Eastern European countries abandon statist developmental systems and adopt market-oriented strategies of their own. Africa's concern over the emergence of a powerful new competition for scarce resources in the Eastern European countries may prod its leaders to move toward market economy models in a more determined manner, thereby overcoming their long-held reservations about the desirability and viability of such economic strategies.

Moreover, mounting bilateral and multilateral pressures on the African states to pattern their institutions and policies after the examples set by the advanced industrialized states extend beyond economics and applies also to the realm of political liberalization. Certainly, as Colin Legum stresses, Africans themselves have been at the forefront in demanding more open democratic systems.[2] Yet bilateral and European Community (EC) donors, concerned about the effectiveness of their aid programs, have not hesitated to pick up this cause and to champion it from the outside. For the World Bank and the major donor countries, more effective "governance" is a quite reasonable condition for further economic assistance, as autocratic systems with their repressive tendencies and lack of political accountability have become identified with poorly considered policies and misallocations of scarce resources. The collapse of communism in the Soviet Union and Eastern Europe and the increasing international pressures for economic and political change in China and the Middle East (see Chapter 10 by Naomi Chazan and Victor T. LeVine) have removed the practical alternatives to these bilateral and multilateral programs, leaving Africa with little choice but to work out its own adjustments to these reform programs on a country-by-country basis.

Accompanying this international concern for domestic economic and political structures is a renewed interest in more effective regional economic organizations, something favored by Africans and non-Africans alike. As Carol Lancaster explains in Chapter 12, African countries have invested considerable resources and energy in regional organizations in the past, with generally modest results at best. Regional integration, with its potential for economies of scale and enhanced international leverage, is regarded by Africa's leaders as a means of achieving collective self-reliance. Thus, these African elites look upon regional integration as an alternative to greater dependence on trade with the developed, industrialized countries. Noting this, Thomas M. Callaghy (Chapter 3) points to the increasing IMF–World Bank role in promoting inter-African cooperation through support for African development projects. Such a process of external facilitation of Africa's regional integration is made more plausible by trends toward economic coordination taking place in Europe as well as moves toward strengthened trade regimes in Asia and Latin America.

Finally, the end of the confrontation between the superpowers, with the emerging international agreement on certain basic political and economic norms of relations, may, among other things, lead to greater multilateral cooperation on human and environmental problems. The former category includes difficulties posed by growing numbers of African refugees (estimated in aggregate terms as over five million people[3]), widespread human rights abuses, natural disasters, acute impoverishment exacerbated by unchecked population growth, and the spread of deadly diseases (for example, AIDS). The latter category includes depletion and degradation of soil, water, and air resources and the technical and social obstacles to their alleviation. The cooperation of the Soviets and the Americans in relieving some of the suffering during Ethiopia's famine and drought situations is a precedent that one hopes could be carried over to future human and environmental challenges.

Clearly, in the real world these new agendas and options are inevitably constrained and conditioned by a variety of historical and structural parameters—parameters that can only be modified, not significantly altered, in the foreseeable future. Notable among these relationships that are not easily amenable to transformation is that of Africa's peripheral political and economic status in the contemporary world order. As Achille Mbembe notes: "At the end of the 1980s, the main problem confronting Africa is not just economic dependence but, more importantly, its *strategic depreciation* and decline in international importance. No one knows how long this process of marginalization will continue. Although there is nothing which points to it being irreversible, there is also little which suggests that it will be resolved in the near future."[4] In the next section, we outline the nature of this peripheralization and aspects of the independence process in the early 1960s that contributed to the emerging realities of the post–cold war international order.

THREE PHASES OF AFRICA'S INTERNATIONAL PERIPHERALIZATION

Postcolonial Engagement and Disengagement

In the first two decades of their independence, the new African states emphasized their identification with many of the norms and institutions of the post–Second World War international order, even as they proclaimed their nonalignment in cold-war politics. In part, domestically, African leaders were inclined to reject many of the institutions and values they associated with colonial rule (bills of rights, bicameral legislatures, multiparty systems, federalism, and various other limitations upon executive power), viewing these as alien transplants that obstructed their need for centralized power. They moved promptly to dismantle or recast such legacies, a process described elsewhere as "impedance."[5] In part, however, they accepted with modifications many of the defining features of the contemporary state: political parties, armies, police, bureaucracies, cooperatives, and universities. At the same time, internationally, African states largely endorsed the institutions and values of the inherited state system, including the norm of sovereignty, international law and protocol, membership in the United Nations, and acceptance of the principles enshrined in the U.N. Charter. Acceptance of and participation in the international state system became a significant and continuing source of domestic political legitimacy for the new African countries.[6] In addition, as Stephen D. Krasner notes, the United Nations emerged as an important organizational forum these countries could use to advance their interests.

> The most important organizational manifestation of the principle of sovereign equality has been the United Nations. The U.N. system provided the major forums at which developing countries could present their demands. Developing states have had automatic access to United Nations agencies. With the exception

> of international financial institutions and the Security Council, states have had equal voting power. . . . If the United Nations had not existed, it would have been impossible for the Third World to articulate a general program for altering international regimes.[7]

For their part, the major powers have retained measures of commitment to African and other Third-World countries largely as a consequence of cold war–related strategic and ideological considerations. The United States has also emphasized the importance of trade and investment opportunities in Africa, but, as Thomas M. Callaghy shows in this volume, these tended to decline in most countries in the 1970s and 1980s. To the extent that the two alliances were not sanguine about the prospects of nonalignment, they were inclined to view regional conflicts in zero-sum terms and behaved accordingly. As two Soviet writers put it, the United States and the USSR, intent upon placing their superpower rival at a disadvantage in Africa, pursued risky policies that were not calculated to benefit them directly.[8] In this zero-option game, an adversary's loss represented a gain for the other side. Until their interests and perceptions of one another shifted in the late 1980s, this negative "game" made the great powers vulnerable to pressures from their African allies, unable to pursue mutually beneficial strategies for fear of appearing weak in the eyes of regional and global actors.

The cold war not only led to U.S. and Soviet strategic and ideological alignments, but it also explains in part the involvement of the great powers in Africa's developmental processes. On the one hand, the subtitle of W. W. Rostow's influential work, *The Stages of Economic Growth: A Non-Communist Manifesto,* revealed a linkage, more conscious for some exponents of this approach than others, to be in effect between cold-war bipolarity and thinking on development.[9] Modernization theory projected an evolution from traditional societies to modernity that would involve the incorporation of Western values, including market economies, individualism, pluralism, and political democracy. Whether intended or not, this theory of modernization lent a philosophical and historical rationale to the continued engagement of the United States and other Western countries in the affairs of postcolonial Africa. On the other hand, the Soviet Union and its allies found justification for their activities on the continent in their strong opposition to capitalist practices and in their commitment to fostering a Socialist path to development in Africa. As Marina Ottaway reports in this work, the Soviets moved—albeit with some uncertainty—to encourage the African countries to adopt working concepts of development compatible with Africa's own ultimate ends.

Détente, Changing Priorities, and New Forms of Engagement

Despite sharp military engagements—notably in the war over the Ogaden and in the Angolan civil war—between the different African countries or movements associated with the two superpowers, patterns of major power engagement in Africa began to change in the 1970s. This change came as a consequence of U.S.-Soviet détente,[10] important shifts in the structure of the global economy, the performance of the developing countries, and reflections by non-African and African political actors on these happenings. Some of the switches in preferences regarding alliance patterns and developmental commitments that have come to mark the present period were presaged by the trends already emerging at that time. Bipolar alliances began to loosen, prompting the African and non-African powers to begin to alter their foreign policy agendas. In such areas as economic development, cultural exchange, and communications, the major and middle powers revealed new interests that were not linked to cold-war imperatives. Their disillusionment with Africa's lack of progress also led to a willingness on the part of the great powers to develop new aid and development strategies based on regional realities. As Ottaway indicates, the Soviet Union crafted an approach to development that put increased emphasis upon the peculiar historical circumstances of developing countries. The United States, meanwhile, placed unprecedented emphasis upon "development from below." In its 1973 foreign aid legislation, it encouraged land reform, appropriate technology, participatory development, and broadened access to education and health care at the grass-roots level. Other Western countries shifted their preferences in a similar manner.[11]

In this period, such multilateral organizations as the World Bank and the IMF began to assert greater leadership in shaping a strategy for assisting the developing countries. During Robert McNamara's tenure as president, the World Bank not only emerged as a principal force in drawing attention to the failure of newly independent countries to respond to aid guidelines and to achieve adequate progress; it also charted new directions for developmental assistance.

At the same time, important changes in global economic relations contributed temporarily to an easing of cold-war tensions. These changes were manifested in particular by the rise of Western Europe (most notably West Germany) and Japan as powerful international actors, the steady decline of U.S. economic influence, and the precipitous decline of the Soviet and East European economies. U.S. hegemony "eroded," wrote Kenneth A. Oye, as economic power became dispersed among a number of political actors.[12] This weakening of the U.S. economic hegemony, signaled in part by President Richard Nixon's decision to allow the dollar to float against other currencies, ushered in the dawn of a multipolar economic order. Henceforth the United States would share world leadership with the Western European and Pacific Rim countries, particularly Japan. Such a shift toward economic multipolarity inevitably had important long-term implications for great-power relations with Africa and the Third World generally.

The thaw in the cold war prompted corresponding changes in the way the superpowers began to define their interests vis-à-vis the developing lands. The superpowers, who felt increasingly economically overextended and constrained by domestic political pressures, began the search for ways to move away from costly rivalries in Europe and the Third World and to place greater emphasis upon disengagement and cooperation. It was to prove a slow process marked by repeated setbacks. Yet concern with internal challenges on the part of Soviet and U.S. officials led to an increasing emphasis upon their economic competitiveness in the new global environment. The eventual consequence was a pulling back from security commitments around the world, including a disengagement from regional conflicts in the Third World.

Hence, with the benefit of hindsight it is possible to see that changes were already under way in the 1970s that would lead to a dramatic transformation of superpower relations following the rise of Mikhail Gorbachev to power in the mid-1980s. Although the language of confrontation remained in evidence and regional conflicts continued to erupt in southern Africa and on the Horn, it was nonetheless becoming apparent to all that the rivalry between the great powers was settling into a costly stalemate that was mutually hurtful to the United States and the USSR as well as to Africa. Within Africa itself, independent governments—increasingly overwhelmed with failing economies, weakening state institutions, and declining infrastructures—pressed the industrialized states for additional support to cope with the challenges to their survival. Their appeal for a new international economic order was evidence of a new assertiveness in the face of impending disaster; joining with other Third-World states, Africa's leaders strove to cooperate among themselves to relieve their disadvantageous position in international production and trade. Meanwhile, many states—often committed in principle to some variant of socialism or Afro-Marxism—embarked more aggressively on programs of self-reliant socialism. Thus, at the very time that the superpowers were beginning their lengthy process of disengagement, many African leaders sought to modify the patterns of the past by exerting increasing pressures for external accommodation and support. A disjunction was emerging between Africa's urgent claim for equitable distributions and the preparedness of the First and Second Worlds to respond.

Bilateral Disengagement; Multilateral Engagement

The initial years of the 1980s were marked by mixed signals. At a time when the Reagan administration was ushering in a renewal of cold-war tensions, boosting its expenditures on sophisticated war materiel, and giving increasing military support to African and other anti-Communist insurgent movements, it intensified the search for new ways to increase the competitiveness of the U.S. domestic economy. The Soviets, who for some time had been allocating a significant level of resources to military assistance programs and who were determined to preserve their international credibility as backers of Socialist regimes around the world, maintained their support for their beleaguered Afro-Marxist allies. Even as the wars of Angola and Ethiopia spiraled to new heights of intensity, the superpowers—aware of the mutual damage to them arising from these encounters—began a parallel effort to find new ways of managing their differences. Gradually but perceptibly, the military encounter was transformed into a diplomatic relationship, one that promised a less intense struggle between them in Africa. Yet even while pragmatic perceptions of the national interest were gaining the upper hand, leading in some cases to a cautious reduction in superpower economic as well as military involvement in Africa's affairs, a trend toward expanded multilateral economic assistance was emerging as an increasingly important, externally initiated alternative in the African context. These mixed trends deserve special attention.

Due to changing perceptions regarding each other's intentions, fatigue with Africa's developmental prospects, and the consequences of their various interventions, the superpowers reassessed their interests in Africa and the Third World generally. The result was a slow but perceptible trend toward military disengagement from Africa in the 1980s, facilitated by an increased willingness and ability on the part of the great powers to work together to mediate a variety of international disputes in these areas. Donald Rothchild's chapter examines this phenomenon in depth. U.S.-Soviet cooperation, limited largely to old cold-war confrontations in which they had exercised some influence over the internal actors, has nonetheless enhanced the possibilities for the mediation of intra-African conflict situations, the subject of I. William Zartman's chapter. One byproduct of this new pattern of superpower participation, as René Lemarchand indicates, may have been the isolation of Muammar el-Qaddafi's Libya—a maverick middle-ranking power on the African continent.

In addition, the signs of Western Europe's disengagement from Africa were quite recognizable, as John Ravenhill's chapter makes abundantly clear. The West was in effect delinking, albeit unconsciously for the most part, from Africa while moving toward a globalization of the economies of the industrially and technically advanced countries. Even France—the most aggressive of the Western countries in maintaining its economic, cultural, political, and military ties with the French-speaking states of Africa (see Ali A. Mazrui's discussion of this)—gave indications as of 1990 that it intended to cut back on its aid commitments and to link its contributions to democratic reforms. With the sense of postcolonial burden diminishing (see Jeffrey Herbst's discussion of this phenomenon in the context of the United States), African countries have begun to find themselves in competition with other regions of the world (such as Eastern Europe) for access to the investment capital and aid resources of the developed states.

Trade, aid, and investment flows between Western Europe and Africa are tangible indicators of the process of Africa's marginalization at work. Africa—despite its ties with Europe under the Lome Convention—finds itself in direct competition with other regions of the world for entry into Europe's lucrative market. As John Ravenhill indicates, Western Europe remains Africa's most important trading partner, although Africa's significance for the European market has declined noticeably since 1960. In trade relations, a pattern of diversifications has been occurring, with France and Britain importing a smaller share of commodities and goods from their former colonies but a larger share from their nontraditional African trading partners. Overall, the EC countries have maintained their share of total exports to the African countries but have imported less from them. In the investment field, foreign investors appear to be holding back, wary of what they perceive as the political risks entailed in such ventures. Direct foreign investment in Africa reportedly fell from $2.4 billion in 1982 to $0.8 billion in 1987, presumably reflecting in part divestments in South African companies. With the emergence of competition for scarce capital from Eastern Europe, it seems likely, in the view of at least one observer, that such investments will fall further in the years ahead.[13] Regardless of their reasons (including uneasiness over radical ideologies, corruption, and embarrassment over linkages with apartheid), the reticence of European investors is indicative of a reluctance on the part of Westerners generally to link their fate with that of contemporary Africa. The result is that Africa is left adrift at a time of economic crisis, perpetuating its sense of marginalization, frustration, and anger over its seeming abandonment.

Observers of the African scene have been quick to comment on Europe's delinkage, particularly in the context of the end of the cold war. "With the Cold War virtually behind them," warned Nigerian General Olusegun Obasanjo, "Africa seems to have become of secondary importance to the superpowers."[14] Moreover, in a lead editorial, the influential magazine *West Africa* reflected on the crisis within the franc zone.

> It [the franc zone] is now seriously in deficit, has continuing liquidity problems and is shaken by a banking crisis. France's trade is now declining, its investment is drying up, there are nerves about disengagement and marginalisation. . . . It is perhaps significant that a new report is soon to be published in Paris which apparently recommends a diversification of France's cooperation policy, away from the francophone countries, to elsewhere in Africa and to Asia implying a further trend to the more global development policy outlined by Jean-Pierre Cot as cooperation minister in the early 1980s.[15]

In addition, African leaders have charged that EC officials are losing interest in the Lome Convention, which is a key achievement in European negotiations with the African, Caribbean, and Pacific (ACP) countries. At the March 1990 joint ministerial council meeting in Fiji, only one European minister came to the sessions, and the EC delegation seemed generally unprepared for the talks; this was interpreted by the ACP states as a sign of the Europeans being too distracted by events in Eastern Europe to give full attention to matters affecting them.[16] In brief, such observers discern a diminishing superpower interest in Africa and, notwithstanding its obvious benefits, lay the responsibility for this loss of concern on the ending of the global confrontation between East and West.[17]

Somewhat counterbalancing these trends, Europe continues to be a reasonably steady contributor of economic assistance to Africa, for the most part improving its disbursements to sub-Saharan Africa as a percentage of overseas aid allocations. With the exception of Great Britain, donor fatigue has not yet resulted in significant cutbacks; even so, more and more bilateral and multilateral conditionalities are being placed on the uses to which these aid funds can be put. In this respect, it is significant that the EC under the Lome Convention has quietly begun to press for the acceptance of structural adjustment programs from its African and other Third-World recipients. Moreover, it is apparent that this steady level of EC contributions will not be sufficient to deal with the immense development problems facing the African states. New sources of funding are needed, and it remains to be seen how far such countries as Japan and the other Asian newly industrialized countries (NICs) will go in making additional aid available.

Although the EC and other bilateral donors have conditioned their own programs upon the acceptance of World Bank and IMF guidelines, it is these multilateral agencies themselves that have been most systematic in pressing the African countries to reform their economies. These organizations have emerged as the main economic crisis managers, attempting to cushion the immediate production and distribution difficulties with which these countries are faced and to offer new medium- and long-range alternatives for coping with the grave challenge at hand. Certainly, the dimensions of Africa's development crisis have become well known: per capita growth rates in the 1970s of less than 1 percent, which have been more than counterbalanced by relatively high inflation rates, growing levels of debt, import dependence, and precarious balance of payments difficulties.[18] The essential prescriptions have been applied, with some adaptation to local circumstances, to Africa as a whole: more open, market-driven economies that are less encumbered by state regulation together with measures to devalue inflated currencies, remove urban consumer subsidies, and increase production incentives (especially in the agricultural sector).

Although acknowledging their own misguided efforts to promote African development in the 1960s and 1970s, the World Bank and IMF have looked askance upon Africa's experiments with socialism and self-reliance and have tended to urge the adoption of more liberal economic programs. Their implicit conclusion was that escape from the development trap required African countries to adopt the historical example of the industrialized societies in their early growth period: limiting state expenditures, reducing the size of bureaucracies, privatizing state-owned enterprises, holding down imports, and increasing exports to the industrialized countries. Paradoxically, just as the World Bank and the IMF reform programs intended to promote greater openness to internal and external private investment and increased reliance upon exports are gaining some acceptance in Africa, a number of the developed societies have become absorbed in their own problems of budgetary limitations and international competitiveness and, as a result, are inclined to distance themselves from Africa's pressing concerns. Thus, the reform programs may well have come at an unfortunate juncture in history. Not surprisingly, therefore, World Bank–IMF programs seem limited in their effects, and, after a decade of structural adjustment programs, the sub-Sarahan countries appear to be no better off relative to the world's developing countries as a whole. In fact, during the early and mid-1980s, all but a small handful of countries displayed low, even negative, growth rates.[19]

In referring to contemporary African peripheralization, it is important to recognize that this phenomenon differs to some extent from that described earlier by Samir Amin and other exponents of dependency theory.[20] While the industrialized countries continue to exert an element of hidden control over the late-developing lands, the evidence presented in this book also points to an increasingly determined trend on the part of the rich countries to disengage from the continent, at least in their bilateral economic relations. Instead of a growing dependence upon the exploitation of the periphery, the industrialized countries are focusing more and more on trade among themselves and with some Third-World countries (especially the NICs), allowing their commercial interchanges with the African states to decline in relative, if not in absolute, terms.

Thus, the picture that emerged by the end of the 1980s was one of increasing African peripheralization. The explanation for this phenomenon varied, but it included the end of the cold war, the industrialized countries' disillusionment with the economic and political performance of the African states, and the growing preoccupation of the developed countries with their own domestic problems, especially those relating to their ability to compete effectively with one another. Rather than expand their bilateral assistance programs in any dramatic fashion, therefore, the industrialized countries were inclined to follow behind the leadership of the World Bank and the IMF in seeking an African economic renaissance. This partial disengagement represented no surrendering of hegemony in north-south relations; rather, the industrialized countries adopted a somewhat lower profile in their direct economic encounters with Africa while allowing the World Bank and the IMF to assume the major responsibility for steering African development along pathways consistent with Western experience and preferences.

NEW AGENDAS AND OPPORTUNITIES

What are the prospects that the shifting agendas of post–cold war times will lead to diminished African peripheralization or, failing that, the amelioration of the harsh living conditions with which it is associated? The chapters in this volume explore several critical issues that will influence the manner in which this question will be answered in times to come.

First, a central political issue shaping the nature of Africa's participation in post–cold war world affairs has to do with the nature and role of the state. Central to most contemporary theories of international relations is the continuing centrality of the state as a key unit of action, both internally and externally. Moreover, as noted above, Africa's participation in the international state system has been an important factor in accounting for the stability and survival of some of its fragile states in postcolonial times.[21] Thus, the international state system has been an important political resource in its own right, providing the weak African state with an indispensable legitimacy.[22]

Yet John Harbeson observes in his chapter on the Horn of Africa that the nature, dimensions, and meaning of the state in international relations in at least some African contexts are not givens but variables, outcomes of an extended interactional process rather than axiomatic foundations of international affairs. As both Harbeson and Crawford Young detail in their chapters, the gestation of the state under colonialism played a direct role in shaping these identities in the present period. Such malleability in colonial and postcolonial times is not without its immediate consequences on the African scene, particularly with respect to the process of international exchanges between state-defined identities and those identified along alternative principles in the contemporary period. In this respect, it is necessary to explore the impact of state formation upon various regional experiments (described in this volume by Carol Lancaster) as well as the forms and practices of international conflict mediation examined by I. William Zartman in his chapter on international diplomacy. Moreover, the process by which the major powers are currently disengaging from Africa, analyzed in the chapters by Jeffrey Herbst, Marina Ottaway, Donald Rothchild, and Vitaley Vasilkov, also has an important bearing on the contours of the African state and its relationship to the international community. In brief, international factors are likely to remain important, sometimes critically important, in shaping Africa's ongoing process of state formation and the roles that Africa will play in the post–cold war global order.

Second, the outcomes and effects of the struggle between the multilateral donor agencies and the African countries over structural adjustment will have a powerful impact on the way in which Africa's current peripheralization is modified or intensified (see Thomas M. Callaghy's chapter). They will also affect Africa's success in coping with the consequences of its peripheralization. Certainly, Africa's growing peripheralization will affect its ability to achieve meaningful development in the years ahead. Among other things, an increasing marginalization may complicate the process of regional harmonization and afford less scope to expanded south-south economic linkages. After over a decade of experimentation, no final conclusion has yet been reached regarding the effects of structural adjustment programs; moreover, there is no agreement on the next steps to be taken to achieve an African economic renaissance.

Third, in discussing Africa's participation in the rapidly changing global environment, it is important not to lose sight of a wide range of social and humanitarian issues. These are no longer regarded as exclusively domestic questions but as ones that help to determine Africa's participation in the international arena. In periods of reduced tensions between the global superpowers, the international agenda tends to hold security concerns steady while placing greater emphasis upon pressing social considerations. In this event, a long list of alternative agenda items comes to the fore, including human rights, democratic institutions, AIDS, drugs, pollution control, the management of scarce natural resources, and refugees. A key issue is whether, in the post–cold war order, these issues will be left to Africa's leaders to wrestle with on their own or whether the major powers will adopt a perspective of enlightened self-interest and provide generous support, enabling African governments to develop the capabilities to cope with these challenges on their own.

Finally, Ali A. Mazrui focuses our attention upon an underlying issue that has been long dormant but never wholly forgotten: whether the long cycle of African subordination to cultural as well as political and economic domination will yield to a new cycle that allows for the expression of genuinely African conceptions of state formation and socioeconomic structures. Neither Socialist nor non-Socialist approaches to development have performed effectively in postindependence Africa, providing the African peoples with the breathing room they might utilize to create new definitions of the polity, the developmental process, and international interactions. In this respect, Africa's peripheralization might set the stage for an African cultural renaissance that brings with it legitimate and possibly more viable approaches to political and economic affairs. In time, such a process might well set the foundation for a genuine autonomy, facilitating the transformation of the continent's peripheralized status in times to come.

It is to these issues that this book now turns.

NOTES

1. World Bank, *World Development Report 1990* (New York: Oxford University Press, 1990), Table 14, pp. 204–205.

2. Colin Legum, "Africa: Who Is Behind the Demand for Multi-Party Democracy?" *Third World Reports*, O.C/2 (July 18, 1990):2.

3. Kimberly A. Hamilton, "Africa's Uprooted: A Status Report," CSIS *Africa Notes*, no. 117 (October 29, 1990):5.

4. Achille Mbembe, "Economic Liberalization and the Post-Colonial African State," in Richard Joseph (ed.), *Beyond Autocracy in Africa* (Atlanta: Carter Center, 1989), p. 125.

5. Donald Rothchild and Robert L. Curry, Jr., *Scarcity, Choice and Public Policy in Middle Africa* (Berkeley: University of California Press, 1978), pp. 61–90.

6. Robert H. Jackson and Carl G. Rosberg, "Why Africa's Weak States Persist: The Empirical and the Juridical in Statehood," *World Politics* 35, no. 1 (1982):1–25.

7. Stephen D. Krasner, *Structural Conflict: The Third World Against Global Liberalism* (Berkeley: University of California Press, 1985), p. 8.

8. Andrei Kozyrev and Andrei Shumikhin, "East and West in the Third World," *International Affairs* (Moscow), no. 3 (March 1989):66.

9. W. W. Rostow, *The Stages of Economic Growth: A Non-Communist Manifesto* (Cambridge: Cambridge University Press, 1960).

10. Marita Kaw, "Choosing Sides: Testing a Political Proximity Model," *American Journal of Political Science* 34, no. 2 (May 1990):460.

11. Although there has been no overall analysis of this remarkable period in regard to U.S. foreign assistance policies, its theoretical foundations are articulated in Coralie Bryand and Louise White, *Managing Development in the Third World* (Boulder, Colo.: Westview Press, 1982); Hollis Chenery et al., *Redistribution with Growth* (New York: Oxford University Press, 1974); David Korten and Rudi Klauss, *People-Centered Development* (West Hartford, Conn.: Kumarian Press, 1984); and Milton Esman and Norman Uphoff, *Local Organizations: Intermediaries in Rural Development* (Ithaca: Cornell University Press, 1984).

12. Kenneth A. Oye, "International Systems Structure and American Policy," in Kenneth A. Oye, Robert J. Lieber, and Donald Rothchild (eds.), *Eagle Defiant: United States Foreign Policy in the 1980s* (Boston: Little, Brown and Co., 1983), p. 7.

13. General Olusegun Obasanjo, "Eastern Promises," *West Africa*, May 7–13, 1990, p. 762.

14. General Olusegun Obasanjo, *Africa in Today's World* (Ota, Nigeria: African Leadership Forum, 1988), p. 21.

15. Editorial, "France, Africa, and Democracy," *West Africa*, April 9–15, 1990, p. 567.

16. Shada Islam, "Lome IV: Frayed Tempers," *West Africa*, April 16–22, 1990, p. 636.

17. See Martin Lowenkopf, "If the Cold War Is over in Africa, Will the United States Still Care?" CSIS *Africa Notes*, no. 98 (May 30, 1989):1–2.

18. Among the various World Bank publications on this topic are World Bank, *Accelerated Development in Sub-Saharan Africa: An Agenda for Action* (Washington, D.C.: The World Bank, 1981); and *Sub-Saharan Africa: From Crisis to Sustainable Growth* (Washington, D.C.: The World Bank, 1989).

19. World Bank, *Sub-Saharan Africa: From Crisis to Sustainable Growth*, pp. 221–222. Sub-Saharan Africa's per capita gross national product (GNP) increased an average of 0.1 percent between 1973 and 1980 and decreased 2.8 percent between 1980 and 1987. Excluding Nigeria, the figures were −0.7 percent and −1.2 percent, respectively. In absolute terms, rates of growth in production for the two periods were 2.5 percent and 0.5 percent, respectively, although if Nigeria is excluded, the figures are 1.7 percent and 2.3 percent, respectively.

20. See Samir Amin, *Accumulation on a World Scale: A Critique of the Theory of Underdevelopment*, vols. 1 and 2 (New York: Monthly Review Press, 1974); and *Unequal Development: Essays on the Social Transformation of Peripheral Capitalism* (New York: Monthly Review Press, 1976).

21. Jackson and Rosberg, "Why Africa's Weak States Persist," pp. 1–25.

22. Warren F. Ilchman and Norman Thomas Uphoff, *The Political Economy of Change* (Berkeley: University of California Press, 1969), p. 32.

PART ONE

DETERMINANTS OF AFRICA'S INTERNATIONAL RELATIONS

2
THE HERITAGE OF COLONIALISM

CRAWFORD YOUNG

Africa, in the rhetorical metaphor of imperial jingoism, was a ripe melon awaiting carving in the late nineteenth century. Those who scrambled fastest won the largest slices and the right to consume at their leisure the sweet, succulent flesh. Stragglers snatched only small servings or tasteless portions; Italians, for example, found only deserts on their plate. In this mad moment of imperial atavism—in Schumpeterian terms, the objectless disposition to limitless frontier expansion—no one imagined that a system of states was being created. Colonial rule, assumed by its initiators to be perpetual, later proved to be a mere interlude in the broader sweep of African history; however, the steel grid of territorial partition that colonialism imposed appears permanent.

Colonial heritage is the necessary point of departure for analysis of African international relations. The state system—which is, transnational vectors notwithstanding, the fundamental structural basis of the international realm—inherits the colonial partition. A few African states have a meaningful precolonial identity (Morocco, Tunisia, Egypt, Ethiopia, Burundi, Rwanda, Madagascar, Swaziland, Lesotho, and Botswana), but most are products of the competitive subordination of Africa—mostly between 1875 and 1900—by seven European powers (Great Britain, France, Germany, Belgium, Portugal, Italy, and Spain).

AFRICAN COLONIAL HERITAGE COMPARED

The colonial system totally transformed the historical political geography of Africa in a few years' time, and the depth and intensity of alien penetration of subordinated societies continues to cast its shadow.[1] The comprehensive linkages with the metropolitan economies in many instances were difficult to disentangle. In the majority of cases in which decolonization was negotiated, the colonizer retained some capacity to shape the choice of postcolonial successors and often—especially in the French case—enjoyed extensive networks of access and influence after independence was attained. The cultural and linguistic impact was pervasive, especially in sub-Saharan Africa. Embedded in the institutions of the new states was the deep imprint of the mentalities and routines of their colonial predecessors. Overall, colonial legacy cast its shadow over the emergent African state system to a degree unique among the major world regions.

In Latin America, although colonial administrative subdivisions shaped the state system, Spain and Portugal swiftly ceased to be major regional players after Creole elites won independence in the nineteenth century. Great Britain and, later, the United States were the major external forces impinging upon the region. In Asia, the first target and long the crown jewel of the colonial enterprise, imperial conquest tended to follow the contours of an older state system; not all Asian states have a historical pedigree (the Philippines, Pakistan, Papua New Guinea), but a majority do. The circumstances surrounding Asian independence, the discontinuities imposed by the Japanese wartime occupation of Southeast Asia, and the larger scale of most Asian states and the greater autonomy of their economies all meant that the demise of the colonial order was far more sharp and definitive than was the case in Africa.

Perhaps the closest parallel to Africa in terms of durable and troubled colonial impact on regional international relations is found in the Middle East. The partition of the Ottoman domains in the Levant between Great Britain and France and the imperial calculus employed in territorial definitions and structures of domination left in their wake a series of cancerous conflicts. Thrones had to be found for Great Britain's Hashemite allies; the duplicity of incompatible wartime promises to Arabs and Zionists bore the seeds of inextricable conflict over whether the Palestine mandate awarded to Great Britain by the League of Nations would develop as a Jewish homeland or an Arab state; Great Britain invented Jordan as a territory for its wartime ally Prince Abdullah; Lebanese borders were drawn so as to maximize the zone of dominance for Maronite Christians; Sunni Arab nationalism in Syria was countered by heavy recruitment of minority Alawites for the colonial militia; and Kurdish state demands were denied so that oil-rich zones could be attached to the British-Iraqi mandate.[2] The unending turbulence in this region provides daily confirmation of the colonial roots of many intractable contemporary conflicts. But even here colonial penetration of Middle Eastern Arab societies and economies was much less than was the case in Africa, and the erstwhile colonial connections weigh less heavily.

In the African instance, the shadow of the colonial past falls upon the contemporary state system in several critical features. The sheer number of sovereign units and the weakness and vulnerability of many due to their small scale are the most obvious. The continuing importance of former economic and political colonial linkages, most of all for the twenty states formerly under French rule, significantly shapes regional politics—both as an active channel of influence and a negative point of reference. Most of the festering regional crises that torment the continent—Western Sahara, Eritrea, Sudan, southern Africa—are rooted in one way or another in ill-considered decolonization strategies driven by metropolitan interests. This chapter will consider in turn these components of the colonial heritage.

FRAGMENTATION OF AFRICA

The African continent in 1990 (and its offshore islands) contained no fewer than fifty-two sovereign units (using U.N. membership as the criterion)—nearly one-third of the world total.[3] Although this large number has some advantages in guaranteeing a voice in international forums where the doctrine of sovereign equality assures equal voting rights for states large and small, this is little compensation for the disabilities of being tiny. Sheer economic weakness is one disadvantage; in 1988 in all of Africa only South Africa had a gross national product (GNP) exceeding that of Hong Kong.[4] Most African states had a GNP less than the Harvard University endowment or the profits of a major multinational corporation. The limits of choice imposed by a narrow national market and circumscribed agricultural and mineral resource bases rendered most states highly vulnerable to the vagaries of commodity markets and the workings of the global economic system. Although some minuscule mercantile states elsewhere have achieved prosperity—Singapore is an obvious example—and tiny sovereignties perched on vast oil pools may accumulate enormous wealth—Bahrein, Qatar, and United Arab Emirates are illustrations—the rapid Iraqi military seizure of Kuwait in 1990 amply demonstrated the vulnerability of the small state, however rich. Of the microstates among Africa's fifty-two polities, only Mauritius has prospered.

The full scope of the fragmentation of independent Africa was not apparent until the virtual eve of independence. Most of the vast sub-Saharan domains under French domination were joined in two large administrative federations, *Afrique Occidentale Française* (AOF) and *Afrique Equatoriale Française* (AEF). Political life, however, germinated first at the territorial level; the crucial 1956 *Loi-cadre* (framework law) located the vital institutions of African political autonomy at this echelon. Although some nationalist leaders dreamed of achieving independence within the broader unit, especially in the AOF, the wealthier territories (Ivory Coast, Gabon) were opposed to this. In the final compressed surge to independence, the interaction of divisions among nationalist leaders and movements combined with French interests resulted in twelve states of modest size rather than two large ones.[5] In the 1950s Great Britain did promote federations of its colonial possessions as a formula for self-government in the West Indies, the United Arab Emirates, and Malaysia, as well as east and central Africa, but with indifferent success. In east and central Africa, the fatal flaw was linking the project of broader political units to the entrenchment of special privilege for the European settler communities. Thus contaminated, the federation idea was bound to fail.[6] In instances in which large territories had been governed as single entities—Nigeria, Sudan, Zaire—independence as one polity was possible, although all three countries have at times been beset by separatist pressures.

Once sovereignty gave life to colonial territories as independent nations, the African state system has proven to be singularly refractory to broader movements of unification. The 1964 unification of Tanganyika and Zanzibar to form Tanzania remains the sole case of political amalgamation. This occurred only in extraordinary circumstances—the bizarre overthrow of the first independent Zanzibar government by a small armed band led by Ugandan herder John Okello, who returned to obscurity as swiftly as he emerged to leadership. This unexpected act set in motion events that made amalgamation of these two unequal units suddenly feasible; to this day, however, the integration of Zanzibar with mainland Tanzania remains incomplete.

DREAM OF AFRICAN UNITY

The dream of a broader African unity persists, first nurtured by intellectuals of the diaspora and expressed through a series of pan-African conferences beginning in 1900, then embraced by the radical wing of African nationalism in the 1950s, above all by Kwame Nkrumah of Ghana. The Organization of African Unity (OAU) was created in 1963 to embody this dream, but even its charter demonstrated its contradictions. The OAU was structured as a cartel of states whose territorial integrity was a foundational principle. Rather than transcending the state system, the OAU consolidated it.

The urgency of regional and ultimately continental unification is repeatedly endorsed in solemn documents, including the 1980 Lagos Plan of Action and the 1989 African alternative framework to structural adjustment programs of the Economic Commission for Africa.[7] Innumerable regional integration schemes have been launched, of which the most important are the *Union du Maghreb Arabe*, the Economic Community of West African States, the Southern African Development Coordination Council, and the various customs and monetary unions of the francophonic west African states.[8] But the goal of effective integration remains elusive; the impact of the colonial partition remains an enduring obstacle.

The colonial origins of most African states weighed heavily upon the consciousness of postindependence rulers. Initially, the fundamental illegitimacy of the boundaries was a central tenet of pan-African nationalism; the 1945 Manchester Pan-African Congress excoriated "the artificial divisions and territorial boundaries created by the Imperialist Powers." As late as 1958, the Accra All-African Peoples' Conference denounced "artificial frontiers drawn by the imperialist Powers to divide the peoples of Africa" and called for "the abolition or adjustment of such frontiers at an early date."[9] But once African normative doctrine was enunciated by the states rather than by nationalist movements, the tone changed, and the sanctity of colonial partition frontiers was asserted. The consensus of the first assembly of African independent states—also in Accra in 1958—was expressed by Nkrumah, the leading apostle of African unification: "Our conference came to the conclusion that in the interests of that Peace which is so essential, we should respect the independence, sovereignty and territorial integrity of one another."[10]

The OAU Charter makes reference to territorial integrity no less than three times; at the Cairo OAU summit in 1964, the assembled heads of state made the commitment even more emphatic by a solemn pledge to actively uphold existing borders, a level of responsibility that goes significantly further than the mere passive recognition of the inviolability of frontiers.[11] Although a certain number of boundary disputes have arisen in independent Africa, the principle of the sanctity of colonial partition boundaries—the juridical concept of *uti possidetis*—remains a cornerstone of a solidifying African regional international law.[12] Most of the disputes have been resolved by negotiation, applying the colonial treaties as the point of juridical reference.[13] The enduring fear of the fragility of the African state system paradoxically endows the artificial colonially imposed boundaries with astonishing durability.

The colonial system profoundly reordered economic as well as political space. During their seventy-five years of uncurbed sovereignty, colonial powers viewed their African domains as veritable *chasses gardées*. Metropolitan capital enjoyed privileged access; to varying degrees, other capital was viewed with reserve or even hostility (especially by the Portuguese until the final colonial years). The security logic of the colonial state joined the metropolitan conviction that the occupant was entitled to exclusive economic benefits in return for the "sacrifice" of supplying governance services to foster trade and investment linkages, which tied African territories to metropolitan economies as subordinated appendages. Territorial infrastructures, particularly the communications systems, were shaped by the vision of imperial integration; road nets ran from the centers of production to the ports and colonial capitals. Although over time a shrinkage of the once-exclusive economic ties with the erstwhile colonizers has occurred, these bonds were so pervasive that they have been difficult to disentangle. It is no accident that regional economic integration schemes joining states once under different colonial jurisdictions have had only limited success; the most resilient mechanism of regional economic cooperation has been the CFA franc zone, a product of the economic space defined by the former French empire in sub-Saharan Africa.

INFLUENCE OF FORMER COLONIZERS

The colonial occupation of Africa, which occurred relatively late in the global history of imperial expansion, was comparatively dense and thorough. The multiplex apparatus of domination, which was constructed to assure the "effective occupation" stipulated by the 1884–1885 Berlin Conference as a condition for the security of the proprietary title and to extract from the impoverished subjects the labor service and fiscal tribute to make alien hegemony self-financing, as metropolitan finance ministries required, was unlikely to dissolve instantly once the occupying country's flag was lowered on independence day. Over time, the many linkages—both manifest and submerged—binding the decolonized state to the former metropole have slowly eroded. They were a central dimension in the international relations of new states, especially in the early years of independence. Even more than three decades later, especially in the case of France, colonial connections still play a significant role.

Several factors influence the importance of ties with former colonizers. In those cases in which independence was won through armed liberation struggles rather than bargaining, the power transfer brought initial rupture (Algeria, Guinea-Bissau, Mozambique, Angola). In some other cases (Guinea, Zaire), the circumstances of independence brought immediate crisis and discontinuity in relationships; even though relations were ultimately restored, the degree of intimacy between the two countries could never be the same. Generally, the smaller erstwhile colonial powers played a less visible role than did the two major imperial occupants, Great Britain and France.

Italy was largely eliminated by being on the losing side in World War II. Although it regained a ten-year trust territory mission in Somalia in 1950, Rome was never permitted to return to Libya and Eritrea and quickly ceased to be a factor in either territory. Spain was the last country to enter the colonial scramble, and it had only a superficial hold on its territories in northwest Africa (former Spanish Morocco, Ifni, Western Sahara, Equatorial Guinea). Its minor interests were swallowed up in postcolonial turmoil in its erstwhile domains (the Moroccan annexation of Western Sahara, the Macias Nguema capricious tyranny in Equatorial Guinea from its independence in 1968 until 1979). Emblematic of Spain's elimination from Africa was the affiliation of Equatorial Guinea with the French-tied CFA franc zone after Macias Nguema was overthrown in 1979.[14]

Belgium retained an important and uninterrupted role in its small former colonies of Rwanda and Burundi, but its economic interests in these states were not large. In Zaire, where the financial stake was considerable, relationships were punctuated with repeated crises.[15] The sudden and aborted power transfer left inextricably contentious disputes over the succession to the extensive colonial state holdings in a wide array of colonial corporations. These disputes were seemingly resolved several times, only to reemerge in new forms of contention.[16]

In the Portuguese case, an imperial mythology of the global Lusotropical multiracial community was a keystone of the corporatist authoritarianism of the Salazar-Caetano *Estado Novo*. However, the utter discrediting of this regime by its ruinous and unending colonial wars in Africa from 1961 to 1974 brought it repudiation. More broadly, in the postcolonial era, a common element for the minor participants in the African partition was an abandonment of earlier notions that overseas proprietary domains validated national claims to standing and respect in the international arena.

Particularly intriguing has been the relative effacement over time of Great Britain on the African scene. Great Britain has long seen itself as a great power, although the resources to support such a claim silently ebbed away because of imperial overreach, according to one influential analysis.[17] In the 1950s, as the era of decolonization opened for Africa, conventional wisdom held that Great Britain was the most likely of the colonizers to maintain a permanent role in its vast colonial estates because of the flexible framework for evolution supplied by the British Commonwealth. This illusion proved to be based upon false inferences deduced from the older constellation of self-governing dominions, which had remained closely bound in imperial security relationships with London. Many thought the commonwealth could preserve a British-ordered global ensemble beyond the formal grant of sovereignty in Asia and Africa. The illusion of permanence in which British imperialism so long basked dissipated slowly.[18] The doctrine enunciated at the 1926 Imperial Conference still dominated official thinking as the African hour of self-government approached. This document perceived the future as incorporating "autonomous communities within the British Empire, equal in status, in no way subordinate one to another in any aspect of their domestic or external affairs, though united by a common allegiance to the Crown and freely associated as members of the British Commonwealth of Nations."[19] As one of its commentators then wrote,

"The British Empire is a strange complex. It is a heterogeneous collection of separate entities, and yet it is a political unit. It is wholly unprecedented; it has no written constitution; it is of quite recent growth; and its development has been amazingly rapid."[20]

These lyrical notions of a global commonwealth's operating in a loose way as a political unit in world affairs so that Great Britain's claim to major power status might survive the decolonization of the empire eroded slowly. India's independence in 1947 was a crucial turning point; the true jewel in the imperial crown, its metamorphosis from the pivot of empire security to a self-assertive "neutralist" Asian power should have ended the illusion that an enlarged commonwealth could remain in any sense a "political unit." Yet when African members of the commonwealth began joining Ghanaian independence in 1957, some of the older mystique still persisted.

For most former British territories, joining the commonwealth formed part of the *rite de passage* of independence; only Egypt and Sudan declined to enter its ranks.[21] Paradoxically, as commonwealth membership became numerically dominated by Asian, African, and Caribbean states, it ceased to serve as a loose-knit, worldwide, British-inspired combine, and its meetings became occasions for heated attacks on British policy in Rhodesia and South Africa. Instead of the ingenious instrument for the subtle nurture of British global influence imagined by its designers, the commonwealth thus seemed a funnel for unwelcome pressures upon British diplomacy. Even imperial nostalgia could not stave off recognition of these facts; waning British interest removed the commonwealth's energizing center. In the words of a recent study, "the Commonwealth has survived only in [a] very attenuated form . . . [it is] still a useful argumentative forum for its governments, offering a place for small states to be heard, extending benefits (albeit on a modest scale) to its members, and providing opportunities for discussion of problems of common interest."[22] This adjustment in the British images of the commonwealth goes hand in hand with the gradual reduction of London's self-perception—from global hegemon to middle-sized European power.

The diminishing mystique of the commonwealth as the vessel for a global British role helps to explain the relative effacement of Great Britain on the African scene. In the first years of African independence, British disposition for intervention was still visible. In the army mutinies that swept Uganda, Kenya, and Tanganyika, British troops intervened to check the mutineers, at the request of the embattled regimes. In Nigeria, Great Britain initially had a defense agreement; however, this was annulled in 1962 due to Nigerian nationalist pressure. In a number of cases, national armies remained under British command for a few years after independence; in 1964, the British commander of the Nigerian army refused the solicitation of some Nigerian leaders to intervene after scandal-ridden national elections brought the country to the brink of disintegration. Security assistance and economic aid in modest quantities continue, and in a few cases—most notably Kenya—influence remains significant. But since 1970 the relatively subdued role of Britain, if set against the expectations of 1960, is what stands out.

THE FRENCH CONNECTION

The case of France, which has played a pervasive role in the seventeen sub-Saharan states formerly under its rule, is completely different from that of Great Britain. The political, cultural, economic, and military connection Paris has maintained with the erstwhile *bloc africain de l'empire* has been frequently tutelary, often intrusive, and sometimes overtly interventionist. The intimacy and durability of these linkages are as surprising as the eclipse of the United Kingdom. When African independence loomed on the horizon, France still suffered from its World War II humiliation and bitter internal divisions. The country was weakened by the chronic instability of the Fourth Republic, with one-third of its electorate aligned with the antiregime Stalinist French Communist party and its army locked in unending and unwinnable colonial wars—first in Indochina, then in Algeria. *France Against Itself* was the title of the most influential portrait of the epoch;[23] few anticipated the recapture of its European status and sub-Saharan role as regional hegemon under the Fifth Republic.

In grasping the pervasive African role of the resurrected postcolonial France, one needs first to draw a sharp distinction between the Maghreb and sub-Saharan Africa, which is sometimes overlooked in the fascination with the French connection. In reality, French influence was shattered in what had been the most important parts of the former empire—North Africa and Indochina. In terms of the size of the economic stake, AOF and especially AEF were far behind the core regions of the imperial era. Psychologically, the heart of overseas France was Algeria, whose northern portions were considered to be full French departments. The savagery of the eight-year war for Algerian independence, especially the self-destructive fury of its final phases, compelled the exodus of most of the one million French settlers and the abandonment of much of their stranglehold on the Algerian economy.[24] The independent Algerian state pursued a consistently radical anti-imperial foreign policy, rendered financially possible by its relatively ample oil and natural gas revenues. Although Tunisia and Morocco were less assertive in international politics and leaned to Western positions in their nonalignment, neither accepted the degree of French tutelage that was common in sub-Saharan Africa.

Several factors explain the comprehensive nature of the French relationship with sub-Saharan states formerly under its domination.[25] The terminal colonial effort in this zone to construct an elusive "federalism" as permanent institutional bonding, while failing in its manifest goal of defining political status short of independence, had important consequences. The representation accorded emergent African leaders in the Fourth and (briefly) the Fifth Republics in French institutions drew much of the sub-Saharan independence generation into the heart of French political processes. In the Algerian instance, Paris representation was dominated by settler interests and a small number of collaborating Algerians; Tunisia and Morocco, which had a different international legal status, were not given parliamentary seats.

Although electoral manipulation occurred in sub-Saharan Africa as well, nonetheless those Africans chosen were far more representative of emergent political forces. As early as the 1946 constitutional deliberations, Leopold Senghor of Senegal played an influential role. By the late Fourth Republic, African leaders held ministerial positions (Felix Houphouet-Boigny of the Ivory Coast, Modibo Keita of Mali). Until literally the eve of independence, the "federal" formula the Fifth Republic Constitution sought to institutionalize had the assent of most of the current political class, with the exception of the more radical intelligentsia—especially the students. The referendum approving the Fifth Republic Constitution in 1958 drew large, usually overwhelming majorities in all sub-Saharan territories except Guinea, reflecting the strong wishes of the African leadership for its approval. Jarring as his words now sound, Houphouet-Boigny spoke for a political generation in his often-quoted 1956 statement: "To the mystique of independence we oppose the reality of fraternity." The degree of incorporation of the sub-Saharan African political elite into the French political world has no parallel, and it left a lasting imprint on the texture of postcolonial relationships. Successive French presidents from de Gaulle to Mitterrand brought to office long-standing intimate ties with many sub-Saharan political leaders.

The original Fifth Republic concept of sub-Saharan territorial automony with an array of core sovereign functions (defense, money, and justice, for example) vested in the France-centered French community swiftly vanished.[26] In its place emerged an array of devices giving institutional expression to intimacy. Some form of defense accords was negotiated with fourteen sub-Saharan ex-colonies;[27] French troops were permanently garrisoned in Djibouti, the Central African Republic, Gabon, the Ivory Coast, and Senegal; and a reserve intervention force earmarked for swift African deployment was held in readiness in France. Except for Guinea, Mali, Mauritania, and Madagascar, all these ex-colonies remained within a French currency zone (and Guinea and Mali eventually sought reentry).

By the 1970s, Franco-African summit conferences became a regular and lavish part of the diplomatic landscape; often these attracted more heads of state than the OAU summits. *Francophonie* as a cultural instrument finds expression in the French educational systems and linguistic policies; the nurture of the French language enjoys a priority in French diplomacy that is unique among former colonizers. In the Maghreb, *francophonie* competes with the active policies of affirmation of the Arab language and culture; in sub-Saharan Africa (excepting Madagascar and Mauritania), retention of French as the primary state vehicle has been internalized as a political value by most of the state class.[28] Even a populist leader such as Alphonse Massemba-Debat of Congo-Brazzaville exclaimed in the late 1960s that the Congolese and the French were "Siamese twins," separable only by surgery.[29] Senghor, who was the most intellectually brilliant member of the independence political generation, summed up the pervasive relationship as *francité* (Frenchness, Francehood).[30] Such a neologism has plausible resonance in the Franco-African case, but its analogs would be preposterous in characterizing any other postcolonial ties.

A singular form of tutelary, or dependent, linkages results from this broad-front set of connections, not all of which are well captured in the visible aspect of politics or in the asymmetrical core-periphery economic flows to which "dependency theory" draws attention. The francophonic African community counts upon the senior French partner to defend its interests within the European Community and among the international financial institutions, both public and private. Priority access to French aid is assumed, including periodic budgetary bailouts for the more impoverished states.[31] French willingness to occasionally intervene militarily to protect clients is of crucial importance; between 1963 and 1983, Guy Martin tallies twenty instances of such intervention.[32] As then-President Giscard d'Estaing stated, "We have intervened in Africa whenever an unacceptable situation had to be remedied."[33] Perhaps even more critical to the nurture of tutelary standing are French security services of a more clandestine nature. French intelligence services provide invaluable protection to rulers by their capacity to monitor and penetrate opposition groups and to foil potential conspiracies by providing early warning to incumbents. These security operations have always enjoyed high-level attention in Paris through such presidential advisers as *eminence grise* Jacques Foccart; currently, Mitterrand entrusts these functions to his son, Jean-Christophe Mitterrand.

In the early 1990s, there are some signs that the silken threads binding francophonic Africa to France may begin to fray. France made no move to prevent the overthrow of Hissene Habre by armed insurgents enjoying Libyan support in Chad at the end of 1990, although French troops in Chad could easily have prevented the takeover. Nor did France lift a finger to avert the collapse of the Moussa Traore regime in Mali in April 1991.[34] Supporting the CFA franc zone is more expensive and less profitable than it once was. Pessimism has spread concerning Africa's infirm economic and political condition.[35] Protection of friendly incumbents appears to have lost some of its attractions, as in early 1990 France moved away from its long-held view that single-party rule, with its corollary of life presidency, was the most "realistic" political formula for Africa.[36] But the closely woven fabric of the French connection is too sturdy to quickly unravel.

STRUGGLE TO ELIMINATE COLONIAL INFLUENCE

The importance of the colonial past in shaping contemporary African international relations is thus beyond dispute. At the same time, the colonial system serves—paradoxically—as a negative point of reference for the African concert of nations. The legitimacy of the first generation of African regimes was rooted in the regimes' achievement—by conquest or negotiation—of independence. The two transcendant unifying principles of the pan-African movement from its inception have been opposition to both colonialism and racism, evils that were joined on the African continent. The independent states that assembled to create the OAU in 1963 were divided on many questions of ideology and interpretation of nonalignment; all could rally behind the combat to complete the liberation of Africa from colonial occupation and regimes of white racial domination. The elemental notion of African solidarity arose out of the shared experience of racial oppression, a point made explicit by W.E.B. Dubois many years ago:

> There is slowly arising not only a curiously strong brotherhood of Negro blood throughout the world, but the common cause of the darker races against the intolerable assumption and insults of Europeans has already found expression. Most men in this world are coloured. A belief in humanity means a belief in coloured men. The future world will in all reasonable possibility be what coloured men make of it.[37]

Nearly five decades later, Julius Nyerere translated these thoughts into African nationalist language: "Africans all over the continent, without a word being spoken, either from one individual to another, or from one African country to another, looked at the European, looked at one another, and knew that in relation to the European they were one."[38]

Indeed, at the moment of the OAU's creation, many of the most arduous independence struggles still lay ahead, such as the Portuguese territories, Zimbabwe, Namibia, and the mortal combat with apartheid in South Africa. The OAU has a mediocre record in coping with inter-African conflicts (Eritrea, Western Sahara, the Nigerian civil war, the Zaire rebellions, and Chad-Libya, for example). However, its anticolonial role has been important in providing a continental focus for African liberation diplomacy.

Within their own territorial domain, independent states faced a compulsion to demarcate themselves from their colonial past, to render visible the new status. The superficial symbolic accoutrements of independence—flags and postage stamps—might serve for a time. Africanization of the state apparatus might help as well, although over time the perception could arise that the real benefits of this change accrued above all to state personnel.

The imperative of demarcation eventually spread to the economic realm. In the 1970s, a wave of seizures of foreign assets with potent colonial connotations swept through Africa: Idi Amin's "economic war" against the Asian community in 1972, Mobutu Sese Seko's "Zairianization" and "radicalization" campaigns of 1973 and 1974, Tanzania's socialization measures after the 1967 Arusha Declaration, the 1972 and 1976 Nigerian "indigenization decrees," the copper mine nationalizations in Zambia and Zaire, and parallel measures in many other countries. Measures of expropriation of foreign assets almost exclusively affected holdings associated with the colonial past. This partly reflected a distinction often made between postindependence investments, which involved contractual commitments (presumably) freely made by the African state, and those made under alien sovereignty, which lacked moral standing (and doubtless had been well amortized). More important, moves to indigenize the economy reflected pressures to move beyond purely political independence, which would be denatured if all the structures of economic subordination remained intact. By the 1980s, this surge of economic demarcation had run its course; the deepening economic crisis and heightened vulnerability to external pressures made such measures unfeasible. In addition, the measures were frequently discredited by the chaotic improvisation of their implementation and consequent dislocations (Zaire, Uganda) or by the perception that only narrow mercantile classes had benefited (Nigeria).[39]

The compulsion for demarcation from the colonial past was driven by psychological as well as political and economic factors. Particularly in sub-Saharan Africa, the colonial era brought a broad-front assault upon African culture that was far more comprehensive than similar experiences in the Middle East and Asia. The "colonial situation," to borrow Georges Balandier's evocative concept,[40] was saturated with racism. African culture was for the most part regarded as having little value, and its religious aspect—outside the zones in which Islam was well implanted—was subject to uprooting through intensive Christian evangelical efforts, which were often state-supported. European languages supplanted indigenous ones for most state purposes; for the colonial subject, social mobility required mastering the idiom of the colonizer. In innumerable ways, colonial subjugation in Africa brought not only political oppression and economic exploitation but also profound psychological humiliation. In the nationalist response to colonialism, psychological themes are prevalent to a degree unique in Third-

World anti-imperialist thought. Frantz Fanon, the Martinique psychiatrist who supplied so powerful a voice to the Algerian revolution, was only the most eloquent such spokesman.[41] Such doctrines as *négritude* and "African personality" were central components in nationalist thought, asserting the authenticity and value of African culture. This dimension of African nationalism gave a special emotional edge to the postcolonial quest for demarcation, as well as to the fervor of African state reaction to racism and colonialism.

Colonial heritage as a negative point of reference also influenced the contours of cold-war intrusion into Africa. The United States and the Soviet Union both represented themselves as alternatives to the African nations' exclusive reliance upon the erstwhile colonizers for succor and support. Particularly in the early phases of independence, visible Soviet linkages served as a badge of demarcation. The extravagant fears of all colonizers—and of the West generally—of "Communist penetration" of Africa enhanced the value of Soviet relations, even if Soviet economic assistance was minimal. For those states who wanted (or felt compelled to undertake) a more comprehensive break with the Western colonial system, for a brief moment in the early 1960s and again in the late 1970s, the Soviet bloc appeared to offer an alternative—a hope that quickly proved illusory.

COLONIAL ROOTS OF REGIONAL CRISES

A final legacy of the colonial system is the series of regional crises it has left in its wake, particularly in southern Africa and the Horn. In southern Africa, the roots of conflict can be ultimately traced to the catastrophic British mistake of transferring power to an exclusively white regime in South Africa in 1910. Imperial security calculus at the time focused exclusively upon the relationships between the English and Afrikaner communities. Virtually the only concession to African interests was the retention of colonial sovereignty over the Basutoland, Bechuanaland, and Swaziland protectorates. The terms of the Act of Union ultimately led to apartheid in South Africa. The year before the doctrine of "paramountcy of native interests" was proclaimed for Kenya in 1924, Great Britain granted full internal self-government to the white settlers in Southern Rhodesia (now Zimbabwe), an error that resulted in a costly liberation war before independence based upon equal rights for all Zimbabweans was won in 1980. When the hour of decolonization sounded elsewhere in Africa, South Africa, Rhodesia, and the Portuguese were in a position to construct a solid redoubt of white domination, which left the oppressed no other choices than the passive acceptance of permanent exploitation or armed uprising. The ensuing militarization of society on all sides had far-reaching consequences: Some of these were positive, such as the 1974 army coup that ended corporatist autocracy in Portugal; others were much more negative, such as the entrenchment of competing insurgent movements in Angola. When independence came to Angola and Mozambique after the 1974 Portuguese coup, the white redoubt shrank, but it escalated its efforts to new and more destructive levels by arming, supplying, and guiding insurgent forces—the União Nacional para a Independência Total de Angola and the Resistência Nacional Mozambiquano. The ultimate cost is incalculable: the literal destruction of civil society in Mozambique and endless civil war with heavy external involvement in Angola with a colossal wastage of its precious oil revenues, which are entirely absorbed in military operations.[42] Only the full dismantling of apartheid—deracialization of the South African polity to undo the false decolonization of 1910—can bring this infernal cycle of violence to an end.

In the case of the Horn, the spiral of decomposition affecting both Ethiopia and Sudan reflects choices made at the moment of decolonization when external strategic interests overrode regional considerations. The decision made by the United Nations General Assembly in 1952 to turn Eritrea over to Ethiopia was powerfully influenced by U.S. desires to enjoy an air and communications base at Asmara and to nurture a developing military cooperation with Ethiopia. Eritrean preferences were divided at the time, and significant sentiment in favor of union existed among the highland populations. However, there was overwhelming insistence on distinctive and autonomous institutions for Eritrea (elected assembly; its own government, language rights, and flag); the reluctant and apprehensive acquiescence of coastal Muslims to the federation, as a fait accompli imposed from without, was absolutely conditioned upon this automony. Once the veil of sovereignty enveloped Eritrea, Ethiopia moved to progressively dismantle the autonomous institutions, finally moving to full annexation in 1962 with no protest from the United Nations or the United States, which was the chief sponsor of the settlement. The result has been a thirty-year war for independence, which has taken untold casualties, devastated Eritrea, militarized Ethiopia, and now threatens Ethiopia's very survival.[43]

In the case of Sudan, as Sudanese nationalism—Arab-centered and concentrated in the north—forced the pace of change in the 1950s, British state interests were above all anti-Egyptian, particularly after the Free Officers seized power in Cairo in 1952. The prime British objective in the decolonization negotiations was to ensure that Sudan became independent separate from its "condominium" partner Egypt. The ransom of this goal was deference to the northern Sudanese desire for a unitary state under their control. The deepening fears of southern Sudanese of their subordination to a state that defined itself as Arab and Muslim—identities they did not share—and their marginalization by the northern elite were ignored. As in Eritrea, the reaction was swift; by 1960, a hydra-headed revolt was in evidence in a number of southern zones. Southern insurrection was brought to a momentary halt in 1972 by a creative political settlement; however, by 1983 its terms had been flagrantly violated, and guerrilla war broke out again—this time at a higher level of violence and associated with widespread famine-induced starvation, which took 250,000 lives in 1988. Beyond the guerrilla forces and the national army, diverse groups of armed bands have proliferated, and the banalization of violence permeates daily existence. The indictment of decolonization policy and of earlier colonial policies that encouraged regional division in Sudan cannot cover all of the miscalculations, insensitivities, and repression that have followed 1956 independence in Sudan. Colonial legacy nonetheless is an inseparable element in any pattern of explanation.[44]

The Western Sahara is yet another festering sore in which an aborted decolonization opened the wound. In this instance, although Spain belatedly abandoned its short-lived (1958–1973) experiment to fully incorporate the colony as an "overseas province," the brief effort begun in 1973 to encourage institutions of autonomy was soon caught between the independence demands of the *Frente Popular para la Liberación de Saguia el Hamra y Rio de Oro* and Moroccan annexation claims. With Franco on his death bed and with grave fears about instability that might lie ahead, Spain simply abandoned the territory when faced with the threat of the October 1975 Moroccan *marche verte*.[45]

Thus, in various ways, the colonial heritage intrudes into postindependence African international relations. Perhaps more than three decades after the great surge to independence in 1960, the colonial shadow will begin to fade. Important new trends that may tug colonial legacy further into the background will have a critical impact in the 1990s. The end of the cold war will certainly have a profound influence. The depth of the economic crisis and a widening consensus that regional integration that bridges the old colonial divisions is indispensable to overcoming them may lead to innovations in the state system that will begin to transcend the colonial partition. The prospect of some settlement of the South African crisis could bring peace to a tormented region and permit movement beyond the bitter residues of the colonial situation. For the first thirty-plus years of African independence, however, colonial heritage has powerfully shaped the African international system.

NOTES

1. For a more extended argument on the pathology of the African colonial state, see Crawford Young, "The African Colonial State and Its Political Legacy," in

Donald Rothchild and Naomi Chazan (eds.), *The Precarious Balance: State and Society in Africa* (Boulder, Colo.: Westview Press, 1988), pp. 25–66.

2. Great Britain was awarded a mandate over the former Ottoman provinces, which became Iraq, by the League of Nations; Iraq achieved nominal independence in 1930 but remained within a British sphere of influence until the late 1950s. In the extensive literature on these themes, I have found especially useful Charles Issawi, *An Economic History of the Middle East and North Africa* (New York: Columbia University Press, 1972); Peter Sluglett, *Britain in Iraq 1914–1932* (London: Ithaca Press, 1976); William Roger Louis, *The British Empire in the Middle East 1945–1951: Arab Nationalism, the United States, and Postwar Imperialism* (Oxford: Clarendon Press, 1984); George Antonius, *The Arab Awakening* (New York: Capricorn Books, 1965); and Mary C. Wilson, *King Abdulla, Britain and the Making of Jordan* (Cambridge: Cambridge University Press, 1987).

3. This total does not include Western Sahara, which is recognized as a member state by the Organization of African Unity (OAU) but not by the United Nations (UN). Eritrea is a likely addition to the total in the 1990s.

4. World Bank, *World Development Report 1990* (New York: Oxford University Press, 1990), pp. 178–179.

5. The most careful political history of this process of fragmentation is Joseph-Roger de Benoist, *La Balkanisation de l'Afrique Occidentale Française* (Dakar: Nouvelles Editions Africaines, 1979). His study clearly demonstrates that the balkanization was less a product of Machiavellian French design than the outcome of a complicated interplay of African political competition and French improvised response. Resentment of the distant bureaucratic despotism of the AOF French administrative headquarters was common in the outlying territories. Those nationalist leaders who at various times fought to preserve the unit—Leopold Senghor, Sekou Toure, Modibo Keita—were constrained both by their own rivalries and by the absence of a strong popular attachment to the AOF as a geographical entity.

6. Among the works on this subject, see Arthur Hazlewood (ed.), *African Integration and Disintegration* (London: Oxford University Press, 1967); Joseph S. Nye, *Pan-Africanism and East African Integration* (Cambridge: Cambridge University Press, 1965); Patrick Keatley, *The Politics of Partnership* (Harmondsworth: Penguin Books, 1964); Philip Mason, *Year of Decision: Rhodesia and Nyasaland in 1960* (London: Oxford University Press, 1960); and Donald S. Rothchild, *Toward Unity in Africa: A Study of Federalism in British Africa* (Washington, D.C.: Public Affairs Press, 1960).

7. Robert S. Brown and Robert J. Cummings, *The Lagos Plan of Action vs. the Berg Report* (Lawrenceville, Va.: Brunswick Publishing Company, 1984); and United Nations Economic Commission for Africa, *African Alternative Framework to Structural Adjustment Programmes for Socio-Economic Recovery and Transformation* (AAF-SAP), E/ECA/CM> 15/6/rev. 3, 1989.

8. See, among others, Ahmed Aghrout and Keith Sutton, "Regional Economic Union in the Maghreb," *Journal of Modern African Studies* 28, no. 1 (1990):115–139; and Elaine A. Friedland, "S.A.D.C.C. and the West: Cooperation or Conflict?" *Journal of Modern African Studies* 23, no. 2 (1985):287–314.

9. Saadia Touval, *The Boundary Politics of Independent Africa* (Cambridge, Mass.: Harvard University Press, 1972), pp. 22–23, 56–57.

10. *Ibid.*, p. 54.

11. Onyeonoro S. Kamanu, "Secession and the Right of Self-Determination: An O.A.U. Dilemma," *Journal of Modern African Studies* 12, no. 3 (1974):371–373.

12. *Uti possidetis* is derived from a Roman private law concept, which holds that pending litigation the existing state of possession of immovable property is retained. Translated into international law, the phrase means that irrespective of the legitimacy of the original acquisition of territory, the existing disposition of the territory remains in effect until altered by a freely negotiated treaty. For a passionate attack on this doctrine by a Moroccan jurist, see "'L'uti possidetis' ou le non-sens du 'principe de base' d l'OUA pour le reglement des differends territoriaux," *Mois en Afrique* 217–218 (February-March 1984):3–30.

13. For major studies on African boundary issues, see, in addition to the previously cited Touval work (note 9), Carl Gosta Widstrand (ed.), *African Boundary Problems* (Uppsala: Scandinavian Institute of African Studies, 1969); A. I. Asiwaju, *Partitioned Africans: Ethnic Relations Across Africa's International Boundaries 1884–1984* (London: C. Hurst & Co., 1984); Yves Person, "L'Afrique Noire et ses frontieres," *Revue Française d'Etudes Politiques Africaines* 80 (August 1972):18–42; and Ian Brownlie, *African Boundaries: A Legal and Diplomatic Encyclopedia* (Berkeley: University of California Press, 1979).

14. On the limited nature of Spanish rule, see Ibrahim Sundiata, *Equatorial Guinea* (Boulder, Colo.: Westview Press, 1989); and Tony Hodges, *Western Sahara: The Roots of a Desert War* (Westport, Conn.: Lawrence Hill & Co., 1983).

15. For thorough detail, see Gauthier de Villers, "Belgique-Zaire: Le grand affrontement," *Cahiers du CEDAF* 1–2 (1990).

16. For detail on the *contentieux*, see Crawford Young and Thomas Turner, *The Rise and Decline of the Zairian State* (Madison: University of Wisconsin Press, 1985), pp. 276–325.

17. Paul Kennedy, *The Rise and Fall of the Great Powers: Economic Change and Military Conflict from 1500 to 2000* (New York: Vintage Books, 1987).

18. The phrase is drawn from the intriguing study by Francis G. Hutchins, *The Illusion of Permanence: British Imperialism in India* (Princeton: Princeton University Press, 1967).

19. Cited in Cecil J. B. Hurst et al., *Great Britain and the Dominions* (Chicago: University of Chicago Press, 1928), p. 9.

20. *Ibid.*, p. 3.

21. South Africa, which had been a member since its accession to "dominion" status in 1910, quit in 1961 in the face of increasing attack from the swelling ranks of African members.

22. Dennis Austin, *The Commonwealth and Britain* (London: Routledge and Kegan Paul, 1988), pp. 62, 64.

23. Herbert Luthy, *France Against Itself* (New York: Meridian Books, 1959).

24. For a graphic account of the holocaust during the final year of the Algerian war, with a mutinous army and a murderous settler force—the Organization de l'Armée Secrète—see Paul Henissart, *Wolves in the City: The Death of French Algeria* (New York: Simon and Schuster, 1970).

25. Useful studies on this topic include Edward Corbett, *The French Presence in Black Africa* (Washington, D.C.: Black Orpheus Press, 1972); Guy Martin, "Bases

of France's African Policy," *Journal of Modern African Studies* 23, no. 2 (1985):189–208; George Chaffard, *Les carnets secrets de la decolonisation* (Paris: Calmann-Levy, 1965); Pierre Pean, *Affaires africaines* (Paris: Fayard, 1983); and Charles-Robert Ageron, *Les chemins de la decolonisation de l'empire français 1936–1956* (Paris: Editions du CNRS, 1986).

26. For a painstaking account by a highly informed French observer, see Joseph-Roger de Benoist, *Afrique Occidentale Française de 1944 à 1960* (Dakar: Nouvelles Editions Africaines, 1982).

27. Martin, "Bases of France's African Policy," p. 204.

28. One encounters some exceptions among the intelligentsia; one example was the late Cheikh Anta Diop of Senegal, a cultural nationalist of great influence who strongly urged promotion of the most widely spoken Senegalese language, Wolof. But overall the commitment to French as the cultural medium is far more entrenched in the former French sub-Saharan territories than anywhere else in Africa.

29. Corbett, *The French Presence*, p. 66.

30. Leopold Sedar Senghor, *Ce que je crois: négritude, francité et civilisation de l'universel* (Paris: B. Crasset, 1988).

31. In theory, financial injections to meet budgetary crises—most commonly payments to civil servants—have long ceased; in practice, they continue to occur. For fascinating details on the process and its political importance, see Raymond Webb, "State Politics in the Central African Republic." Ph.D. dissertation, University of Wisconsin–Madison, Department of Political Science, 1990.

32. Martin, "Bases of France's African Policy," p. 194.

33. *Ibid.*

34. See the special issue of *Africa Report* devoted to "France and Africa: The End of an Era" 36, no. 1 (December-January 1991).

35. Symptomatic was the appearance in 1990 of an array of major reportage on the African situation in leading French newspapers, bearing such titles as "The Shipwreck of Africa," "The Failure of Africa," "What to Do About Africa?" More generally, there seems to be reason to expect, as Ravenhill argues, that the gradual pattern of economic disengagement from Africa by former colonizers will continue and perhaps accelerate in the 1990s.

36. See *Africa Confidential* 31, no. 5 (9 March 1990) for details.

37. Quoted in Victor Bakpetu Thompson, *Africa and Unity: The Evolution of Pan-Africanism* (London: Longman, 1969), p. 36.

38. Lecture by the author at Wellesley College, Wellesley, Massachusetts, April 1961; from my notes.

39. For details, see Crawford Young, *Ideology and Development in Africa* (New Haven: Yale University Press, 1982).

40. Georges Balandier, "The Colonial Situation," in Pierre van den Berghe (ed.), *Africa: Social Problems of Change and Conflict* (San Francisco: Chandler Publishing Company, 1965), pp. 36–57.

41. See, for example, Frantz Fanon, *Black Skin, White Masks* (New York: Grove Press, 1967). On this theme, see also O. Mannoni, *Prospero and Caliban: The Psychology of Colonization* (London: Methuen, 1956); and A. Mennoni, *Portrait du colonise, precede du portrait du colonisateur* (Paris: Buchet-Chastel, 1957).

42. For some calculations on the magnitude of the damage done by South African destabilization in the region, see Joseph Hanlon, *Beggar Your Neighbors: Apartheid Power in Southern Africa* (Bloomington: Indiana University Press, 1986).

43. On the Eritrean case, see Berekhet Habte Selassie, *Conflict and Intervention in the Horn of Africa* (New York: Monthly Review Press, 1980); I. M. Lewis (ed.), *Nationalism and Self-Determination in the Horn of Africa* (London: Ithaca Press, 1983); Richard Sherman, *Eritrea: The Unfinished Revolution* (New York: Praeger, 1980); John Markakis, "The Nationalist Revolution in Eritrea," *Journal of Modern African Studies* 26, no. 4 (1987):643–668; and Mesfin Araya, "The Eritrean Question: An Alternative Explanation," *Journal of Modern African Studies* 28, no. 1 (1990):79–100.

44. For two excellent scholarly monographs reflecting southern and northern Sudanese perspectives, see Dunstan M. Wai, *The Africa-Arab Conflict in the Sudan* (New York: Africana Publishing House, 1978); and Mohammed Omar Beshir, *The Southern Sudan: Background to Conflict* (London: William Blackwood and Sons, 1968).

45. Half a million Moroccans signed on to participate in this proposed citizen invasion and annexation of the western Sahara; 145,000 actually began the move to the frontier. For details, see Hodges, *Western Sahara*.

3

AFRICA AND THE WORLD ECONOMY: CAUGHT BETWEEN A ROCK AND A HARD PLACE

THOMAS M. CALLAGHY

MARGINALIZATION AND DEPENDENCE

A leading historian of Africa, in referring to the precolonial era, has pointed to "the paradox of Africa's simultaneous involvement and marginalization in the world economy" and has said that "Africa was becoming less significant to the world economy at the same time as it involved itself more closely in international commercial relationships." This paradox "operates in the opposite direction" as well: The world's "increasing involvement in the African economy . . . is also at odds with the decreasing economic importance of Africa" for the world economy.[1] In the early 1990s, this paradox is still valid; in fact, it is probably more applicable now than it was earlier.

Increased Marginalization: Postneocolonialism

The increased marginalization of Africa is twofold—economic and politico-strategic—and both aspects are tightly linked in their consequences. The first, primarily economic, aspect is that Africa is no longer very important to the major actors in the world economy (multinational corporations, international banks, the economies of the major Western countries, or those of the newly industrializing countries such as Korea, Taiwan, Brazil, and Mexico) and that economy's changing international division of labor. The second aspect of Africa's marginalization is that, with the end of the cold war, African countries have little politico-strategic importance for the major world powers.

Africa produces a declining share of the world's output. The main commodities it produces are becoming less and less important or are being produced more effectively by other Third-World countries. Trade is declining; nobody wants to lend; and few want to invest except in narrowly defined mineral enclave sectors.

Africa's per capita income levels and growth rates have declined since the first oil crisis in 1973, while its percentage of worldwide official development assistance rose from 17 percent in 1970 to about 30 percent in 1987.[2] Nominal gross domestic product (GDP) has risen more slowly than that of other developing countries since 1970 despite terms of trade and export prices that have been, on average, slightly better than those for other regions. In fact, African real GNP growth rates have dropped dramatically since 1965. Other developing countries performed better in spite of the poor world economic climate, especially in the 1980s. African export levels have stayed relatively flat—in some cases actually declining after 1970—while those of other developing countries have risen significantly. The continent's world market share for non-oil primary products declined from 7 to 4 percent between 1970 and 1985. If the 1970 share had been maintained, 1986–1987 export earnings would have been $9 to $10 billion higher a year. Compared to other regions of the world, Africa's average annual growth rates for exports have fared poorly.

The marginalization of African countries becomes even more obvious when their performance is compared with that of other low-income countries. This is particularly true in regard to South Asia, with which Africa has the most in common. (South Asia is composed of Bangladesh, Bhutan, Burma, India, Maldives, Nepal, Pakistan, and Sri Lanka.) The difference in per capita GDP growth between the two regions is striking—Africa's has declined dramatically while that of South Asia has risen slowly but steadily. Africa's population growth rate continues to climb while that of South Asia has begun to decline.

The most startling differences between the two regions relate to the level and quality of investment. Africa's investment as a percentage of GDP declined in the 1980s while that of South Asia continued to increase despite the difficult economic conditions of the decade. South Asia followed better economic policies and, above all, provided a much more propitious socio-economic and politico-administrative context for investment. This is most vividly manifested in the comparative rates of return on investment: Africa's fell from 30.7 percent in the 1960s to just 2.5 percent in the 1980s while South Asia's increased slowly but steadily, if only marginally, from 21.3 percent to 22.4 percent in the same period.

A similar picture emerges from the comparative figures for the growth of production for both agriculture and industry. In 1965 manufacturing accounted for 9 percent of economic activity in Africa, and by the late 1980s it had risen to only 11 percent—much of which was extremely inefficient by world standards. As a result, by the 1980s there was little interest by major actors in the world economy in lending or investing in Africa. From 1983 to 1985, for example, net nonconcessional capital flows to Africa dropped from more than $8 billion to less than $1 billion.

Given this dismal economic performance, both substantively and comparatively, it is not surprising that world business leaders take an increasingly jaundiced view of Africa. As one business executive expressed it, "Who cares about Africa; it is not important to us; leave it to the IMF [International Monetary Fund] and the World Bank."[3] Some observers have referred to this phenomenon as *postneocolonialism*. For the most dynamic actors in a rapidly changing world economy, even a neocolonial Africa is not of much interest, especially after the amazing changes wrought in Eastern Europe and elsewhere beginning in 1989. According to this viewpoint, the African crisis should be left to the international financial institutions as a salvage operation, and if that effort works, fine; if not, so be it; the world economy will hardly notice.

Thus, whatever one thinks about the role of foreign merchant, monopoly, and finance capital, it is important to remember that Africa increasingly imposes enormous difficulties on these actors, such as political arbitrariness and administrative, infrastructural, and economic inefficiency. Foreign capital has considerable ability to select the type of state with which it cooperates; thus, it is doubtful that Africa will play any significant role in current shifts in the patterns of production in the international division of labor. For most external business people, Africa has become a voracious sinkhole that swallows their money with little or no longer-run return. From this perspective, the laments of international organizations and development economists about the intractable underdevelopment of Africa are not just a conspiratorial attempt to conceal the pillage of Africa but are rather a reflection of the fact (although they would not put it this way) that Africa, from the point of view of major private economic actors, is an underexploited continent with weak states and weak markets.

Disinvestment, in fact, has emerged as a new trend. Between 1980 and 1990, for example, 43 of 139 British firms with industrial investments in Africa withdrew their holdings—mostly from Zimbabwe, Nigeria, and Kenya—despite ongoing economic reforms. Ironically, the retrenchment has been due in part to the economic reforms themselves, as they removed overvalued exchange rates and import tariff protection. The British firms were unwilling to inject new capital to make their investments efficient by world standards of competitiveness. Although Japan is now the major donor to Africa, it is not likely to be a major investor. During the 1980s, for example, the number of Japanese commercial companies operating in Kenya declined from fifteen to two.[4] U.S. investment in Kenya has also dropped. A number of African countries—including Ghana and Kenya—are attempting to attract new investment by creating export processing zones, but with little success so far. The dismal lessons learned by Western investors from the dramatic changes in China in 1989 have made them much less willing to consider investment in the Third World, especially in a place such as Africa.

The second aspect of Africa's marginalization is politico-strategic, but with negative economic consequences. Africa has become of much less interest to the major world powers with the dramatic changes in the international arena in the late 1980s, especially the end of the cold war with a seriously weakened Soviet Union and a liberated Eastern Europe, the rise of Japan as a major world power with much more influence in the IMF and the World Bank, the dynamism of other East Asian newly industrializing countries, and the preoccupations of the Latin American debt crisis, which—unlike the African one—is big enough to pose a serious threat to international financial stability. As one senior African diplomat put it, "Eastern Europe is the most sexy beautiful girl, and we are an old tattered lady. People are tired of Africa. So many countries, so many wars."[5] Even the French are beginning to reassess their special relationship with Africa.

Debates about Africa used to pit internationalists concerned about big-power rivalry against regionalists concerned with African issues.[6] Ironically, the internationalists have now voluntarily ceded the field to the regionalists. The latter used to call for the major powers not to turn Africa into an international battlefield but rather to let Africans solve their own problems—to leave Africa alone. Now that the internationalists have declared the game over, the regionalists are desperately searching for a rationale to keep external interest and resources focused on Africa. The dramatic changes of 1989, Africa's politico-strategic marginalization, and the search for a new foreign policy rationale by Western industrial democracies have meant that economic conditionality is now to be joined by forms of political conditionality under the assumption that, as in Eastern Europe, economic and political liberalization must go hand in hand.

Increased Involvement: The New Neocolonialism

Yet, in other ways Africa has become more tightly linked to the world economy. This increased involvement has two aspects: (1) an extreme dependence on external public actors, particularly the IMF and the World

Bank, in the determination of African economic policy, and (2) the liberal or neoclassical thrust of this economic policy conditionality, which pushes the continent toward more intense reliance on and integration with the world economy. Both of these aspects are linked directly to Africa's debt crisis.

In 1974 total African debt was approximately $14.8 billion; by 1989 it had reached an estimated $143.2 billion. For 1988–1989 alone it jumped 2.6 percent, compared to a 1.0 percent increase for total Third-World debt in the same year. Most of this increased amount came from the international financial institutions, especially the IMF and the World Bank. Roughly 80 percent of Africa's debt is government or government-guaranteed medium- and long-term debt and thus is rescheduled by Western governments through the Paris Club, not by the private banks as is the case in Latin America. A key norm of the debt regime is that countries cannot obtain Paris Club rescheduling relief without being in the good graces of the IMF and the World Bank.[7]

By Latin American standards, even the total African debt is small. Despite its small aggregate size by world standards, however, the striking buildup of African debt puts a terrible strain on fragile economies. By the end of the 1980s, the debt was the equivalent of 350 percent of exports or more than 80 percent of total GNP. Africa's debt service ratio averaged nearly 30 percent by the mid-1980s, with some countries having much higher rates. The debt service ratio for 1989 would have been only half as much, however, if African export growth had kept pace with the performance of other less developed countries.

Given these enormous debt burdens in the context of fragile economies, African countries have benefited from rescheduling concessions such as longer repayment and grace periods, lower interest rates, and the rescheduling of previously rescheduled debt. Since the 1988 Group of Seven summit in Toronto, Africa—especially the low-income countries—has also begun to receive some debt cancellation—even from the United States, which strongly opposed it at first. In June 1990 the French announced debt cancellation for four middle-income countries—Cameroon, Côte d'Ivoire, the Congo, and Gabon. Given the speed with which debt to the major international financial institutions is accumulating, however, this relief is quite modest. Arrears to the IMF and the World Bank are becoming an increasingly serious problem. Ongoing economic reform efforts could be threatened if these institutions cease disbursement to countries in arrears, which they are supposed to do according to their bylaws.

As in other areas of the Third World, this difficult external debt burden and the resulting desperate need for foreign exchange have made African countries highly dependent on a variety of external actors, all of whom have used their leverage to "encourage" economic liberalization. This process, which some have referred to as *the new neocolonialism* means intense dependence on the International Monetary Fund, the World Bank, and major Western countries for the design of economic reform packages and the resources needed to implement them. This leverage has been converted into intensive economic policy conditionality: specific economic policy changes in return for borrowed resources. The primary thrust of these reform efforts is to integrate African economies more fully into the world economy by resurrecting the primary-product export economies that existed at the time of independence and making them work better this time by creating a more "liberal" political economy.

One good indicator of this increased international involvement is the number of African countries that have ongoing relationships with the IMF and the World Bank. Between 1970 and 1978 African countries received 3 percent of the total assistance from IMF-approved economic reform programs. Their share of the total number of IMF programs for this period was 17 percent; this rose to 55 percent by 1979. In 1978 only two African countries had agreements with the IMF. In early March 1990, twenty-eight countries had such agreements, which accounted for 60 percent of the agreements at that time. Six of the IMF's sixteen Stand-By agreements were with African countries; none of the four longer-term Extended Fund Facilities, which are often rewards for reform progress, were African, while thirteen of the seventeen Structural Adjustment Facilities and ten of the eleven Enhanced Structural Adjustment Facilities, both on longer and more concessional terms, were with African countries. Zaire had both Stand-By and Structural Adjustment Facility agreements. Most of the countries had simultaneous agreements with the World Bank. African countries have the highest number of repeat programs of any region in the world. Between 1979 and early 1986, twenty-eight African states had a total of ninety-five programs, and twenty-four had more than one program. Seven countries had two programs; two had three programs; eight had four; three had five; three had six; and one had seven. By 1990 the reach of the IMF and the Bank was nearly complete in Africa, as Mozambique, Angola, and Namibia have become members.[8]

In sum, Africa's current dismal situation is not caused predominantly by its relationship to the world economy or to dominant countries or actors in the international state system. Clearly, however, what happens to Africa will be the *combined* result of the effects of world market forces, the international state system, African socioeconomic structures, and the nature and performance of African state structures. Africa has always been relatively marginal to the world economy. It is now becoming even more so, and at an accelerating rate. In many respects, Africa is lost between state and market. It wanders between an ineffective state and weak markets, both domestic and international, and the latter are increasingly indifferent. Many

African officials fail to realize just how unimportant Africa is becoming to the world economy; they still fear this economy and seek to run from it. Many of them are still looking for a shortcut, a quick fix, while world events since 1980 show that one does not exist. If African countries are to survive, changes must be made. If not, changes in the world political economy will continue to pass Africa by, with very serious long-term consequences for the people of the continent.

This was made clear by the World Bank in the summer of 1990 when it announced that poverty would be in decline in every region of the Third World except Africa by the year 2000. In Africa, poverty is expected to increase significantly, even with optimistic assumptions about policy reform, aid, and world economic conditions. Even with such assumptions, Africa's share of the world's poor is expected to double from 16 to 32 percent. The Bank admits, however, that the outcome could be "much worse."[9]

In the context of Africa's increased marginalization, dependence, and poverty, I will look first at the experience with economic reform in the 1980s, the factors that facilitated and impeded it, the near collapse of an "implicit bargain" between African governments and external actors about resource flows, and the nature and extent of policy learning over the decade. With the frustratingly modest results of these efforts in mind, I will then examine the debate that raged between African and Western officials at the end of the 1980s and the beginning of the 1990s over what to do. The early 1990s brought the threat of an even more intrusive form of conditionality. I will assess this new political conditionality, which is supposed to improve African governance, thereby increasing the chances of successful economic reform. I will conclude by discussing some prospects for the future, particularly the increasing differentiation between African countries and two key factors that will affect it—levels of state capacity and the nature and openness of the world economy.

THE POLITICAL ECONOMY OF ATTEMPTED ECONOMIC REFORM IN THE 1980s

By the early 1980s the key question was not whether Africa had a serious economic crisis, but rather what to do about it. Avoiding the problem and policy drift were common reactions despite external warnings and pressure. Much of the African response was to rail against the prescriptions of external actors. For those governments that did decide—out of conviction or a desperate need for foreign exchange and debt rescheduling—to attack the problem, the dilemmas were enormous, the risks great, and the uncertainties pervasive. Throughout the 1980s economic reform did take place in Africa in large and small ways. Many countries went through the motions of reform or at least appeared to do so, resulting in a series of small reforms. Few cases of large reform—that is, multisector and sustained over time—appeared, however.

Ghana, in fact, is the only clearcut example of large reform, and it illustrates the enormous difficultes entailed in such reform. Dr. Kwesi Botchwey, Ghana's longtime finance minister, portrays the problems vividly:

> We were faced with two options, which we debated very fiercely before we finally chose this path. I know because I participated very actively in these debates. Two choices: We had to maneuver our way around the naiveties of leftism, which has a sort of disdain for any talk of financial discipline, which seeks refuge in some vague concept of structuralism in which everything doable is possible. . . . Moreover, [we had to find a way between] this naivete and the crudities and rigidities and dogma of monetarism, which behaves as if once you set the monetary incentives everybody will do the right thing and the market will be perfect.[10]

As the Rawlings regime in Ghana discovered, neither position is fully correct: Everything is not possible, and policy incentives do not ensure that markets will work well. In addition, a revenue imperative exists whatever path is chosen. Resources have to come from somewhere. In 1982 and early 1983, the Rawlings government engaged in a series of radical mobilization efforts, such as using students to harvest and transport food and repair roads, and turned to the Soviets and East Europeans for assistance. While the radical mobilization efforts had some success, the government realized that they could not be sustained over time, and the Soviets and East Europeans politely but firmly suggested that Ghana should turn to the Western countries, the IMF, and the World Bank for assistance. A rare conjuncture of factors has allowed the economic reform efforts in Ghana to be sustained, and Ghana's success at large reform—itself still fragile—is rare on the continent.[11]

How, then, do we explain the varied abilities of African governments, caught as they are between strong and often contradictory internal and external pressures, to engage in sustained economic reform? The degree to which an African government can adjust appears to be determined by its ability to insulate itself from the political logics, characteristics, and effects of the statist syndrome that has dominated Africa since independence. The ability to insulate is affected primarily by the following variables: (1) the manner in which the economic crisis is perceived by African rulers—particularly whether it is caused by external or internal factors and is temporary or systemic; (2) the degree to which decision-making is influenced by technocratic rather than political considerations—patron-client politics and rent-seeking, for example; (3) the degree of the government's autonomy from powerful sociopolitical forces and groups, particularly relating to distributional demands; (4) the administrative capabilities of the state apparatus and the overall level of economic development; and (5) the nature, dependence on, and extent of external influence, support, and resource flows, including the market forces of the world economy.

This argument maintains a balance between voluntarist perspectives that stress political will—so common to external actors—on the one hand, and pessimistic ones that stress structural constraints—so common to academic and African analyses—on the other. Adequate levels of understanding, commitment, and statecraft skill (plus luck—a variable we greatly underestimate) are necessary but not sufficient; state capacity, sociopolitical insulation, and adequate external resources are also necessary but not sufficient. Some combination of both sets of factors is required. Given this argument and the nature of African postcolonial political economies, it is not surprising that there have been few cases of sustained neoorthodox economic reform in Africa.

Economic Reform and the Implicit Bargain

Africans and external actors alike have asked how serious attempts at economic reform can be prevented from collapsing, as one such program discussed below did in dramatic fashion in Zambia in 1987. How can others that are limping along become more effective and sustainable? How can the enormous burdens of such efforts be softened, ameliorated? In a very real sense, these are classic issues of statecraft at both the national and international levels.

Africans have long maintained that substantial resource flows and debt relief are required for sustained reform. One of the lessons of Ghana is that this is a necessary but not sufficient condition. By the late 1980s, external actors began to realize that increased resource flows and debt relief were going to be required for Africa. This realization began to sink in as the enormous obstacles to reform and the possibility of widespread failure became increasingly apparent. Whether the resource flows and debt relief will come is another matter. The special new lending facilities of the IMF and the World Bank, including the Structural Adjustment Facilities and Enhanced Structural Adjustment Facilities mentioned above, are steps in that direction, but substantial support for them will be needed from all donor countries.

A larger problem exists, however, that is directly linked to Africa's increasing marginalization from the world economy. An implicit bargain has existed between the international financial institutions and the major Western countries on the one hand and the Africans on the other. The provisions of the bargain are that if African countries would reform their economies in a neoorthodox direction with the help and direction of the IMF and the World Bank, then new international private bank lending and direct foreign investment would be available to underpin and sustain the reform efforts.

This implicit bargain is likely to collapse, if it has not already. If it does, it will not be the fault of the IMF and the World Bank, both of which have worked to increase voluntary lending and direct foreign investment, or of the reforming African governments. It will be a legacy of Africa's thirty-year history of dismal economic performance, a track record banks and investors do not forget easily; it will also be due to structural shifts in the world economy and state system that make other areas of the world more attractive to investors. Proponents of neoorthodox reform in Africa have argued that the track record of poor performance can be overcome if Africa provides relatively predictable opportunities for profit. Even if the African end of the bargain were to be fulfilled (which is not likely), the bargain would hold only if other areas of the world did not provide better opportunities.

In a speech in March 1990, Michel Camdessus, the managing director of the IMF, provided a good description of the implicit bargain—what he called "the unwritten contract"—and, seemingly without intending to do so, the precarious nature of it. The speech is worth quoting at length.

> In other words, we must all strive to come back to what I would call the core idea of the *unwritten contract* of international cooperation: that countries adopt good policies, and that these [are] supported by adequate internal and external financing. . . . [But] foreign investment and other assistance can *only* supplement the actions of the country itself. . . .
>
> In view of the rapid growth in Africa's debt-servicing burden, strenuous efforts to reduce the debt overhang must continue. For the future, African countries will *need to be prudent* about their borrowing, both as regards its scale and terms, and be careful to use new resources wisely and efficiently, so that they contribute to growth and external viability.
>
> The availability of the traditional types of finance will be *limited*. But I am sure that the Fund itself will be able to continue to play successfully its role as a catalyst of international financing, *if* African countries come forward with economic programs that are *strong enough*, and *credible enough*, to convince *Africans* themselves to invest in Africa. *If* this occurs—and it is possible—then the banks can be expected to overcome their *hesitations*, to support their long-term customers, and to direct their new lending to those countries that are creating growth and good business opportunities. They will lend on a *very selective basis*, and *within limits*, although these limits *may* expand for countries that succeed in their adjustment efforts.
>
> Other forms of private lending can become more important. For example, there *may* be wider scope for direct and portfolio investment in many African

> countries. *But* this will happen *only* for those countries that consistently show a good economic performance, *and* that attract and welcome financing from abroad. This includes, not least, their own flight capital. By *persevering* with sound policies, any African country can *gradually* increase the confidence of its own population and of foreign investors in its long-term potential. . . .
>
> You all know that the Fund also has heavy ongoing responsibilities in the global debt strategy, and *new challenges in helping Eastern European countries* to reform. Despite these demands on our resources, we shall be able to continue to support all African countries that are prepared to *persevere* with far-reaching reforms *and* that back up these reforms with firm financial discipline.[12]

Note the degree to which this description of the terms of the "unwritten contract" is hedged by repeated and careful qualifications. These are a reflection of the degree of Africa's marginalization, the larger changes in the international division of labor and state system, and the enormity of the economic and political obstacles to restructuring African political economies after over thirty years of decline. The message is that it is indeed a self-help international system and that resources will flow only to those who help themselves.

Assuming that resources continue to flow at least at current levels from the IMF, the World Bank, and Western governments—even if not from international private banks and investors—conditionality is likely to continue. Even the exceptions make this point. Between 1985 and early 1987, the Kaunda government in Zambia half-heartedly attempted to implement a very unpopular IMF–World Bank economic reform package. After deadly food riots, strikes, and protests, Kaunda terminated the program in May 1987, announcing that Zambia would formulate and implement its own reform package without external resources and the conditionality that comes with them. If Zambia after May 1987 is an example of what African economic reform would look like without conditionality, Africa is in serious trouble. The tough decisions were simply not made, the economy continued to decline, and external actors essentially cut off resource flows. Economic conditionality, then, is an international fact of life and a key element of the implicit bargain. But conditionality went wild in the 1980s. By the end of the decade, overly minute and cross-cutting conditionality stimulated game playing by both African and external officials that tended to undermine the efficacy of reform and the scarce resources that existed to support it.[13]

In addition, the capacity of African states to absorb new resources effectively can be easily overloaded. Although more resources are definitely needed to increase the chances of sustained economic reform, only so much can be absorbed, both technically and politically. Inefficient programs and renewed rent-seeking are real possibilities. One of the ways of coping with this problem has been to use expatriates. A striking new expatriatization has quietly taken place in many African countries. In mid-1990, the head of the World Bank noted "the extraordinary fact that there are more expatriate advisors in Africa today than at the end of the colonial period. This fact is even more extraordinary, given the evidence that some $7 per head or $4 billion a year is spent on technical assistance."[14] Although this renewed expatriatization has increased the technical capacity of African governments, it has also become a very sensitive political issue. In Ghana, for example, the country's largest union—the Industrial and Commercial Workers Union—demanded that the Rawlings government make public all of its agreements with the IMF and the World Bank *and* disclose the cost of maintaining all foreign advisers.

Learning: The Fear of Failure

By the mid-1980s, some international officials began to realize that many efforts at economic reform in Africa would fail unless changes were made in how the programs were designed and implemented. This often palpable fear of failure became an impetus to international learning. One senior World Bank official addressed this problem bluntly and honestly in 1987.

> The alternative—a series of failed programs in Africa—is not worth thinking about, and not only because of the human suffering. . . . The basic idea of moving to a market economy, shifting policies out of grandiosity to step-by-step solid progress, will be discredited. If they fail in a series of countries . . . then it is a failure of our approach to the economy, a failure of our institutions, a failure of our political will, and there's no way that we'll be able to say that it is just the failure of Africa! So we have a very, very big stake in this.[15]

This realization prompted some reassessment of the economic reform process, and by the end of the decade important learning was taking place—slowly and unevenly—by both external actors and some African officials.

External officials began to realize that stop-go cycles of reform were a fact of life and that they needed to learn to adjust to them. Both sides became more attuned to the need for the politics of fine-tuning—the more careful calibration of policy measures, instruments, pace, timing, and sequencing, especially for the sensitive issues of food, health, fuel, and wages—in order to modulate the socioeconomic and political impacts of adjustment measures and thereby increase the chances of sustained reform. Some external officials now believe, for example, that Zambia's 1985–1987 effort at reform might not have failed if these lessons had been learned earlier.[16]

Structural adjustment is an enormously difficult and politically sensitive task in Africa, especially as the benefits are often uncertain and come far down the road. Reform is often complicated by other factors, such as drought, famine, civil and regional wars, destabilization, and AIDS. The hardest point to accept is that even successful neoorthodox reform will not eliminate Africa's marginality to the world economy in the short and medium runs. It might, however, begin to lessen and prevent the continent, or parts of it at least, from becoming totally unimportant to the world economy.

Although some policy lessons are being learned, Africa's problems are larger still. Even if proper policy lessons are implemented and resources found to support them, it is not clear that they would result in a high number of sustained large reform efforts. A link clearly exists between debt and structural adjustment in Africa, but it is not predominantly a causal one. The need for structural adjustment long predated the debt crisis; the latter merely brought the structural adjustment crisis to a head. Even if the debt crisis were somehow miraculously solved tomorrow—through a total writeoff, for example—the structural adjustment crisis would remain. The case of Nigeria has shown that massive new resources from oil can intensify rather than ameliorate economic decline.

The task of confronting this decline is enormous, much more so than for any other region of the world. External actors have learned that Africa is a special case; it has not responded as neoclassical theory predicted it should. In 1988 the World Bank noted that:

> The supply response to adjustment lending in low-income countries, especially in SSA [Sub-Saharan Africa], has been slow because of the legacy of deep-seated structural problems. Inadequate infrastructure, poorly developed markets, rudimentary industrial sectors, and severe institutional and managerial weaknesses in the public *and* the private sectors have proved *unexpectedly* serious as constraints to better performance—especially in the poorer countries of SSA. Greater recognition thus needs to be given to the time and attention for structural changes, especially institutional reforms and their effects.[17]

Note the revealing use of *unexpectedly;* it indicates a changed perception—that Africa is a particularly difficult case.

It is not just a case of reordering policies, but rather one of constructing a whole new context[18]—what the World Bank is now calling an "enabling environment." By the early 1980s, liberal neoorthodoxy had become, as had radical structuralism before it, explicitly linked to economic development concerns. Its two central tenets are export-led growth and a minimalist state. The new orthodoxy views the state itself as a key obstacle to development, whereas for the structuralists the main obstacles are to be found in socioeconomic patterns, both internal and external.

In a sense, for Africa *both* sides are right: As the structuralists maintain, there are enormous economic and social structure obstacles to development, internal and external; and, as the adherents of neoorthodoxy maintain, the state is also an impediment. *And* both sets of obstacles inhibit both import substitution and industrialization and export-oriented economic activity, public and private. The structuralists are correct that socioeconomic obstacles prevent neoclassical monoeconomics—the presumption that economic pressures work the same everywhere—from being fully operative in Africa, as the World Bank has "unexpectedly" discovered; and the proponents of neoorthodoxy are correct that the nature of the state in Africa makes import substitution industrialization ineffective and wasteful, as many African structuralists still have not admitted.

Structuralists do have a theory of reform; it is a weak one, however, because its instrument of reform—the state—is itself terribly ineffective in Africa. Yet, in the course of attempted reform, the external proponents of neoclassical change have confronted an orthodox paradox—in order to implement such reform, they, too, have to use what they perceive to be the major obstacle to reform, the African state, as the primary instrument of reform. Everybody knows what kind of state they would like to have, but nobody knows how to obtain it. Other than getting the state out of the economy, the neoclassical strategists do not have a theory of state reform, and they are finding that getting the state out of the economy is much more difficult than they expected—politically, administratively, and technically. In addition, the adherents of neoorthodoxy are learning that their own proclaimed instrument of reform, the market, is also terribly weak in Africa. Over time it becomes increasingly clear that nobody understands the functioning of African economies; even the basic data set for the formal economy is extremely limited and unreliable, and systematic data on the informal economy are almost nonexistent.

After over thirty years of independence, most of Africa is neither effectively Socialist nor capitalist; it is not even statist. Socialist and statist efforts have yielded few results, and modern capitalism hardly exists. Current liberalization efforts may not have a major impact in many places, and the rest of the world increasingly passes the continent by. In many ways, then, African countries are still lost between state and market, and although—as Ghana demonstrates—successful large reform is not impossible, it takes an extraordinary confluence of forces to bring it about and to sustain it.

THE DEBATE: INTO THE 1990s

Despite the learning discussed above, however, by the end of the 1980s—with obstacles to reform apparent on all sides—the key question remained (or reemerged, depending on one's point of view): What should Africa do to cope with its devastating economic crisis? The answer of the external actors, led by the World Bank, is to persevere with the neoorthodox thrust of reforms, with modifications to make them work more effectively. Many Africans remain unconvinced. This fundamental disagreement simmered quietly throughout the 1980s behind what appeared to many as an increasing consensus around a modified neoorthodox position. The disagreement burst forth with surprising vigor in what can be called "the bloody spring of 1989."[19]

Starting at least by the middle of the decade, the World Bank and other external actors proclaimed that a new consensus had emerged about the need for systematic structural adjustment in Africa along neoorthodox lines. In addition, the Bank began to assert that its reforms were working, even in the short run. In order to demonstrate this, the Bank issued a report in March 1989, *Africa's Adjustment and Growth in the 1980s,* which maintained that for the period 1985–1987, countries that adopted externally approved economic reform programs performed better than countries that did not.[20] The Bank wished to demonstrate that such reforms could indeed have a direct payoff, despite the often intense political and social difficulties the reforms generated. It hoped that the report would encourage those already engaged in economic reforms to persevere and stimulate those who did not have such programs to start them.

The Economic Commission for Africa (ECA) reacted very strongly to the report. The ECA felt a sense of betrayal, both as to the report's conclusions and the fact that it was released without warning or consultation. It feared that a World Bank assertion of progress would threaten external support and resource flows to Africa by implying that its problems were well on the way to being solved. Above all, the ECA still did not believe that the IMF–World Bank strategy was the correct one or that it was indeed working. In April 1989 it issued a stinging attack on *Africa's Adjustment and Growth.* Entitled "Statistics and Policies," it came to the exact opposite conclusion of the World Bank report: African countries that engaged in strong efforts at neoorthodox reform did less well than those that did not have such reform programs.[21] In addition, "Statistics and Policies" charged that the World Bank report engaged in serious data manipulation, failed to provide adequate documentation, and did not agree with the Bank's own worldwide assessment of adjustment experience.[22] According to the press release for "Statistics and Policies," the ECA's executive secretary, Adebayo Adedeji, said that "a falsely optimistic portrayal of Africa's economic situation which might need to be reversed later would jeopardize the international support for Africa that is now developing."

After initially giving *Africa's Adjustment and Growth* considerable play, the World Bank attempted to paper over the dispute with the ECA. Conciliatory meetings were held with ECA and other African and U.N.

officials. A detailed Bank response to "Statistics and Policies" was prepared but never made public. Many African officials appeared pleased by the vigorous ECA response; only officials from strongly adjusting countries, such as Ghana and Nigeria, reacted negatively to "Statistics and Policies" and its implication of the futility of following neoorthodox prescriptions.

What the Bank had hoped would be a boost to continued neoorthodox reforms in Africa had become the reverse—an object of major controversy that demonstrated that a consensus on IMF–World Bank reforms clearly did not exist. In fact, the alleged consensus probably never really existed. What was taken as consensus by powerful external actors was really a quiet waiting game generated by the desperate need of African countries for external resources and the hope of a major bailout through substantial debt relief, higher export prices, greatly increased bilateral and multilateral aid, commercial bank lending, or direct foreign investment. When these failed to materialize, a sense of betrayal set in for many African officials that, linked to serious disagreements about strategy, set in place the ingredients for a major explosion.

For their part, the World Bank and other external actors had helped to generate this crisis by being unduly optimistic about the expected results of the reform efforts in order to sell them. As part of an effort to sustain positive expectations, the Bank fell victim to what I have elsewhere called the "fault of analytic hurry"—wanting to see things as real before they are.[23] A backlash from failed expectations should not have been a surprise. The time frame was too narrow; the data were unreliable; reform measures were not fully or consistently implemented; and designating strong versus weak reformers, other than for a clear-cut case such as Ghana, was arbitrary and misleading. In addition, expectations about positive outcomes have nearly always been out of line with what could realistically be expected. Even if all reform measures were fully implemented in a sustained manner, the results would not be spectacular; they would be modest at best. Although modest results would be a major accomplishment, it would unfortunately not be perceived that way by most Africans.

The fact that an African–external actor consensus on neoorthodox reforms still did not exist was demonstrated dramatically in July 1989 when the ECA issued its long-anticipated attempt at a counterfactual strategy, *African Alternative Framework to Structural Adjustment Programmes for Socio-Economic Recovery and Transformation* (AAF-SAP).[24] Some of the turmoil of the bloody spring had, in fact, been generated by a belief on the part of African officials that the World Bank's release of *Africa's Adjustment and Growth* was an attempt to upstage and blunt the release of *AAF-SAP.* This endeavor by an African-dominated organization to put forward its own viable alternative merely underscored the degree to which most Africans are still running away from the world economy, still see it as the enemy, and are still looking for the easy way, the quick fix.

The press release announcing *AAF-SAP* was entitled "Africa Proposes Bold New Plan for Economic Revival." In reality, the ECA's counterfactual strategy is not bold, new, a plan, or likely to lead to economic revival. It is a warmed-over version of the Lagos Plan of Action with vague and contradictory, largely statist, policy proposals that could not be implemented under the best of conditions, all of which are linked to renewed demands for substantially increased external resource flows and debt relief. Above all, *AAF-SAP* illustrates the continued fear of the world economy.

> Fundamentally, these [ECA] reforms aim to lessen Africa's extreme dependence on external trade and financing, a dependence that renders the continent vulnerable to an unstable and unfavourable world economic environment and obstructs its efforts toward balanced development. African countries . . . should reorient their economies in a more self-reliant direction, looking both domestically and to other African countries for markets, sources of finance and technical co-operation.
>
> Concerned about "the increasing role of foreign experts and managers in national economic decision-making in Africa" and the narrowing of policy options implied by the conditionalities usually attached to much of Africa's external financing, AAF-SAP also urges African governments to shoulder the main responsibility for drawing up their economic programmes. This . . . will help ensure that the programmes are more in line with Africa's basic development goals. . . . Overall, Africa sees self-reliance as both the goal and the means through which the region will eventually find its true identity, full dignity and historic strength.[25]

As this passage indicates, many Africans are still running away from the dual dependence laid out at the beginning of this chapter—dependence on the markets and players of the world economy and on the economic policy advice of external actors in the international state system, especially the IMF and the World Bank. The instinctive African response to these dependencies is to flee the world economy rather than to attempt to use it to lessen dependence. The likely result of this flight reaction will be increased dependence, marginalization, and decline rather than the development, self-reliance, and "true identity, full dignity and historic strength" that *AAF-SAP* claims as its goals.

By late 1989, the visceral emotions of the bloody spring had been substantially tamed, but without resolving many of the underlying disagreements. One of the main pacifying factors was the November release by the World Bank of its long-awaited "long-term perspective study," *Sub-Saharan Africa: From Crisis to Sustainable Growth.* The report demonstrated a realization on the part of the Bank that it was necessary to go beyond policy change toward the construction of a more propitious context for reform. It incorporated many of the lessons derived from the experiences of the 1980s, above all the desperate need for institutional change and for a slower, more sequenced transition that recognizes the sociopolitical obstacles to change. Its major themes are that Africa requires an enabling environment, more technical and administrative capacity (both state and private), and better governance.

> A central theme of the report is that although sound macroeconomic policies and an efficient infrastructure are essential to provide an *enabling environment* for the productive use of resources, they alone are not sufficient to transform the structure of African economies. At the same time major efforts are needed to *build African capacities*—to produce a better trained, more healthy population and to greatly strengthen the institutional framework within which development can take place. . . . African governments . . . need to go beyond the issues of public finance, monetary policy, prices, and markets to address fundamental questions relating to human capacities, institutions, governance, the environment, population growth and distribution, and technology.[26]

The report appeared to take seriously many of the lessons of the 1980s; thus, it was initially welcomed by many African officials. It had, after all, been drafted following extensive consultation with Africans from many diverse backgrounds—from government officials and entrepreneurs in both formal and informal economies to the heads of private African volunteer organizations.

The welcome was reinforced by the fact that the report also appeared to represent an ambivalent shift away from the more vehement antistatist aspects of neoorthodoxy toward a more balanced view of the relationship between state and market. It seemed to represent a tacit admission that earlier versions of neoorthodoxy had, to use Tony Killick's phrase, been "a reaction too far."[27] Although fluctuating, fragile, and often contradictory, this shift in tone is reflected in the report's favorable discussion of what is called "the Nordic development paradigm." This model, according to the Bank, rejects the "dichotomy between capitalist and socialist development models" and "offers an alternative development model where the state assumes a leading role in building human resources, administrative, and physical infrastructure capacity, while the goods-producing and noninfrastructure service sectors are left to the flexibility and incentives of private enterprise and market discipline." This model contrasts with "the planned economies of the Third World" and "the more top-down mercantilist policies of Japan and Korea."[28] The report thus seeks a second-generation development strategy in which the state listens carefully to the market even if it does not always precisely follow the market. Although not put in these terms, this strategy would attempt a move away from the predatory and inefficient mercantilism of the first thirty-plus years of independence toward a more productive and efficient, although distinctly limited, version of what has been called "benign mercantilism"[29]—that is, toward a more balanced tension between state and market.

In reality, this effort would take African political economies back to their position at the time of independence and make them work correctly this time. From the African point of view, this second-generation strategy is clearly a second-best one. The primary point remains, however, that the Africans have no viable counterfactual strategy to this modification version of neoorthodoxy. As indicated above, recent African efforts to provide such a strategy are still riddled with incredible levels of state voluntarism of the kind mentioned by Kwesi Botchwey. The model African state does not have the capabilities for the more interventionist versions of benign mercantilism represented by Korea and Taiwan. It can and should work in that direction, but the transition will be slow and uneven. As Goran Hyden has stressed, there are "no shortcuts," especially to developing productive linkages to the world economy.[30] Creative tinkering with the neoorthodox strategy by *both* African governments and the IMF and the World Bank could begin to move the continent in beneficial directions. The long-term perspective study may represent a step down that road. Ultimately, it is not just a question of finding the precarious balance between state and market or state and society but rather of searching for the precarious trialectic between state, market, and the international arena.

GOVERNANCE AND DEMOCRACY: THE NEW POLITICAL CONDITIONALITY

Such a precarious trialectic may be difficult to achieve, however, as the international arena tends to present new and unexpected challenges for African rulers. While *From Economic Crisis to Sustainable Growth* was initially well received by many Africans, it contained a quiet time bomb—governance, which has brought considerable new tension and uncertainty to African–external actor relations in regard to economic policy. The World Bank's emphasis on governance emerged from its learning about the primary importance of creating a more facilitative sociopolitical context for structural adjustment in Africa. Due to the dramatic changes in the world in 1989–1990—especially in Eastern Europe but also in Central America and South Africa—and the search for a new foreign policy thrust to replace anticommunism, governance is being transformed by the major Western industrial democracies into political conditionality focusing on the promotion of democracy. The convergence of these two policy thrusts—one largely technocratic, the other distinctly political—poses a real dilemma for African leaders committed to economic reform.

In its long-term perspective study, the World Bank—and indirectly the IMF and the major donor countries—raised governance as a major issue for the first time.

> Efforts to create an enabling environment and to build capacities will be wasted if the political context is not favorable. . . . Ultimately, better governance requires political renewal. This means a concerted attack on corruption from the highest to lowest levels. This can be done be setting a good example, by strengthening accountability, by encouraging public debate, and by nurturing a free press. It also means . . . fostering grassroots and nongovernmental organizations (NGOs), such as farmers' associations, cooperatives, and women's groups.[31]

For the Bank, better governance also means less unpredictability and uncertainty in policy and administration, more rule of law, maintenance of judicial independence, and transparency and accountability to representative bodies.

Warnings about governance and political liberalization have come from the highest levels of the international financial institutions and the most important Western industrial democracies. In April 1990, Barber B. Conable, the president of the World Bank, put the case in blunt terms.

> The development of many Sub-Saharan African countries has been quite unnecessarily constrained by their political systems. Africans can and must tackle this issue. . . . Indisputably, three decades after independence too many African countries have failed to produce political and economic systems in which development can flourish. . . . People need freedom to realize individual and collective potential. . . . Open political participation has been restricted and even condemned, and those brave enough to speak their minds have too frequently taken grave political risks. I fear that many of Africa's leaders have been more concerned about retaining power than about the long-term development interests of their people. The cost to millions of Africans . . . has been unforgiveably high.[32]

Douglas Hurd, the British foreign secretary, asserted that the distribution of aid should favor countries tending toward pluralism, public accountability and human rights, and market principles. In saying that France does not intend to impose models, President François Mitterrand made a similar declaration and noted that for him democracy would include free elections, multiparty systems, press freedom, and an independent judiciary.[33] U.S. officials are treading a similar path, which is being vigorously pushed by Congress.

The ECA inadvertently abetted such an emphasis by noting in its press release for *AAF-SAP* that "programmes for economic recovery can only be successful if African governments, drawing on the support and democratic participation of their people, take on the prime responsibility for determining their own country programmes." In fact, however, the World Bank and the ECA have quite different perspectives about governance and democratic participation. The ECA means to use the notion of democratic participation to fend off the *existing* challenges of economic conditionality, which, in its view, leads to a "gradual erosion of sovereignty" because the "external development agencies play a principal role in the formulation, design, implementation and monitoring of adjustment programmes." The ECA asserts that "Africa has particularly suffered from such conditionality because the weakness of its economies gave it very little negotiating leverage."[34]

Political conditionality *would* greatly increase African dependence on external actors. Many African leaders fear it, including some who are committed to economic reform. Senegal's President Diouf almost fell from power due to economic discontent on the part of social groups adversely affected by economic reform, expressed through partially liberal political structures, whereas Nigeria's President Babangida struggles to protect his economic reforms from his own political liberalization efforts and Ghana's Jerry Rawlings attempts to avoid the issue altogether. African leaders are also being pushed by internal societal pressure, as events in Kenya, Côte d'Ivoire, Zambia, and Zaire, among others, demonstrated vividly in 1990. Some leaders resist energetically; others stall; and still others play charades with both internal and external critics. Is Africa now becoming politically as well as economically marginalized and dependent? Is political conditionality a good idea, especially regarding the prospects for major economic change?

A major contradiction between economic and political conditionality may indeed exist, one that the major Western governments either do not see or choose to ignore. The primary assumptions appear to be that economic structural adjustment and political liberalization are mutually reinforcing processes and that since authoritarian politics in large part caused the economic malaise, democratic politics can help change it. These assumptions may be incorrect, however. Eastern Europe aside, evidence from the Third World in the 1980s does not support optimism about the mutually reinforcing character of economic reform and political liberalization. This is not to say that authoritarian regimes can guarantee economic reform or even produce it very often. Nor is it to say that economic reform under democratic conditions is impossible; it is just very difficult.

There is evidence from other regions of the Third World that economic reform can take place in existing democracies. Two such examples are Costa Rica and Jamaica. In Costa Rica, however, there was much more economic stabilization than structural adjustment; and in Jamaica under Edward Seaga particular institutions and circumstances existed that reinforced executive autonomy and fragmented the opposition. Evidence also exists that new democracies that replace hated and inefficient authoritarian regimes may have a honeymoon period that can be used to launch, if not sustain, major economic reform (the Philippines under Aquino, Argentina under Alfonsin, Brazil under Sarney). Military regimes already engaging in successful economic reform can become democratic, as demonstrated by Turkey under Ozal and post-Pinochet Chile; but again institutions and circumstances that reinforce executive autonomy and controlled opposition appear essential. Turkey also demonstrates that such a transition can require considerable financial resource slack in order to make the political side payments necessary to maintain stability in fragile coalitions.[35]

The assumption of the mutually reinforcing character of political and economic reform in Africa rests on an extension of neoclassical economic logic: Economic liberalization creates sustained growth; growth produces winners as well as losers; winners will organize to defend their new-found welfare and create sociopolitical coalitions to support continued economic reform. This logic, however, does not appear to hold for Africa under authoritarian, much less democratic, conditions.

As argued above, given the evidence from Africa so far, successful economic reform requires a rare conjuncture of factors, such as those that have existed in Ghana since 1983. Central to this argument is that successful reform comes from insulating the policy process from the rent-seeking and distributional pressures that so dominated the first thirty years of independence in Africa. Ghana under Rawlings demonstrates that successful and sustained economic reform is possible without the presence of an *existing* societal support coalition. By the late 1980s, however, after seven years of impressive growth (especially by African standards), the main dilemma facing Rawlings was his inability to translate successful economic reform into a viable political support base. He has hesitated to liberalize politically for fear that the economic reform program his government has struggled so mightily to start and sustain would disappear. There have been winners in Ghana, especially cocoa farmers and resident expatriates; but the former are difficult to organize specifically to support the economic reforms of the government, and the latter cannot form a viable element in a new support coalition.

The winners of economic reform in Africa are few; they appear only slowly over time and are difficult to organize politically. The neoclassical political logic of reform is too mechanistic for the African context; there are real transaction costs to organizing winners, not just infrastructural ones. Cocoa farmers, for example, have other interests, political loyalties, and histories of organization that make direct political organization in support of a given set of economic policies difficult. Other organizational bases of political solidarity exist—ethnic, regional, religious, linguistic, and patron-client—that make mobilization around policy-specific economic interests difficult. Even where groups might so organize, they would not be likely to support the full range of economic measures, thereby threatening the viability of reform.

Some have argued that Africa does not have a democratic legacy; but it does have one. It was brief, vivid, and a failure, and the reasons for its demise have not disappeared. The periodic reemergence of democratic regimes in Ghana and Nigeria since the late 1960s indicates that old patterns of political organization reappear with amazing vigor under conditions of free political association. Political liberalization is not likely to guarantee the appearance of new political alignments that favor sustained economic reform. No strong evidence exists that African politics has shifted from distributional to productionist logics and forms of behavior. Nigeria's scheduled return to democratic politics in 1992 might well terminate the relatively impressive economic reforms undertaken by the Babangida military government. Neoorthodox economic reform in Africa is very unpopular because its political, social, and distributional effects are negative for most of the population, as Ghana shows even in the medium run. Economic learning by political leaders and societal groups is possible, as Chile, Jamaica, and Turkey demonstrate, but it is usually a fragile creature that requires special circumstances in order to survive and that can be easily upset. Renewed democratic politics on a still-shrinking production base might be even more difficult to sustain than in the 1960s, making such learning very difficult indeed.

Is this version of the "thesis of the perverse effect"—that political liberalization might have a negative impact on the chances for sustained economic reform—likely to hold across the board for Africa?[36] No, it is not. It is important to assess particular country cases. Kenya, for example, might be a case where political liberalization could allow formerly powerful political actors, who had to retreat into the private economy to survive under the Moi government, to return to political influence without impeding continued economic reform, but such a return would have to occur carefully and without allowing the older political forces to again totally dominate political and economic life. In the Kenyan case, little might be lost by political liberalization. In Ghana, however, a good deal could be lost. Careful and clever political engineering might facilitate economic reform under certain democratic conditions. It might be possible, for example, to shield key areas of policy from distributional and other political pressures by delegating them to autonomous institutions or processes, such as auctions for exchange rate fluctuations and central banks for types of monetary policy.

Thus, a probabilistic rather than a deterministic perverse effect is likely to operate in Africa if political conditionality becomes a substantive rather than merely a rhetorical element of the new foreign policies of Western industrial democracies and the international financial institutions they control. If not handled properly, political conditionality might impede rather than facilitate the productive relinking of Africa to the world economy. The widespread emergence of what Richard L. Sklar has called "developmental democracies" is not likely in Africa anytime soon, however.[37]

PROSPECTS FOR THE FUTURE

Given the enormous constraints discussed here, with or without political conditionality, what are the prospects that African countries will engage successfully in economic reform and establish more effective linkages to the world economy? The answer appears to be that simultaneous marginalization and dependence are likely to continue and probably increase for most countries. A few—with hard work, propitious facilitating circumstances, and luck—may begin to lessen their marginalization and dependence. Differentiation among African states, already long evident, will increase. A few will stay in the Third World and do relatively better economically, while most will continue to descend into the Fourth and Fifth Worlds—fulfilling the ECA's nightmare scenario.[38] The countries that are likely to do better are those that are already more advantaged, partly because of better performance since the early 1960s—Kenya, Côte d'Ivoire, Cameroon, Nigeria, Zimbabwe, and possibly Senegal. Even these cases are fragile, however, as has become evident since the late 1980s. A small number of countries in serious decline, such as Ghana, may be able to reverse course, but these prospects are even more fragile.

A quiet debate about Africa under these circumstances is underway among Western officials and business people: Do you provide some resources to all countries across the board to create a sort of international social safety net for declining countries who then become de facto wards of the world community, or do you "pick a few and work with them," as one Western official put it?[39] With the first option, it is not clear how effective such an international safety net would be. With the second option, countries are chosen that have some eventual prospects for better and sustained economic performance and possibly some strategic importance—Nigeria and Zimbabwe, for example. Resources would then be concentrated in these countries. Clearly it is a tough world and will probably become more so as the last decade of the century continues to unfold.

The trajectory of individual countries will be affected by both internal and external factors. On the internal side, the degree of effective "stateness" will be crucial. On average, Africa has the lowest level of state capabilities and overall development of any region in the world. As the IMF and the World Bank have begun to realize, it takes a relatively capable state to implement successful neoorthodox economic reform consistently over time. High degrees of stateness are central to better position a country in the international political economy; a country especially needs the ability to bargain with all types of actors—private business groups, states, and the international financial institutions. The World Bank's long-term perspective study tacitly asserts the importance of the state. Whether increased stateness will emerge in many places, however, is questionable. Certainly, political dynamics will play a central role in arriving at a productive balanced tension between state and market, between state and society. Some African leaders have begun to understand this. They know that it is a self-help world and that one should not wait for external miracles. As President Babangida put it, "Ever since the majority of our countries became independent in the 1960s we have conducted our lives as if the world owes us a living."[40] The outside world does not believe that it does.

Although it is largely a self-help world, external factors affecting country trajectories are also important. They revolve around two central issues: (1) the degree of openness of the world political economy, and (2) the degree to which the implicit bargain discussed earlier is fulfilled. John Gerard Ruggie has characterized the current international political economy as one of "embedded liberalism," in which the relative international economic openness of the postwar era is maintained by the major Western countries intervening in their own domestic arenas to buffer the costs of adjusting to shifts in the world economy. A precarious openness based on liberal economic norms is maintained despite increasing tensions. Others, such as Robert Gilpin, see the world moving toward an increasingly conflictual and closed international political economy, which might be characterized as "malign mercantilism." Still other analysts—Kenneth Oye and Susan Strange, for example—do not dispute the assessment that the international political economy is moving in a more mercantilist direction, but they dispute its effect on openness. According to them, the world has always been more mercantilist than liberal theorists have maintained, and they feel that considerable openness can be sustained as liberal economic norms continue to recede in practice, if not in rhetoric. They stress the importance of bilateral bargaining and a regionalization of the world economy as crucial to the maintenance of openness. Again, the role of the state is absolutely essential.[41]

Africa's prospects under a shift from embedded liberalism to malign mercantilism would not be bright. Despite its marginalization and dependence, Africa desperately needs openness in the world economy. In fact, the neoorthodox adjustment strategy is predicated on it. Whether some form of benign mercantilism would benefit Africa is open to question. The usual presumption is that Africa would be increasingly included in a European-dominated regional sphere. With the changes of 1989–1990 in Europe, however, it is less clear that European interest in Africa will be important or sustained.

European officials regularly prompt Africans to prepare for 1992. In late 1989, for example, Jacques Pelletier, the French minister of cooperation and development, urged African officials to build up their own regional cooperation efforts: "The changes in Europe are, to my mind, a model. Without a regional market, sub-Saharan Africa will not be organised on a sufficient scale to become an area of economic growth. Without political co-ordination in all areas—fiscal, social and legal—it will remain too weak in the face of the large groupings which are being established everywhere in the world."[42]

Clearly, then, such an international political economy would put a very high premium on state capabilities, ones that are already weak in Africa and that are not likely to increase significantly in the short to medium run. Africans fear a "fortress Europe" and delay preparing for it. A leading African banker has warned of the consequences of such myopic behavior: "The Western world has changed so much in the handling of economic and financial matters that Africa is in danger of being left behind. By 1992 we will have to think differently."[43] But the track record of regional cooperation and economic reform in Africa does not inspire confidence that such warnings will be heeded.

Prospects for the fulfillment of the implicit bargain may not be much brighter. As private actors in the world economy increasingly pass Africa by, Western countries—even with declining interest—and the international financial institutions will continue to play central roles. If African countries are to have any chance of making economic progress, these actors must help to fulfill the implicit bargain, primarily through increased aid levels and substantial debt relief. Given the domestic politics of Western industrial democracies, debt relief might be the easier route to take, for it is more politically malleable. As resources are scarce, aid and debt relief should be given only to those actually undertaking these difficult changes, *and* they should not be tied automatically to political conditionality. African rulers such as Jerry Rawlings should be supported; the Mobutus should not. It is not clear, however, how many such rulers external actors can actually support at the level required for sustained economic change. Such reform is difficult; thus, stop-go cycles are a fact of life, and external actors need to learn to adjust to them. Some lessons have been learned and creative proposals put forward for Zambia since it ended its externally sponsored reform effort in May 1987, but the progress has been halting. The primary obstacle is how to cope with a huge debt overhang and substantial arrears to the IMF and the World Bank without setting precedents that have worldwide implications.

Finally, external actors should avoid the "faults of analytic and policy hurry" and not create undue expectations about what can be achieved in Africa over the medium run. Given the enormous obstacles confronting African countries, overly optimistic expectations can be dangerous. Slow, steady, consistent progress is preferable. There are no shortcuts. The lessons of the development administration movement of the late 1960s and the 1970s should not be forgotten—that is, that productive change in state capabilities and contextual variables comes about slowly and unevenly. Neither international nor African policymakers can unduly hasten, control, or speed up social progresses such as institution and capacity building. Change is incremental, uneven, often contradictory, and dependent on the outcome of unpredictable socioeconomic and political struggles. Policymakers—both international and African—must try to bring about important changes, but they need to retain a sense of the historical complexity involved. If they do not, undue expectations can get in the way of making slow but steady progress on difficult obstacles. Today's policy fads can easily become tomorrow's failed initiatives.

External actors, then, need to work closely with Africans to find ways to effectively implement the lessons learned from the experience with structural adjustment in the 1980s, lessons apparent in the World Bank's long-term perspective study. If not, adjustment with a human face, capacity building, and governance will just become the latest in international passing fancies. Another of the current panacea buzz words is *policy dialogue*, a term used mostly by external actors to mean that intensified consultation with a reforming government will lead to more effective adjustment because the African government will then "own" the reforms. Policy dialogue is based, however, on the tacit assumptions that greater discussion leads to greater agreement and that the parties that need to be convinced are the African actors. More consultation does not necessarily increase agreement; thus, policy dialogue can only be effective if *both* sides are willing to learn and to give ground.

One phenomenon that has been the most subject to the "faults of analytic and policy hurry" is the informal economy. Undue expectations about the salvation potential of the informal economy and the ability of policymakers to relink it effectively to the formal economy, including the world economy, need to be avoided. The informal economy *is* a bright spot on the African scene. Entrepreneurial groups might emerge from it to provide the basis of coalitional support needed to sustain economic reform, reorder the state, and link African countries to the world economy more productively, but this will not happen in many places overnight, easily, or evenly.[44] Africa is caught between a rock and a hard place in regard to the world economy, and all actors will have to work hard to alter that fact. But try they must, for not trying could have even worse consequences for Africa's long-suffering peoples.

NOTES

1. Ralph Austen, *African Economic History* (London: James Currey, 1987), pp. 102, 109.

2. The data in this section come from *IMF Survey* 18, no. 23 (December 11, 1989) and 19, no. 14 (July 16, 1990); World Bank, *Sub-Saharan Africa: From Crisis to Sustainable Growth* (Washington, D.C.: World Bank, 1989); World Bank and United Nations Development Programme, *Africa's Adjustment and Growth in the 1980s* (Washington, D.C.: World Bank, 1989); World Bank, *World Development Report 1989* (New York: Oxford University Press, 1989); World Bank, *World Development Report 1990* (New York: Oxford University Press, 1990); and Tony Killick and Matthew Martin, "African Debt: The Search for Solutions," United Nations Africa Recovery Programme Briefing Paper no. 1, New York, June 1989.

3. Confidential interview, New York, April 26, 1990.

4. "UK Companies Sell African Investments," *Financial Times* (London), June 28, 1990, p. 4, based on a recent study by the Overseas Development Institute.

5. B. A. Kiplagat, quoted in "Africa Fears Its Needs Will Become Secondary," *New York Times*, December 26, 1989, p. A6.

6. See Gerald Bender, James S. Coleman, and Richard Sklar (eds.), *African Crisis Areas and U.S. Foreign Policy* (Berkeley: University of California Press, 1985).

7. On Africa's debt problems, see Killick and Martin, "African Debt"; Charles Humphreys and John Underwood, "The External Debt Difficulties of Low-Income Africa," pp. 45–68 in Ishrat Husain and Ishac Diwan (eds.), *Dealing with the Debt Crisis* (Washington, D.C.: World Bank, 1989); and Thomas M. Callaghy, "Debt and Structural Adjustment in Africa: Realities and Possibilities," *Issue* 16, no. 2 (1988):11–18.

8. Callaghy, "Debt and Structural Adjustment," pp. 13–14; *IMF Survey* 19, no. 7 (April 2, 1990):110.

9. See World Bank, *World Development Report 1990*; and *IMF Survey* 19, no. 14, pp. 210–213.

10. Quoted in "Ghana: High Stakes Gamble," *Africa News* 31, no. 2 (January 23, 1989):10.

11. For a more detailed analysis of the Ghana case and the nature of African reform efforts discussed below, see Thomas M. Callaghy, "Lost Between State and Market: The Politics of Economic Adjustment in Ghana, Zambia, and Nigeria," in Joan M. Nelson (ed.), *Economic Crisis and Policy Choice* (Princeton: Princeton University Press, 1990), pp. 257–319.

12. Excerpts from the speech are reprinted in *IMF Survey* 19, no. 7, pp. 108–111, emphases added.

13. See Miles Kahler, "International Financial Institutions and the Politics of Adjustment," in Joan M. Nelson (ed.), *Fragile Coalitions* (New Brunswick: Transaction Books and the Overseas Development Council, 1989), pp. 139–159.

14. Barber B. Conable, "Address as Prepared for Delivery to the Bretton Woods Conference on Africa's Finance and Development Crisis," Washington, D.C., April 25, 1990, World Bank, mimeograph, p. 3.

15. Margaret A. Novicki, "Interview with Edward V. K. Jaycox, Vice-President, Africa Region, The World Bank," *Africa Report* 32, no. 6 (November-December 1987):32.

16. See Ravi Gulhati, *Impasse in Zambia: The Economics and Politics of Policy Reform*, EDI Development Policy Case Studies no. 2 (Washington, D.C.: World Bank, 1989).

17. World Bank, *Adjustment Lending* (Washington, D.C.: World Bank, 1988), p. 3, emphases added.

18. See Thomas M. Callaghy, "The State and the Development of Capitalism in Africa" in Donald Rothchild and Naomi Chazan (eds.), *The Precarious Balance: State and Society in Africa* (Boulder, Colo.: Westview Press, 1988), pp. 67–99.

19. This section is based in part on confidential interviews with officials of African governments, the United Nations, the IMF, and the World Bank in New York and Washington, D.C., conducted between May 1989 and July 1990.

20. World Bank and UNDP, *Africa's Adjustment and Growth.*

21. United Nations Economic Commission for Africa, "Statistics and Policies: ECA Preliminary Observations on the World Bank Report: 'Africa's Adjustment and Growth in the 1980s,'" Addis Ababa, April 1989.

22. World Bank, *Adjustment Lending.*

23. Callaghy, "The State and the Development of Capitalism," p. 92.

24. United Naitons Economic Commission for Africa (ECA), *African Alternative Framework to Structural Adjustment Programmes for Socio-Economic Recovery and Transformation* (Addis Ababa: ECA, 1989).

25. United Nations Economic Commission for Africa, press release for *African Alternative Framework*, New York, July 6, 1989, p. 7.

26. World Bank, *From Crisis to Sustainable Growth*, pp. xii, 1.

27. Tony Killick, *A Reaction Too Far* (Boulder, Colo.: Westview Press, 1990).

28. World Bank, *From Crisis to Sustainable Growth*, pp. 186–187.

29. Robert Gilpin, *The Political Economy of International Relations* (Princeton: Princeton University Press, 1987), pp. 404–405.

30. Goran Hyden, *No Shortcuts to Progress* (Berkeley: University of California Press, 1983).

31. World Bank, *From Crisis to Sustainable Growth*, pp. 192, 6.

32. Conable, "Address," pp. 2–3.

33. "A Fresh Wind in Africa," *Financial Times* (London), July 10, 1990, p. 18; "France Ties Africa Aid to Democracy," *New York Times*, June 22, 1990, p. A3.

34. ECA, press release for *African Alternative Framework*, p. 2.

35. On these cases, see Nelson, *Economic Crisis and Policy Choice;* and Stephan Haggard and Robert Kaufman, "Economic Adjustment in New Democracies," in Nelson (ed.), *Fragile Coalitions*, pp. 57–77.

36. On the "thesis of the perverse effect," see Albert O. Hirschman, "Reactionary Rhetoric," *The Atlantic Monthly* 263, no. 5 (May 1989):63–70.

37. See Richard L. Sklar, "Democracy in Africa," in Patrick Chabal (ed.), *Political Domination in Africa* (Cambridge: Cambridge University Press, 1986), pp. 17–29.

38. On the "nightmare scenario," see ECA, "ECA and Africa's Development: 1983–2008," Addis Ababa, April 1983; and "Beyond Recovery: ECA—Revised Perspective of Africa's Development, 1988–2008," Addis Ababa, March 1988.

39. Confidential interview, Washington, D.C., May 4, 1990.

40. "OAU Promotes Greater Democracy," *Financial Times* (London), July 12, 1990, p. 18.

41. See John Gerard Ruggie, "International Regimes, Transactions and Change," *International Organization* 36, no. 2 (Spring 1982):379–415; Gilpin, *Political Economy;* Kenneth Oye, *The World Political Economy in the 1930s and the 1980s* (Princeton: Princeton University Press, forthcoming); Susan Strange, "Protectionism and World Politics," *International Organization* 36, no. 2 (Spring 1982):417–455; and Susan Strange, *States and Markets* (New York: Blackwell, 1988).

42. "Africa Ill-Prepared for Challenge from Europe," *Financial Times* (London), November 16, 1989, p. 6.

43. Dr. B. E. Kipkorir, executive chairman of Kenya Commercial Bank, quoted in Baffour Ankomah, "Who Isn't Afraid of 1992?" *New African* (February 1989):25.

44. On the informal economy, see Janet MacGaffey, *Entrepreneurs and Parasites: The Struggle for Indigenous Capitalism in Zaire* (Cambridge: Cambridge University Press, 1987).

4

AFRICA AND OTHER CIVILIZATIONS: CONQUEST AND COUNTERCONQUEST

ALI A. MAZRUI

CULTURAL RECEPTIVITY

One of the most intriguing aspects of the historical sociology of Africa in recent times has been its remarkable cultural receptivity. For example, Christianity has spread faster in a single century in Africa than it did in several centuries in Asia. European languages have acquired political legitimacy in Africa more completely than in formerly colonized Asian countries such as India, Indonesia, and Vietnam. Indeed, while nobody talks about English-speaking Asian countries or francophone Asia, African countries are routinely categorized in terms of the European language they have adopted as their official medium (lusophone, English-speaking, and francophone African states).

North Africa and much of the Nile Valley were not only converted to the Muslim religion, but millions of the inhabitants were linguistically transformed into Arabs. Elsewhere in Africa the Muslim faith has continued to attract new converts in spite of the competitive impact of Euro-Christian colonial rule following the Berlin Conference of 1884–1885.

Linguistic nationalism in favor of indigenous languages in postcolonial Africa has been relatively weak. Only a handful of African countries allocate much money toward developing African languages for modern needs, even though most African governments south of the Sahara give high priority to teaching European languages in African schools.

No African country has officially allocated a national holiday in honor of the gods of indigenous religions. All African countries, on the other hand, have a national holiday that either favors Christian festivals (especially Christmas), Muslim festivals (such as Idd el Fitr), or both categories of imported festivals. The Semitic religions (Christianity and Islam) are nationally honored in much of Africa; the indigenous religions are at best ethnic rather than national occasions.

TOWARD CONQUERING THE CONQUERORS

Africa's readiness to welcome new cultures is both its strength and its weakness. Africa is prepared to learn from others, but danger also looms that Africa will depend upon and intellectually imitate these others.

Often overlooked is the third dimension of this equation—that those who have culturally conquered Africa have, over time, become culturally dependent upon Africa. The conqueror has sometimes been counterconquered. This chapter is about this boomerang effect in acculturation and assimilation.

The process of Africa's counterpenetration has sometimes been facilitated by Africa's political fragmentation in the egalitarian age. The majority of the members of the nonaligned movement are from Africa. Almost half of the members of the Organization of the Islamic Conference are also members of the Organization of African Unity. Much of the agenda of the British Commonwealth since the 1960s has been set by its African members, as they have used the Britannic fraternity to help liberate southern Africa and dismantle apartheid. Although fewer than a third of the forty-seven members of the commonwealth are African countries, this group has been by far the most influential regional group in shaping the commonwealth's agenda and decisions. African influence has been further enhanced by the election of the first African secretary-general of the commonwealth, Chief Eleazar Emeka Anyaoku of Nigeria. In the United Nations, African countries make up almost a third of the total global membership. Africa's fragmentation in an egalitarian age has helped its voting power in the General Assembly.

However, there are limits to the egalitarianism of the age in terms of power. The United States almost single-handedly prevented the election of the first African secretary-general of the United Nations, Ambassador Salim Ahmed Salem of Tanzania. The United States and Great Britain also succeeded in driving out of power the first African director-general of the United Nations Economic, Social, and Cultural Organization (UNESCO), Moukhtar M'Bow. Even in this relatively egalitarian age in human history, real power continues to be decisive when there is enough at stake to invoke it.

Nevertheless, Africa's weakness has been a source of power on other occasions. As indicated earlier, Africa's territorial fragmentation has translated into voting influence even in UNESCO, in spite of what happened to M'Bow. And the General Assembly of the United Nations continues to take into account the liberation concerns of the African group.

Similarly, Africa's cultural receptivity, although often excessive and a cause of intellectual dependency, has sometimes become the basis of its counterinfluence on its conquerors. This chapter on Africa's counterpenetration will examine Africa's relationship with two interrelated civilizations—Arab and the politics of identity, and Islamic and the politics of religion. It will then examine the French connection and the politics of language as an illustration of Africa's potential in counterinfluencing the Western world. The chapter concludes with Africa's interaction with India—with special reference to the legacies of Mahatma Gandhi and Jawaharlal Nehru—and the politics of liberation.

Africa Conquers the Arabs

In the seventh century A.D., parts of Africa were captured by the Arabs in the name of Islam. Three factors hastened the Arabization of North Africa and the Lower Nile Valley. One factor was Africa's cultural receptivity—a remarkable degree of assimilability. The second factor was the Arab lineage system and the way it defined the offspring of mixed marriages. The third factor behind Arabization was the widespread use of the Arabic language and its role in defining what constitutes an Arab.

At first glance it seems clear that the Arabs took over large chunks of Africa. But on closer scrutiny, the Afro-Arab saga involves both conquest and counterconquest. It is similar to the British colonization of North America. Much later imperial Great Britain was being protected and led by her former colony—the United States of America. But there is one important difference in the case of reciprocal conquest between the Arabs and the Africans: The actual creation of new Arabs still continues. Let us examine this remarkable process of "Arab-formation" in Africa across the centuries more closely.

The Arab conquest of North Africa in the seventh and eighth centuries initiated two processes—Arabization (through language) and Islamization (through religion). The spread of Arabic as a native language created new Semites (the Arabs of North Africa). The diffusion of Islam created new monotheists but not necessarily new Semites. The Copts of Egypt are linguistically Arabized, but they are not Muslims. On the other hand, the Wolof and Hausa are predominantly Islamized, but they are not Arabs.

The process by which the majority of North Africans became Arabized was partly biological and partly cultural. The biological process involved intermarriage and was considerably facilitated by the upward lineage system of the Arabs. Basically, if the father of a child is an Arab, the child is an

Arab regardless of the ethnic or racial origins of the mother. This lineage system could be described as *ascending miscegenation*, as the offspring ascends to the lineage of the more privileged parent.

This is in sharp contrast to the lineage system of the United States, for example, where the child of a white father and a black mother *descends* to the less privileged race of that society. Indeed, in a system of descending miscegenation, it does not matter whether the father or the mother is black. An offspring of such racial mixture descends to black underprivilege. The U.S. system therefore does not coopt "impurities" upward across the racial barrier to higher status; it pushes them downward into disadvantaged status.

It is precisely because the Arabs have the opposite lineage system that North Africa was so rapidly transformed into part of the Arab world (and not merely the Muslim world). The Arab lineage system permitted considerable racial cooptation. Children of mixed parentage were admitted to higher echelons as full members, provided the father was an Arab. Thus, the colors in the Arab world range from the whites of Syria and Iraq to the browns of Yemen and from blonde-haired Lebanese to the black Arabs of Sudan.

Within Africa the valley of the White Nile is a fascinating story of evolving Arabization. The Egyptians were not Arabs when the Muslim conquest occurred in the seventh century A.D. The process of Islamization in the sense of actual change of religion took place rapidly after the Arab conquerors had consolidated their hold on the country.

The Arabization of Egypt, however, occurred significantly slower than its Islamization. The Egyptians changed from Christianity to Islam more quickly than they changed linguistically from ancient Egyptian and ancient Greek to Arabic. Even when Arabic became the mother tongue of the majority of Egyptians, it took centuries before Egyptians began to call themselves Arabs.

When one considers the pace of Arabization in the first millennium of Islam, however, it occurred significantly faster than is typical in the history of human acculturation. The number of people in the Middle East who called themselves Arabs grew dramatically in a relatively short period—due partly to the exuberance of the new religion, partly to the rising prestige of the Arabic language, and partly to the rewards of belonging to a conquering civilization. Religious, political, and psychological factors transformed Arabism into an expansionist culture that absorbed the conquered into the body politic of the conquerors. In the beginning, there was an island or a peninsula called Arabia, but in time there were far more Arabs outside Arabia than within. In the end there was an "Arab world."

Along the valley of the White Nile, northern Sudan was also gradually Islamized and more recently has been increasingly Arabized. Again people who were not originally Arabs have come to see themselves increasingly as such.

The question that arises is whether there is a manifest destiny of the White Nile that is pushing it toward further Arabization. It began with the Egyptians and their gradual acquisition of an Arab identity. The northern Sudanese have been in the process of similar Arabization. Are the southern Sudanese the next target of the conquering wave of Arabization? Will the twin forces of biological mixture (intermarriage between northerners and southerners) and cultural assimilation transform the Dinkas and Nuers of today into the black Arabs of tomorrow?

This is not inconceivable, provided the country as a whole holds together. As intermarriage increases, northern Sudanese will become more black in color. As acculturation increases in the south, southerners will become more Arab. Biological Africanization of the north and cultural Arabization of the south will reinforce each other and help to forge a more integrated Sudan.

Southern Sudanese are the only sub-Saharan Africans who are being Arabized faster than they are being Islamized. This is in sharp contrast to the experience of such sub-Saharan peoples as the Wolof, the Yoruba, the Hausa, or even the Somali—among all of whom the religion of Islam has become much more infused than the language of the Arabs. This rapid Arabization of the southern Sudanese linguistically has two possible outcomes. The southern Sudanese could become Sudan's equivalent of the Copts of Egypt—a Christian minority whose mother tongue would then be Arabic. Or, the Arabization of the southern Sudanese could be followed by their religious Islamization—in time, making southern and northern Sudanese truly intermingled and eventually indistinguishable.

Meanwhile, the Swahili language has been creeping northward toward Juba from East Africa as surely as Arabic has been creeping southward from the Mediterranean. The Swahilization of Tanzania, Kenya, Uganda, and eastern Zaire has been gathering momentum. With Arabic coming up the Nile toward Juba and Kiswahili moving down the same valley, southern Sudanese will find themselves caught between the forces of Arabization and those of Swahilization. Historically, these two cultures can easily reinforce each other; thus, the manifest destiny of the Valley of the White Nile appears to be a slow but definite assimilation into the Arab fold.

But racial ambivalence will maintain a linkage with Africanity. Indeed, the southern Sudanese are likely to be the most negritudist of all Sudanese even if they do become Arabized. There is also a precedent of black nationalism among northern Sudanese; few realize how strong such sentiment is among important sectors of northern Sudanese. Muhammad al-Mahdi al-Majdhub, for example, has been described as "probably the first Sudanese poet to tap the possibility of writing poetry in the Arabic language with a consciousness of a profound belonging to a 'Negro' tradition."[1] The poet al-Mahdi has affirmed: "In the Negroes I am firmly rooted though the Arabs may boastfully claim my origin. . . . My tradition is: beads, feathers, and a palm-tree which I embrace, and the forest is singing around us."[2]

Muhammad Miftah al-Fayturi is another Arab negritudist. Information about his ancestry is somewhat contradictory. His father was probably Libyan and his mother Egyptian, but of southern Sudanese ancestry. In his words:

> Do not be a coward
> Do not be a coward
> say it in the face
> of the human race:
> My father is of a Negro father,
> My mother is a Negro woman,
> and I am black.[3]

In some notes about al-Fayturi's early poetic experiences is the anguished cry "I have unriddled the mystery, the mystery of my tragedy: I am short, black and ugly."

There are also Arab negritudists who sometimes revel in the fact that they are racially mixed. They can also be defiant and angrily defensive about that mixture. Salah A. Ibrahim, in his piece on "The Anger of the Al-Hababy Sandstorm," declared:

> Liar is he who proclaims:
> "I am the unmixed. . . ." Yes, a liar![4]

The Sudan of the future may have even less room for such "lies" than it has at present. Almost by definition, Arabization is a process of creating mixture, and its relentless force along the White Nile is heading southward toward Juba and beyond.

How has the boomerang effect worked in relation to the Arabization of Africa? In what sense has there been an Africanization of the Arab world? We must remember that the majority of the Arab people live in Africa. Over 60 percent of the population of the Arab world now resides west of the Red Sea on African soil. The largest Arab country in population is Egypt, which in 1989 became the presiding country in the Organization of African Unity while its president was simultaneously seeking a resolution of the Palestinian-Israeli impasse. The headquarters of the Arab League is in Africa—currently in Tunis and previously in Cairo. If this headquarter symbolizes the capital of the entire Arab world, then the capital of the Arabs during the entire second half of the twentieth century has been located on the African continent.

When the Palestine Liberation Organization and its warriors were expelled from Lebanon by the Israeli military invasion of 1982, the headquarters of the Palestinian movement moved to Africa. Major decisions about the Palestinians, including the declaration of the Palestinian state, were now made in Tunis. It was partly because of this evolving Afro-Palestinian solidarity that Yassir Arafat was in Lusaka in 1990 to embrace Nelson Mandela when the latter made his first trip outside South Africa in thirty years.

The largest city in the Arab world—Cairo—is located on its African side. The population of Cairo is more than double that of Saudi Arabia as a whole. Cairo has become the cultural capital of the Arab world. Its greatest singers and musicians—including Umm Kulthum, affectionately known as "the Star at Sunrise"—have mesmerized the Middle East from the studios of the Voice of the Arabs Broadcasting System in Cairo. Kulthum's funeral was second only to President Nasser's in 1970 in terms of the size of the crowds and the passions and public grief displayed.

The most famous twentieth-century Arab composer also came from the African side of the Arab world. Al-Ustadh Muhammad Abdul Wahab started primarily as a singer and an instrumentalist. His musical compositions were initially simple, but after more intense study of Western classical music—especially Beethoven—Muhammad Adbul Wahab took Egyptian music to new levels of cross-cultural complexity. He developed new styles of Arab orchestral and symphonic music. All this innovative work was done on the African side of the Arab world.

Culture has a technological and professional infrastructure. Egypt is by far the most important film-making country in both Africa and the Arab world. Egyptian shows are featured prominently on cinema screens and television on both sides of the Red Sea.

Other skills of the Arab people also emanate disproportionately from the African side. Boutros Boutros-Ghali, Egypt's minister of state for foreign affairs, has estimated that sometimes as many as two million Egyptians provide technical assistance to other Arab countries.[5]

Egypt has also been important in the Arab military equation in at least four of the Arab-Israeli wars. Until the 1973 war, the Arab armies were no match for the Israelis. Even in 1973, Arab victories came mainly at the beginning of the conflict. The nearest thing to Arab military credibility against Israel came from the African side of the Arab region, which is why the United States invested so heavily in the Camp David Accords and the neutralization of Egypt as a confrontation state against Israel.

In the year A.D. 639, the Arabs crossed into Africa and conquered Egypt. By the second half of the twentieth century, Egypt had become the most important pillar of the Arab military defense. History has once again boomeranged in the interaction between Africa and its conquerors. The ancestral home of the Arabs in Asia is now heavily dependent—culturally and militarily—on the African side of the Arab nation.

The ancestral home of Islam—Saudi Arabia—has thus far retained a preponderance of oil reserves and petro-power. Perhaps only the petro-factor has prevented the African side of the Arab nation from attaining complete dominance. Arabized Africa does lead the way demographically, culturally, technologically, militarily, and artistically.

Africa: The First Islamic Continent?

Why are Islam and Christianity continuing to spread so fast in sub-Saharan Africa? Why has religious receptivity in Africa been so remarkable? The spread of Christianity during Africa's colonial period was particularly spectacular. The Christian gospel spread faster in a single century in Africa than it did in several centuries in places such as India and China. Christianity in southern India is almost two thousand years old—going back to the days of the disciples of Jesus. Yet the present-day Christian population in India is only 20 million out of a total population of 820 million.[6]

When we turn to Islam, Africa may become to Islam what Europe became to Christianity—the first continent to have a majority of believers. It is possible that Africa will become the first continent to have a majority of Muslims.

Since independence, two issues have been central to religious speculation in Africa—Islamic expansion and Islamic revivalism. Expansion deals with the spread of religion and the scale of new conversions. Revivalism involves the rebirth of faith among those who are already converted. Expansion is a matter of geography and populations—of new worlds to conquer. Revivalism is a matter of history and nostalgia—of ancient worlds to reenact. The spread of Islam in postcolonial Africa is basically a peaceful process of persuasion and consent. The revival of Islam is often an angry process of rediscovered fundamentalism.

In Arab Africa, little expansion is taking place, although some Egyptian Muslim fundamentalists regard the Coptic church as a historical anachronism that ought to end. For North Africa as a whole, Islamic revivalism is the main issue. The widespread belief by revisionists that Sadat abandoned Islam by making peace with Israel probably cost Sadat his life in 1981 and has sometimes threatened the ruling regimes of Tunisia, Algeria, and Morocco.

Outside Arab Africa the central issue concerning Islam is not merely its revival, it is also the speed of its expansion. There are more Muslims in Nigeria than in any Arab country, including Egypt. Muslims in Ethiopia make up nearly half the population. Elsewhere in Africa, Islam has spread—however unevenly—all the way to the Cape of Good Hope. Islam has existed in South Africa for three hundred years, having first come from Southeast Asia with Malay immigrants.

The largest countries in Africa in terms of population are Nigeria, Egypt, Ethiopia, and Zaire. Among them these four countries account for over 120 million Muslims. Virtually half of the population of the continent is now Muslim.

But religion in Africa does not exist in isolation. The world of religious experience in Africa is rich in diversity. It is even affected by the rivalry between the written word and the oral tradition. The written word and literacy are often regarded as allies of modernization. But the written word can also be an adversary to modernization, particularly in situations where a holy book or sacred text commands so much loyalty that it hinders the process of secularization. The primordial power of the Qur'an (Koran) on Muslim believers has tended to make modernization in the Muslim world more difficult.

Religions of the oral tradition, on the other hand, tend to be more receptive to new religious influences. African traditional religions are particularly ecumenical. The same African citizen may combine either Islam or Christianity with his or her ethnic religion in what is called *syncretism*. However, while an African may be both a Muslim and a follower of a traditional creed, he or she is unlikely to be both a Muslim and a Christian. One religion of sacred text (such as Islam) can be combined with a religion of oral message (the Yoruba religion), but rarely can two religions of sacred text (Sunni Islam and Roman Catholicism) be adhered to by the same individual.

Of the three principal religious legacies in Africa (indigenous, Islamic, and Christian), the most tolerant has been the indigenous tradition. It is arguable that Africa did not have religious wars before the arrival of Christianity and Islam. Indigenous religions were neither *universalist* (seeking to convert the entire human race) nor *competitive* (in bitter rivalry against other creeds). Christianity and Islam, on the other hand, were both universalist and competitive—perhaps especially in black Africa where Christianity and Islam have often been in competition for the soul of the continent. Rivalry has sometimes resulted in conflict.

Indigenous African religions, on the other hand, are basically communal rather than universalist. As with Hinduism and modern Judaism—and unlike Christianity and Islam—indigenous African traditions have not sought to convert all of mankind. The Yoruba do not seek to convert the Ibo to the Yoruba religion, or vice versa. Nor do the Yoruba or the Ibo compete with each other for the souls of a third group. By not being proselytizing religions, indigenous African creeds have not fought with each other.

The indigenous toleration today has often mitigated the competitiveness of the imported Semitic religions (Christianity and Islam). Let us illustrate this point with Senegal, which is over 80 percent Muslim. The founder of this predominantly Islamic society was Leopold Sedar Senghor—a Roman Catholic. He presided over postcolonial Senegal for two decades (1960–1980) in basic political partnership with the Muslim leaders of the country, the Marabouts.

Contrast this with the history of the United States as a predominantly Protestant society. In spite of a constitution that ostensibly separated church from state in the eighteenth century, it was not until 1960 that the U.S. electorate elected a Roman Catholic as president. When will the United States elect a Jew to that highest office? Although U.S. Jews have occupied some of the highest offices in the land and have been represented on the Supreme Court, it seems unlikely that there will be a Jewish U.S. president in the twentieth century.

Muslims in the United States may now equal Jews in number (although not in influence and power). Although the constitution still separates church from state, the prospect of a *Muslim* president of the United States seems incomprehensible.

And yet in 1960 newly independent Senegal calmly accepted a Roman Catholic to preside over a basically Muslim country. Senghor was not a fellow Muslim but was from a different denomination (as Kennedy was a fellow Christian to most Americans but from a different sect). And yet he served as president of a stable Muslim country for some twenty years.

His successor as president was Abdou Diouf, finally a Muslim ruler of a Muslim society. But the tradition of ecumenical tolerance continued in Senegal. The first lady, Madame Elizabeth Diouf, was Roman Catholic, and several of the new president's ministers were Christian.

Senegalese religious tolerance has continued in other spheres since that time. What might be regarded as provocative in Islamic countries elsewhere in the world has been tolerated in Senegal. There have been occasions when a Christian festival such as the First Communion—with feasting, merrymaking, and singing—has been held publicly in Dakar right in the middle of the Islamic fast of Ramadhan, and the Christian merrymakers have been left undisturbed.

To summarize, predominantly Muslim countries south of the Sahara have had above-average religious toleration. The capacity to accommodate other faiths may to some extent be part of the historical tradition of Islam in multireligious empires. But indigenous African traditions have been far more tolerant of religious differences than either Islam or Christianity, especially since these traditions do not aspire to universalism and are not inherently competitive. In black Africa this indigenous tolerance has, as indicated, often moderated the competitive propensities of Christianity and Islam.

As president of Uganda in his first administration, Milton Obote (a Protestant) boasted that his extended family in Lango consisted of Muslims, Catholics, and Protestants "at peace with each other." Obote's successor, Idi Amin Dada (a Muslim), also had a multireligious extended family and once declared that he planned to have at least one of his sons trained for the Christian priesthood. (Amin may have reconsidered the matter when, upon losing office, he found political refuge in Saudi Arabia as a guest of the custodians of the Islamic holy cities of Mecca and Medina.) Religious ecumenicalism and cultural receptivity continue to moderate the sensibilities of contemporary Africa.

When we place Islam in the context of the African continent as a whole, the cultural boomerang effect is again discernible. The most influential Islamic university in the world, Al-Azhar University, is on the African continent in Cairo and is credited with some of the most important *fatwa* under the Shari'a (legal opinions under Islamic law) in the last six hundred years. Al-Azhar was founded by the Fatimids in A.D. 970, which makes it one of the oldest and most durable universities in the world. The basic program of studies through the ages has been Islamic law, theology, and the Arabic language, with other subjects added more recently. Women have been admitted since 1962. The university has continued to attract Muslim students from as far away as China and Indonesia. It is widely regarded as the principal center of Islamic learning in the world.

Islamic modernism also developed on the African side of the Muslim world. Muhammad Abduh (1849–1905) is still widely acclaimed as the primary architect of the modernization and reform of Islam. Born in the Nile Delta, he was influenced by the great pan-Islamic revolutionary, Jamal al Din al-Afghani, who had settled in Cairo before being expelled for political activity in 1879. Abduh himself suffered exile more than once. He became the leading jurist of the Arab world, a professor at Al-Azhar University, and eventually *Mufti* (chief Islamic chancellor) of Egypt. His doctrinal reforms included freedom of will in Islam, the harmony of reason with revelation, the primacy of ethics over ritual and dogma in religion, and the legitimacy of interest on loans under Islamic law.

A more recent disciple of Abduh and al-Afghani was the Sudanese scholar, Mahmoud Muhammad Taha. Taha's version of Islamic modernism in Sudan earned him a punishment more severe than those suffered by Abduh and al-Afghani in nineteenth-century Egypt. Under the presidency of Jaafar el-Nimeiry in Sudan, Taha was executed in his old age in January 1985 on charges of apostasy and heresy.[7]

While this history of Islamic modernism includes personal tragedy as well as intellectual originality, the role of Africa in the reformation of Islam is apparent. Africa has often been in the vanguard of Islamic innovation and doctrinal review. Africa's remarkable presence in the global Islamic equation includes the scale of its membership in the Organization of the Islamic Conference (OIC). Almost half of the members of this global Islamic organization are also members of the Organization of African Unity. Africa has produced some of the leaders of the OIC. The late Ahmed Sekou Toure of Guinea (Conakry) was chairman of the OIC when he attempted to mediate between Iraq and Iran in the earlier phases of the Iran-Iraq war.

In terms of distribution, Islam is indeed an Afro-Asian religion. Almost all Muslim countries are located in Africa or in Asia. In 1988 the world's Muslim population was estimated at 984 million. Early in the twenty-first century, the Muslim population may reach 25 percent of the human race. The fastest rate of increase in the world's Muslim population is currently in Africa, partly because Africa is undergoing the fastest rate of Islamic conversion of any major region on earth. Also, natural fertility rates in Africa are higher than anywhere else in the world, and Muslims in Africa are reproducing at a faster rate than most other Africans. As one study has demonstrated:

> The single most remarkable demographic aspect of Islamic societies is the nearly universal high level of fertility—the average of childbearing in Islamic nations is 6 children per woman. . . . Fertility rataes are highest for those Islamic nations in sub-Saharan Africa—an average of 6.6 births per woman. Furthermore, African Islamic nations south of the Sahara have higher fertility on average than do other developing nations in that region.[8]

There is evidence not only that Muslim women marry significantly earlier than women in other developing countries but also that they aspire to have more children. The Kenya Fertility Survey of 1977 (part of the World Fertility Survey) helped to demonstrate that among currently married Muslim women in that country, the average desired family size was 8.4 children: "This was the highest of any religious grouping, with Catholic women preferring 7.1 children and Protestant women an average of 7.0 children."[9]

Although many millions more Muslims are found in Asia than in Africa, the demographic indicators show that the gap is narrowing dramatically. Before the end of this century, Africa may become the only continent with a Muslim majority. A part of Asia once conquered Africa in the name of Islam. Africa is now overshadowing Asia in the advancement of Islam. The cultural boomerang effect has again been at work.[10]

History is playing out a remarkable prophetic destiny. The first great Muezzin of Islam was a black man, Bilal, of Ethiopian extraction. Bilal called Muslim believers to prayer in seventh-century Arabia.

Symbolically, this call to prayer has echoed down the centuries. In the twentieth century, has Bilal been heard particularly clearly in his ancestral continent of Africa? Perhaps the cultural boomerang effect has now taken the form of echoes of an African Muezzin reverberating back across the centuries. What of the echoes from that other great civilization in Africa's destiny—the Western heritage? Our next case study concerns the French version of the idea of *Eurafrica.*

Eurafrica: The French Connection

France invented the concept of *Eurafrica,* asserting an organic relationship between Europe and Africa deep enough to transform the two continents into a single integrated international subsystem. How does this concept relate to the French language?

The majority of French-speaking people in the world live in the Western world, mainly in France itself. However, the majority of French-speaking *states* are in Africa. Over twenty members of the Organization of African Unity are French-speaking: Algeria, Benin, Burundi, Chad, Cameroon, Central African Republic, Comoros, Congo, Côte d'Ivoire, Djibouti, Burkina Faso, Gabon, Guinea, Madagascar, Mali, Mauritania, Morocco, Niger, Rwanda, Senegal, Réunion, Togo, Tunisia, and Zaire.

Without Africa the French language would be almost provincial. Zaire is the largest French-speaking country in population after France and is destined to be the largest early in the twenty-first century. If Zaire succeeds in stabilizing itself and in assuming effective control over its resources, it may become France's rival in influence and power in French-speaking Africa. When we look at the global scene as a whole, use of the French language is declining in the Northern Hemisphere. On the other hand, it is spreading and gaining in influence in the Southern Hemisphere, especially in Africa.

The most important challenge to the French language in the Northern Hemisphere has been the vast expansion of U.S. influence, with a corresponding use of the English language, in the twentieth century. While the spread of the English language in Africa has been due primarily to the impact of imperial Great Britain, the spread of English in Europe and its expanding role in international affairs have been due largely to the new U.S. hegemony in the Northern Hemisphere. The triumph of the English language globally has ranged from its increasing usage in diplomacy to its role as the supreme language of aviation and air control.

A second reason for the diminishing usage of French in the Northern Hemisphere concerns the computer revolution. The amount of information circulating in English is much greater than that transmitted in French. The global influence of U.S. computer firms such as IBM has reinforced the Anglo computer revolution.

Another factor is the decline of the cultural influence of Europe's upper classes. Royal houses in continental Europe once spoke French extensively. In the aftermath of the Russian revolution in 1917 and the subsequent development of social egalitarianism in Europe as a whole, linguistic snobbery—which favored the use of French—declined, and linguistic pragmatism—which ultimately favored the use of English—became the norm.

The fourth factor behind the decline of French in the Northern Hemisphere was Great Britain's entry into the European Economic Community. This made English more clearly an official language of the community. It became increasingly influential in the affairs of the community, in both written and oral forms. Smaller members of the community have increasingly turned to English rather than French in the post-Gaullist era.

A final factor in the decline of the usage of French is linked to the decline of the power of the French-speaking Walloons in Belgium. The days of French preeminence in Belgium were coming to an end by the 1980s, although francophone Brussels still remained the capital. Belgium moved toward a neofederal structure rooted in the principle of linguistic parity between French and Flemish.

It is arguable that the French language has made some gains in North America as a result of the greater recognition of bilingualism in the federation of Canada. On the other hand, a decline of linguistic nationalism in Quebec has occurred since the old militancy of the 1960s.

The decline of the role of German in Europe has also tended to favor English rather than French. When the Scandinavian countries regarded German as their first foreign language, they tended to use French as well for a sense of balance. But when Scandinavians turned to English as their first foreign language, both German and French suffered. English was more widely used internationally than German; thus, its adoption by Scandinavians as their premier foreign language reduced the need to balance it with French. Scandinavian schools are still aware of the importance of French and German as well as English, but linguistic priorities have changed in the Nordic syllabi and curricula and in class enrollments.

Japan has also experienced shifts in emphasis that have demoted German and French and advanced the role of English in educational and linguistic priorities. Between the Meiji Restoration in 1868 and Japan's defeat in World War II in 1945, Japan's main Western role models were Germany and France. This Franco-German orientation influenced Japan's curricula and syllabi and its legal system and civil code.

The U.S. occupation of Japan after World War II decisively shifted Japan from a Franco-German to an Anglo-Saxon orientation. The continuing

U.S. relationship with Japan after the occupation consolidated Japan's cultural reorientation. While the Americans under Douglas MacArthur imposed upon Japan a national constitution basically drawn from continental European experience, much of the rest of the Westernization of Japan has been a case of cultural Americanization—from Japan's introduction to baseball to its enthusiasm for U.S. pop stars. The economies of the two countries have become interlocked. The confirmation of English as Japan's first Western language in the postwar era has been part of this U.S. phase of Japan's transformation. The decline of the use of French and German in Japan was an inevitable consequence of the Americanization of Japan. A surprising development was the decision of the Socialist party of Japan to adopt a campaign anthem written in English in the election campaign for the Lower House in 1989–1990.

If these have been the main factors that have resulted in the decline of the French language in the Northern Hemisphere, which factors have contributed to its expansion in the South? What must be emphasized first is that the Southern expansion has occurred mainly in Africa. On the whole, the distribution of the French language is bicontinental, with a large number of French-speaking *individuals* in Europe and a large number of French-speaking *states* in Africa. There are smaller francophone constituencies in Quebec, Lebanon, Syria, Indochina, and elsewhere, but these are peripheries of the francophone world. The main francophone theater is in Europe and Africa.

Factors that have favored expansion in Africa include the type of states French and Belgian imperialism created during the colonial period. These were often multiethnic countries that needed a lingua franca. Colonial policy had chosen the French language as the lingua franca, and the entire educational system and domestic political process consolidaated that linguistic choice.

A related factor was the assimilationist policy of France as an imperial power. This created an elite mesmerized by French culture and civilization. A surprising number of persons retained dual citizenship with France even after independence. Some African heads of state may still secretly be citizens of France. Annual holidays in France continue to be part of the elite cultures of francophone West and North Africa.

With some subsidies and technical assistance, the French language is also increasingly taught in classrooms in anglophone Africa. Before independence British educational policymakers were more committed to the promotion of indigenous African languages than to the rival French legacy in British colonies. French offers to send language teachers to schools in British colonies were also not welcome. The difference made by Africa's independence partly consists of greater readiness on the part of anglophone governments to accept France's offers to supply teachers of the French language. Many African universities in the commonwealth have been the beneficiaries of technical assistance and cultural subsidies from the local French Embassy or directly from France.

France's policy in Africa is consolidated partly through an aggressive cultural diplomacy. Considerable amounts of money are spent on French-style syllabi and curricula in African schools and on the provision of French teachers, advisers, and reading materials. A residual French economic and administrative presence in most former French colonies has deepened Africa's orientation toward Paris.

In addition, every French president since Charles de Gaulle has attempted to cultivate special personal relationships with at least some of the African leaders. There is little doubt that French-speaking African presidents have greater and more personalized access to the French president than their anglophone counterparts have had to either the British prime minister or the British head of state in spite of commonwealth conferences.

Here is another case of reciprocal conquest. There is little doubt that the French language and culture have conquered large parts of Africa. Many decisions about the future of Africa are being made by people deeply imbued with French values and perspectives.

Moreover, France is expanding its constituency in Africa, at least outside Algeria. The postcolonial policy of re-Arabization in Algeria is designed to increase the use of Arabic in schools and public affairs at the expense of the preeminent colonial role of the French language. Also, Mobutu Sese Seko's policy of promoting regional languages in Zaire (Lingala, Kikongo, Tchiluba, and Kiswahili) is partly responsible for the decline of the use of French in Zairean curricula. But such a setback for the use of French in Africa is the exception rather than the rule.

However, France's aspiration to remain a global power requires a cultural as well as an economic constituency. Its cultural constituency in Europe has been declining; its cultural constituency in Africa has become more valuable than ever. A remarkable interdependence has emerged—still imperfect and uneven but real enough to make Africa indispensable in the recognition of France as a truly global power and the acceptance of the French language as a credible world language. *Eurafrica* as a concept obtains its maximum meaningfulness in the destiny of the French language. But there is also a concept of *Afrindia*, which will be explored next.

Afrindia: Between Gandhi and Nehru

Early in his life, Mahatma Gandhi saw nonviolent resistance as a method that would be well suited for the African as well as the Indian. In 1924 Gandhi said that if the black people "caught the spirit of the Indian movement their progress must be rapid."[11] In 1936 Gandhi went even further. To understand his claim, it should perhaps be linked with something that was said later by his disciple, Jawaharlal Nehru: "Reading through history I think the agony of the African continent . . . has not been equalled anywhere."[12]

To the extent that black men had more to be angry about than other men, they would need greater self-discipline than others to be "passive" in their resistance. But by the same token, to the extent that black men in the last three centuries had suffered more than any others, passive but purposeful self-sacrifice for the cause should come more easily to them. And to the extent that black men had more for which to forgive the rest of the world, that forgiveness when it came should be all the more weighty. Perhaps in response to these considerations, Gandhi came to the conclusion by 1936 that it was "maybe through the Negroes that the unadulterated message of non-violence will be delivered to the world."[13]

Thus, in the United States the torch was passed to Martin Luther King, Jr. And in South Africa, where Gandhi first experimented with his methods, it passed to Albert Luthuli and later to Desmond Tutu. In Northern Rhodesia (Zambia after independence), Kenneth Kaunda became a vigorous Gandhian: "I reject absolutely violence in any of its forms as a solution to our problems."[14] In the Gold Coast (Ghana before independence), Nkrumah had translated *satyagraha* (soul force) into a program of "positive action," a program he defined as "non-cooperation based on the principle of absolute non-violence, as used by Gandhi in India."[15] In 1949 *The Morning Telegraph* of Accra went so far as to call Nkrumah the "Gandhi of Ghana."[16]

African conceptions of dignity now seemed very different from that old ceremonial affirmation of young Kikuyu initiates about which Kenyatta spoke—the glorification of the spear as "the symbol of our courageous and fighting spirit." But these new conceptions of dignity could also be differentiated from the submissive virtues of early missionary teachings. Yet, one question remained to be answered: Could passive resistance survive the attainment of independence? Would Gandhism retain political relevance once its immediate objective of liberation from colonialism was achieved?

It is perhaps not entirely accidental that the two most important Indian contributions to African political thought were the doctrines of nonviolence and nonalignment. Gandhi contributed passive resistance to one school of African thought; Nehru contributed nonalignment to almost all African countries. Uganda's President Milton Obote, in his tribute to Nehru on his death, said: "Nehru will be remembered as a founder of nonalignment. . . . The new nations of the world owe him a debt of gratitude in this respect."[17] However, Gandhi and Nehru both taught and learned from Africa.

How related are the two doctrines in their assumptions? For India Gandhi's nonviolence was a method of seeking freedom, while Nehru's nonalignment came to be a method of seeking peace. And yet nonalignment was, in some ways, a translation into foreign policy of some of the moral assumptions that underlay passive resistance in the domestic struggle for India's independence.

Nehru's armed ejection of Portuguese colonialism from Goa in 1961 had a significant impact on Africa. In the United Nations, Foreign Minister Khrishna Menon described colonialism as "permanent aggression." Particularly permanent was the colonialism of those who regarded their colonies as part of the metropole, as Portugal had pretended to do. In a situation in which colonialism threatened to be more durable than even permanent, a military solution was a necessary option.

Nehru's use of armed force against the Portuguese set a precedent for an Africa still shackled by Portuguese imperialism in Angola, Mozambique, and Guinea-Bissau. Had Gandhi's *satyagraha* been replaced in 1961 by Nehru's *satya-Goa?* Was Nehru's negation of nonviolence a legitimation of the violence of liberation? If Gandhi had taught Africa civil disobedience, had Nehru now taught Africa armed liberation? Had the armed ejection of Portugal from the Indian subcontinent strengthened Africa's resolve to eject Portugal from Angola, Mozambique, and Guinea-Bissau?

The impact of India upon twentieth-century Africa goes beyond even such towering figures as Mahatma Gandhi and Jawaharlal Nehru. But there is no doubt about the special significance for Africa of Gandhi's strategies of civil disobedience and Nehru's principles of both nonalignment and armed liberation. Gandhi's *satyagraha* inspired African political figures as diverse as Nobel laureate Albert Luthuli of South Africa and Ivorian president Felix Houphouet-Boigny. Nehru's ideas about what used to be called "positive neutralism" helped to shape African approaches to foreign policy in the entire postcolonial era.

Africa's Reverse Impact on Gandhi and Nehru

What has seldom been adequately examined is the reverse flow of influence *from* Africa *into* both Gandhi's vision of *satyagraha* and Nehru's concept of nonalignment. Experience in the southern part of Africa must be counted as part of the genesis of Gandhi's political philosophy. And the 1956 Suez war in the northern part of Africa was probably a major influence on Nehru's vision of nonalignment.

South Africa was the cradle and threatened to be the grave of passive resistance as a strategy of Africa's liberation. Gandhi first confronted the problem of politicized evil in the context of racism in South Africa. Racial humiliation in that part of the continent helped to radicalize him and therefore to prepare him for his more decisive historical role in British India later in the century.

Gandhi's political philosophy developed from both the world of ideas and the world of experience. Moreover, in the realm of ideas he relied heavily on both Western liberalism and Indian thought. But what helped to radicalize Gandhi's own interpretation of those ideas was the power of experience. And within that crucible of experience we must include his exposure to sustained segregation in South Africa—a deeper form of racism than even the racist horrors of British India at that time.

Under the stimulus of activated evil and the need to combat it, Gandhi radically reinterpreted important concepts in Indian thought. For example, he reinterpreted *Ahimsa,* transforming it from nonresistance to passive resistance. This provoked the criticism of such Western students of Indian philosophy as Albert Schweitzer, who was also deeply fascinated by Africa. Schweitzer objected to Gandhi's reformulation of *Ahimsa* on the following grounds.

> Gandhi places Ahimsa at the services of world-affirmation and life-affirmation, directly to activity within the world, and in this way it ceases to be what in essence it is. Passive resistance is a non-violent use of force. The idea is that, by circumstances brought about without violence, pressure is brought to bear on the opponent and he is forced to yield. Being an attack that is more difficult to parry than an active attack, passive resistance may be the more successful method. But there is also a danger that this concealed application of force may cause more bitterness than an open use of violence. In any case the difference between passive and active resistance is only quite relative.[18]

Schweitzer and Gandhi were both profound humanitarians, and both retained a fascination with Africa. But while Schweitzer sought to serve humanity ultimately by curing the physical body of disease, Gandhi sought to serve humanity by curing the social condition of injustice. Schweitzer approached his physiological mission through medical work in Gabon. Gandhi approached his sociological mission through passive resistance—first in South Africa and later in British India.

If Gandhi's *satyagraha* was a response to the moral confrontation between good and evil and to racial intolerance, Nehru's nonalignment was a response to the militarized confrontation between capitalism and socialism and to ideological intolerance. The regime in South Africa became the symbol of racial bigotry for Gandhi. The cold war between East and West became the essence of ideological bigotry for Nehru.

South Africa as an inspiration for Gandhi is well documented. North Africa as an inspiration for Nehru's nonalignment has been less explored. Two wars in North Africa in the 1950s were particularly important in Afro-Asian interaction. The Algerian war from 1954 to 1962 took African resistance beyond the passive level into the militarized active domain. African Gandhiism was in crisis. Had *satyagraha* been rejected as no longer relevant for the struggle against colonialism?

The second great war in North Africa in the 1950s was the Suez conflict of 1956. If the Algerian war marked a possible end to *satyagraha* as a strategy for African liberation movements, the Suez war marked a possible birth of nonalignment as a policy of the postcolonial era. Gamal Abdel Nasser of Egypt was economically punished by the United States, Great Britain, and the World Bank for purchasing arms from the Communist bloc. Washington, London, and the Bank reneged on their commitment to help Egypt build the Aswan Dam. Nasser's nationalization of the Suez Canal was an assertion of self-reliance. Revenue from the canal was going to help Egypt construct the Aswan Dam. Egypt's sovereign right to purchase arms from either East or West was not for sale. In retrospect, Nasser's nationalization of the Suez Canal was a kind of unilateral declaration of nonalignment before the nonaligned movement was formally constituted.

Before the actual outbreak of the Suez hostilities, the diplomatic division at the level of the big powers was indeed East-West. Socialist governments supported Nasser, while the capitalist world was alarmed by his nationalization of the canal. However, when Great Britain, France, and Israel actually invaded Egypt, the Western world was divided. The United States was strongly opposed to the military action taken by its closest allies.

The Soviet Union went further than merely condemning the aggression by Great Britain, France, and Israel. When the Western powers withdrew their canal pilots in an attempt to sabotage Egypt's efforts to operate the canal after the nationalization, the Soviet Union lent Egypt its pilots until Nasser could train his own. And in the wake of the West's reneging on the commitment to build the Aswan High Dam, the Soviet Union stepped into the breach and became the builder of the dam. What emerged from the entire experience was the value of trying to balance traditional Egyptian dependence on the West with readiness to find areas of cooperation with the East. The central principle of nonalignment was in the process of being conceived at Suez.

Nehru helped to mobilize Third-World opinion on the side of Nasser during the entire crisis. Although there was not as yet a nonalignment movement in world politics, the Suez conflict was part of its birth—and Nehru was the leading midwife in attendance.

These factors have made the Suez crisis part of the genesis of Nehru's diplomatic thought and vision, just as racism in South Africa remains part of the genesis of Gandhi's principle of *satyagraha*. Suez was the most dramatic test of a Third-World country when invaded by two members of the North Atlantic Treaty Organization (NATO) (France and Britain). Never before had a Third-World country been the subject of aggression by *two* members of NATO with the leader of NATO—the United States—protesting against its allies.

Mahatma Gandhi inspired many Africans to pursue the path of passive resistance, but Nehru's liberation of Goa in 1961–1962 converted even more Africans south of the Sahara to the use of military action. Gandhi was the prophet of nonviolence; Nehru became the symbol of armed struggle. Were the two Indians contradicting each other in the corridors of history? Or were passive resistance and armed struggle two sides of the same coin of liberation?

The answer probably lies in the unfolding struggle in the Republic of South Africa in the concluding years of the twentieth century. Both civil disobedience and armed struggle are still at play in South Africa, and they appear to be at once complementary and contradictory. We have noted that, in a sense, South Africa was the cradle of Gandhi's *satyagraha*. Is it about to become the graveyard of passive resistance, as violence subsequently escalates? Or will *satyagraha* receive a new moral validation in the process of dismantling apartheid?

The answer lies in the womb of history. Two things about South Africa are almost totally predictable. First, when the fires of struggle are put out, a new black-ruled republic will join the community of nations. Almost equally predictable is the foreign policy the new Republic of South Africa will adopt—one of nonalignment. When the Republic of South Africa joins the nonaligned movement, the heritage of Gandhi and the legacy of Nehru will at last be fused in Africa. Morally, Afrindia is about to be vindicated.

By a strange twist of fate, Mahatma Gandhi never won the Nobel prize, but four of his black disciples did. They are Ralph Bunche (1950), Albert Luthuli (1960), Martin Luther King, Jr. (1964), and Desmond Tutu (1984).

Africa's capacity to turn weakness into a form of influence has found a new arena of fulfillment. Fragmentation and excessive cultural receptivity are weaknesses, and weakness is not an adequate currency in the marketplace of power. But often the power of the weak is, in human terms, less dangerous than the weakness of the powerful—their arrogance.

CONCLUSION

I have sought to demonstrate in this chapter the paradox of counter-penetration and the boomerang effect in Africa's interaction with other civilizations. Africa's cultural receptivity to its Arab conquerors has now tilted the demographic balance and changed the Arab cultural equation. The majority of Arabs are now in Africa, and the African side of the Arab world has become the most innovative in the fields of art and science.

Africa's receptivity to Islam may make it the first truly Islamic continent. What Europe was to Christianity may be what Africa becomes to Islam—the first continent to have a preponderance of believers. Since the nineteenth century, African Islam has also been in the vanguard of the Islamic reformation and modernism, especially since the time of the Egyptian thinker, Muhammad Abduh. The martyrdom of Mahmoud Muhammad Taha in Sudan in 1985 is part of the story of daring innovation within the African constituency of Islam.

Africa's cultural receptivity to the French language and culture has made it the second-most-important home of French civilization after France itself. The majority of French–speaking countries are in Africa, and Zaire may one day become the largest French-speaking country in the world in population and possibly in material resources.

Africa's response to Gandhian ideas, reinforced by Christian pacifism, has resulted in more Nobel Peace Prizes being awarded to Africans than to Indians. Gandhi had once predicted that the torch of *satyagraha* would one day be borne by the black world. Black winners of the Nobel Prize for Peace in the second half of the twentieth century have included two South Africans (Albert Luthuli and Desmond Tutu) and two African-Americans (Ralph Bunche and Martin Luther King, Jr.).

Africa's response to Nehru's ideas of nonalignment has resulted in a majority of nonaligned countries being located in Africa. Africa was in fact the first continent to become almost completely nonaligned. If nonalignment once penetrated Africa, Africa has now truly penetrated the nonalignment movement.

In the future, Africa's cultural receptivity must be more systematically moderated by cultural selectivity. Counterpenetrating one's conquerors may be one worthy trend. But at least as important for Africa is avoiding being excessively penetrated by others.

Perhaps one day the sequence of cultural penetration will be reversed. Instead of Africans being Arabized so completely that the majority of Arabs are in Africa, some Asians may be Africanized so completely that they are indistinguishable from native Africans. Instead of Zaire being the largest French-speaking nation after France, some other European nation may become the second heartland of Yoruba civilization after West Africa.

NOTES

1. See Muhammed Abdul-Hai, *Conflict and Identity: The Cultural Poetics of Contemporary Sudanese Poetry* (Khartoum: Institute of African and Asian Studies, University of Khartoum, 1976), pp. 26–27.

2. *Nar al Majadhib* (Khartoum: 1969), pp. 195, 287; see also p. 24.

3. Cited by Abdul-Hai, *Conflict and Identity,* pp. 40–41.

4. *Ghadhbat al Hababy* (Beirut: 1968); Abdul-Hai, *Conflict and Identity,* p. 52.

5. Boutros-Ghali, interviewed by the author in Cairo, February 1986.

6. V. A. Panadiker and P. K. Umashaker, "Politics of Population Control in a Diverse, Federal Democratic Polity: The Case of India," Conference paper at international symposium on "The Politics of Induced Fertility Change," sponsored by the University of Michigan, Villa Serbelloni, Rockefeller Foundation Conference Center, Bellagio, Italy, February 19–23, 1990.

7. See Taha's book, *The Second Message of Islam* (Evanston, Ill.: Northwestern University Press, 1987).

8. John R. Weeks, "The Demography of Islamic Nations," *Population Bulletin* (a publication of the Population Reference Bureau, Inc.) 43, no. 4 (December 1988):15.

9. *Ibid.*, p. 20.

10. It is widely believed in African Muslim circles that Islam is already the majority religion on the African continent. This claim was often repeated at an international conference on "Islam in Africa," Abuja, Nigeria, November 1989. See *Africa Events* (London) 6, no. 2 (February 1990).

11. *Young India* (Madras: S. Ganesan, 1927), pp. 839–840. See also Pyarelal, "Gandhi and the African Question," *Africa Quarterly* 2, no. 2 (July-September 1962). See also the selection entitled "Mahatma Gandhi on Freedom in Africa," *Africa Quarterly* 1, no. 2 (July-September 1961). For a more extensive discussion by Gandhi on nonviolence, see M. Gandhi, *Non-Violence in Peace and War,* 2nd ed. (Ahmedabad: Navajivan Publishing House, 1944).

12. Jawaharlal Nehru, "Portuguese Colonialism: An Anachronism," *Africa Quarterly* 1, no. 3 (October-December 1961):9. See also Nehru, "Emergent Africa," *Africa Quarterly* 1, no. 1 (April-June 1961):7–9.

13. *Harijan,* 14 October 1939.

14. See *Black Government* (Lusaka: United Society for Christian Literature, 1960).

15. *Autobiography,* p. 92.

16. The *Morning Telegraph,* 27 June 1949.

17. See *Uganda Argus,* 29 May 1964.

18. Albert Schweitzer, *Indian Thought and Its Development,* trans. Mrs. C.E.B. Russell (1936), pp. 231–232. See also George Seaver, *Albert Schweitzer: The Man and His Mind* (London: Adam and Charles Black, 1951), p. 275.

PART TWO

CONTEMPORARY INTERNATIONAL CONFLICT AREAS IN AFRICA

5

SOUTHERN AFRICA: THE REVOLUTION PROLONGED

KENNETH W. GRUNDY

Viewed in broad historical terms, the focus of southern African interstate politics is becoming sharper. Slowly but undeniably, the southward thrust of African nationalism is coming closer and closer to the Republic of South Africa. The tide of African nationalism is reaching its flood, starting with the independence of the Congo (now Zaire) in 1960 and Tanganyika (now Tanzania) in 1961, followed by Malawi and Zambia in 1964, Botswana and Lesotho two years later, Swaziland in 1968, Mozambique and Angola in 1975, Zimbabwe in 1980 (after fifteen years of bogus "independence" as the settler state of Rhodesia), and most recently Namibia in 1990. The last four states gained their independence after protracted armed struggles and strenuous diplomatic efforts.

For defenders of minority rule or simply for those content with the status quo, the prospect of majoritarian government for South Africa is frightening. In fact, many white reactionary South Africans still deny the inevitability of the arrival of black rule in South Africa. The privilege, advantage, and power of white South Africans, in their view, need not be sacrificed if only their government in Pretoria would stand firm against concessions to the militant black majority. They feel they have the economic strength to maintain their regime in the face of foreign sanctions, hostility, and resistance from vulnerable black interests. They are convinced that in security terms they are without serious equal in the region. They perceive a genuine threat from surrounding black governments, especially from Zimbabwe. But they think that what their government needs is the will to hold power in the face of mounting demands for a transfer of that power.[1] A selective reading of history bears out this view. As they see it, South Africa successfully weathered past uprisings and efforts to ostracize it. The ability of independent Black Africa to challenge South Africa economically and militarily is declining. Disorder, chaos, and administrative failure bedevil neighboring states. The Western powers and the Socialist bloc seem to be losing interest in the region.

It is true that too frequently hope and expectations have been raised by proponents of radical change, only to be dashed by the authorities and their harsh, unbending opposition to demands for change. After Sharpeville and related protests in 1960, Soweto and its national spillover in 1976, and the nationwide uprising from 1983 to 1986, government forces sought to destroy and discredit the resistance and to reestablish their firm control of the situation. At Sharpeville, protesters sought to turn in their identity documents (passbooks) at a township police station. Panicky policemen fired on the crowd and killed sixty-nine people. Soweto is the generic term for the nationwide violence, the catalyst of which was a massive demonstration by school children protesting the compulsory use of the Afrikaans language as a medium of instruction. Altogether more than one thousand protesters died at the hands of the police in two months of confrontation. The 1983 to 1986 resistance was more widespread and diffuse in its opposition to apartheid and economic conditions, specifically to the government's plans for a tricameral legislature without black representation and to the active application of repressive security laws. In those three years, some three thousand deaths were attributed to the political violence. Government was eventually able to assert its control over most of the townships by declaring states of emergency, deploying police and defense force units, forming new, black units, including vigilante forces; and, in general, ruthlessly enforcing laws aimed at political dissent and organization. The authorities were able to regain control after each challenge, although less convincingly each time and not without a measure of reform designed to divide opponents, defuse the tensions, and win over fence hangers, cautious foreign critics, and shocked and embarrassed supporters. To the unrepentant racist, the message is clear—be firm and politically shrewd, and black nationalist demands can be deflected and denied.

Simultaneous with the southward push of nationalism has been a northward reach of South Africa, primarily but not only in the economic arena.[2] Almost from the time of the settlement at the Cape in 1652 and certainly since British hegemony in the region after 1806, settlers and eventually their governments have looked northward beyond the borders. The motivations were part escapist and part expansionist.

When the National party government first came to power in 1948, a defensive mood developed in South African foreign policy. Pretoria sought to support colonial rule to the north yet to gain greater independence from Great Britain and the British Commonwealth, particularly as the commonwealth became a more multiracial organization. To Prime Minister D. F. Malan, South Africa could not allow "Negro States" to arise within South Africa's borders (he was referring to the British High Commission Territories of Bechuanaland, Basutoland, and Swaziland). Later, under J. G. Strijdom, South Africa took a more realistic view of the independence process to the north. Steps were to be taken to normalize relations with the "nonwhite states of Africa." But policy pronouncement was at variance with the inflexible diplomatic style and performance of Pretoria.

Under Dr. Hendrik Verwoerd and later leaders, South Africa maintained the position that it was ready to deal openly and correctly with Black Africa only after black Africans abandoned their "feud" with Pretoria. Once these states emerged from their "mistaken course," discovered the folly of socialism and hostility to South Africa, and "learned to appreciate the value of South Africa," then South Africa would be prepared to establish relationships with Black Africa and black states would be encouraged to turn to South Africa for friendship, trade and investment, protection, and assistance.

In the mid-1960s it became clear to Pretoria that a dynamic defense of the white-dominated regional status quo demanded active initiatives. On the one hand, this took the form of a perspective that South Africa's defense perimeter extended at least to the Zambezi. By establishing relations with black governments, one minister said in 1970 that the government was protecting the borders of the republic against "terrorist incursions." Terms such as a "Monroe Doctrine" for southern Africa, a "buffer" of friendly black states, and a South African "sphere of influence" became common. The military component of policy took precedence. This was reflected especially in expanded defense budgets and greater cooperation with Portugal in its wars in Angola and Mozambique and with the white government in Rhodesia, all combined with a consistent anti-Communist line. In various forms it touched upon Communist ideology in Africa, Soviet naval power in the Indian Ocean, Chinese presence in Tanzania and Zambia, Soviet and Chinese aid to "terrorists," and even at one point an expressed fear of massive Chinese migration to Africa.

Simultaneously, as these proactive defensive themes were heard, there was also a more benign call for peaceful coexistence, mutual assistance, noninterference, and normal, cordial relations—an early manifestation of South Africa's dual strategy. In public South Africa stressed regional security, stability, cooperation, and economic growth. Who better to power and direct these goals than Pretoria? The fact was that independent Black Africa was not buying into these temptations, at least insofar as South African regional leadership was concerned, largely because it experienced more directly the aggressive face of Pretoria.

To some extent this appeal to Black Africa was, indirectly, an appeal to Europe and North America. By demonstrating to the West that South Africa wanted to live at peace with and to help black Africans, Pretoria hoped to forestall an emerging rejection or distancing and to maintain and enlarge economic, political, and military links with the West. By getting along with Black Africa, Pretoria sought to disarm its critics in the West and, if possible, to enlist them in trying to stabilize minority rule in South Africa. For a relatively small investment, it was thought, South Africa could divide Black Africa, precipitate debate within key African and Western states, and even galvanize support within South Africa among conservative blacks and the white business community. "We are of Africa," Prime Minister John Vorster said, "and our destiny lies in Africa." This statement of mission hid a multitude of foreign policy abuses—among them racism, paternalism, interference in the domestic affairs of neighboring governments, exploitation, and dominance. But it and similar expressions did mislead many of Pretoria's critics throughout the 1960s and 1970s. What had been called the "outward-looking policy" and sometimes "détente" in the end was not successful, but it did give critics pause to consider that, perhaps, South Africa was prepared to be flexible and to become a fully participating member of the world community.

SOUTH AFRICAN ECONOMIC HEGEMONY

Seen from the secure perspective of aggregate data, South Africa is an economic heavyweight among neighboring flyweights. Several of the nearby black-governed states (Zimbabwe, Angola, Zambia, and Mozambique) have the potential to improve their economic performance significantly. Taken as a group, they might at some future point challenge South Africa's economic dominance of the region. But for now, their efforts to restructure their economies seem inadequate to the challenge. In addition, South Africa's earlier economic takeoff (particularly the development of an economic infrastructure such as railways, roads, ports, telecommunications, and electricity production and distribution) had served throughout the colonial and independence periods to attract capital and entrepreneurial talent to South Africa and to enable that country to become the focus of regional economic growth.[3]

One could recite a litany of data and economic facts to demonstrate this historical asymmetry. A few examples will illustrate the depth and extent of South Africa's economic advantages.

- In 1969, South Africa's gross domestic product constituted 65.5 percent of the combined GDPs of the twelve states in the region. By 1978 that proportion had risen to 70.7 percent. The 1988 figure was 84.4 percent.

- South Africa remains the only industrialized country in the region. Although Zimbabwe has started to industrialize, the other countries are largely producers and exporters of primary products. In most cases, just one or two commodities dominate their trade. In one or two instances, the export of labor to South Africa is the major foreign exchange earner for the countries' economies.
- Except for Botswana—which has shifted from a cattle-raising economy to one powered largely by mining—and Angola—which moved from agriculture to petroleum—there has been little fundamental alteration of state economies since 1970.
- Prior to 1982, 95 percent of Malawi's overseas trade went through Mozambican ports. By 1986, 95 percent passed through South Africa.
- Botswana, Lesotho, and Swaziland have formalized trading patterns with South Africa through a regional customs union agreement.

The region's economic infrastructure has long been dominated by South Africa. Efforts to alter these patterns, including the development of new railway lines and ports, have been undermined by wars in the region and by South African efforts to destabilize black governments—either directly or through proxy forces. Since the 1930s, the principal railway lines have run through South Africa to its ports of Durban, Port Elizabeth, Cape Town, and Richards Bay. This meant that until the Rhodesian Unilateral Declaration of Independence (UDI), the predominant flow from as far north as the Zambia-Zaire copper belt was southward through Portuguese-controlled Angola to Lobito, through Zimbabwe to South Africa, or through the colony of Mozambique to Beira or Maputo. The landlocked situations of Zambia, Malawi, Zimbabwe, Botswana, Lesotho, and Swaziland and the difficult transport situation of Zaire virtually dictated that those states be dependent on routes and ports under the control of colonial and settler governments and later of South Africa.

Likewise, functional cooperation—the development of the hydroelectric facilities in Mozambique (Cahorra Bassa), the operation of the port of Maputo, the construction of the dam on the Cunene River dividing Angola and Namibia, the long-in-coming Lesotho Highlands water scheme for the supply of water to South Africa, the new rail link between Zimbabwe and South Africa that opened in 1974, and the 1979 connection between the Swazi and South African railway systems—added to South Africa's pivotal role in the region. Infrastructural links in turn contributed to deeply entrenched flows of trade, investment, and labor. Considerable efforts are being made to shift these ties and patterns, but they have proven difficult to break. The years since the creation of the Southern African Development Coordination

Conference (SADCC) in 1980 have been unsettling. SADCC has tried to redraw the economic map of the region—that is, to end the economic dependence of SADCC member states on South Africa. But despite hard-won changes, South Africa's advantages seem as constraining as ever.

The South African business community requires investment capital, and there is no question that sanctions and disinvestment campaigns have pushed some Western firms into abandoning their facilities and markets in South Africa. They have also posed difficult problems for the government and for South African firms in paying debts, finding finance capital, and developing state-of-the-art technologies. However, South African investment capital is still active in neighboring countries. This pattern of extensive regional outreach is particularly apparent in mining and related industries. As Namibia tries to consolidate its independence, the issue of South African investment will again be more starkly posed. Should black governments committed to the destruction of apartheid accept capital investment and technology from the most reviled state? So far their answer has been largely "yes." Angola, Mozambique, and Zimbabwe have recently revised their investment codes to encourage greater foreign inputs. Botswana's impressive growth has been dependent on South African investments in its extractive industries. What is needed is an appropriate investment vehicle to generate jobs and greater local income shares.

Other instruments of leverage exist. South Africa is still a major destination for large numbers of migrant laborers from the region, many of whom end up working in the gold mines. At one time, 78 percent of Africans employed were from outside South Africa. Most came from Lesotho, Botswana, and Swaziland, but large numbers also came from Malawi and Mozambique. After major cutbacks of foreign labor by Pretoria in the late 1970s, those numbers leveled off in the 1980s at around 350,000 officially registered alien workers. Illegal aliens could boost that figure to over 550,000.

With regard to the countries that export labor, the departure of workers relieves population pressures on the land, thereby reducing domestic levels of discontent and marginally reducing the chances for internal unrest. Moreover, labor is a commodity that can be a vital source of foreign exchange when exported, source of government revenue when taxed, and a contributor to the level of economic productivity. Nevertheless, it removes the healthiest and most ambitious workers, and their absence stifles overall levels of economic initiative.

From the perspective of the labor-importing country, the impact of an extensive foreign labor pool is profound. First, foreign labor tends to be cheaper, and it helps depress the economic conditions and bargaining power of the indigenous workers. The total fabric of temporary migrant labor (largely with no families) enables the South African authorities to avoid a variety of social welfare costs generally provided in industrialized states.

Foreign laborers are vulnerable. They tend to not be organized, although that is changing. They are easier to police than local labor. The promise of deferred earnings and the interaction between Pretoria and their home governments, especially when deferred pay is returned in gold or hard currencies, enables South Africa to pressure uncooperative politicians. The ultimate threat of a return of large numbers of contract laborers is a powerful implied weapon. This pattern during the postwar period from the 1940s to the 1970s underlay South Africa's confidence that it would continue to attract cheap labor, often with the collaboration of source governments.

These conditions, forged in the colonial period, led Samora Machel, the late president of Mozambique, to say that black states in southern Africa were "chained to the dungeons of apartheid."[4] Countries cannot abandon patterns of trade, investment, labor flow, and transport overnight, nor can they replace them with new patterns without tremendous cost and sacrifice. Familiar economic relationships, fashioned originally by and for the benefit of colonial and settler interests, were the economic givens from which a new political economy of southern Africa would eventually emerge. The end of Portuguese rule in the region, the demise of the white Rhodesian regime, and the resulting independence of Mozambique, Angola, Zimbabwe, and Namibia provided opportunities to alter old patterns of economic exchange. Yet try as they might, black governments could not entirely sever the old links. Indeed, a combination of difficulties—floods and droughts, economic and political mismanagement, all compounded by Rhodesian and South African campaigns to destabilize nearby governments and economies—rendered their efforts very costly and not entirely successful.

SOUTH AFRICA'S SHRINKING POLITICAL HINTERLAND

During the days of European colonialism, South Africa could interact regularly with the colonial administrations to the north and could use such diplomatic and political contacts to facilitate economic dealings in the region. South Africans conspired to overcome their political rejection in the region. Their isolation was not total. To be socially rejected as a pariah, an outcast, among states did not mean that no one would deal with South Africa. Rather, it meant that there were costs associated with political and economic relations, costs that states more acceptable to the international community need not bear. But since 1990, Pretoria has sought to parlay domestic progress toward negotiations with its black majority into renewed and correct relations with other states in Africa.

Prior to the demise of the British and Portuguese colonial empires in southern Africa, South Africa was a hub of activity. Linkages radiated outward from South Africa, and colonial and settler regimes around southern

Africa looked to Pretoria for assistance and direction. Major European and U.S. firms located their regional headquarters in South Africa, from which sales, service, and even production facilities were managed and controlled. International banks, news operations, travel organizations, airlines, and voluntary service organizations used South African bases to project their operations outward.

Governments had their diplomatic operatives in South Africa serve neighboring territories. Most apparent, for example, was the role that Britain's high commissioner in South Africa played in the administration of the so-called High Commission Territories prior to their independence. Since 1910 the British high commissioner (after 1960 the ambassador) to South Africa administered the High Commission Territories as British protectorates. By so doing, Great Britain was able to resist Pretoria's requests and demands that Great Britain turn these extensive lands over to South Africa. Earlier in the century, various British officials had committed the government to transferring these lands to South African jurisdiction. Later, however, when they realized the National party government was following a policy of apartheid, the British determined instead to grant independence to Botswana, Lesotho, and Swaziland. As for years it had been the only independent sovereign state south of the Zambezi, South Africa had been the key to the region.

In part this network was founded on the expectation in Pretoria that South Africa would eventually replace the departing colonial powers as the dominant force in the southern half of Africa and even as the sovereign power in some of these territories. South African diplomatic representation ranged throughout Africa. South Africa was also an active and valued participant in a number of regional and interterritorial organizations for technical cooperation—among them the Commission for Technical Cooperation in Africa South of the Sahara and its auxiliary organizations and the Southern African Regional Commission for the Conservation and Utilization of the Soil, headquartered in South Africa. In addition, South Africa regularly participated in diverse broader organizations to which the colonial powers and the newly emerging African states belonged, including the United Nations, the Commonwealth of Nations, and their many ancillary bodies.

Although there was considerable criticism of its domestic racial policies, until the 1960s South Africa fully expected to participate in the affairs of Africa and to be regarded as the leader in the subcontinent. The Department of External Affairs was reorganized to accommodate an Africa section, and in 1959 a separate Africa division was established—the first geographically based division in a department chiefly organized along functional lines. Occasionally top-ranking government officials would state that South Africa was an African state and that its future role in Africa must be twofold:

(1) to develop ties with Africa in order to facilitate the development of its own hinterland, and (2) to serve as a "link between the Western nations on the one hand and the population of Africa south of the Sahara on the other."[5] These were the utterances of a government that, although not pleased by the decolonization process and certainly not at ease with the prospect of dealing with black governments and their representatives, was determined to make the most of the potentially awkward and rapidly evolving international scene.[6]

The policymakers, however, did not seem to realize the extent to which the international context of values and power had shifted as a result of World War II. The demise of the colonial empires was imminent. Human rights and national self-determination, thanks in large part to Hitler's obsession with racial purity and dominance and to the rise of the United States and the Soviet Union as superpowers with global interests, had come to be regarded as central issues in postwar relations. The allegiance of the newly emerging states became a crucial policy aim of the superpowers and their allies. Third-World states quickly realized the potential value of organizations such as the United Nations and the Commonwealth of Nations. The technical revolution in mass communications and transport, coupled with the commitment to liberal values, increasingly contributed to pushing South Africa and the remaining settler regimes in Africa to the periphery of the diplomatic circle, although—paradoxically—to the center of the political maelstrom. As these regimes were losing influence in world forums, the content of their rule became more controversial.

The election of a nationalist government in 1948 and its aggressive championing of racial separation and domination—the apartheid issue—served to intensify criticism abroad. As Pretoria fashioned legislation to refine and implement the instruments of separation and social control through the 1950s, the world responded by progressively ostracizing South Africa. It was, perhaps, the most celebrated instance of a regime's domestic order and policies contributing to its fundamental international posture, or at least to the posture of outsiders toward the regime.

South Africa's response to this ostracization was to try to expand its economic relations with the Western capitalist economy. "Each trade agreement, each bank loan, each new investment," Prime Minister John Vorster said in 1972, "is another brick in the wall of our continued existence."[7] At the same time, Pretoria periodically sought breakthroughs with Black African states on the assumption that if South Africa could demonstrate its acceptance among its black neighbors, Europe and North America would be less reluctant to deal openly with South Africa. In other words, South Africa's ticket to expanded economic links with the West and to frustrating the aims of boycotts, expulsions, sanctions, divestment, and disinvestment campaigns was ostensibly to "prove" its accessibility to the very peoples who were presumably exploited and denigrated by Pretoria. In the end, this strategy did not work, but it enabled fence sitters to persist for a long while in their dealings with South Africa.

The bottom line—a crucial one—was that the domestic racial order in South Africa, compounded by Pretoria's violent suppression of protest and of the peaceful appeals of proponents of majority rule, served to highlight the extent to which South Africa was out of step with the times. Apartheid, marked and punctuated by spasmodic popular uprisings, is not only not a salable commodity worldwide, it is not even one to be tolerated.

Over time, South Africa found it increasingly difficult to deal with—even to make political contact with—the states of Africa. As the peoples of southern Africa gained their independence, as a more militant mood toward South Africa festered in these governments, and as governments founded on the military defeat of colonial and settler rule took their places, South Africa's hinterland shrunk and its dealings with even economically vulnerable neighbors became more secretive, more costly, and more troublesome. Despite a rhetoric of inclusion and outwardness, South Africa was forced to look inward for the causes of its ostracization.

SOUTH AFRICA'S MILITARY OPTION

Although its political choices and leverage had narrowed, South Africa bolstered, displayed, and deployed its military strength.[8] For governments and peoples in the region, this meant that South Africa was prepared not only to use its considerable economic clout openly to try to extract more favorable political and economic concessions from weaker neighbors but that Pretoria would use its overwhelming military muscle (overwhelming solely in relation to the military preparedness of other states in southern Africa) to achieve a number of regional policy aims. Among those goals were: (1) to destabilize and discredit black governments and societies; (2) to intimidate and thereby persuade them to continue to do business with South Africa; (3) to bring about major governmental changes if possible and, short of that, to force policy shifts on these governments; (4) to attack South West African People's Organization (SWAPO) and African National Congress (ANC) bases, facilities, and personnel so as to deny these groups sanctuary near South Africa's borders; and (5) to do all these things without triggering either higher levels of fighting (which would be costly politically within South Africa) or greater pressures for economic sanctions and diplomatic isolation in the West and among South Africa's major business partners.

A considerable record of hostile actions into neighboring territories could be compiled to document the accusations about destabilization.[9] Rather than detail those instances, it should be sufficient to list the types of operations South Africa has engaged in or fostered.

- Assassinations and attempted assassinations of ANC officials as far afield as Europe, but mostly in neighboring states
- Bombings (letter bombs and aerial bombardment) of suspected or alleged ANC and SWAPO centers, some of this large scale (as in the systematic destruction of the civilian economy and infrastructure in southern Angola)
- Short-term cross-border strikes into foreign capitals (Harare, Gaberone, Maputo, Lusaka) and at alleged concentrations of refugees and alleged liberation movement bases
- Large-scale (up to 10,000 troops) cross-border invasions (especially into Angola) in putatively hot-pursuit or preemptive strikes against enemies
- Occupation of territory of foreign states for extensive periods (for example, 40,000 square kilometers of the Cunene Province of Angola from 1981 to 1984)
- Extensive support (financial, diplomatic, military, training, logistical, material, and armaments) for dissident political movements hostile to recognized black governments and for disruptive armed groups created and sustained by South Africans or white Rhodesians. These groups—most notably Resistência National Moçambicana (Renamo) against Mozambique, União National para a Independência Total de Angola (UNITA) against Angola, and the Lesotho Liberation Army against Lesotho, as well as those that have challenged the governments in Zambia and Zimbabwe—have caused extensive damage and death throughout the region, almost to the point of bringing down the regimes in Mozambique and Lesotho and undermining the security of that in Angola.

Since 1975–1976, destruction by South African Defense Force (SADF) operatives or groups assisted by the SADF has been extensive, reaching a peak between 1980 and 1984. Although military operations contributed to forcing international agreements with Mozambique (the Nkomati Accord, an agreement on nonaggression and "good neighborliness") and Angola (regarding troop withdrawal and later with regard to the implementation of U.N. resolution no. 435 for the independence of Namibia), South African military operations and surreptitious assistance to militarized proxy groups have not ended although they have been considerably reduced. Pretoria denies all assistance to Renamo and UNITA, but evidence continues to be unveiled that shows links with the SADF or with other South African and freelance operatives. The United States also continues to aid UNITA. Thus, although the military scene in southern Africa may not be at a rolling boil, it simmers beneath the surface.

Through the 1980s, South Africa sought to pursue what may be called a double dual strategy. This was a carrot-and-stick policy that involved simultaneously (1) a policy of military readiness and the application of coercion to force and intimidate its opponents, and (2) a policy of ostensibly correct, peaceful relations with neighbors—even including economic and social inducements and rewards—in order to coopt possible opponents into defending or cooperating in the defense and maintenance of the status quo. This dual strategy may be regarded as double in the sense that it was pursued in both the domestic and the regional political arenas. Before the accession of F. W. de Klerk in 1989, the police and defense forces asserted themselves domestically. Violence was a mode of control. Regime opponents were detained, and police were ruthless in putting down protests. Regime-fostered vigilante groups killed and attacked critics and political opponents.[10] The recently dismantled national security management system sought to defuse protest and unrest by offering rewards and blandishment to local communities and leaders who were prepared to cooperate and be identified with reformist policies and with government-sponsored agencies.[11] But there is still evidence that clandestine units of the police and the SADF continue to organize and assist vigilante-like black forces.

The carrot and stick have also long coexisted as parts of South Africa's regional policy. At the same time that Pretoria helped Mozambique to rebuild and modernize the railway from the Witwatersrand industrial center to Maputo and to manage that port, South African operatives raided ANC offices and housing in Maputo and assisted Renamo forces in the Mozambique interior. It reached the point in 1988 where Pretoria supplied military material to the Mozambican army while South Africans secretly abetted Renamo. Calls for treaties of nonaggression were interspersed with threats and cross-border raids. Widening trade relations were accompanied by slowdowns on the rail lines and at the ports. "Live with us in peace," Pretoria seemed to say. "Do not take steps to influence our domestic order, or else we will make you pay dearly for your meddling. If you accept South Africa as is, we are prepared to reward you. Our businesses will invest in your economy, and in general we will continue along the lines that have marked our relations (asymmetrical) through the years." It is not a message that black southern African governments are buying openly.

DETERMINED DECADE OF THE SOUTHERN AFRICAN DEVELOPMENT COORDINATION CONFERENCE

To rectify the imbalances and dependencies posed by South Africa's power, black governments have sought to improve their performance through a number of cooperative efforts in order to strengthen their collective hand and to bypass South Africa's strengths. Since 1974 the frontline states (FLS) of Angola, Botswana, Mozambique, Tanzania, and Zambia, and later Zimbabwe and Namibia have sought to coordinate their diplomatic stances by meeting, planning, and adopting joint policies and by involving themselves in political and military efforts to defend themselves and to liberate minority-ruled southern Africans.[12] Their collective diplomatic skills, surprisingly cohesive and influential, contributed to the independence of Zimbabwe and to a consensus approach to dealing with South Africa over Namibia. In June 1985 they also arrived at a joint security arrangement to support the Frelimo government in its fight against Renamo's efforts to destroy the social fabric of Mozambique. In the fall of 1988, the group pressured Malawi to end its sanctuary for Renamo or face an economic blockade. In response, Malawian President H. Kamuzu Banda expelled thousands of Renamo supporters. But SADCC governments have found that without economic and military stability and power, their diplomatic enterprise remains limited.

A summit in Lusaka in April 1980 sought to focus on regional development and to reduce the black states' dependence on South Africa, especially upon South Africa's infrastructure. The nine states represented (the five original FLS plus Zimbabwe, Lesotho, Malawi, and Swaziland) approved a declaration drawn up at a SADCC meeting held nine months earlier in Tanzania. The declaration called for greater integration of the states' economies and included a seven-point plan to reduce their economic dependency upon South Africa. Additional proposals included the creation of a Southern African Transport and Communications Committee; development of measures to control foot and mouth disease; establishment of a regional agriculture research station, a regional development fund, and permanent administrative machinery; harmonization of industrial and energy policies; and coordination of other joint economic concerns.

The creation of SADCC symbolized a realistic awareness of the need to strengthen cooperative institutions in order to reduce individual member state's growing reliance on economic contacts with South Africa (see Chapter 12 by Carol Lancaster). Given the extent to which Zambia, Mozambique, and Angola suffered in the struggle for the independence of Zimbabwe and Namibia, the economic strength to weather the approaching contest for majority government in South Africa itself and the need for economic achievement in its own right are imperative. It is an irony of modern regional relations that the presence of a hostile South Africa and the antagonisms that relations with that country evoke are among the factors that contribute to cooperation and coordination among black-governed states. As the South Africans appear to switch domestic racial policies and regional policies, the need for SADCC cooperation on economic development is still real, but the anti-apartheid focus is blurred and the defensive stimulus less immediate.

SADCC is an idea whose time has come. The most impressive aspect of its meetings has been the sober perspective that it will take a long time to get the nine states' own economic houses in order and that short-term solutions, scapegoating, and excuse making will serve no practical ends. Economic independence is not, for these reasons, strictly an anti–South African policy but a reasonable long-term aim. It is central to domestic political stability and to the social well-being of the citizens of the member states.

SADCC is a modest experiment based on the need to locate ultimate decision-making with each member state and to coordinate diverse economic and social sectors in the long-range planning. This approach, it is hoped, will overcome the failures of earlier efforts at regional cooperation in Africa, the most recent of which tended to favor overly ambitious programs leading to individual state reluctance to cooperate because the costs and benefits of cooperation fell unevenly on different members. At Blantyre in 1981, each member was assigned its own sector to coordinate. Angola was responsible for energy; Lesotho, soil conservation and land utilization; Mozambique, transport and communication; and so forth. SADCC's loose structure, minimal administrative machinery, and division of labor that involves every member state seem to keep the group together.

The result has been a series of small-scale successes but an overall frustration at being unable to change regional economic patterns appreciably. Of the ninety-seven projects approved in 1980 in the transport sector, for example, about twenty were completed by 1984; thirty were in process; and twenty were actively being negotiated for financial support. And yet trade between southern African countries represents only about 5 percent of their total trade.

The SADCC approach to raising funds is particularly distinctive. SADCC calls major conferences (Maputo in 1980 was the first) to explain its aims and projects to potential donors and to elicit firm pledges of financial support (which totaled $3 billion in 1980–1990). Representatives of industrialized states and international organizations have attended, and specific projects have been floated. By linking aid to specific projects, the fund raising has been more successful and follow-up on implementation more likely. Although aid has appeared to dwindle elsewhere in Africa, SADCC has managed to raise a large proportion of its projected needs, especially for transportation plans.

GREAT-POWER INTERESTS IN SOUTHERN AFRICA

In a way, the great powers share similar interests in southern Africa. They may express and rationalize them differently and emphasize different concerns at different times, but the basic attraction of the region and the concerns of the powers there are the same. Expressed at their most fundamental levels, these interests fall into four categories—strategic, economic, political-psychological, and moral.

There is no question that so-called strategic considerations and governments' perceptions of them change over the years. What may appear to be a pressing need today can fade into insignificance and, invariably, must be considered in relation to how one's rivals look at the same issue.

One such changing issue has been the so-called Cape sea route. At one time it was regarded as vital that the United States and its European allies have access to the ports in southern Africa, particularly the superior facilities of Cape Town and Durban. But the United States has not used South African ports since 1967, and the State Department has said that they are not vital to U.S. defense needs. After the closure of the Suez Canal in 1967 and the introduction and dependence on very large crude carriers rounding the Cape of Good Hope, arguments were again offered in Europe, North America, and South Africa about the need to keep the sea lanes open to transport petroleum from the Persian Gulf to consumers in the West. The Cape was regarded as a potential "choke point," vulnerable to Soviet naval interdiction. These arguments were rerun after Marxist governments were installed in Maputo and Luanda. What is more, because of the rising tide of African nationalism and the apparent popularity of Socialist doctrine at that time, defense planners and cold-war politicians warned that a revolutionary takeover in South Africa would provide the Soviet Union with naval bases in the region.

The alarmists were geopolitically naive. The Strait of Hormuz is more vulnerable and is closer to Soviet naval and air power. Instabilities and rivalries among Gulf-area governments sharpen that focus. Alarmists misunderstood the nature of black nationalism. Even radical or Marxist regimes in southern Africa—even those aided by the USSR—have had little desire to surrender their independence and freedom of action. So far no permanent Soviet military or naval facilities have been authorized by Mozambique or Angola. The motive that forced these leaders into collaboration with the Soviet Union was the fear of South African attacks and civil violence fomented by South Africa's proxies. The leaders wanted to save their own political skins, but lending their territories to Soviet military purposes did not guarantee their continued rule.

The basic flaw in proposals of this sort is the insistence upon interpreting southern African events in East-West terms. By so doing, local and regional imperatives are ignored. But for years Western, Soviet, and Chinese policies in southern Africa have been propelled by the fear that rivals might make breakthroughs in the region, gain solid footholds, and seek to exclude one's own country and its agents and private businesses from key potentially friendly countries.

Southern Africa was among several regions of the world in which a domino theory was thought to dictate policy. Each successive weakening of Western interests strengthened the Socialist bloc and made the ultimate outcome more difficult to control, and vice versa. It was often seen as a zero-sum game—what one side lost, the other gained. Such a simplistic geopolitical perspective was also applied to the question of strategic minerals.

On the surface, secure access to minerals is an economic issue. But the fortuitous combination of the particular minerals produced in southern Africa (many of which are vital to the specialized steel industry and hence to jet aircraft construction and the automotive industry, while others are valuable in the chemical and oil refining industries) coupled with the fact that the major alternative sources for many of these minerals are Socialist countries (notably the USSR and China) causes the East-West planners to see minerals as a strategic issue. In 1989, for example, South Africa supplied 83 percent of the world's exports of platinum, 76 percent of rhodium, 92 percent of vanadium pentoxide, 42 percent of chromium, and 58 percent of ferrochromium.

There are other vital minerals and suppliers in the region, including Angola (petroleum), Zaire (copper, nickel, and cobalt), Zambia (copper and cobalt), Zimbabwe (chromium), Namibia (diamonds, copper, and uranium), and Botswana (diamonds), but they are deemed less important strategically, as they represent proportionately smaller market shares than does South Africa. Still, if the West were cut off from access to southern Africa's minerals, it is felt that its principal alternative in many cases would be Communist countries. Thus, the risk is that the West's perceived chief rival in world politics would be able to withhold vital resources or, alternatively, be in a position—in concert with its alleged client states in southern Africa—to withhold minerals from the market and thereby increase the prices beyond strictly economic or market levels. There is a third, less obvious, dimension to the problem, which is seldom discussed in the literature.[13] Most centralized economies are capital deficient and are not export-oriented. Government policies do not generally expand production to keep pace with demand. In capital-intensive mineral exploitation, where long-range planning is imperative, the real danger is that Socialist countries would not be able or even inclined to produce sufficient supplies to satisfy projected capitalist world demands.

There are other economic linkages that shape great-power interests in the region. Despite sanctions, trade with the capitalist countries is vital to the maintenance of the South African economy and of other national economies in the region. In addition, Western-based corporations have been heavily involved in the economies of southern Africa. In late 1985, there were 350 U.S.-based firms operating in South Africa, representing $2.8 billion in direct investment. There was another $8 billion in indirect investment, mostly U.S.-owned shares in the South African stock exchange, and some $4.8 billion in U.S. bank loans—a total of over $15 billion in U.S. investments. This figure is not great in terms of total U.S. investments abroad, nor is it that massive for South Africa. But U.S. money played a major role in key industries—computers, petroleum, and automotive, for example.

The domestic violence that escalated in 1983 highlighted the sensitivity of U.S. firms to pressures of public opinion at home and to economic signals in the field. Corporations began to take into account political pressure to withdraw from South Africa, and many did depart. The combination of falling profit margins, South African instability, and the "hassle factor" among customers, stockholders, and protestors (institutional and individual) led to a major capital outflow from the country. The Comprehensive Anti-Apartheid Act of 1986 contributed to that flight. Overall, international economic pressures on South Africa have resulted in a cumulative foreign exchange loss of more than $15 billion since 1985.

The European share of the South African economy is deeper and wider than the U.S. share in terms of trade, loans, and investment. South Africa needs these links in order to survive. Some European countries, particularly certain firms and industries, profit from and depend on their ties to South Africa. It is a symbiotic relationship that would be difficult and costly to end. So, despite repeated calls for sanctions, disinvestment, divestment, and economic isolation, there is considerable opposition to severing ties, and obvious efforts are undertaken to elude sanctions and other economic measures. The same sort of resistance met the far more determined sanctions campaign against Rhodesia in the 1960s and 1970s.

The Socialist bloc has no economic links with southern Africa that are remotely comparable to those of European countries. For the Soviet Union, it has been sufficient to embarrass the West, to drive up costs to Western corporations and governments, and to weaken apartheid and South Africa in the region. Thus, Soviet and Eastern European support to the enemies of apartheid has been largely military and strategic (before and after liberation movements gained power), economic (in the form of marginal foreign aid programs and some trade), technical, diplomatic, and psychological. Even these forms of support are declining. There is no question that without Cuban and Soviet assistance, the Movimento Popular de Libertação de Angola (MPLA) government in Angola would be shaky, SWAPO would have been even more vulnerable in its Angolan sanctuary, and the ANC would be far less effective in focusing opposition against Pretoria. As long as the East-West competition was keen, southern Africa was a cockpit of world (as distinguished from regional) tension.

This contest has also had a psychological dimension. Washington feared "losing" another region to the Soviet bloc, an event that would have contributed to a sense of momentum and dynamism unfavorable to the West. Given all that had taken place since the end of World War II, another Soviet success—this one in a region remote from the borders of the Socialist bloc—would have demonstrated Western weakness, division, and confusion and shown a Socialist determination and ability to project its influence far beyond the traditional confines of Soviet power. It would have lent credence to the Soviet claim in the 1970s that the "correlation of forces" in the world had indeed shifted against the West. Although agreeing on the need to contain the menace of Socialist bloc expansion, various U.S. administrations have differed on how best to prevent further Socialist bloc gains.

Southern Africa is strategically important, although less so now that the Soviet bloc and the Western allies downplay their competition. In other words, a presence in southern Africa had been thought to be crucial primarily when the parties were actively engaged in a cold war. But even then, does it necessarily follow that in order to protect or improve their strategic position, the Western governments should have identified with Pretoria? Just because the South African government regards itself as anti-Communist, is it wise to welcome self-proclaimed enemies of one's enemies into one's own camp?

Conventional wisdom had been that the status quo West should prevent revolutionary political transformation in South Africa. A change to majority rule, or at least the process of conflict leading to it, would presumably mean that the United States and its allies would be denied supplies and markets, their investments would be expropriated, and their loans would be renounced or lost. Cold warriors in Washington still talk of "resource wars." They sometimes follow this analysis with a plea to defend or at least not to pressure the white regime in Pretoria instead of pursuing a more valid policy of preparing for shortages by stockpiling, finding substitutes for South African products, and developing solid relations with potentially popular governments.

The argument that radical governments will jeopardize the West's access to essential raw materials is not sound. The fact is that for most southern African countries (including South Africa), extractive industries geared to producing minerals for export are indispensible to each economy. These industries are major foreign exchange earners. They provide employment, tax revenues, fees, and royalties. The only viable market for these products is in the industrialized West. Governments in these countries would have to sell their raw materials to the West, ideology notwithstanding. The West needs to buy them; the countries need to sell to the West. In order to pay their bills, revolutionary regimes committed to expanding employment and state services and to meeting the popular demands they earlier encouraged would have to expand exports and raise the prices, or both. They would have to attract more, not less, foreign capital and foreign technology. Rapidly increased prices would not serve their long-term interests of encouraging greater usage of and dependence on their commodities. The governments of Angola, Mozambique, and Zimbabwe are beginning to learn this fact. Their new investment codes seek to attract investment by providing the inducements their rhetoric so recently discouraged. If the Soviet Union has neither the will nor the capacity to subsidize economies as close and strategically vital as Eastern Europe, why would it take risks in order to sustain friendly and ideologically sympathetic regimes in faraway southern Africa?

Morally, apartheid has few defenders outside of South Africa. A state founded on the principle of the legal separation and exploitation of people of different races is hard to defend in an era of democracy, egalitarianism, and enlightenment. Apartheid has become so discredited that even South Africa's ruling National party maintains that it will be dismantled. Although the NP's five-year political "plan of action" for the 1989 elections referred to the need to define "groups" (that is, races) in law, it insists that South Africa must prove that it is a democracy and that it no longer believes in "group" dominance. It says it cannot blatantly justify the social and legal order it has so carefully erected since 1948 even to its own white voters.

If this is so, then clearly the West faces an awkward policy dilemma. Apartheid must go. Minority rule is unacceptable. Yet the prospects for a peaceful transition to majority rule seem slim. Moreover, the most likely parties to lead the black majority have shown Marxist and Socialist tendencies. Hence, majority rule seems to include a rejection of the sort of capitalist economic system South Africa presently has.[14] Not only would an economic changeover compound the insecurities of a political revolution, but it would appear to jeopardize the special advantages Western capitalist governments, their corporations, and their citizens presently enjoy in South Africa. The dilemma is clear—to do what is morally right may threaten what has proven to be profitable and may raise the further moral issues of the use of violence in the transition and possibly risk another form of repression after the transition. Fortunately for the West, the unrest since 1983 coupled with the poor economic performance of South Africa has diminished the profitability for foreign firms; many have decided to disinvest and to close or sell their South African operations. Likewise, lessened East-West competition in southern Africa also diminishes the short-term impact of a setback for foreign capitalists in South Africa, especially given the poor economic performance of the Socialist bloc states in Europe and Asia.

CONTENTIOUS POLICY ISSUES

If what is desired is the establishment of sovereign governments representing majorities, then progress has been made since 1960. When one considers the magnitude of opposition to change in the region, the acquisition of self-rule in Angola, Mozambique, Zimbabwe, and Namibia is an achievement of major proportions.[15]

For the liberation movements in each of these territories, independence and majoritarian government were the culmination of long and costly struggles. For South Africans, especially for the government in Pretoria, however, each of these struggles has been viewed in terms of the way in which changes in the regional power alignments would affect the power equation in South Africa itself. South Africa is the ultimate target. The military coup in Lisbon in 1974 and the subsequent takeover by officers determined to end Portugal's colonial empire so weakened the forces of white minority rule and so isolated settler governments that it established an unmistakable momentum for majority rule. But trends and momentum do not necessarily mean that victory is easy or even inevitable. Progress in these cases is not linear. Setbacks, such as those that occurred in the period 1978 to 1988, make celebration premature. During the 1978–1988 period, South Africa's armed forces destabilized the social and governmental fabric of neighboring independent states. Within South Africa itself, champions of revolution and resistance to minority government were also arrested, detained, and even murdered. Elements of the arm of the state still threaten the transitional process. Corruption and economic mismanagement demonstrate that self-rule does not in itself translate directly into material or political well-being. The election of conservative governments in the West (the United States, Great Britain, and Germany) gave heart to the advocates of the status quo in the region.

There is an ebb and flow to southern African international relations that contributes to periods of both euphoria and depression among the advocates of revolution. High points followed the coup in Portugal, the independence of Zimbabwe after the difficult British-chaired Lancaster House constitutional negotiations leading to a ceasefire and a transition to majority rule, and the 1980 election of the government of Robert Mugabe and his Zimbabwe African National Union Patriotic Front party. The release of Mandela, the independence of Namibia, and the start of the negotiation process in South Africa have also been positive milestones. Low points have been associated with the repeated disappointments over the negotiations on Namibia, South Africa's military incursions into neighboring states, and the Nkomati Accord between South Africa and Mozambique in March 1984 in which each party agreed not to assist or give permission to operate on its soil to parties or movements opposed to the other signatory to the accord. In the implementation of the accord, Mozambique forced the ANC to close down its operations; but South Africa apparently continued to assist Renamo.

The fact that South Africa appeared ready to resolve the dispute with Mozambique diplomatically opened doors for its president. P. W. Botha was received in European capitals. Outsiders seemed prepared to believe that Pretoria was positioning itself to reform apartheid. It appeared that South Africa's hardline coercion had paid off. For a time, its neighbors were compelled by force of arms to postpone the agenda for revolution in South Africa. F. W. de Klerk has built upon these openings. He has sought to gain control over the security establishment, visited regional heads of government, and—at least publicly—ended government aid to proxy dissidents.

Parallel and somewhat paradoxical tendencies have prevailed. At the very time when South Africa appeared to be militarily unassailable, it became increasingly evident that the country had lost its political credibility—among its own black citizens and many of its white ones, among its neighbors, and outside of Africa. Recent events in southern Africa and in South Africa have seemed to provide Pretoria with opportunities to reduce hostilities in the region and to address the demands for profound changes in the power structure, albeit grudgingly.

To advocates of change, greater clarity appears in the struggle than at any time in the recent past. First, the ultimate target—apartheid South Africa—appears within their sights. Independence for Namibia means that all of Africa's sub-Saharan territories have gained their independence. South Africa, with its two-tiered version of domestic colonialism (the system of "independent" homelands and the structured racial divisions within so-called "white" South Africa) remains Africa's last bastion of white minority rule.

Second, partisan and leadership changes in white South Africa itself indicate that the power structure is searching for an alternative mode to maintain concurrent power. Such changes point to a period of transition that presents opportunities. Modulated reform of the status quo may be seen in Pretoria as a substitute for majoritarian revolution. This is only partly correct, however, for existing conditions still make revolution the only long-range hope for real stability in South Africa.

F. W. de Klerk replaced P. W. Botha, first as leader of the NP in February 1989 and then as state president in September of that year. De Klerk's party then contested the September general election as a party of "change." He interpreted his party's victory, but with a considerably smaller majority than in the 1987 general election, as a mandate for reform. Only 6 percent of the people of voting age actually cast ballots for the NP. Still, de Klerk said that 70 percent of the white voters (he combined NP and Democratic party votes) supported an end to apartheid. He promised to end racial domination and to institute black votes and black participation in the organs of central government. The negotiation process raises hopes even as the violence in Natal and in the townships on the Reef threatens to undermine the modus operandi. The white power structure is on shaky ground, and it knows it. The rules of the game must be changed in order to break down racial solidarity and to offer opportunities to the divided white populace as well as to divided blacks.[16]

After the 1989 election, de Klerk began a series of gestures to demonstrate tangibly the changing mood in Pretoria. The granting of permission for demonstrations and marches, the release of some prisoners and detainees, the unbanning of anti-apartheid organizations, the dismantling of the national security management system, and the general and oft-repeated statement that the door to a new South Africa was now open and that it would not be necessary to batter it down were the most evident gestures. But change in South Africa can be sabotaged.

Third, recent regional changes have contributed to a momentum that generates expectations and that demands progress in South Africa. Related to this is the fact that the Soviet Union is clearly preoccupied with domestic and Socialist bloc issues.[17] In this context, regional foreign policy issues have a lower priority. Moscow is prepared to downplay matters that sap its energies and that show little promise of positive resolution from its point of view. The superpowers—eager to build upon the reduced cold-war tension and the budding mood of cooperation—together are pressuring their clients, allies, and friends in the region to reach accommodation on various disputes in Angola, Mozambique, and South Africa. What is more, when the superpowers can agree, the United Nations can function more actively and effectively; for example, the U.S.-brokered agreement on southwestern Africa regarding Angola and Namibia was administered by the United Nations with a minimum of disruption of the transition to independence. The near-ceasefire in Angola between the MPLA government and UNITA and the possibility of an end to Renamo's banditry in Mozambique reflect the pressures and propitious conditions for the resolution of conflicts.

This, in turn, encourages regional governments to think in terms that tempt Pretoria to consider concessions to black demands. Some governments seem prepared to deal more openly with Pretoria than do others. De Klerk visited Mozambique, Zambia, and Zaire in August 1989 and has also visited the Ivory Coast, Madagascar, and Namibia since assuming power. He has made state visits to nine European countries (in May 1990) and to the United States. Other South African officials now deal with governments long hostile to Pretoria. Thanks to the reforms, diplomatic doors are now opening, and commercial and financial ties are being explored. De Klerk has started a feeling-out process that may lead to a development of trust and possibly more. But the political ground can shift. The irony is that although South Africa is militarily stronger than ever, geopolitically it is more and more isolated—both in the region and globally. Another tightening of sanctions might well contribute to a sense of loneliness that would make accommodation more imperative.

This is a crucial period for South Africa. Expectations are high and, hence, are in danger of being disappointed—by delay, by retrograde acts that include calculated violence designed to derail NP-ANC cooperation, and by the ultimate realization that white minority rule and black majority rule are irreconcilable. Meanwhile, outsiders watch as the principals seek to strengthen their bargaining hands in a fluid and multifaceted struggle. The real conditions for negotiation have not yet been established. Coercion is still the major vehicle for white power in South Africa. Elements of the regime are not yet prepared to relinquish that leverage, regardless of the changing constellation of power—globally, regionally, or even within South Africa.

NOTES

1. André du Pisani, *What Do We Think?: A Survey of White Opinion on Foreign Policy Issues*, no. 4 (Braamfontein: South African Institute of International Affairs, May 1988), esp. pp. 5–21.

2. Kenneth W. Grundy, *Confrontation and Accommodation in Southern Africa: The Limits of Independence* (Berkeley: University of California Press, 1973), pp. 228–275; and Joseph Hanlon, *Beggar Your Neighbours: Apartheid Power in Southern Africa* (Bloomington: Indiana University Press, 1986).

3. Grundy, *Confrontation*, pp. 28–82; and Kenneth W. Grundy, "Economic Patterns in the New Southern African Balance," in Gwendolen M. Carter and Patrick O'Meara (eds.), *Southern Africa: The Continuing Crisis*, 2nd ed. (Bloomington: Indiana University Press, 1982). See also, Ronald T. Libby, *The Politics of Economic Power in Southern Africa* (Princeton: Princeton University Press, 1987).

4. As quoted in *Africa Research Bulletin* (Econ. series) 17, no. 11 (Dec. 31, 1980), p. 5733A.

5. Foreign Minister Eric Louw, quoted in Deon Geldenhuys, *The Diplomacy of Isolation: South African Foreign Policy Making* (Johannesburg: Macmillan, 1984), p. 13.

6. A summary of South Africa's postwar foreign policy can be found in Jack Spence, "South Africa's Foreign Policy: The Evolution, 1945–1986," *Energos* 14 (1986):5–16.

7. As quoted in *ibid.*, p. 9.

8. See Jacklyn Cock and Laurie Nathan (eds.), *War and Society: The Militarization of South Africa* (Cape Town: David Philip, 1989); Philip H. Frankel, *Pretoria's Praetorians: Civil-Military Relations in South Africa* (Cambridge: Cambridge University Press, 1984); Gavin Cawthra, *Brutal Force: The Apartheid War Machine* (London: International Defence and Aid for Southern Africa, 1986); Christopher Coke, *South Africa's Security Dilemmas*, the Washington Papers, no. 126 (New York: Praeger,

1987); and Kenneth W. Grundy, *The Militarization of South African Politics* (Oxford: Oxford University Press, 1988).

9. See especially Hanlon, *Beggar Your Neighbours;* and Cock and Nathan (eds.), *War and Society,* especially Ch. 7–9.

10. Nicholas Haysom, *Mabangalala: The Rise of Right-Wing Vigilantes in South Africa* (Johannesburg: University of the Witwatersrand, Centre for Applied Legal Studies, 1986); and *Weekly Mail* (Johannesburg) 5, no. 50 (Dec. 21, 1989):6, 13.

11. Cock and Nathan (eds.), *War and Society,* Ch. 11–12.

12. Carol B. Thompson, *Challenge to Imperialism: The Frontline States in the Liberation of Zimbabwe* (Boulder, Colo.: Westview Press, 1986).

13. An exception is Robert M. Price, "U.S. Policy Toward Southern Africa: Interests, Choices, and Constraints," in Carter and O'Meara (eds.), *International Politics in Southern Africa,* pp. 62–67.

14. The debate over the relationships between capitalism and apartheid is ongoing. See, for example, Stanley B. Greenberg, *Race and State in Capitalist Development: Comparative Perspectives*

6

THE INTERNATIONAL POLITICS OF IDENTITY IN THE HORN OF AFRICA

JOHN W. HARBESON

The Horn of Africa is today one of the world's poorest and most politically unsettled regions. The causes of its instability and its poverty and their interrelationship are multiple, complex, and seemingly intractable. However, among the factors bearing on the region's political and economic distress has been the interrelationship between regional and extraregional international politics, historically as well as at present. One of the features defining the Horn of Africa has been the extensive and persistent entanglement of its international politics with the competition among European powers for imperial influence. Similarly, in more recent times the Horn of Africa has been more directly caught in cold-war political and military competition between the Warsaw and NATO alliances than has much of Africa, with the exception of parts of southern Africa.

The thesis of this chapter is that this historical and contemporary linkage between the politics of the European and northeast African theaters has been an important but not determinative factor shaping both the international and domestic political development of the Horn countries.[1] That linkage has been a critical influence on the activity of those powers (including the United States and the Soviet Union) that have participated in the regional politics of the Horn. Moreover, the unstable character of the international politics of the Horn, abetted by the relationship with big-power international politics, has been and remains a prominent cause of mutually reinforcing underdevelopment and political instability on the Horn.

The relationship between major-power international relations and regional international political turbulence and underdevelopment is of considerable contemporary importance. In some quarters the incipient transformation of superpower relations in the Gorbachev era is being hailed as a key to resolving at least one of the Horn's longest-running and most intractable wars, the Eritrean-Ethiopian conflict. This is the case because with the end of the cold war, the USSR is no longer interested in bankrolling its former ideological allies. Therefore, the Ethiopian government can rely only on its own military resources in the conflict as an alternative to negotiations. Moreover, if resolution of this war were to come into view, it would at a minimum remove a complicating and escalating factor in the Sudanese civil war—the fact that the Ethiopian government has been backing the Sudanese rebels because the Sudanese government has been perceived as lending aid to the Eritreans. The Sudanese government has done so because of its perception that Ethiopia has assisted the Sudanese rebels. Resolution of the Eritrean conflict might break this vicious cycle. Finally, such contributions to regional international peace would liberate resources previously diverted to military activity for use in peaceful developmental purposes.

This string of hypotheses rests on several important premises. First, it assumes that external international competition is a sufficient condition for the continuation of at least some of the major regional international conflicts. Second, it supposes that greater superpower cooperation in the region will produce more favorable political and, by extension, economic outcomes than has their competition in the past. Third, this set of hypotheses rests upon the assumption that both the regional and the external actors will identify mutual interests consonant with the objectives of peace and development in the region and will pursue them rationally.

This last assumption in particular carries considerable theoretical significance. According to realist and neorealist theories of international relations, actors' identification and rational pursuit of interests—including converging interests—depend upon at least two conditions: (1) the existence of defined and established actors, if not nation-state actors; and (2) the existence of some form of international system whose central features shape the interests of participating actors.[2] But what has been at work in the history of the entanglement of Horn and European international politics is the convergence of two groups of international actors with markedly different characteristics. One of the most important such differences has been the nature of the participating actors. The actors in the international politics of the Horn have not all had settled and established identities, and all have not been nation-states, as the term is conventionally employed. Indeed, the international politics of the Horn of Africa has largely been a struggle of competing actors to establish just such settled identities.

Relatively little theoretical investigation has been devoted to the reality of multiple, simultaneous, and dissimilar international systems involving global and regional powers. There has been a lack of research on what happens when actors in such different systems cause the systems to converge or on what happens when there are fundamental dissimilarities in the characteristics of the actors in such different systems.[3] It follows that there is little basis for predicting the impact of changes in the relationship of actors in one system on the behavior of actors in another that has distinctive characteristics. Thus, as complex as may be the impact of changing Soviet-U.S. relations on those of other industrial powers, the impact on relations among actors on the Horn of Africa may be even more complex and unpredictable.

The entanglement of European and Horn theaters of international politics offers us the opportunity to explore the foregoing theoretical issues. In particular, the outcomes of the convergence of these two theaters of international relations suggest the weakness or absence of basic parameters employed by realist and neorealist theories to explain international behavior. If the assumptions of the existence of (1) established actors operating within (2) a common system are relaxed, how are international relations to be explained and predicted, and how is stability resting on the accommodation of particular actors' interests to be achieved? How do actors specify and pursue their interests in such circumstances, and with what results?

More fundamentally, to what extent and in what ways do actors in such circumstances move to develop what realist and neorealist theories of international relations have assumed as givens: established actors and a common system of relations among them guiding the pursuit and accommodation of their respective interests? Underlying this empirically researchable question is an issue fundamental to theories of international relations: the chicken-egg question of whether actors define the systems in which they participate or whether in some sense preexisting systems define the positions and interests of participating actors. In the former case, systems are the creations of actors; in the latter case, systems become objective realities defining the parameters of individual actors' behavior. In general, theories of international relations appear to rely upon the latter perspective, thus begging the question of how such systems develop in places such as the Horn of Africa.

The remainder of this chapter will explore the convergence of European and Horn international politics with the foregoing questions in mind. After a brief description of the Horn of Africa as a region, I will consider the nature and consequences of the historical convergence of European and Horn systems of international relations. I will then consider how this convergence of such systems has affected the political and economic development of the Horn. Against this background, I will consider the prospects that Soviet-U.S. collaboration will promote greater political stability and economic development in the Horn, focusing on the specific case of the Eritrean conflict. (On this point, see Chapter 14 by Donald Rothchild in this volume.) Finally, I will offer some preliminary thoughts concerning the implications of Horn-European relationships for some of the theoretical questions just identified.

DEFINING THE HORN OF AFRICA

One direct consequence of the incomplete process of establishing the stable, settled identity of the major international actors in the Horn of Africa is that the boundaries of the region itself are somewhat inchoate and are, therefore, open to differences of opinion. It is agreed that Ethiopia (including Eritrea), Djibouti, and Somalia are part of the Horn. Whether Egypt, Sudan, and Kenya should also be included is open to question. In this chapter, only Sudan will be included on the grounds that one of the defining features of the Horn is the thin, even non-existent line between domestic and international politics, each profoundly influencing the other. By such a definition, Kenya and Egypt might reasonably be excluded. Although both have played prominent roles in the international politics of the Horn, domestic politics in these countries would not appear to have been as greatly influenced and disrupted by international politics involving the other countries as has been the case for those countries themselves.

In the Horn's struggles over the geographical and juridical identities of its actors, the boundaries between "domestic" and "international" political spheres have remained unusually permeable. Disputed boundaries have both reflected and fueled complex, fundamental, and revolutionary conflict over who constitute the legitimate political actors and whom they are entitled to rule. Sudan has been mired in one of the continent's longest-running—albeit on occasion quiescent—civil wars, which has both influenced and been influenced by the Eritrean and Tigrean liberation wars with the Mengistu regime in Ethiopia.[4] (These wars are discussed later in this chapter.) The disputed border between Ethiopia and Somalia is more than a question of territorial adjustment. In a more fundamental way than elsewhere on the continent, it poses the question of whether ethnicity or territoriality is to define the state. For Ethiopia, the stakes were much larger than the potential loss of territory, for the withdrawal of ethnic Somalis would have reverberated throughout Ethiopia, setting a bold precedent for other peoples in the 75 percent of the land annexed to the empire by Menelik II's conquests in the late nineteenth and early twentieth centuries. Finally, tiny Djibouti is composed of peoples closely identified with their kin in Ethiopia and Somalia. Djibouti's existence as an independent state since 1977 has rested on a rough power balance between Ethiopia and Somalia and on a continued French military presence in the country.

With a few notable exceptions, such as Gezira in Sudan and the Chilalo Agricultural Development Unit (now the Arsi Rural Development Unit) in Ethiopia (the most famous externally supported agricultural projects in the region), the direct impact of European powers on the socioeconomic structures and fortunes of these countries appears to have been modest. In part, the ambitions of the European powers in this region have characteristically been more limited than in other regions of the continent. At least partly for this historical reason, the region remains perhaps the poorest on the continent and one of the poorest in the world. Per capita incomes in Somalia and Ethiopia have been among the lowest in the world, with Sudan and Djibouti only modestly higher. Until recently educational levels have been low, even by African standards. With some significant, localized exceptions (primarily in Ethiopia), the region has attracted significantly less overseas private investment than other regions of Africa.

Exposure to European influence appears to have been qualitatively different in the Horn than elsewhere in Africa. Although the machinations of the powers complicated, disrupted, and profoundly altered the politics of the Horn, their impact on the region's socioeconomic and cultural structures was in many respects less intensive and profound than elsewhere on the continent. The peoples of the Horn region displayed a singular capacity to resist imperial intrusions. The prior spread of Islam in the Horn and the strength of Coptic Christianity in Ethiopia appear to have stiffened local peoples' resistance to European cultural influence.[5]

Substantial areas of all the Horn countries—southern Sudan, the interior of Somalia, and 80 percent of the land area of Ethiopia—have remained largely unpenetrated by roads and other modern means of communication longer than has been the case in much of the rest of Africa. Mountainous terrain in Ethiopia has also impeded the spread of transport and other communications networks. This prolonged inaccessibility of significant areas of the region has both helped it to resist imperial influences and perpetuated strongly centrifugal domestic political tendencies in all of the countries, with the possible exception of tiny Djibouti. In addition, one apparent important consequence of the relatively limited European socioeconomic impact during the colonial era was that educational levels remained notably low, although in Italy's Eritrean colony educational levels appear to have been above those of independent Ethiopia.

While the region by no means lacks economic potential, ecological fragility is one of its distinguishing features, one that has contributed powerfully to recurrent drought and famine. At present, large areas are suitable primarily for pastoralism; other areas cannot be cultivated intensively; and still other zones—notably in Ethiopia—have suffered from centuries of erosion. Desertification and deforestation have been characteristic of this region, posing further threats to the natural resource base. At the same time, river-based agriculture along the Nile as well as significant irrigation projects and the potential for their expansion—notably along the Awash and the Wabe Shebelle in Ethiopia—offer important bases and further prospects for agricultural development.

Ethnically, the region is one of enormous diversity. This is the case even in Somalia, where the Islamic faith and the Arabic language contribute greatly to cultural homogeneity—important class divisions notwithstanding. Politically dominant groups, such as the Amhara in Ethiopia, are in fact sharply divided along territorial lines. Innumerable small communities with their distinct dialects and traditions, many of them still relatively isolated, are found throughout the region, especially in Ethiopia. Pastoralists constitute important minorities in both Ethiopia and Sudan and may represent a majority within Somalia. Their indifference to political boundaries in the movement of their herds has further complicated the international politics of the region. Historically, conflict among these diverse communities has been substantially exacerbated by their involvement with European interests. The socioeconomic bases and costs of such conflict have been profoundly magnified by drought and famine, stimulating some of the largest movements of refugees to be found anywhere in the Third World. Such displacement has greatly complicated and burdened the already troubled processes of state formation and development in the region.

Finally, with the possible exception of Somalia, population expansion rates have ranged well above GDP growth rates.[6] These unfavorable ratios must be reversed if ecological calamity and magnified socioeconomic distress, with all their attendant political ramifications, are to be avoided.

THE HISTORY OF INTERNATIONAL POLITICS ON THE HORN

The international politics of the Horn and those of European countries began to converge in the nineteenth century, although this was preceded much earlier by the region's exposure to external influence from another source: the world of Islam. For Ethiopia, this exposure began in the sixteenth century when, with Portuguese assistance, it barely survived the *jihad* of Ahmed Gran. The Portuguese remained in Ethiopia at the invitation of the emperors, where they applied their technological capabilities. However, they overextended their welcome and were expelled when they sought to convert the Coptic kingdom to Roman Catholicism.[7] On the heels of this international triumph followed by domestic trauma came an external challenge from another source: Oromo expansion from the south. The combined effect of the Amhara kingdom's wars with and more peaceful interpenetration by the Oromo was to reduce the authority of the monarchy to little more than symbolic proportions by the latter decades of the eighteenth century. During this period of radical decentralization (known as the "era of princes"), Ethiopia nevertheless successfully preserved its independence. Sven Rubenson has argued persuasively that national identity, not merely forbidding topography as Arnold Toynbee asserted, enabled the Ethiopian state to survive, although the nature of that political identity and how it was perceived by the actors themselves remain subjects of further historical research.[8]

The beginnings of European imperial intrusion in the Horn as a whole roughly coincide with the renaissance of the Ethiopian state around 1850 under Emperors Teodros, Johannes, and Menelik II. In this process the interests of Ethiopia collided with those of its neighbors. Simultaneously, all of the countries were struggling to come to terms with the expanding European powers, whose competition with each other in the region was a reflection of the dynamics of the European balance of power. If the outcomes of these struggles may have had substantial bearing on the European balance of power, the European powers' competition with each other even more profoundly shaped the development of international politics in the Horn in Africa.

The broadening and deepening of the Horn's exposure to the European powers' expanding competition in the nineteenth century was an offshoot of the powers' rivalry over Egypt. France's invasion and occupation of Egypt under Napoleon Bonaparte awakened long-dormant European interest in the area. Indirectly, the new focus of European international relations upon Egypt provoked a fundamental change in the relations among the peoples of northeastern Africa, for—in the wake of Egyptian disarray following France's departure—Muhammad Ali emerged not only to consolidate his rule in Egypt and promote European-style reforms but to extend his rule by the middle of the century over much of what is now the Sudanese republic. Within a generation, however, Egyptian influence expanded further south as well as eastward, threatening parts of Ethiopia and the Somali coast.[9]

Egypt became a focal point of European expansion in the first decades of the nineteenth century as Great Britain made increasing use of the Red Sea as a pathway to India. Within a generation, France and Italy responded by acquiring their own outposts on the Red Sea coast, thus initiating a rivalry that was to transform the politics of the Horn. Serbian and Bulgarian revolts dramatized the weakness of the Ottoman Empire and highlighted the possibility of a major clash of interests in the eastern Mediterranean area among all the parties to the European balance of power in the event of a vacuum that would be created by the empire's collapse. Meanwhile, at the high point of its territorial expansion, Egyptian external debt led first to British and French administrative intervention and then in 1882 to a British military strike.

The dynamics of the European balance of power determined how Great Britain employed its enhanced influence in the region. In order to avoid upsetting the increasingly strained and frayed international relations within the European theater, as well as in response to domestic pressures, the British government chose to prop up and exert influence through the existing Ottoman rulers rather than to establish more direct formal colonial authority. That pattern of limited, indirect involvement was to continue and to shape fundamentally the nature of the influence of European international relations on the Horn. Elsewhere in Africa and in the Third World, colonial powers ultimately excluded European competition in their respective spheres of influence through formal colonization. By contrast, Great Britain's constrained role in Egypt by extension circumscribed its influence in the part of the Sudan that Egypt controlled at least nominally on behalf of the Ottoman Empire. That limited intervention created a sense of a power vacuum from a European perspective. This contributed greatly to continued European competition for influence in the Horn, with attendant important consequences for relations among the Horn actors themselves.

While Egypt was preoccupied with escalating European involvement in its affairs and competition in its neighborhood that involved Italy as well as France, the Mahdist revolution broke out in the Sudan, fueled by a combination of religious idealism and resentment of heavy-handed Egyptian administration.[10] The Mahdist movement challenged not only a weakened and distracted Egypt but threatened Ethiopia, where Emperor Johannes was struggling with major internal centrifugal tendencies integrally related to Ethiopia's growing involvement with European powers and their international competition. Johannes died leading his armies against Mahdist forces who were suspected of quietly collaborating with Teclehaimanot of Gojjam, one of Johannes's two principal domestic rivals. The other rival, Menelik II—who was to become Johannes's successor—was beginning what was to be the vast expansion of the Ethiopian empire, made possible in part by his arms trade with Italy.

The Mahdist revolution dramatized the weakness of Egypt and, by extension, of Great Britain's position vis-à-vis competition from other European powers in the Sudan. The European perception of a vacuum in the region was heightened by Britain's geopolitical notion that control of the upper Nile was the key to control of Egypt. The resultant convergence of British, French, and Italian interests in the region came to a climax in the Fashoda crisis at the turn of the century. The subsequent Anglo-French agreements ceded colonial hegemony in Egypt and the Sudan to Great Britain. My concern here is not with the European diplomacy that produced this result but with its significance for relationships among actors in the Horn itself.

European competition in the Horn during the last decades of the nineteenth century influenced international relations within the Horn of Africa long after the European powers withdrew formally from their spheres of imperial influence. These influences can be seen in three subtheaters: the Sudan, Ethiopia, and Somalia.

The Sudan

First, in the Sudan the memory of the Mahdist revolution lived on to influence Sudanese nationalist politics during the colonial period. At the time, however, the embryonic Mahdist state failed to establish itself as a separate actor capable of joining and sustaining its own interests in the European competition for power in the region. Preoccupied with a bitter and violent struggle to consolidate his power among rivals who united behind the Mahdi, his successor, Adallahi, chose to assert the embryonic state's unity in international relations through continuation of the *jihad* rather than through attempted negotiations with European powers. His eventual defeat by Anglo-Egyptian forces resulted in the perpetuation of Egyptian as well as British influence through the Anglo-Egyptian Condominium.

As a consequence, ambivalence on the issue of whether Sudan would or should be an independent state or, alternatively, should merge with Egypt remained central to Sudanese politics throughout the colonial period. Egyptian nationalists encouraged nationalism in Sudan. Great Britain sought to manage regional international relations by using divide-and-conquer tactics against Sudanese and Egyptian nationalism. In the latter case, Great Britain created divisions among the Sudanese as well as between pan-Arab nationalists who sought common cause with Egypt and the Mahdists. Although the Mahdists preferred an independent course, they found it prudent to make common cause with the British against both Egypt and their domestic rivals, who viewed this unholy alliance with contempt. Nasser's renunciation of Farouk's pretensions to be king of Egypt and Sudan and his recognition of Sudan's right to self-determination cleared the way for Sudanese independence in 1956.

Meanwhile, the British had previously set out to cordon off the southern provinces from the influence of either the Mahdists or their rivals, a policy that was not abandoned until the decade between the conclusion of World War II and Sudanese independence, by which time the fruits of separate development had ripened into glaring socioeconomic inequalities. Thus, in important ways British recognition of Sudan's independence may be said to have represented a juridical fig leaf poorly concealing the sacrifice of any emergent Sudanese statehood to British manipulation of regional politics on the Horn for its imperial ends.

Ethiopia

From the mid-nineteenth to the late twentieth century, Ethiopia's rulers courted international recognition both to confirm the country's historic independence in a world of intensifying international conflict and to buttress the domestic legitimacy of their regimes. However, the most lasting consequences of Ethiopia's engagement with the expanding European competition in the Horn was to lay the foundations of a contemporary thirty-year war over the existence and definition of the Ethiopian state. In the mid-nineteenth century, Teodros emerged from obscurity to initiate the revival and reunification of the Ethiopian empire. His shining vision was secular where the Mahdi's was sacred, but its revolutionary fervor was no less intense.[11] Teodros sought the purification of the Ethiopian state from the corrupting influences of the church and of the nobility and its armies. He pursued this vision with a militancy that undermined the unity he had begun to build and the international acceptance he sought. Thus, his successor, Johannes, was left the twin tasks of consolidating a reunited Ethiopia and preserving its independence and territorial integrity in the face of European imperial competition.[12]

Ethiopia both gained and lost in the international competition of European and regional actors on the Horn. As *nequsa neqast*—King of Kings—Johannes succeeded diplomatically in consolidating Ethiopian unity on the basis of a federal-type relationship with the kings of Shoa and Gojjam—Menelik II and Teclehaimanot, respectively. But it was a fragile unity. I have already mentioned Teclehaimanot's possible involvement with the Mahdists at the point of their military challenge to Ethiopia. Meanwhile, Menelik increased his power relative to that of Johannes by beginning the imperial expansion of Ethiopia from his Shoan base, an expansion that ultimately involved nearly three-fourths of the country's present land area. He did so with the help of an arms trade with the Italians, who judged that a strengthened Menelik weakened Johannes in any effort he might make to obstruct their incursion into what is now Eritrea.

Early in his reign, Johannes's own military strength was sufficient to expel a weakened Egypt and defeat a small Italian force in Eritrea in pursuit of Ethiopia's claim to be a Red Sea power. In the complicated politics of the European balance of power, however, Great Britain found it in its interests to encourage Italian advances in the Horn as a means of checking French pretensions. Johannes's diplomacy did not prevent the Italian inheritance of Massawa from a retreating Egypt—with British concurrence. In the 1880s, Italy moved to expand its sphere to include most of what is now Eritrea. Emperor Menelik, accepting realities, confirmed this with his erstwhile partner, Italy, in the Treaty of Ucciali in 1889. From that time on, Eritrea proceeded on a course separate and distinct from that of Ethiopia, laying the foundations for the present war.[13]

Italy's imperial thirst, encouraged by Great Britain for its own purposes, was not quenched. Menelik renounced the Treaty of Ucciali when France pointed out to him that the Italian version of the treaty suggested that he had agreed in effect to an Italian protectorate and to allow Italy to represent Ethiopia in international relations. The resulting war, climaxed by an Ethiopian victory at Adwa in 1896, confirmed for Ethiopia a stature in Eurocentric international relations enjoyed by no other African power. However, this newly won status counted for little when, forty years later, Emperor Haile Selassie appealed to the League of Nations for support in a new Italian war on Ethiopia. Italy occupied Ethiopia from 1936 until British armies liberated the country and restored Selassie to his throne in 1941. Great Britain, however, had its own colonial designs on Ethiopia, but they were thwarted primarily by the emperor's determined efforts and a lack of U.S. encouragement.[14]

Undeterred by past experience, Haile Selassie calculated that enhancement of Ethiopian interests—the interests of his regime—and Ethiopia's standing in world affairs dictated that his country actively participate in both regional international relations and the cold war on the side of the Western alliance. As a historically independent state in an otherwise colonized continent, Ethiopia came to symbolize African liberation even to nationalist leaders a generation removed and politically a pole apart from Selassie.[15] In cultivating this role, Selassie gained a measure of legitimacy for his African empire from African leaders bent on rolling back European imperialism, an irony Somalia (with its claims to the Ogaden) has never successfully impressed on the OAU collectively or on other African leaders individually.[16] Selassie's traditionalism gained him patronage from the United States, which feared that the Soviet Union would capitalize on nationalism in northeastern Africa and the Middle East to expand its influence. U.S. patronage included training Selassie's armed forces and developing a communications base in Asmara, Eritrea, for monitoring activities in the Soviet Union and the Middle East.

Haile Selassie may also have calculated that such international prestige would dampen any adverse international reaction to his deliberate cashiering of the Eritrean federation by 1962 in favor of full incorporation in Ethiopia. Whether that calculation will prove to be valid remains to be seen, for in setting aside the federation hammered out by the United Nations in 1951, Selassie provoked a challenge not only to the definition of the Ethiopian state but also to its very existence. In challenging what it claims is imperial subjugation, Eritrea challenges the basis upon which most of the Ethiopian state was established through the conquests of Menelik II—an issue with which the Mengistu regime has struggled inconclusively and at fearful cost since it came to power in 1974.[17]

Somalia

In contrast to Ethiopia and Sudan, the future Somalian state was affected more directly at the turn of the century by the expanding Ethiopian empire than by European empires (which limited their activities to coastal Red Sea outposts). Strengthened by success at Adwa, Menelik won acceptance from all three European powers for Ethiopia's claims to and appropriation of much of what is now the Ogaden region. Inland Somalia rallied to the oratory and vision of Muhammad Abdille Hassan in launching a twenty-year *jihad* against alien incursions.[18] The Sayyid, as he was known, proved adept in playing the European powers against each other, gaining some German assistance in his war with Great Britain and—during an interlude in the war—finding protection from the Italians. In the end, British military power proved superior. Although the Sayyid made an enduring contribution to Somali nationalism, the nascent state he started to build did not survive his death. Italy, France, Great Britain, and Ethiopia parceled the domain of the Somali nation he envisioned, most of which was temporarily reunited as Italian East Africa during World War II.

The reinstatement of these divisions after World War II by the United Nations included the restoration to Italy of its Somali holdings as a trust for a ten-year term. The renewed divisions spurred the Somali Youth League to demand the incorporation in a single independent state of all Somalis then parceled out to three European empires, an African empire, and a British colony (Kenya). This vision fueled twenty-five years of cold and hot wars with Ethiopia over the definition of the Horn's political map.

THE INFLUENCE OF HISTORY ON CONTEMPORARY HORN POLITICS

A century's exposure to the politics of the major world powers has continued to weigh heavily upon the Horn of Africa. The nature of that legacy has differed from that experienced by much of the rest of Africa in two respects. First, the three Horn countries (other than Djibouti) experienced continuing competition among the major powers within their borders rather than the established hegemony of single powers within defined boundaries. Second, one of the three—Ethiopia—was itself an imperial power with which nationalist movements in each of the others clashed.

The major consequence of this legacy has been that the very definition of all three states has presented more profound and international issues than has been the case elsewhere in the continent. This has been true particularly since Sudan's and Somalia's independence—in 1956 and 1960, respectively—and the fall of Emperor Haile Selassie's government in Ethiopia in 1974. Upon the prolonged struggles since 1975 to determine how states on the Horn shall be defined and bounded has been superimposed continuing rivalry among external super- and secondary powers. This multidimensional struggle has consumed resources that might have been devoted to lifting the region as a whole out of its grinding poverty. Equally important, however, the course of the state definition and building struggles has governed the ends and means of utilizing the available development resources. The results have generally been unfortunate and often counterproductive.

Ethiopia has been the epicenter of the contemporary crisis in the Horn because of both its size and the nature of the issues it has confronted, particularly since the revolution. In geopolitical terms, it is central; the conflicts between the countries have been bilateral, involving Ethiopia with both Sudan and Somalia but not the latter two with each other; Ethiopia's population (including Eritrea) is 70 percent of that of the entire region; and Ethiopia's army has been the largest in the region—ahead of Sudan's and Somalia's although theirs are large by African standards, making the Horn the most militarized region on the continent. Although Ethiopia is the poorest of the countries in per capita income, it is widely believed by agricultural economists to have significant economic potential—perhaps more than the other countries. However, the Ethiopian revolution is what has made the country the center of the crisis of the Horn of Africa, for the revolution has opened wide a Pandora's box of possible reconfigurations of states.[19]

The Mengistu regime's blueprint for transforming a traditional empire into a Marxist-Leninist republic was profoundly undermined not only by those contesting the regime's legitimacy but by challenges to its presumption that an Ethiopian state survived the demise of Haile Selassie's imperial government. The Eritrean liberation movement emerged in the late 1950s when it became apparent that Selassie was about to cashier the federation and force unification with Ethiopia. The Eritrean Liberation Front (ELF) launched an armed struggle in 1961 and rapidly attracted broadly based support among students, teachers, and urban workers. Organizational difficulties and ideological differences led to its being supplanted by the more radical Ethiopian People's Liberation Front (EPLF) in the 1970s. Despite continuing and sometimes violent divisions within its ranks, the EPLF became (and has remained) the vanguard of Eritrean insurgency. By the eve of the fall of Selassie's government, Eritrean liberation armies controlled most of the area except for the major cities and towns, including Asmara and Massawa.

The Eritrean-Ethiopian conflict became enmeshed in the complexities of Middle Eastern politics. Eritrean liberation forces drew assistance from a number of Middle Eastern states and from Eritrean communities in exile elsewhere in the region, while Selassie's government remained closely associated with Israel and the United States. In recent years, the EPLF has become increasingly independent of Middle Eastern support, sustaining its military activities in large part with equipment it has captured from fleeing Ethiopian units. Meanwhile, changing U.S. policies toward the Middle East transformed the Ethiopian-U.S. relationship at the very end of Selassie's years. As U.S. foreign policy in the Kissinger years shifted toward less unquestioning support for Israeli positions, Ethiopia's value as a U.S. ally diminished in importance. At the same time, with changes in intelligence-gathering technology, the Kagnew base lost its importance as a communications outpost.

Ethiopia had been the principal U.S. client on the continent in military assistance terms since World War II. In the 1970s, with the United States having increased communications with Arab countries, Ethiopia became less important to the United States as an ally useful in helping Israel resist the Arab countries. The communications post in Asmara, used to monitor developments in the region, became technologically obsolete. Ethiopia's altered relationship with the United States was reflected in Selassie's failure to work out a new arms agreement on his final U.S. visit in 1973. The failure of the emperor's negotiations undermined his domestic position even before his government's handling of the 1973 drought sealed his fate.[20] Meanwhile, Ethiopia felt its position was vulnerable in light of continued large-scale Soviet military assistance to Somalia. In fact the Somalian arms buildup may have been a factor in the Ethiopian military's decision to claim leadership of the 1974 revolution.

After a decade of armed conflict that was largely unaccompanied by significant diplomatic initiatives to mediate the differences, the possibilities for Eritrean reconciliation with Ethiopia remained slim. The first Ethiopian head of state following Haile Selassie was Eritrean-born General Aman Andom. Aman's visits to Eritrea suggested the possibility of negotiations on some basis other than complete Eritrean independence. However, with his execution in the coup that brought Mengistu toward leadership of the military regime, those hopes were dashed for the foreseeable future. Although informal talks did take place between Ethiopia and the Eritrean insurgents, Mengistu's regime was never prepared to negotiate seriously, and the EPLF appeared to accept nothing short of independence.

In the late 1970s and again in the late 1980s and early 1990s, the EPLF seemed on the verge of being able to wrest all of Eritrea from Ethiopian jurisdiction and to establish at least de facto independence. Meanwhile, the prosecution of the war led the Mengistu regime to adopt increasingly authoritarian practices domestically, prompting the emergence of another separatist movement in Eritrea's southern neighbor, Tigre. The Tigrean People's Liberation Front (TPLF) had won control of most of that province by the early 1990s, and secessionist contagion spread into parts of neighboring Welo and Gondar as well.

The course of the Ethiopian civil war in the north has also intersected with that of the Sudanese civil war. Previously, the two wars had been kept somewhat insulated from each other, in part by Haile Selassie's role in mediating the Sudanese conflict. Since 1974, each government has accused the other of aiding and abetting the other's secessionist adversaries. Large numbers of Eritreans, Tigreans, and peoples from other bordering provinces sought refuge in Sudan, leading to accusations by the Ethiopian government of Sudanese government assistance to the two northern secessionist movements. Ethiopia, in turn, has both encouraged southern Sudanese in their civil war with successive Khartoum governments and created an alliance with Yemen and Libya to counter Sudan's alignment with Egypt, moderate Arab states, and the United States. Sudan's tacit cooperation in the extraction of Bete Israel peoples—Ethiopian Jews recently recognized as such by Israel—has further inflamed Ethiopia–Sudan relationships, although confusion generated by another coup in Sudan in 1986 may have served to cool tempers in the two foreign ministries.

Observing the increasing disarray of the Mengistu regime in the face of intensifying and expanding northern wars of secession, the Somali government of Siad Barre saw an opportunity to wrest the Ogaden from Ethiopia by supporting Ogaden liberation movements. The resulting 1977 war between Somalia and Ethiopia for control of the Ogaden occurred against a background of considerable international pressure. Ethiopia's close cooperation with Kenya (whose increase in military expenditures had been one of the fastest-growing on the continent) in checking Somalian irredentism survived the fall of Selassie's government, even though ideologically the two countries became polar opposites. On the eve of the outbreak of the 1977 war, the Soviet Union and Cuba explored the possibility of creating a regional political consensus around Ethiopia's and Somalia's common professions of socialism as their objective. This initiative backfired, leading to Somalia's expulsion of its Soviet patrons of more than a decade. In so doing, Somalia also yielded to pressure from Saudi Arabia and other conservative Arab states that were fearful of Soviet influence in the Middle East.

Once again the dynamics of big-power politics were superimposed upon the international politics of the Middle East and the Horn regions. The expulsion of the Soviet Union from Somalia coincided with Mengistu's success in persuading the Soviet leadership that Ethiopia had embarked upon a true Marxist-Leninist course and that having Ethiopia as a client was in its interests. In shifting alliances, moreover, the Soviet Union was able to align itself with OAU doctrine concerning the alteration of imperial boundaries. The Soviet Union gave over a billion dollars in military assistance to Ethiopia immediately to enable it to survive the challenge to its territorial integrity. Without that Soviet assistance, it is doubtful that Ethiopia could have prevented the de facto demise of the imperial patrimony, which the Mengistu government struggled to preserve intact.

Ethiopia had found itself vulnerable vis-à-vis Soviet-supported Somalia when the United States shifted its posture during the last days of Haile Selassie's government; Somalia now faced a Soviet-backed Ethiopia with no superpower patron of its own. The Carter administration moved cautiously and with qualifications to help Somalia with military assistance for its defensive purposes against a potential Ethiopian counterinvasion. The Carter administration's caution reflected official skepticism that Somalia could be deterred from using this assistance to fulfill its irredentist agenda.

A central question is how, if at all, the superpowers' exchange of client states affected long-term patterns of international politics on the Horn. Such analysis cannot be conducted without some resort to speculation over what might have happened had this exchange not occurred. It is at least plausible that the Soviets might have been successful in persuading Somalia to stay its hand in the Ogaden out of a combination of caution and regard for the Marxist-Leninist orientation of the Mengistu government. If the Soviets had been unable to restrain Somalia through their own efforts or with the help of whatever influence the OAU and the United States might have been able to exert, it seems unlikely that the Carter administration or any other power would have offered Ethiopia the levels of assistance the Soviets contributed. At a minimum, Ethiopia's territorial dimensions would have shrunk significantly. At worst, a war-weakened Ethiopia might have succumbed to several liberation movements and virtually disappeared from the map.

The same observation applies to the northern Ethiopian theater. Although articulations of the Reagan doctrine almost always omitted any reference to Eritrea, it is doubtful that U.S. assistance would have been available—let alone sought or welcomed—to help Ethiopia against Eritrean and Tigrean insurgencies for a decade, as the Soviets have done. Even if the superpower role switch had not occurred, only the Soviets were in a position to influence the self-proclaimed Marxist-Leninist Mengistu government to negotiate. It is thus plausible to argue that the superpowers' role switch was a necessary precondition for the viability of the Mengistu regime's effort to transform the empire and at least temporarily deter the opposition of those who would have dismantled it.

Soviet and Cuban intervention to restore the Ethiopia-Somalia military balance appeared to have established necessary but not sufficient conditions for broader stabilization and equilibrium in the international politics of the Horn. First, the forced withdrawal of the Somali armies from the Ogaden may have encouraged the Somali government to limit the scope of its irredentism, but it did not by itself bring about peace between Somalia and its neighbors. On the one hand, Somalia took steps to achieve peace with Djibouti even as it prepared for war with Ethiopia. At the height of tension between Somalia and Ethiopia in 1977, both countries—by separate treaties—agreed not to extend their conflict to newly independent Djibouti. Somalia appeared to renounce ethnic-based claims to suzerainty over Djibouti's citizens. The Ethiopian treaty pledged maintenance of the Djibouti–Addis Ababa rail link, which was vitally important to both countries, and noninterference in Djibouti's affairs so long as Afar refugees from Ethiopia were not permitted to use Djibouti as a base for insurgency against Ethiopia. On the other hand, the end of the war did not lead directly to any cessation of the long history of tension between Kenya and Somalia. Somalia did not renounce its claims upon Kenya's ethnic Somalis until a 1984 treaty between the two countries.

Second, Soviet support in the Ogaden and Eritrean wars may have been a necessary precondition for the Mengistu regime to be able to pursue the transformation of the empire, but again it was not a sufficient condition. Soviet support for the Mengistu regime in the Ogaden and Eritrea preserved the outer boundaries of Ethiopia as established by Menelik's conquests without decisively influencing the outcome of contests over whether one state or many would exist within its boundaries. On the other hand, the outcome of the war did not deter any liberation groups from pursuing autonomy or independence from Ethiopia. A case in point was the Western Somali Liberation Front (WSLF), which was actively supported by Somali army regulars in their (presumably shared) goal of detaching the Ogaden from Ethiopia. At the point when Somali troops had advanced their furthest into Ethiopia, the Somali government invited the Oromo Liberation Front (OLF) to make common cause with Somalia and the WSLF. The OLF represented peoples elsewhere in southern and western Ethiopia who had also been incorporated in the empire by Menelik's conquests. But the OLF was suspicious of the WSLF's links with Somalia and did not wish to exchange an Ethiopian for a Somalian overlord. Ethnic differences in the constituencies of the two organizations were not overcome. Subsequently, the WSLF began to distance itself from Somalia and to move toward a position of nonaligned self-determination, although not without serious divisions in its ranks. Both the WSLF and the OLF thus appear to have chosen to pursue self-determination independently of each other and of Somalia in the Ogaden War.

On the other hand, Soviet support for the Mengistu government in Eritrea did not promote a sense of postimperial political unity even among those sharing opposition to a regime they regarded as symbolizing the continuation of an empire. Neither the WSLF nor the OLF appeared to trust the Eritrean and Tigrean movements, which—at least at the time—

they considered to be the heirs of their conquerers as much as the Mengistu regime.[21]

Soviet and Cuban support for Ethiopia in its war with Somalia, through its effects on the domestic politics of Somalia and Ethiopia, appears to have both promoted and undermined international peace on the Horn. First, although dissuaded from a counterinvasion of Somalia, continued Soviet backing of its northern campaigns may have emboldened Ethiopia to maintain its support of guerrilla attacks against the Barre regime within Somalia. At the same time, the negative impact of these wars on the country's severely depressed economy may have played some role in eventually encouraging Somalia to come to terms with Kenya.

Also, continued Soviet military support for the Mengistu regime appears to have reinforced a negative cycle of "domestic" authoritarianism and "international" insurgency. The Mengistu regime was challenged at the outset both by primarily urban opponents who insisted on civilian leadership of the revolution and by Eritrean separatists soon joined by the Tigrean and Oromo movements.[22] In response, the Mengistu regime treated implementation of its domestic socioeconomic reform program as another theater of its military campaigns against these opponents. However, the regime's determination to bring about rapid development through martial law and forced marches proved counterproductive, leaving the country little better off economically in 1990 than it had been in 1975—some promising blueprints for reform notwithstanding.

These policies, in combination with the diversion of more than 50 percent of the public budget to military purposes, did not enable the country to cushion itself against natural calamities of drought and famine. Moreover, the wars have diminished the availability of resources to address the man-made causes of these calamities through reforestation, soil conservation, and irrigation. Thus, the country's famine relief requirements continue to be massive and recurring. Frustration on the part of relief agencies with the impact of the civil wars on their work has further mirrored the primacy of fundamental unresolved issues concerning the shape of the "state" system in the Horn of Africa.

Herein may lie one of the most important contributions of the Ethiopian revolution to the history of modern revolutions. In Ethiopia, to a much greater extent than in other revolutionary contexts, the very identity and existence of the polity within which the revolution was launched has been at issue. At least in this case, the conflicting actors appear to have reached tacit consensus with one another that defining the state system in the region would determine the content and course of the socioeconomic revolution more than would the reverse.

After more than a decade of continuing military assistance to the Mengistu government, the Soviet Union has appeared to change its course. It has signaled that Ethiopia will be no exception to the extension of its domestic policies of glasnost and perestroika to relations with its international adversaries and allies. Mengistu received what one highly placed official termed a "head scrubbing" on a 1989 arms shopping trip to Moscow. The Soviet leadership has resisted sending more support for the Eritrean and Tigrean campaigns, encouraged negotiations with the liberation movements, and urged the Mengistu government to follow World Bank–IMF guides in restructuring the Ethiopian economy. It has not, however, suspended military shipments to Ethiopia.

Since at least 1986, the Mengistu government has participated in diplomatic forays in the Somali theater. Initiatives by other governments within the Horn have contributed to these encouraging developments. In 1986, for example, the Djibouti government organized a regional conference that produced a Permanent Intergovernmental Authority on Drought and Development in East Africa. The conference featured the first face-to-face meeting between Siad Barre and Mengistu Haile Mariam since the 1977 Ogaden War and also brought together the governments of Kenya, Sudan, and Uganda. Djibouti President Hassan Gouled subsequently mediated further talks between Somalia and Ethiopia. In early 1988, perhaps under the influence of both Soviet pressure and serious military reversals in the north, Mengistu reached an agreement for military disengagement and separation with Siad Barre, who was also under a serious military challenge from his domestic opponents. However, the agreement did not address the border question itself. Nevertheless, these conversations led in late 1989 and early 1990 to the normalization of diplomatic relations between the two countries, no doubt heavily influenced by the seriousness of the domestic insurgencies challenging both the Siad and Mengistu regimes.

Private, informal conversations between Ethiopian government and Eritrean People's Liberation Front representatives have occurred intermittently for many years, but to no avail.[23] However, in September 1989 a preannounced meeting between Ethiopian government and Eritrean representatives took place at the Carter Center in Atlanta under the auspices of former president Jimmy Carter. Further talks occurred in Nairobi in December 1989, with the cooperation of Kenya's president Moi and former Tanzanian president Julius Nyerere. The meetings focused primarily upon procedural preliminaries. The two sides agreed publicly to further talks in November 1990. At the end of October 1990, the Mengistu government also agreed to preliminary peace talks with the Tigrean People's Liberation Front under Italian auspices in Rome. Meanwhile, North Yemen convened a meeting of dissident Eritreans with Ethiopian representatives in Sana.

Parallel to these developments, in early 1988 the Ethiopian government finally agreed to accept some aspects of a World Bank structural adjustment program, thereby ending years of delay in renewing an agreement for Bank support of agricultural development in the country. Neither the Bank nor the Ethiopian government gained complete acceptance of its requirements, but the agreement did merit cautious optimism that renewed multilateral support for the country's economic development might eventually lead to tangible, favorable outcomes. And late in 1989, the Ethiopian government agreed to facilitate relief efforts for famine victims in rebel-held areas.

However, events in 1990 and 1991 demonstrated that the ongoing crises of state formation shaped the course of "international" relations within the Horn of Africa independent of the official exertions of the major powers, multilateral agencies, and private voluntary groups such as the Carter Center. External criticism and pressure may have helped domestic groups in their efforts to overthrow the government of Siad Barre in Somalia, which succeeded in early 1991, but external forces have appeared unable or unwilling to influence the protracted competition among the regionally based factions to establish a successor regime. The TPLF's poorly timed endorsement of Albanian-style socialism, just as the Berlin Wall came down, helped the Mengistu government by making it appear a lesser as well as known evil, but its recognition of Eritrea's right to secede provoked strong nationalist responses—even from Mengistu's opponents—from which his regime drew new strength. The regime's desperate struggle to retain power and uphold its definition of the Ethiopian state, more than World Bank entreaties or events in Eastern Europe, led the Mengistu government in March 1990 to abandon most features of the socioeconomic transformations it had sought to impose since 1976. Similarly, the conflicting interests of the combatants in both the Sudanese and Ethiopian civil wars have taken precedence over their common interests in distributing famine relief, in part because it has been external donors who have sought to define that common interest. Finally, regional international relations on the Horn have not lacked influence on global politics: The Sudan government's Islamic fundamentalism has undermined the Arab League's support in the struggle against Iraq, and Ethiopia has diminished superpower capacities to mediate its civil war by drawing once again on military support from Israel.

Finally, in May 1991 Mengistu fled into exile and his government collapsed in the face of its imminent overthrow by a Tigrean-led coalition of northern-based opposition forces, the Ethiopian People's Revolutionary Democratic Front (EPRDF). Simultaneously, the EPLF gained full military control of Eritrea. The end of the cold war made U.S. mediation of the transition to a new order acceptable to all parties. The United States, along with European countries, used its influence to encourage the EPRDF to organize an all-party conference to establish a broadly based transitional regime and a process for building a new political order that would honor basic human rights. The attendance of all major groups, including the Eritreans, at the July 1, 1991, convening of the conference augured well for its, and Ethiopia's, future. But the tenor of at least some of the EPRDF's early policy statements suggested strongly that it, and not the Western states, would determine the contours of the new Ethiopian state and, to that extent, leave uncertain the future shape of the region as a whole.[24]

Thus, a major lesson of more than a century of diplomatic and military history appears to be that major-power interventions have heavily influenced but not decisively or comprehensively determined the course of international politics on the Horn. Soviet pressure clearly helped move the Mengistu regime toward negotiations it had previously adamantly rejected. However, contemporary events appear to confirm a fundamental pattern in the Horn that has been apparent for at least the last century and a half: International relations in the Horn have been defined by conflicting struggles over state formation that are independent of and that influence global patterns of international relations at least as much as they are influenced by them.

The Ethiopian government's war with Eritrean and Tigrean movements long predates the cold war, and the protagonists have in no way been mere proxies for their superpower patrons. It should not be surprising, therefore, that the diminishing of superpower conflict in the region has not appeared ipso facto to influence the parties automatically to settle their differences. Conceivably, although not necessarily, such disengagement might alter the outcome of the struggle. However, when and the extent to which the Soviet Union winds down its military support for the Mengistu regime may significantly influence whether the regime continues or collapses and therefore, perhaps, influence the outcome of the Eritrean independence campaign. As in Somalia, however, the major powers are likely to lack both the will and the capacity to significantly influence the complex processes of state re-formation that are likely to ensue. They will lack the will primarily because of the decline of global superpower competition in the post–cold war era. They may lack the capacity because the complexity of the issues is beyond their comprehension and because the actors involved see great-power interests as largely irrelevant to the substance and resolution of those issues.

The replacement of the Mengistu government through a successful coup may bring in its wake a regime prepared to negotiate measures of regional autonomy short of independence, particularly in view of the 1990 political and economic reforms at the national level. Eritrean and Tigrean movements might be prepared to accept such an outcome. Yet it remains unclear whether Ethiopian opposition to the TPLF and to Eritrean independence will evaporate with an end to the Mengistu government; the victory of either or both is not likely to resolve issues of state formation per se, for the definition of neither Eritrea nor Ethiopia has been ipso facto settled.

Indeed, the ensuing struggle may resemble the "era of princes" in Ethiopia between about 1775 and 1850. During that period, power struggles among the peoples of the region nearly eclipsed a central Ethiopian government and prevented its reemergence for most of a century. In the case of the northern wars, important and somewhat unpredictable exogenous factors will affect the eventual outcome: (1) the present and likely future status of other regional autonomy movements in the south and west, (2) the strength of these movements, and (3) their dispositions to align with either party or remain unaligned. The record documents the difficulty of real collaboration among the liberation movements, notwithstanding efforts and steps taken periodically in that direction. The prospects, then, are for a lengthy and complicated sorting-out process under the most favorable circumstances. An unfortunate consequence may be that the time when substantial military resources can be reallocated to peaceful development efforts will be postponed some distance into the future.

CONCLUSION

How does the foregoing analysis bear upon the theoretical questions posed at the outset of this chapter? The record suggests the following hypotheses. First, the Horn remains a distinctive regional international system resisting full assimilation into big-power-dominated global politics. Contact between the Horn actors and major global powers has influenced and helped define the emergence of new state actors and, thereby, the shape of international politics on the Horn. However, such intervention has not resulted in the elimination of important nonstate actors, which continue to influence Horn international politics. Their presence has continued a mixed system of state and nonstate actors that has resisted direction by major powers. This situation is analogous to bilateral settings, such as Vietnam and Afghanistan, where guerrilla warfare has checked much greater conventional big-power military establishments.

Second, although the activities of the major powers have greatly stimulated change in the Horn of Africa international system, it is not clear that they have decisively shaped the direction of the processes of change over the long term. It is uncertain that the direction of change is toward a system of state actors identical to that of the major external actors, given the precarious situation of the three larger states in the Horn (and perhaps also of Djibouti as well) vis-à-vis the "domestic" forces within them that threaten their dissolution and that may augur eventual political constellations of a very different nature. The direction and outcome of processes of "state" formation in the Horn, therefore, are not necessarily a given.

Third, the evidence suggests that within distinctive regional international systems, political actors pursue their interests and develop international equilibria independent of, as well as within, the frameworks established by major-power competition in their midst. Their interests as they perceive them are shaped by factors independent of, although in some cases consonant with, those that animate the major powers.

Fourth, it follows that patterns of major-power conflict and cooperation in regional theaters shape but do not determine what regional actors define as being in their interests. It also follows that the outcomes of the influence regional and major-power actors exert upon each other can be only partially predictable at best. Thus, the changing relations of the superpowers toward each other outside as well as within the Horn have set in motion possibly significant and potentially positive changes in the behavior of regional actors. However, even if those new patterns of behavior continue, contemporary theories of international relations do not yet enable us to envisage clearly their long-term consequences.

NOTES

1. The complexity of politics on the Horn of Africa is such that strictly speaking it is inappropriate, albeit unavoidable, to categorize these politics as "domestic" or "international." In the case of the Eritrean conflict, for example, the choice of either term automatically creates a bias in favor of one side or the other—"domestic" favoring Ethiopia, "international" favoring Eritrea.

2. Use of the term *international* to describe political relations among the actors on the Horn is also, strictly speaking, a misnomer, as the nation-state status of some of the actors involved is precisely what is at issue in their conflicts. Major sources on realist and neorealist theories of international relations include Robert Keohane (ed.), *Neo-Realism and Its Critics* (New York: Columbia University Press, 1986); Hedley Bull, *The Anarchical Society: A Study of Order in World Politics* (New York: Columbia University Press, 1977); J. E. Dougherty and Robert Pfaltzgraff, *Contending Theories of International Relations*, 2nd ed. (Philadelphia: Lippincott, 1981); Robert Jervis, *Perception and Misperception in World Politics* (Princeton: Princeton University Press, 1976); Morton Kaplan, *System and Process in International Relations* (New York: John Wiley & Sons, 1957); *International Organization* 36 (special issue on international regimes, 1986); Stephen Krasner, *International Regimes* (Ithaca: Cornell University Press, 1983); Hans Morganthau, *Scientific Man Versus Power Politics* (Chicago: University of Chicago Press, 1946); William H. Riker, *The Theory of Political Coalitions* (New Haven: Yale University Press, 1962); and Kenneth Waltz, *The Theory of International Politics* (Reading, Mass.: Addison-Wesley, 1979).

3. The extent to which it is appropriate to define an international system in terms of the characteristics of its component actors is one of the prime issues between Kenneth Waltz and his critics. See Keohane, *Neo-Realism and Its Critics*. Implicitly, this chapter weighs in on the side of the critics. The argument, here, however is that the relationship of Horn and European international politics provides an opportunity to advance theory on this issue.

4. The term *Ethiopia* is also very much at issue in this discussion, for the struggles in that country have been about the very definition of a postimperial polity. See my *The Ethiopian Transformation: The Quest for the Post-Imperial State*

(Boulder, Colo.: Westview Press, 1988). The use of the term *Ethiopia* as though it did not include Eritrea is for purposes of semantic clarity only and does not imply any judgment by me on the merits of the issue at stake.

5. Sven Rubenson, *The Survival of Ethiopian Independence* (London: Heinemann, 1976).

6. World Bank, *World Development Report 1988* (New York: Oxford University Press, 1988).

7. One of the best sources on this episode remains A.H.M. Jones and Elizabeth Monroe, *A History of Ethiopia* (London: Oxford University, Clarendon Press, 1935).

8. Rubenson, *Survival;* Arnold Toynbee, *A Study of History* (New York: Cambridge University Press, 1934).

9. A good source is P. Vatikotis, *The Modern History of Egypt* (New York: Praeger, 1969).

10. On the Sudan, see P. M. Holt and M. W. Daly, *The History of Sudan: From the Coming of Islam to the Present,* 3rd ed. (Boulder, Colo: Westview Press, 1979).

11. On Teodros, see S. Rubenson (ed.), *Teodros: King of Kings* (London: Oxford University Press, 1981); and Donald Crummey, "Teodros as Reformer and Modernizer," *Journal of African History* 10, no. 3 (1969):457–469.

12. A good source on Johannes is Zewde Gebre Sellassie, *Johannes IV of Ethiopia* (London: Oxford University Press, 1975). On Menelik, see Harold Marcus, *The Life and Times of Menelik II* (New York: Oxford University Press, 1975); and Kofi Darkwah, *Shewa, Menelik and the Ethiopian Empire 1813–1889* (London: Heinemann, 1975).

13. S. Rubenson, *Wichale XVIII: The Attempt to Establish a Protectorate over Ethiopia,* Historical Studies no. 1 (Addis Ababa: Haile Selassie I University, 1964).

14. Harold Marcus, *Ethiopia, Great Britain and the United States* (Berkeley: University of California Press, 1983).

15. The single best source on postwar Ethiopia under Haile Selassie is John Markakis, *Ethiopia: Anatomy of a Traditional Polity* (New York: Oxford University Press, 1974).

16. The irony is that Haile Selassie, an emperor, was defending his empire against irredentist Somalia nationalism but managed at the same time to be respected as a friend of nationalist movements in other countries on the continent. He accomplished this because Ethiopia was admired as a country that had never been colonized and that had defeated a European army (Italy's) at the Battle of Adwa in 1896. Selassie's diplomatic skill also helped.

17. On Eritrea, see Richard Sherman, *Eritrea: The Unfinished Revolution* (New York: Praeger, 1980); G.K.N. Trevaskis, *Eritrea: A Colony in Transition* (London: Oxford University Press, 1960); Berekhet Habte Selassie, *Conflict and Intervention in the Horn of Africa* (Addis Ababa: Monthly Review, 1980); and Jordan Gebre Medhin, *Peasants and Nationalism in Eritrea* (Trenton: Red Sea, 1989).

18. On Somalia, see David Laitin, *Politics, Language and Thought: The Somalia Experience* (Chicago: University of Chicago Press, 1977); R. L. Hess, *Italian Colonialism in Somalia* (Chicago: University of Chicago Press, 1966); and I. M. Lewis, *A Modern History of Somalia: Nation and State in the Horn of Africa* (London: Longman, 1980).

19. On the revolution, see recent books by Christopher Clapham, *Transformation and Continuity in Revolutionary Ethiopia* (Cambridge: Cambridge University Press, 1988); Harbeson, *Ethiopian Transformation*; Edmond Keller, *Revolutionary Ethiopia: From Empire to People's Republic* (Bloomington: Indiana University Press, 1989); and John Markakis, *National and Class Conflict in the Horn of Africa* (Cambridge: Cambridge University Press, 1987).

20. Jack Shepherd, *The Politics of Starvation* (Washington, D.C.: Carnegie Endowment for International Peace, 1975).

21. See my "Multilateral Approaches to Multidimensional Conflict Resolution: Lessons from the Horn of Africa," in Arthur Day and Michael Doyle (eds.), *Escalation and Intervention: Multilateral Security and Its Alternatives* (Boulder, Colo: Westview Press, 1985), pp. 74–97.

22. Harbeson, *Ethiopian Transformation*.

23. Dawit Wolde Ghiorgis, *Red Tears: War, Famine, and Revolution in Ethiopia* (Trenton: Red Sea, 1989).

24. Statement by Meles Zenawi, leader of the EPRDF, reported in the *Los Angeles Times*, June 24, 1991.

7
LIBYAN ADVENTURISM

RENÉ LEMARCHAND

Libyan policies in Africa are Janus-faced: There is the erratic face, the element of rashness and unpredictability that figures so prominently in Muammar Qadhafi's record of destabilization; and there is the ideological face, the pan-Arab, anti-imperialist vision that provides the rationale for Libya's long-term policy goals. It is the former that has attracted public controversy and that evoked doubts about Qadhafi's sanity from the Reagan administration; it is the latter, however, that has prompted some observers to see in Qadhafi the embodiment of wisdom or, as Ali Mazrui and Michael Tidy put it, the personification of the sage in African leadership traditions.[1] Where some detect wisdom, others denounce crimes.

Much of our everyday discourse about Qadhafi revolves around one or the other of these images, each setting mental boundaries for radically different interpretations of his foreign policies. What follows is an attempt to cross these boundaries, or at least reduce the conceptual distance between them, and to suggest possible connections between the adventurist and the pan-Arab streaks in the Libyan foreign policy mold. The aim, in brief, is to shift the ground of debate away from the usual catalog of sins attributed to the leader of the *Jamahiriya* (state of the masses) and instead focus attention on the cognitive underpinnings of his policies.

What this cognitive map reveals is an ideological frame that informs and structures Libyan policy choices around the two-fold imperative of pan-Arab unity and anti-imperialism. At a more general level of analysis, it also reflects a way of ordering political reality, of sorting out tactics and strategies in which that reality is deeply anchored and yet transcends the historical and cultural particularities of the Libyan arena. Here attention shifts to the characteristics of statelessness embedded in the Libyan political culture and to the absence of a coherent institutional framework implicit in the notion of a "hydrocarbon society,"[2] which will be discussed below.

The element of consistency between the ideology of pan-Arabism and the political culture of statelessness is transparently evident in Qadhafi's repeated strictures against the concept of the state both as an organizing principle and as a focus of popular loyalties. Consistency evaporates at the level of the strategies employed to bring reality into line with ideology. Here the political and cultural determinants of statelessness and hydrocarbon society combine to invite tactical and strategic moves that seem strangely inconsistent with the primacy of Arab-Muslim unity. Why, for instance, after 1975 did Qadhafi support the Addis authorities—ostensibly Christian—against the predominantly Muslim Eritrean secession? Why did he throw his weight behind Mengistu against Siad Barre's Somalia—a member of the Arab League—and, at times in the Sudan, behind the Christian south against the Muslim north? Why, after repeatedly unleashing his wrath against King Hassan of Morocco, did he suddenly agree in 1986 to a union with his former rival? And why in Chad did he at one point support a major faction of the Christian south against Hissene Habre, a Muslim from the north?

The answers, in part, lie in the potential for conflict inherent in Qadhafi's twin commitments to pan-Arab unity and anti-imperialism. By giving immediate priority—after 1974—to the second of these objectives, Qadhafi found himself in the astonishing position of castigating as neoimperialists (and hence enemies of the Arab nation) those very elements that were most susceptible to the appeals of Arab-Islamic solidarity. The policy choices forced upon him created their own inner contradictions. I am reminded of the general observation made by a student of Arab politics that "it is a notable fact that while the Arab value system demands absolute solidarity within the group, it at the same time encourages among its members a kind of rivalry that is destructive of that very solidarity."[3]

ADVENTURISM RECONSIDERED

What does *adventurism* mean in the context of Libyan foreign policy? The term is heavily freighted with negative moral overtones. Generally meant to refer to "an ill-considered or rash adoption of expedients in the absence or in defiance of consistent plans or principles,"[4] it applies to a variety of foreign policy initiatives, including the April 1986 U.S. bombing raid on Tripoli. Yet the term seldom enters the language of the U.S. media to describe the seamier side of U.S. foreign policy. With this caveat in mind, and insofar as it connotes the erosion of international norms of behavior and accepted diplomatic practice, there can be little question that adventurism is nowhere more palpably evident than in Qadhafi's propensity to use subversion as a major instrument of his foreign policy.

There is more to Libyan adventurism than Qadhafi's own murderous idiosyncrasies. At the broadest level of generalization, the phenomenon may conceivably be viewed as the product of a persistent contradiction between dream and reality, ambition and capability. It reflects Qadhafi's obsessive determination to adapt his long-range pan-Arab goals to the constraints of his environment, to the point where force becomes an adjunct to or a substitute for diplomacy. Seen from this perspective, Libyan adventurism is only the expression of thwarted ambitions.

Plausible as it may sound, the argument calls for several major qualifications. First, if adventurism is indeed an irreducible component of Libyan policies, the term—although of convenient shorthand usage—is hardly adequate to convey the full range of strategies and instrumentalities that have accompanied the implementation of such policies. There is evidently more to Qadhafi's modus operandi than an endless series of provocations, aggressions, and unwarranted interventions in the domestic politics of African states. For all the publicity given to Qadhafi's "unconventional" style of diplomacy, the evidence shows that, where practical or strategically advisable, conventional forms of diplomacy—including conference diplomacy—remain to this day part of his foreign policy arsenal. Nor is adventurism a random phenomenon. It is perhaps best understood as a calculated response to the perceived threats and opportunities that have arisen at specific points in time in specific contexts. What is involved here is less an abdication of rationality than a logic of opportunity.[5] Finally, and most important, insofar as it translates into a consistent disregard of international boundaries and a categorical rejection of the institutions of power built around the state, adventurism, as noted earlier, reflects the enduring impact of the Libyan setting on Qadhafi's cognitive map.

The political economy of contemporary Libya intersects with its traditional milieu in ways that have profoundly influenced Qadhafi's perspectives on his political environment. One aspect of this phenomenon refers to the absence of institutional constraints on the exercise of power, a phenomenon associated with what some have referred to as the "hydrocarbon society" and others as the "rentier state";[6] another brings into focus the element of statelessness inherent in the history and social structure of Libyan society and the apparent ease with which it has been incorporated into Qadhafi's vision of the international order.

QADHAFI AS HYDROCARBON PRINCE

The hallmark of the hydrocarbon society is its overwhelming dependence on external sources of revenue and its absence of accountability to a domestic constituency. Freed of the institutional constraints that in most other instances shape political choices, the hydrocarbon prince, to use John Davis's felicitous expression,[7] is accountable to no one but himself. Only a small body of advisers and technical assistants is needed to handle the flow of revenue from petroleum companies; policy choices have little to do with the institutional restraints of representative bodies; the hallowed principle of "no taxation without representation" is conspicuously irrelevant to policy-making.

From this vantage point, Libya is not a unique case but one that nonetheless differs significantly from the normal pattern of state-society relations. Here, as Lisa Anderson reminds us, "the state [is] virtually completely autonomous from its society, winning popular acquiescence through distribution rather than support through taxation and representation."[8] As the incarnation of the hydrocarbon society, Qadhafi is under no obligation to render accounts; his vulnerability to public opinion is nil: "The social contract, if there is one, is not between Prince and citizen, but between Prince and petroleum company."[9]

Several implications immediately come to mind. For one, the rentier state phenomenon helps illuminate both the centrality of Qadhafi's role as the sole and omnipotent architect of Libyan policies and the practical costs involved in a style of governance so utterly divorced from institutional limitations. The penalties of adventurism, made painfully clear by the outcome of Qadhafi's involvement in Chad, are inscribed in the constitution of the rentier state. Furthermore, the sheer capriciousness of the distributive patterns associated with the rentier state, involving a catch-as-catch-can application of the carrot-and-stick principle, is not atypical of how Qadhafi handles both friends and enemies at the international level. The buying off of foreign clients, along with the use of force to eliminate enemies, reflects a style of diplomacy that is forcefully reminiscent of the dominant motif of his domestic politics. Finally, the rentier state is one that by definition does little or nothing to expand and legitimize state institutions. In a sense the rentier state is a contradiction in terms. If only because it obviates the need for internal resource extraction, it can also dispense with the institutional mechanisms normally designed to enhance state capabilities. This brings us to a consideration of statelessness as another component of Qadhafi's cognitive frame.

STATELESSNESS AS A VARIABLE

For Qadhafi the realization of pan-Arab unity is entirely consonant with his relentless denigration of the state. The Arab nation is the only significant historical reality. The presence in Africa of a state system inherited from the West has no historical validation any more than do the forms of nationalist self-expression that brought the system into existence. Both are the products of Western imperialism, whose impact on the map of Africa is consistently denied in the name of a higher historical reality, the *umma*—the community of the faithful.

Echoes of Nasser resonate through the pages of the Green Book devoted to the imperative of Arab unity: "Everything is inferred from, connected with or subordinated to this version of the future—an independent, unified and socialist Arab nation, for only then can the existence of Israel, the expression of US imperialism, be brought to an end."[10] One wonders, however, whether the Nasserist message would have made as profound an impact on Qadhafi's mindset had it not been for the fact that, as Davis puts it, "notions of statelessness are endemic in Libyan society."[11] The exposure of most Libyans to something resembling a state system has been exceedingly brief. Only during the seven years preceding the 1969 coup did a legitimate state come into being. Even so, its reach into the vast Libyan hinterland was at best intermittent, leaving much of the rural sectors under the sway of tribal sheikhs and kinship structures: "With the support [of kinship] men do not need the state and can manage their affairs without government."[12]

Nor did Ottoman rule leave much in the way of even a diffuse consciousness of the state as an institution. There was the notion of *al hukumia al arabiya*—of an Arab government—but as Davis shrewdly observed, the phrase is better translated as "people's government" or better still, as "no government."[13] At best the concept refers to little more than a set of organizing principles. Nowhere is this lack of awareness of and perceived need for state institutions more evident than among nomads, whose lifestyle implies—among other things—autonomy, mobility, and to this day a considerable measure of boundary crossing. It is perhaps not irrelevant to note here that hundreds of families of the al-Qadhadhfia tribe (Qadhafi's group of origin) migrated into the northern region of Chad in the course of the Libyan conquest, only to be "repatriated" after World War II along with thousands of other displaced Libyans.[14]

One must concur with the observation that there is "an important correspondence between the image of the stateless past and the rhetoric with which Qadhafi supports his attempts to abolish representation"[15]—and ultimately to do away with the very notion of the state. The functions government normally performs are best left to the clan and the family, which Qadhafi sees as the only significant participatory structures. In these conditions, government is not only redundant but, in a sense, is contrary to the interests of the local communities.

Furthermore, the image of the stateless past translates into an image of conflict situations where, in the absence of corporate sources of arbitration, ad hoc alliances—dictated by reasons of convenience or opportunism—are the rule rather than the exception. The pattern that comes to mind is that of segmentary conflicts in which alliances among groups are constantly recalculated, the prizes at stake reassessed, and new alignments tested. It is much the same pattern that transpires from the incessant probings, tactical moves and countermoves, and shifting combinations worked out by Qadhafi in his quest for external allies. In short, the element of unpredictability that characterizes Libyan adventurism is perhaps best understood in the light of the remarkable fluidity of the conflict situations confronting most stateless societies.

IDEOLOGY AS A FRAME OF REFERENCE: PAN-ARABISM VERSUS ANTI-IMPERIALISM

If the style and texture of Libyan policies are traceable in part to the cultural parameters within which policy choices are made, ideology is the crucial variable that defines the range of foreign policy options confronting Qadhafi in his attempt to promote pan-Arab unity and eliminate all vestiges of imperialism from the map of Africa. Should immediate priority be given to policies designed to counteract the spread of neoimperialism as a necessary first step toward pan-Arab unity, or the other way around? Are the prime vectors of imperialism to be identified with Israel, the United States, and France, or with those African regimes whose survival depends on continued economic, technical, or military support from one or the other of the foregoing? Should diplomacy serve as the principal means of achieving pan-Arab unity, or should force be substituted for diplomacy?

Until 1974 the answers were reasonably clear: Pan-Arab unity assumed first priority; Israel was seen as the primary villain; and diplomacy was the preferred instrumentality to achieve regional unity and counteract Israel's influence in the continent. The consistency with which Qadhafi used diplomacy in pursuing his unitarist goals is made abundantly clear by the series of regional unification agreements signed with Egypt and the Sudan in 1969 (Tripoli Charter), with Egypt and Syria in 1971 (Benghazi Treaty), again with Egypt in 1972, with Algeria in 1973 (Hassi Messaoud Accords), and with Tunisia in 1974 (Djerba Treaty). Equally evident are the consistent setbacks that have accompanied Qadhafi's brand of "conference diplomacy" and his growing conviction by 1974 that the forging of Arab unity required an entirely different strategy.

There is more, however, to the rethinking of Libyan strategies than a tacit admission of failed diplomacy; it also reflects Qadhafi's attempt to extend to the international arena the basic ingredients of his Third Universal Theory. By making the concept of *direct democracy* the central operating principle of the *Jamahiriya*, Qadhafi saw as his first priority the elimination of the formal institutions of power that stood between the masses and their leader. The Zuwara speech of April 15, 1975, articulates the essence of his cultural revolution: "The masses are, after this day, no longer in need of any deceiving hypocritical intermediaries. . . . The masses have no need for the deception of the right or the left! The masses today are in need of destroying their fetters, of governing themselves, and of building their own future according to their own will!"[16] Projected into the international arena, the message is equally clear: The destruction of reactionary state systems makes it imperative to vest untrammeled power in the hands of the African masses; only then can they be expected to fulfill their historic mission and lay the foundation for direct democracy as the first step toward the construction of an Arab-Islamic community.

Thus, from 1974 onward, a radically different way of identifying "relevant enemies" emerged from Qadhafi's cognitive map. Although never departing from his visceral hatred of Israel or from his deep suspicion of U.S. motives, by 1974 "reactionary" African regimes had become a top priority on Qadhafi's hit list. As unity through diplomacy proved unfeasible, striking at the root of obstructionism was now seen as the most sensible course. This is not to suggest that diplomacy was henceforth systematically ruled out but only that it would be employed selectively—in conjunction with or as an alternative to force, depending on the circumstances. Finally, and most important, many of the alliances sealed in the name of Arab-Islamic solidarity were about to be dissolved for the sake of a higher priority—the struggle against neoimperialism. That some of the states and opposition movements eventually singled out for Libyan subversion happened to be, culturally or linguistically, members of the Arab nation is not the least of the ironies brought to light by this reordering of priorities.

The choices forced upon Qadhafi by changing power configurations in the Sudan and in the Horn are illustrative of the contradictions inherent in his two-pronged effort to promote Arab unity and combat the forces of imperialism. Consider the case of Ethiopia. Until the fall of the monarchy in 1974, Ethiopia was the preeminent example of a state whose domestic and foreign policies were ideally orchestrated to attract Libyan hostility. The closeness of military and diplomatic ties between Haile Selassie and his two principal external patrons—the United States and Israel—coupled with the pro-Arab sentiment of at least one faction of the Eritrean insurgency (Ousman Saleh's Eritrean Liberation Front [ELF]), and Somalia's irredentist claims to Ogaden made Ethiopia the most likely candidate for Libyan subversion.[17]

Libyan deliveries of arms and financial assistance to Somali irredentists and Eritrean nationalists were entirely in keeping with Qadhafi's repeated denunciations of "imperialist and Sionist" maneuvers in the Horn. With the overthrow of Haile Selassie, however, and the reversal of East-West alliances that followed the coming to power of a Marxist regime in Addis Ababa, the logic of anti-imperialism called for a drastic reorientation of Libyan policies. Recognition of the Mengistu regime by Tripoli implied a cessation of Libyan support to Eritrean insurgents as well as an open condemnation of Somali claims to Ogaden. Thus, by free recourse to the logic of anti-imperialism, Libyan policies came full circle. Yesterday's foes became today's friends, and vice versa. A predominantly Christian Orthodox society, Ethiopia was now seen as a friend of the Arab nation, and its domestic Arab-Islamic opponents became Qadhafi's declared enemies.

Much the same paradox emerges from the record of Libyan policies in the Sudan following Numeiri's tilt to the West in 1976. Until then, the Khartoum authorities were doubly qualified to stand as Libya's closest ally for precisely the same reasons that, until 1974, Ethiopia stood as its foremost enemy. Here the state was seen as the embodiment of Arab-Islamic legitimacy and its regional opponents as the incarnation of an "unholy alliance" between Christianity and Zionism. By 1976, however, Numeiri's growing receptivity to Western overtures had become unmistakable. Furthermore, his reticence to join hands with Libya in a regional unification scheme had become apparent as early as 1971, when Qadhafi's offer to the Sudan to become a member of the Federation of Arab Republics was politely declined on the grounds that it would greatly compromise Khartoum's ability to deal effectively with the southern insurgency.[18]

If the 1976 mutual defense pact with Egypt left few doubts as to the pro-Western inclination of the Khartoum regime, the abortive Libyan-sponsored coup attempt against Numeiri, also in 1976, made Libyan distaste for his brand of regional diplomacy dramatically clear. As Numeiri's ties with Washington hardened into a politico-military alliance, the exigencies of the anti-imperialist struggle meant that Qadhafi had no other choice but to throw his weight behind the southern-based and predominantly Christian Southern Peoples Liberation Army (SPLA) and against the Khartoum regime. Speaking on the seventh anniversary of the founding of the *Jamahiriya* in April 1984, Qadhafi made clear his unqualified support for the "revolutionary forces" of southern Sudan: "We are allied with the popular revolution in the southern Sudan for the sake of liberating Sudan inch by inch—just as Lebanon was liberated. The US cannot save that man who is hiding in Khartoum. . . . The people will march forward and will develop the people's war of liberation in Sudan and tomorrow in Egypt and in every part of Africa that America seeks to dominate!"[19] Three years later Qadhafi's prediction had proved partially correct: Numeiri was out of office, and the coming to power of Prime Minister Sadiq al-Mahdi saw yet another spectacular permutation of alliances when Qadhafi decided once again to normalize relations with Khartoum after a long period of open enmity, thus bringing to a halt the march of the Libyan-supported "people's war of liberation." By November 1988, units of the SPLA bore the full brunt of the air attacks launched by Libyan planes flown by Libyan pilots on behalf of the Khartoum regime.[20]

Clearly, the perils of incoherence are nowhere more evident than in the case where a basic choice has to be made between the appeals of pan-Arab unity and the exigencies of the anti-imperialist struggle. The dilemmas confronting Libyan policies in the Horn and in the Sudan reflect the different priorities accorded to one or the other of these goals in response to changing power configurations. Elsewhere, however, Libyan policy choices were generally informed by a simple dichotomy between the forces of "progressivism"—perhaps best incarnated by Thomas Sankara in Burkina Faso and Jerry Rawlings in Ghana—and the clients of Western imperialism—epitomized by Sese Seko Mobutu of Zaire. The progressive versus reactionary frame of reference is the key to understanding Libyan support to personalities as different as Idi Amin in Uganda, Sankara in Burkina Faso, Rawlings in Ghana, and Jean-Pierre Bagaza in Burundi and, by the same token, of Libyan animus toward Mobutu of Zaire and Felix Houphouet-Boigny in the Côte d'Ivoire. The dichotomy is not without certain limitations, both in terms of its applicability to concrete situations and of its explanatory force, as the case of Chad demonstrates with striking clarity.

ADVENTURISM AT HIGH TIDE: THE CASE OF CHAD

Chad is where Libyan adventurism exacted its heaviest toll and the disproportion between performance and ambition was most cruelly revealed. No other state has had a higher priority on Qadhafi's foreign policy agenda.[21] There are no parallels anywhere on the continent for the scale and duration of Libyan intervention in northern Chad; nor is there any equivalent to the severity of the losses suffered by the *Jamahiriya* in the course of its armed confrontation with the Chadian army. Between 1973—when a handful of Libyan troops crossed the Chadian-Libyan border into Aouzou—and 1987—when the Libyan army was forced back into Aouzou after occupying almost the entire northern half of the country, leaving behind over 3,600 killed, 1,165 prisoners, and $1 billion worth of military equipment—Tripoli has consistently upped the ante in terms of ground forces, defense systems, armory, and infrastructural developments. From 1980 to 1987, between 5,000 and 7,000 Libyan troops saw military action in Chad in engagements ranging from isolated skirmishes to pitched battles involving T-54 and T-62 tanks, heavy artillery, and air strikes against enemy positions.

The magnitude of the Libyan effort, like the severity of its costs, cannot be explained by reference to any single set of factors. Nonetheless, the geopolitical dimension of the Chadian arena and the history of the region are critical elements in the spectrum of forces that have shaped Qadhafi's perception of the Libyan national interest in northern Chad. Few other regions provide a more compelling illustration of the arbitrariness of colonial boundaries. Rooted in part in the cultural affinities shared by Toubou and Arab elements on both sides of the Chadian-Libyan border, Libyan perceptions of northern Chad as a strategic political space are further reinforced by historical precedents going back to the Ottoman period when parts of the Tibesti area came under Turkish control, albeit intermittently, as well as by the countless litigations that have arisen between France and Italy over the demarcation of their colonial boundaries. Even though the Mussolini-Laval Accords of January 7, 1935 (the Rome Treaty)—designed to assign the Aouzou strip to Italy—were never ratified, Libyan claims to this contested area continue to rest on this slender juridical reed.[22]

The circumstances of postindependence politics in Chad added a new dimension to Libyan motives. With the emergence in Ndjamena of a predominantly Sara, Christian-dominated government headed by François Tombalbaye and the subsequent outbreak of a major insurgency in the Muslim north, new opportunities suddenly arose for bringing ideology in line with the exigencies of the Libyan national interest. Although Qadhafi's commitment to Arab-Islamic solidarity made intervention on the side of the insurgents a foregone conclusion, the joint efforts of France and Israel to bolster the authority of the pro-Christian, Sara-based government of François Tombalbaye made such intervention all the more consonant with the ideological goals of the *Jamahiriya.* The configuration of forces at work in the Chadian arena was the mirror image of what could be observed in the Sudan; thus, it is easy to see why the pattern of alliances in Chad should have been exactly the opposite of those in the Sudan. And yet, in the end, Libyan policies in Chad came to exhibit the same kinds of contradictions that were brought to light in the Sudan, and for precisely the same reasons. Just as Numeiri's tilt to the West caused Qadhafi to shift partners, Habre's growing ties with Paris and Washington—not to mention the decisive role played by U.S. covert assistance in facilitating Habre's seizure of power in 1982—made the ex-rebel leader from the north (and devout Muslim) the declared enemy of the *Jamahiriya,* while some of the Christian factions from the south ended up seeking Libyan support in their trial of strength with Habre.

It is not the purpose of this chapter to provide a detailed account of Libyan misadventures in Chad. A more useful way of assessing their significance is to examine the factors and circumstances that lie in the background of the Libyan nemesis. The first and most obvious has to do with the sheer fragmentation of rebel elements, reflecting in part the fissiparous forces at work in the societies of northern Chad—not only between Toubous and Arabs but also within each group—and in part the existence of genuine differences of opinion among their respective leaders over the wisdom of a tactical alliance with Libya. The turning point in the process of fragmentation came in 1973 with the de facto occupation of Aouzou by Libya. The Libyan troops had scarcely taken position in the strip when bitter rivalries erupted within the Front de Liberation National Tchadien (Frolinat) between its two major operational Toubou-led armies—headed respectively by Habre and Goukouni Oueddei—with the former growing increasingly disillusioned over the usefulness of his Libyan connection. As factionalism gained momentum and ramified into an ever-more complex pattern of fragmentation, Qadhafi never missed an opportunity to play one faction against another in order to advance his own strategic objective—to convert Chad into a Libyan sphere of influence. Here as elsewhere, his tactics were disarmingly simple: to reward the faithful and penalize the recalcitrant. In so doing, however, Qadhafi overplayed his hand, not only turning Habre into his bitterest enemy but also prompting him to cast about for alternative sources of external support.

France's carefully calibrated military response to the Libyan challenge played a crucial role in bolstering the Habre regime after Goukouni was routed from Ndjamena in June 1982, but not without prompting renewed Libyan efforts on behalf of Goukouni. Libyan intervention paved the way for a process of escalation that began with covert U.S. support for Habre in 1981 (with the full cooperation of Numeiri's Sudan) and reached its culmination in 1983 with the deployment of French troops and air support under the code name Operation Manta. By then Libyan troops controlled much of the Borkou-Ennedi-Tibesti (BET) northern prefecture, which covered approximately half of Chad's national territory, with units of the so-called Gouvernement d'Union Nationale Transitoire (GUNT)—consisting of Toubou and Arab elements as well as a generous sprinkling of Sara dissidents from the south—acting as auxiliaries. Although there can be little question that Manta's protective shield played a decisive part in containing Libyan forces north of the 16th parallel, the unmitigated dislike of the Libyan occupation forces displayed by the Chadian populations of the BET and the innumerable tiffs and misunderstandings that beset the relationship of the Libyan army with GUNT units go far in explaining Qadhafi's inability to consolidate his military gains into a viable partnership with his Chadian allies.

As for the military side of the equation, the Libyan record is not nearly as impressive as might have been expected at the height of the Libyan thrust into the BET. The devastating defeat suffered by the Libyan army at the hands of Habre's Chadian National Armed Forces (FANT)—first in Fada on January 2, 1987, and then in Ouadi Doum on March 22—is as much a commentary on the fighting skills of the FANT, which at the time caught everybody by surprise, as it is a reflection on the inability of the Libyan army to accommodate the Soviet model of ground warfare to the conditions of the desert *blitzkrieg* forced upon it by its Chadian adversaries. As one observer commented, "In defeating the Libyans the Chadians did more than achieve a major victory. They also showed that the weapons and tactics of advanced industrial nations are not necessarily appropriate, offensively or defensively, for poorly trained armies of less developed countries. The Chadians fought the desert battles in their own fashion. ... The Libyans, for their part, apparently believed that by simply transferring Soviet technology and tactics to their army, they had a magic formula for military success without the need for hard fighting."[23] In their desperate attempt to retake Aouzou in August 1987, the FANT encountered a more determined and better-positioned enemy. After capturing the oasis on August 8, they held their ground for twenty days until a massive land and air assault by the Libyan army delivered the town back into Libyan hands.

As the foregoing plainly suggests, the manipulation of client factions and the willingness and ability to use force on their behalf are two critical features of Libyan policies in Chad; a third involves the use of diplomacy. If the use of military capabilities proves unavailing in furthering Libyan interests, diplomacy is the next-best thing; alternatively, if diplomacy fails, recourse to force is a likely response. Consider, for example, the intricate sequence of events preceding the 1983 armed intervention on behalf of the GUNT forces. The timing of the intervention testified to the egregious failure of Qadhafi's OAU diplomacy, in particular his inability to gain for his client the recognition of the OAU—first at the Tripoli summit in 1982 and then at the Addis Ababa summit in 1983. But diplomacy also played a supportive role in his decision to unleash his armed forces against the FANT. After leaving the Addis Ababa summit in July 1983, he traveled to Saudi Arabia, Morocco, and Algeria, and in the course of these visits a deal was struck "whereby Saudi Arabia and Morocco would look the other way when the Qadhafi-Goukouni team would move into Chad if Libya would reduce its arms and cash supplies to the Popular Front for the Liberation of Saguia al-Hamra and Rio de Oro (Polisario) fighting Moroccan troops in the Western Sahara."[24] Thus, only after securing the benevolent neutrality of Morocco and Saudi Arabia was the decision made to organize a major military thrust in the direction of the 16th parallel.

By the same token, when faced with major military setbacks, Qadhafi's receptivity to diplomacy increases in proportion to his losses. Thus, the crippling blows delivered by the FANT against the Libyan forces in 1987 must be seen as the decisive factor behind the Habre-Qadhafi peace accords of 1988 and the subsequent exchange of ambassadors between Tripoli and Ndjamena. In short, force and diplomacy are strategically related to each other. Just as the former may set the stage for diplomatic advantage, diplomacy is intended to create the conditions that will enable Qadhafi to draw maximum benefits from the use of military power (as happened in 1983) or, if the going gets rough, to cut his losses.

The centrality of Chad on the Libyan foreign policy agenda is plainly revealed by the magnitude of Qadhafi's political and military investments on behalf of his Chadian clients. It is equally apparent in his efforts to either forge tactical alliances with or destabilize those regimes that are seen as strategically located (Niger and Sudan) or as willing to comply with Libyan requests for "technical assistance" (Benin). Thus, there is every reason to believe that the aborted 1975 coup against Seydou Kountche in Niger was motivated in part by Qadhafi's hope of acquiring a privileged sanctuary in an area of critical strategic significance for his Chadian allies. Similarly, his decision to normalize relations with Sadiq al-Mahdi's Sudan in 1986 was inspired by much the same kind of calculation, as shown by the subsequent infiltration of units of the Islamic Legion and Centre Democratique Revolutionnaire along the Chadian-Sudanese border. Again, the attempted coup against Mathieu Kerekou's Benin in 1988, through the good offices of the Libyan People's Bureau in Cotonou, came about in response to Kerekou's decision—presumably under joint pressures from France and the United States—to close down the training facilities heretofore made available to GUNT guerrillas. Finally, given the unqualified support of Mobutu to the Habre regime, there is probably more to allegations of a Libyan-sponsored plot against Mobutu in 1985 than mere rumor. The ripple effects of the Chadian imbroglio thus go far beyond the Chadian arena. Much of Qadhafi's incessant meddling in the internal affairs of African states is traceable to the strategic priority assigned to Libyan interests in Chad.

At the diplomatic level, Qadhafi's sustained efforts to extract from the OAU a sanction of legitimacy for his Chadian policies point to the same conclusion. By forcefully insisting in 1982 on OAU recognition of the Goukouni faction as the sole legitimate representative of the Chadian state, Qadhafi not only compromised his chances of assuming the chairmanship of the organization but virtually paralyzed the debates. As the split between moderates and radicals hardened into a prolonged stalemate, the result, according to one observer, was "to throw the organization into something of a tailspin."[25] Commenting on the net effect of Libyan obstructionism in the OAU, Emmanel Pondi offers the following assessment: "After the formidable impediments posed to the OAU by Qadhafi's vindictiveness, that the organization was able to survive the many crises thrust upon it from Tripoli is not the least of its achievements."[26]

The compliment could be returned to Qadhafi: His ability to survive the domestic and international crises that he himself has engineered is no mean achievement. Measured against the costs of his policies, however, Qadhafi's notoriety takes on a singularly ominous coloration. No attempt to properly assess the Qadhafian legacy in Chad can overlook the immense sufferings and continuing economic hardships—for Libyans and others—

that have attended Libya's "imperial temptation."[27] Nor can we ignore the threats to the stability of African states posed by Libyan attempts at destabilization, the chronic paralysis suffered by the OAU, or the monumental economic costs and agonizing choices confronted by the French in their effort to maintain a measure of credibility in the face of the Libyan challenge. Whether Libyan adventurism has changed its spots remains a moot point. What is beyond dispute is the fact that the Libyan crusade against neoimperialism has brought its instigator little sympathy and its presumptive beneficiaries, in Chad and elsewhere, more liabilities than most would care to admit.

NOTES

1. Ali Mazrui and Michael Tidy, *Nationalism and New States in Africa* (London: Heinemann, 1984), p. 88.
2. The phrase is borrowed from John Davis, *Libyan Politics: Tribe and Revolution* (London: I. B. Tauris, 1987), p. 15.
3. Harold Glidden, "The Arab World," *American Journal of Psychiatry* 128, no. 8 (February 1972):984–988, quoted in Edward W. Said, *Orientalism* (New York: Vintage Books, 1978), p. 48.
4. *Webster's Third New International Dictionary* (Springfield, Mass.: Merriam Co., 1976).
5. For further elaboration on this theme, see I. William Zartman and A. G. Kluge, "Heroic Politics: The Foreign Policy of Libya," in Bahgat Korany and Ali E. Hillal Dessouki (eds.), *The Foreign Policies of Arab States,* 2d ed. (Boulder, Colo.: Westview Press, 1991), p. 245.
6. On the concept of the rentier state, see Lisa Anderson, "The State in the Middle East and North Africa," *Comparative Politics* 20, no. 1 (October 1987):9 ff; Theda Skocpol, "Rentier State and Shi'a Islam in the Iranian Revolution," *Theory and Society* 11, no. 1 (January 1982):265–300; and Hazem Beblawi and Giacomo Luciani (eds.), *The Rentier State* (New York: Croom Helm, 1987). I am grateful to Ruth Iyob for drawing my attention to the latter.
7. Davis, *Libyan Politics,* p. 15.
8. Anderson, "The State in the Middle East," p. 10.
9. Davis, *Libyan Politics,* p. 19.
10. Herve Bleuchot and Taoufik Monastiri, "La logique unitaire libyenne et les mobiles du colonel Qadhafi," *Herodote* 36, no. 2 (March 1980):82.
11. Davis, *Libyan Politics,* p. 40.
12. *Ibid.,* p. 42.
13. *Ibid.,* p. 43.
14. Archives Nationales, République du Tchad. Ndjamena. "Rapport de H. Montchamp au sujet d'un voyage dans l'Erguei du 28 février au 15 mars 1950."
15. Davis, *Libyan Politics,* p. 44.
16. Cited in Mahamoud A. Ayoub, *Islam and the Third Universal Theory* (London: KPI Ltd., 1987), p. 33.

17. For further details see Rene Otayek, *La Politique Africaine de la Libya* (Paris: Editions Karthala, 1986), pp. 144 ff.

18. See John Waterbury, *Hydropolitics of the Nile Valley* (Syracuse, N.Y.: Syracuse University Press, 1979), p. 82.

19. Cited in Anon., "The Involvement of Ethiopia and Libya," *Horn of Africa* 8, no. 1 (1985):56.

20. Jane Perlez, "Sudan's Premier Is Visiting Libya After Proposal for Unity Is Signed," *New York Times*, November 14, 1988, p. A-10.

21. Much of the information in this section is drawn from my chapter on Chad in R. Lemarchand (ed.), *The Green and the Black: Qadhafi's Policies in Africa* (Bloomington: Indiana University Press, 1988), pp. 106–122.

22. On the historical backdrop of the Rome Treaty and its provisions, see Bernard Lanne, *Tchad-Libye: La Querelle des Frontieres* (Paris: Editions Karthala, 1982).

23. Bernard Trainor, "In Desert Much Evidence of Rout of Libyans," *New York Times*, April 13, 1987, pp. A-1, A-12.

24. John Cooley, "Qadhafi's War," *The New Republic* 189, no. 10 (September 5, 1983):11–13.

25. Jennifer S. Whitaker, "Africa Beset," *Foreign Affairs* 62, no. 3 (1983):749.

26. Emmanel Pondi, "Qadhafi and the OAU," in Lemarchand, *The Green and the Black*, p. 148.

27. The phrase is borrowed from Otayek, *La Politique Africaine*, p. 177.

PART THREE

AFRICA AND THE POWERS

8

THE UNITED STATES AND AFRICA: ISSUES FOR THE FUTURE

JEFFREY HERBST

In his cogent review of geopolitics, Patrick O'Sullivan makes the classic argument for the importance of spatial relations in international relations. "The strength of sympathetic and influential ties between the governments of nations," he argues, "is as much a matter of geographic distance as of political and cultural distance."[1] In the U.S. relationship with Africa, in which traditionally there have been few political, economic, or cultural ties, the great physical distance between the two continents has meant that political relations—except in a few cases—have existed at a very low level.[2] There is little reason to believe that the nature of the relationship will change in the near future. Rather, there is some evidence that with declining concerns about the cold war, the end of colonialism, and the poor economic performance of African countries, relations between the United States and Africa will become more attenuated in the future.

However, there will be important developments in Africa in the next decade that will pose challenges the United States cannot ignore. More than thirty years after the winds of change blew through the continent, Africa is at last moving beyond decolonization into a new era in which economic, political, and international arrangements will, we hope, be based less on the need to consolidate newly won political sovereignty and more on the desire to increase the general welfare. Thus, a proper understanding of how relations between the United States and Africa will evolve is important if U.S. diplomacy is to perform up to its potential. In addition, studying the relationship between the United States and Africa can tell us, at a more theoretical level, something about how international relations will develop in a post-cold war world.

THE UNITED STATES AND AFRICA: AN INCREASINGLY MARGINAL RELATIONSHIP

The success in the implementation of the New York Accords, which the United States brokered between South Africa, Cuba, and Angola in December 1988, will undoubtedly mark the high point of U.S. diplomacy in Africa for some time to come. Indeed, the success in southwestern Africa may, somewhat paradoxically, mark the beginning of a decline in U.S. involvement in Africa, as both the cold war and colonialism ended in 1989.

Undoubtedly, one of the primary concerns of the United States in Africa has been to deny the Soviet Union important strategic advantages. Indeed, emphasizing Africa's role in the cold war sometimes appeared to be the only way to focus attention on the continent. As David D. Newsom noted in his valuable review of U.S. foreign policy toward Africa, "The East-West confrontation theme appeared to assure the greatest justification for broad-based and long-term support for an African policy."[3] The emphasis on the cold war became especially noticeable after 1975 with the Soviet and Cuban successes in Ethiopia and Angola. Indeed, the Soviet-Cuban advances in Africa in the mid-1970s made many U.S. policymakers, notably then-U.S. Secretary of State Henry Kissinger, concentrate on Africa for the first time.

Now, however, the cold war is over in Africa. The open cooperation between the superpowers during the South Africa–Cuba–Angola talks in 1988, the withdrawal of the Cubans from Angola (as well as their previous withdrawal from Ethiopia), and Gorbachev's "new thinking" all made it clear that after 1989 there would not be any great-power competition in Africa. U.S. Assistant Secretary of State Herman Cohen was probably correct to note that, in retrospect, there has not been serious competition between the United States and the Soviet Union in Africa since the 1970s other than in Angola.[4] The Soviet Union, with so many problems of its own, seems to be trying desperately to leave Africa, and it has suggested to some African countries that their only hope for significant aid is to turn to the West.[5] The abandonment of scientific socialism as a doctrine by such countries as Mozambique and Benin is both a reflection of the Soviet Union's decreasing interest in Africa and a further acknowledgment that socialism has no future on the continent.

Therefore, one of the primary driving forces behind the U.S. Africa policy for more than thirty years has disappeared. Observers are entitled to ask, as did Martin Lowenkopf, "If the cold war is over in Africa, will the United States still care?"[6] Clearly, the United States does have some strategic interests in Africa; however, they are small, and they may become even less important if the cold war continues to wind down in other parts of the world. The United States, for instance, only has "important military interests" in the Horn countries—Kenya, Chad, and Zaire.[7] It remains concerned about Libya, but at least for the time being, Libya does not seem to pose the threat to its neighbors that it once did.

The United States may also become more concerned about the increasing role middle-level powers are playing in Africa. In particular, Iran appears to have an increasingly active foreign policy in Africa, notably among Islamic countries, and this could attract U.S. interest at a later date. However, it is unlikely that any middle-level power involvement in Africa will ever be as much a concern to U.S. policymakers as the Soviet and Cuban presence was in the 1970s. Therefore, it seems as though Africa will become even less important to U.S. strategic interests in the next few years.

The independence of Namibia, Africa's last colony, also marked the end of the decolonization process in Africa. For over thirty years, many of the most difficult problems confronting U.S. diplomacy in Africa—the Congo crisis, Angola, Rhodesia, Namibia—were essentially questions of how to resolve the decolonization issue. These questions immediately became international issues, and the United States was almost always forced to adopt a position because of its leading role in world affairs. Concerns about the results of decolonization almost inevitably interacted with cold-war fears, as the Soviet Union was usually willing to devote resources to those involved in protracted wars against settler regimes in the 1970s and 1980s. Now that decolonization is complete, this particular type of international instability will no longer occur.

South Africa, the only remaining country in Africa in which control of the government has not been resolved, is not a colonial question, as everyone—including South African blacks—has long recognized. I feel it is clear that when a settlement is finally reached in South Africa, it will not be brokered in the same way as was the case with Great Britain at Lancaster House or the United States in Namibia. There may be a role for outside mediation in South Africa, but the conflict will not immediately call for international mediation as did Rhodesia and Namibia. Nor will South Africa, especially in the new global environment, become a major issue of dispute between the United States and the USSR. This is not to say that the road to peace and political stability in South Africa will be easy or that all actors inside the country will eventually work for peace. Rather, if conflict resolution is to occur in South Africa, it will be due fundamentally to successful negotiation by the domestic parties to the dispute rather than to the actions of outside mediators.

U.S. Economic Aid

The United States therefore needs to redefine fundamentally why it is involved in Africa. The decreasing strategic role of Africa has been noted by U.S. policymakers who argue that the United States has a major role to play in helping African countries to restructure their economies. Indeed, the United States can seek at least some credit as the intellectual godfather of reform programs that have been adopted by at least two dozen countries across the continent since 1981. However, as U.S. policymakers also note, just when Africa is adopting the kinds of policies the United States has long suggested, the United States is becoming less involved economically in the continent. Since 1985, total U.S. aid to Africa has stagnated at just below a billion dollars a year. The high in 1985 was $1.25 billion, while the administration requested $905 million for 1990. Of this total, $820 million was to be in economic aid and $85 million in military assistance.[8] In 1988, France, Germany, Italy, and Japan all gave more to Africa in absolute dollars than did the United States. Only 13.9 percent of total U.S. aid goes to Africa. The average developed country gives 32 percent of its aid to Africa, and only Japan, Australia, and New Zealand give a lower percentage of their total aid budget to Africa than does the United States.[9]

These figures are not likely to increase significantly in the near future because of the U.S. deficit and because any aid money that does become available will probably be devoted to the countries of Eastern Europe. Indeed, a clear indication of the difficulty of mobilizing resources for Africa outside of the cold-war context can be gained by comparing U.S. military aid in Africa to the amount of U.S. aid UNITA receives. U.S. officials bemoan the fact that they only have $85 million to allocate to military aid programs in Africa and that this level of funding is not even adequate to help those countries that have traditionally cooperated with the United States on military issues. The level of funding is low in part because the United States cannot develop a strong strategic rationale for an increase in military aid. However, UNITA, which can still fall back on the logic of the cold war, seems to have had little trouble acquiring $50 million in U.S. military aid—more than the amount any single African nation receives.

The United States, in conjunction with the other major industrialized countries, did adopt a program to relieve the debt burden of African countries. Of the $4.5 billion sub-Saharan countries owe to the United States, approximately $1 billion is in development loans the United States is now willing to cancel. For a country to be eligible for debt relief, it must demonstrate its intention to reform its economy by signing an agreement with the International Monetary Fund or the World Bank.[10] As of January 1990, countries that had external liabilities equal to $600 million were eligible for debt relief. Another $400 million is held by countries that have not yet enacted persuasive economic reform programs.[11]

The U.S. budget crisis affects U.S. relations in Africa in numerous other ways. For instance, due to fiscal shortfalls at the United States Information

Agency, the Swahili service of the Voice of America was eliminated in 1990. Tens of millions of people who speak Swahili will no longer have any definite contact with the United States. Reductions in other programs due to budgetary pressures will almost inevitably decrease contact at the personal level between Americans and Africans.

Economic Ties

In addition, the United States will find it difficult to develop a rationale for a relationship with Africa based on economic ties because U.S. trade and investment have traditionally been extremely low. Indeed, the United States is trading less with Africa that it was a few years ago. In 1983, for instance, U.S. exports to Africa amounted to 2.2 percent of total U.S. exports, and imports from Africa accounted for 4.1 percent of total imports. In 1988, exports to Africa accounted for only 1.2 percent of total U.S. exports and imports from Africa for only 2.0 percent of the total value of goods the United States bought from the rest of the world.[12] The decline seems to have come about because of U.S. sanctions imposed on South Africa, the decline in oil prices, and the general economic crisis that gripped Africa throughout the 1980s. Similarly, U.S. investment in Africa is extremely low. In 1987—the latest year for which data are available—U.S. nonbank foreign affiliates in Africa accounted for 1.2 percent of worldwide U.S. nonbank foreign affiliates' assets, 1.2 percent of worldwide net income, and 1.4 percent of worldwide employees.[13]

Given the economic crisis in Africa and the impressive growth rates of other countries, notably in East Asia, it is unlikely that Africa will increase its share of U.S. foreign investment in the near future. Indeed, the World Bank now estimates that the total amount of economic activity in sub-Saharan Africa is 10 percent less than that which occurs in Belgium. Similarly, Hong Kong has an economy that is 50 percent larger than Nigeria's, which is the largest economy in sub-Saharan Africa outside of South Africa.[14] There is little incentive to invest in markets that are this small.

A DOMESTIC CONSTITUENCY FOR AFRICA?

If there were a domestic constituency for Africa in the United States, these factors might be less important. However, in the early 1990s, there are few indications that a new constituency will be developed for Africa. For example, the promotion by the Reverend Jesse Jackson of the use of the term *African-Americans* could have been expected to lead to greater attention being focused on Africa. Indeed, Jackson has said that one of his aims in giving attention to the term is to promote a greater association with Africa. However, there is no evidence that African-Americans are especially interested in Africa, outside of South Africa. On the issue of South Africa, African-Americans have played an important role out of proportion to their percentage of the population in convincing the U.S. Congress to adopt sanctions against South Africa, but this is the case because the issue in South Africa is racism, which fits in with the African-American domestic agenda. Thus, the very visible actions undertaken by the Congressional Black Caucus, TransAfrica, and prominent members of the African-American community to protest apartheid should not be seen as significant political activity on an African issue but rather as a continuation of the intense politics revolving around civil rights in the United States. Indeed, at least in the mid-1980s, a public official's stand on South Africa (or, rather, sanctions on South Africa) was something of a proxy for his or her position on civil rights generally. The very visible politics that revolve around South Africa are rooted in domestic concerns; thus, it would be incorrect to suggest that African-American interest in apartheid reflects an overall desire to become more involved in Africa.

Indeed, African-Americans' domestic interests have not been particularly concerned with events in countries south of the Sahara. African-Americans have a broad domestic agenda that leaves little time for foreign affairs. Further, Africa is not a country but a collection of over forty countries. It is therefore much harder to promote ties between the United States and Africa than between the United States and Ireland, Israel, or Italy, for example. Thus, there seems little reason to believe that African-Americans will pressure the United States to become more involved in the continent other than in South Africa. For instance, African-Americans show no particular interest in the oppression of southern Sudanese by northerners or of Senegalese by Mauritanians along the Mauritanian border, although both groups are being oppressed in part because they are African. Nor do African-Americans seem particularly concerned about gross violations of human rights by African leaders in Ethiopia, Somalia, Burundi, or Liberia. The few efforts in Congress to act against these countries have received little public support.

African-Americans have also shown little interest in developing the kind of domestic constituency for foreign aid to Africa that Jewish, Greek, and Turkish groups—among others—have been so successful in doing. Even attempts by those in Congress to aid countries in southern Africa, who are among apartheid's victims, have stalled due to lack of public support. For instance, there has been little public pressure to provide significant economic aid to newly independent Namibia. African-Americans may someday form a constituency for Africa, but it will not likely have a serious impact on policy in the near future.

ALTERNATIVE RATIONALES FOR INVOLVEMENT IN AFRICA

Faced with declining political, economic, and cultural ties with Africa, sympathetic observers have attempted to develop rationales for continued U.S. involvement in the world's poorest continent. Some of these new rationales are particularly interesting, as they reflect a much larger debate over how the United States should formulate the national interest following the end of the cold war. Pauline H. Baker argues, "As the United States becomes more involved in global issues, redefined from a geo-social rather than a geo-strategic perspective, Africa may assume larger importance. Especially with the development challenge, public health concerns, environmental issues, and the desire to spread democracy replacing traditional geopolitical concerns."[15] There is, in fact, little reason to believe that the fundamental factors that drive U.S. foreign policy have changed. The fact that the geopolitical threat to the United States has eased does not mean that it and other nations will suddenly stop acting primarily on geopolitical concerns.

Indeed, arguably the most likely outcome of the decrease in the geopolitical threat facing the United States is that it will simply become less engaged in foreign issues. Without the cold war, U.S. administrations will have a much harder time justifying U.S. engagement in international issues or peripheral areas such as Africa unless the national interest is clearly threatened. Thus, U.S. intervention in the Persian Gulf after the Iraqi invasion of Kuwait is not necessarily evidence of a new U.S. willingness to become involved in other issues, as the control of oil was the central issue. If one African country had overrun another, the United States may have opposed the conquest, but, as in the case of East Timor, the world's response would likely have been much less dramatic. There is reason to believe that the United States will fundamentally reformulate its agenda only if the social concerns in Africa, such as environmental degradation, can be shown to have a direct link to the U.S. welfare—and such evidence is tenuous at the moment.

Others who have examined possibilities for the post–cold war world have argued that there are significant opportunities for cooperation between the superpowers in Africa. C. S. Whitaker argues that because both superpowers agreed on decolonization, supported the Nigerian federal government during its civil war, and provided aid during natural disasters, there is reason to believe that the post–cold war era could become a period in which the superpowers actively cooperate to help Africa.[16]

However, the superpowers cooperated on these issues not to cooperate per se but because their disparate interests happened to drive them to the same positions. Active cooperation will come about only if real interests are present that cause the superpowers to have the same position. Thus, the superpowers did cooperate in the negotiations over Namibia because the United States had an interest in getting the Cubans out of Angola and the Soviets wanted to eliminate Angola as an irritant to superpower relations as well as reduce aid to the Angolan government. This cooperation was propelled by high-level policymakers precisely because both superpowers had significant strategic interests in Angola and Namibia, the kind of interests that are not present elsewhere on the continent.

It is unlikely that resources (either money or the time of senior policymakers) freed up from the cold war will go to Africa, for, when designing their public policy agendas, government officials in the United States and the Soviet Union face a mix of foreign and domestic issues. It is not a case, as some would believe, where resources saved in one area of foreign policy (for example, military spending) can only be devoted to another foreign policy issue (development spending on Africa). Even time, a crucial resource for top-level policymakers, can be shifted between foreign and domestic issues depending on the total public policy agenda. In the Soviet Union especially, it is obvious that all free resources will be devoted to the country's enormous domestic problems. Therefore, simply because resources are no longer being devoted to the top of the foreign policy agenda it does not mean that funds or time, both of which are fungible, will go to the next most important foreign policy issue. Indeed, many domestic issues are perceived as more important than Africa.

Unless Africa gains importance to the United States because of reasons related to the traditional notion of the national interest (such as economic trade or national defense) or develops a domestic constituency, it is not likely to become more important to the United States and may become substantially less so. How much of a real impact this will have on Africa is unclear. The United States never provided enough resources to make a significant difference to Africa's economic prospects. Correspondingly, there was little U.S. investment in Africa before the cold war ended. If companies exist that are dedicated to investing in Africa, they will not be concerned with how much attention Africa is getting from public policy officials. After all, U.S. oil companies did not hesitate to invest and continue operations in Libya and Angola, even though both of those countries were subject to considerable hostility from the U.S. government. In fact, the U.S. government had to expend considerable energy to get U.S. oil companies out of Libya.

U.S.-AFRICAN RELATIONS IN A NEW ERA

Even if Africa becomes less important, the United States will continue to be involved due to its political position in the world. In addition, U.S.

involvement in Africa through multilateral organizations—especially the World Bank and the International Monetary Fund—will continue and may even increase. It is therefore necessary to analyze the types of issues with which the United States will be confronted in the coming years in its relationships with African countries.

In the following sections, I examine three areas—promoting trade, promoting democracy, and dealing with boundary changes—in which U.S. diplomacy could be particularly important to Africa. All three areas reflect a fundamental reality: Africa must make the transition from reacting to the inheritance of the colonial period to adopting policies that are more economically and politically beneficial. It is understandable that in the first thirty years of independence, many African countries adopted economic and political policies that were aimed at strengthening the insecure state apparatus inherited from the former colonial powers. In addition, the colonial boundaries were declared inviolate so that African nations would not have to face internal or external threats to their national integrity, although it was widely recognized that these boundaries caused some states to be nonviable economic propositions. Now, African governments are being asked by international donors to change economic policies so that they benefit the state less and help promote private economic activity. Similarly, many donors and Africans (including a generation that has grown up with essentially no memory of the colonial period) are demanding that states drop the authoritarian practices of the past and liberalize their political systems.[17] Finally, in the near future many Africans may begin to focus on the continent's boundary system as a source of national weakness rather than a vestige of colonialism that is convenient to retain.

Promoting African Economic Trade

The United States has a continuing interest in promoting economic liberalization in Africa. In part, the U.S. involvement in economic liberalization stems from a wish for existing foreign aid to have more of an impact. The United States is also the major funder of the World Bank and the International Monetary Fund (IMF), the multilateral agencies that have been at the forefront of the effort to promote economic reform. Finally, U.S. involvement in economic reform is an important way in which the United States can remain engaged with Africa in the expectation that, one day, the continent will begin to grow again and will offer real possibilities for commercial trade.

Efforts by the IMF and the World Bank to promote economic reform have engendered a huge body of literature that need not be reviewed here. However, one aspect of economic reform has not been thoroughly examined in the literature, and it is an aspect on which the United States can have an impact: increasing the prospects for African exports. This issue is particularly important because the economic reforms that have been suggested to Africa demand that countries become more export-oriented.[18] At the same time, there has been little discussion of how the international economy can be made more amenable to African countries who do try to increase their exports. In fact, Africans have argued that efforts to reform their domestic economies may stumble because of failure to alter key international economic practices. These barriers include domestic subsidies to farmers and tariff and nontariff barriers. Pessimism over the prospects for African exporters has been a major factor in the reluctance of some countries to adopt structural adjustment programs.

African trade performance in the 1980s was extremely poor. At the beginning of the decade, the African continent accounted for almost 6 percent of total world exports (by value); by 1988, this number had fallen to 2.5 percent. Between 1980 and 1988, the continent's total exports decreased by 6 percent annually.[19] A large part of this decrease was due to a sharp drop in the price of oil and fewer shipments from Africa's large oil producers, especially Nigeria and Libya. Exports (in constant U.S. dollars) from sub-Saharan African countries, excluding Nigeria, were almost exactly the same in 1987 as they were in 1980 ($26.2 billion).[20] The three dozen smallest African exporters suffered a 7 percent annual decrease in their exports.[21] Only some middle-income African countries were able to preserve their share of total world trade. In the latter part of the 1980s, when world trade growth was buoyant and there were few hostile external developments, African countries continued to stagnate.[22] This market share loss has been devastating. If sub-Saharan African countries, excluding Nigeria, had retained their share of world exports, by 1987 they would have exported approximately $10 billion more than they actually did.[23] Total debt service for all of sub-Saharan Africa, excluding Nigeria, was estimated to be $7.5 billion in 1987.[24]

African countries have experienced decreases in export prices, but these decreases (except in the case of Nigeria) have not been large enough to explain their export failures. African countries increased the volume of their exports by only 29 percent between 1980 and 1987, a performance so poor that it left them extremely vulnerable to price fluctuations in their major exports. If African countries had increased the volume of their exports by 51 percent between 1980 and 1987, as developing countries that are neither oil exporters nor major exporters of manufactured goods were able to, they could have overwhelmed the decrease in the price of their exports and still produced a reasonable export growth.[25]

The inability to increase trade has had a deleterious effect on African countries, which are in desperate need of the foreign exchange generated by exports to provide industries with badly needed imports. The shortage of foreign exchange has been one of the factors most commonly cited for

Africa's overall economic decline. In addition, trade is important to African countries because they will have difficulty attracting other significant sources of foreign exchange, such as direct investment or foreign aid.

When suggesting possible reforms of the international economy, some useful lessons can be learned from the debate over the New International Economic Order (NIEO) in the 1970s. The first is that there will not be any dramatic, comprehensive reform of the international economy and that developed countries are not going to allocate more funds outright to help the poorest nations. Rather than the grandiose schemes proposed in the 1970s, any realistic program of reform to help African countries will be composed of a large number of elements that can be adopted incrementally with as little outright cost to the United States and other developed countries as possible. To say otherwise is to be politically unrealistic. Second, the proposed reforms should take advantage of market forces rather than, as NIEO did, seeking to suppress them at every turn. The fate of the coffee, cocoa, and tin cartels demonstrates again that reforms that do not realistically evaluate how the international market works will fail, as these cartels were not able to defend the prices of their commodities.

The first step that can be taken to increase African exports is for the United States to continue to reform its system of agriculture and to press other developed countries, notably the EC, to finally act on the problem of subsidized agriculture. The EC is particularly important for Africa because Europe is Africa's natural market and the level of agricultural protection is noticeably higher in the EC than in other countries. The EC currently spends $55 billion on subsidizing farmers for food they would not otherwise grow competitively.[26] These subsidies have two direct effects on African farmers: They are unable to export goods to Europe in which they would have an advantage (the classic example is sugar), and the prices of their exports globally are depressed as the EC dumps excess commodities (for example, cereals) on the world market in order not to incur storage costs.

Next, the United States and other developed countries must work to reduce other tariff and nontariff barriers that affect poor countries. For instance, when Zimbabwe attempted to increase its ferrochrome exports to Europe, it was accused of dumping by the EC.[27] These restrictions have two pernicious effects. First, they are a severe burden on the poor countries that are beginning to export more, as the IMF and World Bank have demanded. Second, and perhaps more important in the long run, ad hoc developed country restrictions on poor country exports have created an atmosphere in which African government officials have come to believe that it is not worthwhile to try to export more.

Resisting protection is not a financial problem; indeed, the developed world would be better off if it were to give African exporters a cost advantage to export more. However, many developed countries are under significant political pressure from select industries to introduce protectionism. Protectionism has been successfully resisted in the past by governments that were politically courageous and that could educate the public about the overall costs of quotas and tariffs. One additional strategy that could be used is to link openness to African exports directly to the welfare of poor Africans themselves. The problem with promoting a liberal trade policy is that the victims of protectionism are usually atomistically dispersed and not able to speak for themselves. However, those who promote free trade with Africa have a particularly good case, for they can point to the dramatic suffering countries that are trying to help themselves will endure if protectionist measures are adopted.[28]

Third, there must be a serious rethinking of aid given by the United States and other donors for export promotion. A significant amount of aid to African countries in recent years has been given to rehabilitate a primary crop or mineral export. For instance, in Ghana, when the Economic Recovery Program began, top priority was given to rehabilitating cocoa. Some aid to products that are already major exports is important, as African countries need to augment their foreign exchange supplies immediately. However, given the poor prospects for raw material exports—especially when the entire continent is trying to increase the amount of the same exports—this type of aid will be of limited value. As an example, how useful were the tens of millions of dollars spent on cocoa rehabilitation in Ghana if, because of price decreases, the country does not earn a great deal more money for its exports?

Finally, U.S. aid can play an important role in giving potential exporters in Africa information about the complex and difficult U.S. and Western European markets. African entrepreneurs, in markets in which price and other information signals have long been distorted by governments and inadequate communications systems, are in a particularly poor position to understand the workings of foreign markets in which there are constantly changing opportunities. If African countries are willing to provide an atmosphere in which exporters are viable, then providing information about developed country markets will be of critical importance in helping these poor countries to export more.

Promotion of Democracy

After the Eastern European revolutions of 1989, there has been increased pressure on the United States to promote democracy in Africa. Pressure for democratization in Africa from Congress and the U.S. public may be particularly strong because the wave of democratization that has affected so many countries across the world has been notably absent in Africa.

Although there are increasing protests involving both peaceful gatherings and riots in many countries (including Kenya, Côte d'Ivoire, Cameroon), the events in Eastern Europe have considerably raised expectations about how quickly democratization can occur and what individuals and governments can accomplish. Thus, Africa is perceived as lagging behind the tide of history. In addition, many people in Africa and the West are beginning to notice that there is much more open political discourse and debate about the future in South Africa than in most other African countries. If the South African government and the black opposition make progress in dismantling apartheid and adopting nonracial rule, the discrepancy between South Africa and the rest of the continent will become even more glaring in the years to come. Of course, promoting democracy is only one goal of U.S. foreign policy in Africa; however, that goal is important in and of itself. In addition, promoting democracy is vital to placing Africa higher on the public policy agenda. The presence of many old-style, authoritarian one-party states on the African continent in a world that is rapidly moving toward democracy may be the major impetus for the marginalization of Africa.

Given limited resources and competing goals, perhaps the most important step the United States can take is to try to influence the "atmospherics" that surround the debate over political alternatives in Africa. It can be made repeatedly clear to Africans in many different forums that the one-party state has failed globally and that much of the rest of the world has found an alternative in multiparty democracy. In addition, the importance of political liberalization accompanying the economic reform that many African governments have already accepted could be significant. The United States already attempts to promote the idea of democracy through greater aid to those countries that do not violate human rights and similar measures, and it can do more in the future. Thus, the United States can amplify the pressures brought about by Africans themselves who are increasingly demanding steps toward democracy. Some countries—notably Zimbabwe and Kenya, which are not becoming more democratic, at the moment—may choose to ignore current trends, and there is little the United States can do except to tell them repeatedly how out of step they are with the rest of the world.

The United States must also help promote indigenous democratic thinking. Theories such as "African socialism" or "humanism" can be criticized on many accounts, but they were serious attempts to adjust political institutions to African realities. A new wave of indigenous political thinking is necessary because African attempts simply to graft Western democratic structures to their own countries will fail just as they did in the 1960s. Africans need to develop their own political structures to account for their particular realities: large peasant communities, ethnic cleavages, and low economic development. Unfortunately, African intellectuals are under continuous assault from their own governments and from overpopulated universities and, at best, possess inadequate research facilities to help them attack pervading problems. Special attention to promoting local political theory is therefore justified.

Some may question the legitimacy of external actors supporting the development of African democratic theory. In fact, these types of actions are the exact opposite of cultural imperialism. Rather, policies that enhance the capabilities of Africans to develop indigenous democratic practices and institutions explicitly recognize the inappropriateness of simply attempting to artificially graft Western institutions onto other societies.

Third, the United States can use its sectoral aid programs, which are usually designed in conjunction with the World Bank, to promote local agents who might be especially important in furthering democratic practice. For instance, U.S. agricultural reform programs should attempt to include the views of peasant organizations and try to aid those associations as much as possible. During consultative group meetings and other forums, all donors can also be encouraged to use their sectoral programs to promote political liberalization.

There should also be some limited attempt to aid the more democratic African countries by redirecting development assistance. Inevitably, this will mean penalizing undemocratic countries, but the U.S. Congress is already doing this. An official administration policy would be more helpful than ad hoc congressional action. The reprogramming of development assistance from authoritarian to relatively democratic countries would send a strong signal. It should be noted that U.S. threats to reduce aid because of severe human rights abuses or particularly undemocratic practices are now much more credible, as African countries can no longer appeal to U.S. cold-war interests.

The United States should be humble about its ability to promote democracy in Africa. However, it can add its voice constructively to increasing cries within the continent to end the dysfunctional rule of authoritarian one-party states. Indeed, one of the ways Africa can become more important on the public policy agenda is for it to no longer appear to be the continent that has the greatest number of old-style, authoritarian one-party states. The credibility of U.S. policy in the years to come may depend upon future U.S. governments making it clear that not only are they pushing for democratization in Africa but also that such democratization is possible.

Boundary Changes

One of the effects of the cold war was to freeze boundaries across the world. Since 1945, there have been remarkably few boundary changes, and only the Bengalis have been able to form a new state.[29] Now, after the cold war, boundaries are changing. Germany has already united, Yugoslavia is about to dissolve, the Baltic states will eventually gain independence, and a more or less independent Quebec may emerge. Other frontier changes may occur as ethnic groups are finally allowed to form their own homelands. Inevitably, these examples will have an important effect on Africa, where a new generation may be less wedded to Organization of African Unity (OAU) declarations concerning boundary integrity. In fact, an increasing number of Africans may realize that preservation of the colonial boundaries locks many states into permanent weakness.[30] The specter of a militarily victorious Eritrean People's Liberation Front may hasten thinking as to the advisability of keeping the current system of boundaries. Indeed, as the revolt of Charles Taylor and other dissidents that eventually overthrew the regime of President Samuel Doe in Liberia indicates, many African governments can be threatened with far fewer military resources and less prowess than had previously been thought.

The prospect of large-scale boundary changes is some time away, but the United States should be thinking now about how it will react. So far, the United States has been able to essentially avoid the question of boundary changes because it has simply followed OAU norms, which consider any attempt at changing frontiers to be illegitimate. However, if there were a few successful boundary changes, the OAU consensus might break down rapidly. The United States and the rest of the West might be faced with nations that forcibly implement boundary changes, that could legitimately claim to have physical control over their new territories, and that could successfully defend themselves against former central governments.

Issues related to the creation of new states may present the United States with exceptional dilemmas. Certainly, policy will have to be made on a case-by-case basis depending on the local conditions. The best that can be said is that, now that the cold war is over, the United States will be able to decide these issues without having to worry about how its position will affect its global competition with the Soviet Union. Indeed, on a more general basis, one of the great advantages of decreased superpower tensions is that the United States will increasingly be able to take positions on African issues based almost entirely on the realities on the ground.

Although U.S. policy toward boundary changes should be nuanced and based on local realities, the United States should appreciate the importance of changing fundamental political structures in Africa. For over a decade, the United States and other Western countries have argued for changes in basic economic institutions, and they will undoubtedly continue to do so for the foreseeable future. However, simply focusing on economic structures implies that, in the final analysis, the political institutions are viable if the right policies are adopted. Yet, in many African countries—

notably the very small ones and many in the Sahel, such as Mali and Mauritania—it is increasingly obvious that the nation-states as currently designed are not viable. In the future, the automatic mind-set against boundary changes may therefore not be justified.

An international environment fostered by the United States and others that encouraged African countries to experiment peacefully with changing basic political structures such as boundaries might, in the end, be more beneficial for the continent than changes in boundaries forcibly imposed by a few states or ethnic subgroups. If African leaders realize at some point that the boundaries do more harm than good by locking them into positions of weakness, they may begin to forcibly change them with chaotic results. Fostering peaceful alterations in boundaries might prevent potential disasters on the continent and prepare the United States to deal with some potentially difficult issues.

AFRICA AND THE UNITED STATES IN THE POSTDECOLONIZATION ERA

As the cold war ends, an era is also coming to a close in Africa. Since 1960, Africans have been adjusting to the end of colonialism. Now African countries and the United States face problems with which Africa will have to cope as it moves away from simply reacting to the end of colonialism and starts to face the future. Thus, economic systems will finally have to be designed to promote growth, political systems developed to cultivate democracy, and boundaries drawn so that nations have a chance to develop. Hopefully, the fact that Africa will not be high on the U.S. policy agenda will not mean that it is unable to successfully confront the problems of a new era.

NOTES

1. Patrick O'Sullivan, *Geopolitics* (London: Croom Helm, 1986), p. 1.
2. In this chapter, I will use *Africa* to refer to the countries south of the Sahara.
3. David D. Newsom, "U.S. and Africa in the Post-Cold War Era." *Washington Quarterly* 13, no. 1 (Winter 1990):104.
4. See the interview with Cohen in "Bush Messenger," *West Africa* 3781 (February 12, 1990):208.
5. Such was its advice to Ghana as early as 1982.
6. "If the Cold War Is Over in Africa, Will the United States Still Care?" *CSIS Africa Notes* 98 (May 30, 1989):1.
7. See Deputy Assistant Secretary for Africa Alison Rosenberg's statement, "FY 1990 Assistance Request for Sub-Saharan Africa," *Department of State Bulletin*, July 1989, p. 41.
8. Ibid., pp. 39–40.

9. Statistics are from the Organization for Economic Cooperation and Development (OECD), *Development Cooperation in the 1990's* (Paris: OECD, 1989), p. 242.

10. "Bush Acts to Ease African Debt," *New York Times*, 7 July 1989, Sec. IV, p. 1.

11. "Forging a Bipartisan Policy," *Africa Report* 34 (September-October 1989): 19.

12. Statistics are for countries south of the Sahara. International Monetary Fund, *Direction of Trade Statistics 1989* (Washington, D.C.: International Monetary Fund, 1989), p. 402.

13. Statistics include investments in some North African countries. "U.S. Multinational Companies: Operations in 1987," *Survey of Current Business* 69, no. 6 (June 1989):32.

14. World Bank, *World Development Report 1989* (Washington, D.C.: World Bank, 1989), pp. 168–169.

15. Pauline H. Baker, "Africa in the New World Order," *SAIS Review* 10, no. 2 (Summer-Fall 1990):151–152.

16. C. S. Whitaker, "An Agenda for Cooperative Action in Africa," in Anatoly A. Gromyko and C. S. Whitaker (eds.), *Agenda for Action: African-Soviet-U.S. Cooperation* (Boulder, Colo.: Lynne Rienner, 1990), p. 3.

17. Forty-five percent of the people in Africa were born after 1972. United Nations, *Demographic Yearbook* (New York: United Nations, 1989), p. 171.

18. World Bank, *Accelerated Development in Sub-Saharan Africa* (Washington, D.C.: World Bank, 1981).

19. General Agreement on Tariffs and Trade, *International Trade 1988–1989*, vol. 2 (Geneva: GATT, 1989), p. 28.

20. World Bank, *African Economic and Financial Data* (Washington, D.C.: World Bank, 1989), p. 50.

21. GATT, *International Trade 1988–1989*, p. 29.

22. United Nations, *World Economic Survey, 1989* (New York: United Nations, 1989), p. 7.

23. Figures from GATT, *International Trade 1988–1989*, vol. 1 (Geneva: GATT, 1989), p. 51; and World Bank, *Sub-Saharan Africa: A Long-Term Perspective Study* (Washington, D.C.: World Bank, 1989), p. 240.

24. World Bank, *World Debt Tables*, first supplement (Washington, D.C.: World Bank, 1989), pp. 4, 44.

25. Figures are calculated from United Nations Conference on Trade and Development, *Trade and Development Report 1989* (New York: United Nations, 1989), p. 60.

26. "Farm Spending on the Rise Again," *The Economist* 315, no. 7654 (May 12, 1990):51.

27. Cadman Atta Mills, *Structural Adjustment in Sub-Saharan Africa*, EDI Policy Seminar Report no. 18 (Washington, D.C.: World Bank, 1989), p. 7.

28. This proposition parallels Milner's argument that one of the most important ways policymakers can prevent protectionist pressures from growing is for international economic ties to be kept open. See Helen V. Milner, *Resisting Protectionism:*

Global Industries and the Politics of International Trade (Princeton: Princeton University Press, 1988), p. 300.

29. I discuss African boundaries in Jeffrey Herbst, "The Creation and Maintenance of National Boundaries in Africa," *International Organization* 43, no. 4 (Autumn 1989):673–692.

30. Jeffrey Herbst, "War and the State in Africa," *International Security* 14, no. 4 (Spring 1990):117–139.

9

AFRICA AND EUROPE: THE DILUTION OF A "SPECIAL RELATIONSHIP"

JOHN RAVENHILL

Fifteen years after most African states gained their independence, I. William Zartman suggested that decolonization had facilitated a reduction in their dependence on Europe.[1] More than fifteen years later, we may pose the question of whether the processes Zartman identified have led to a normalization of relations between Africa and Europe—that is, whether the "special relationship" that existed between African countries and their former colonial metropoles has been diluted to such an extent that it is no different from their relationships with other major external actors.

As we will see, the evidence is mixed. Europe has become considerably less important as an economic partner for Africa, yet it remains the single most important trading partner for all African states. European Community countries alone continue to provide close to half of all the overseas development assistance received by sub-Saharan Africa (SSA). But perhaps of greatest significance in determining the nature of the relationship is Europe's perception of the value of Africa as an economic partner. Africa has become a far less significant market for Europe since 1960 and a less important source of supply of critical raw materials. Together with disappointment at the political evolution of many African countries and a certain growth in "donor fatigue," the relative decline of the SSA market explains the growing disinterest of many European countries in Africa. But just as continent-wide generalizations are dangerous for Africa, so they are for Europe; France, for example, remains as active as ever in its efforts not merely to preserve but to extend its African sphere of influence.

TRADE RELATIONS

Africa's trading relations have undergone a remarkable diversification since independence. This generalization—particularly in terms of export markets—applies equally to countries regardless of their colonial background, their regimes' development ideologies, or the commodity composition of their exports.[2] The share of the European Community (which, of course, includes the principal former colonial powers) in African exports declined from an average of 63 percent in 1958–1963 to 45 percent in 1974–1986.[3] The reduction in the importance of the EC as a purchaser of African exports occurred despite the preferential access African countries enjoyed to the European market initially through the Treaty of Rome and subsequently through the Yaounde and Lome Conventions.[4] The only African states for which Europe did not decline in importance as an export market were Liberia and Ethiopia—countries that had not been colonies of the EC. For these two, a larger export market share for Europe may be consistent with trade diversification.

Trading partner concentration is one of the indicators most frequently employed in empirical studies of dependency. Most economists and political scientists would argue that a diversification of export markets is desirable. The greater the concentration of export trade, the more vulnerable are export receipts to fluctuations arising from such developments in the principal market as changes in the level of imports or devaluations. When, for instance, exports are directed predominantly toward a relatively slowly growing market (as was the case with the EC in the late 1970s and early 1980s), the exporting country would be worse off than if its markets were less concentrated. Countries with geographically concentrated export markets are vulnerable to pressures to increase their purchases from their trading partners and are particularly poorly placed in tariff disputes.[5]

The reduction in the importance of the European market for Africa's exports is itself an important step toward normalizing Africa's external economic relations. The extent to which trade diversification has occurred is disguised, however, by treating the EC as a single group. When the data for the EC are disaggregated into figures for the individual member states, the full extent of diversification becomes apparent. Particularly noticeable is the decline in the shares of the former metropoles in the exports of their ex-colonies. This has been most marked for Great Britain: Its share of total African exports declined from an average of 22 percent in 1958–1963 to only 7 percent in 1974–1986. Some—but by no means all—of this fall is explained by Great Britain's move to self-sufficiency in oil (its share of the exports of Africa's minerals and agriculture also dropped markedly). The most pronounced reduction occurred in Great Britain's share of the exports of its former African colonies—down from 36 percent to under 10 percent. In contrast, its share of the exports of former French colonies increased in a statistically significant manner over this period.

Perhaps more surprising, given France's continued close ties with its former colonies, was the decline in the importance of the French market for the exports of the francophone African states. The percentage of the exports of former French colonies absorbed by France fell from an average of 56 to 25 percent in the years 1958–1963 to 1974–1986, respectively; in contrast, France's share of the exports of former British colonies rose from 2 to 9 percent for the same period. Similarly, the most marked reduction in Belgian and Portuguese shares of African exports occurred in those of their former colonies.

To some extent, these data may reflect the improved access to the markets of nontraditional trading partners within the EC that was provided to African states by the Lome Conventions (discussed in the final section of this chapter). More than three decades after independence, African exports are far less vulnerable to trade threats from any single European country. Europe as a whole, however—particularly the EC—remains by far the most important single export market. In contrast to the European Community's 45 percent share of African exports, the next most important market was the United States, which absorbed an average of 23 percent of African exports in the period 1974–1986 (15.5 percent, if Nigeria's oil exports are excluded from the analysis). The third of the major trading giants, Japan, is a pygmy as far as African exports are concerned. Between 1974 and 1986 it provided a market for less than 3 percent of Africa's total exports. And despite the emphasis that has been given to South-South trade in general and to African regional trade in particular, other developing countries absorbed 11 percent and African countries less than 7 percent of all African exports. Thus, to the extent that European Community countries act as a single bloc for trade purposes, they still constitute by far the most important export market for all African countries, and they might be expected to enjoy considerable leverage in any trade dispute.

A similar concentration is found in Africa's imports. Indeed, the European Community as a whole has been markedly successful since 1960 in maintaining its share of African markets—this declined only from 53 to 49 percent between 1958–1963 and 1974–1986. Again the aggregate data mask changes that have occurred in the relationships between individual European countries and their former colonies. Whereas, for instance, France maintained a 15 percent share of total African imports throughout the period, its share of the market in its ex-colonies declined from an average of 58 percent in 1958–1963 to 38 percent in 1974–1986. In the same period it tripled its share of the market in former British colonies (albeit only to 6 percent). In a similar vein, Great Britain increased its share in the imports of former French colonies, but it lost close to half its share of the markets of its

TABLE 9.1 Sub-Saharan Africa's Share of European Exports (in percentages)

	1960	*1965*	*1970*	*1975*	*1980*	*1985*	*1987*
Belgium	3.0	2.5	2.1	2.0	2.2	1.7	1.6
France	8.1	7.7	5.5	6.3	6.0	4.7	4.2
Germany	2.3	1.9	1.6	1.9	1.9	1.1	1.6
Portugal	27.5	25.8	24.9	9.2	6.6	4.7	2.9
United Kingdom	7.9	6.1	5.1	5.4	5.1	2.7	3.2
European Community	8.5	6.0	6.1	6.6	7.5	4.9	5.5

Source: International Monetary Fund, *Direction of Trade* (Washington, D.C.: IMF, various years).

former African colonies (down from 35 to 17.5 percent). The contributions of Japan and the United States to Africa's imports remained fairly constant throughout the entire period, at 7 and 8 percent, respectively.

Despite the European Community's having maintained its share of sub-Saharan Africa's imports in the postindependence period, the region's importance as a market for European exports underwent a significant decline (Table 9.1).

Africa's declining significance as an outlet for European exports, the product in part of the continent's poor economic performance in relation to the performances of other developing countries, is one of the principal reasons some European governments appear to have lost interest in the continent, as discussed later. For governments and corporations pursuing more rapidly growing markets elsewhere, there appears to be little economic logic to preserving the advantages—for example, in market access—that Africa enjoys in Europe compared to those afforded other developing countries.

Although Africa's share of aggregate European imports has changed little since independence (Table 9.2), there has been a major shift in commodity composition. The principal factor in this shift was the emergence of petroleum in the 1970s, which by the end of the decade accounted for more than one-third of Europe's total imports from Africa. Without petroleum, Africa would be even more marginalized in the European market than it is at present.

Europe relies more heavily on African minerals than do other major industrialized importing countries, and the European Community has occasionally expressed concern about the lack of expenditure by European companies on exploration in Africa. But the declining resource intensity of industrial production, the evaporation of fears about resource security, and the reputation of many African countries as inhospitable business

TABLE 9.2 Sub-Saharan Africa's Share of European Imports (in percentages)

	1960	1965	1970	1975	1980	1985	1987
Belgium	8.4	4.8	5.3	2.7	3.1	3.4	2.8
France	9.4	7.2	5.0	5.1	5.1	4.7	3.0
Germany	3.8	3.4	2.8	2.9	2.9	2.6	1.9
Portugal	15.4	16.0	14.7	6.1	4.1	7.4	4.3
United Kingdom	6.5	6.9	5.6	3.8	2.4	2.3	1.9
European Community	6.6	7.5	7.8	6.6	6.7	6.9	5.7

[a]Excludes intra-European Community trade.

Source: International Monetary Fund, *Direction of Trade* (Washington, D.C.: IMF, various years).

environments and unreliable sources of supply have contributed to a European loss of interest in Africa's mineral wealth.

AID RELATIONSHIPS

Europe may have lost some of its importance as a trading partner to Africa but not as a source of aid. As Table 9.3 shows, the EEC's share in total overseas development assistance (ODA) to SSA, after falling somewhat in the mid-1970s to mid-1980s, has returned to the level of the early 1970s. The European Community alone provides more than half of the aid Africa currently receives. Europe's share of aid provided to Africa is disproportionate to its overall contribution to global overseas development assistance.

In 1987, France was by far the largest single source of aid to SSA. Its contribution of over $2 billion exceeded that of the World Bank (whose International Development Association [IDA] subsidiary provided approximately $1.4 billion). Of the ten largest aid donors, five were EC countries (with Italy, perhaps surprisingly, the third-largest of all sources). The European Development Fund—the European Community's aid fund—was the sixth-largest source; its 1987 contribution of $712 million was close to that provided by all U.N. agencies combined, including the U.N. Development

TABLE 9.3 European Community Share of Sub-Saharan Africa's Total Net ODA Receipts (in percentages)

1970	1973	1977	1981	1985	1987
53	53	48	47	43	52

Source: Derived from data in *Geographical Distribution of Financial Flows to Developing Countries* (Paris: Organization for Economic Cooperation and Development, various years).

TABLE 9.4 Major Aid Donors to Sub-Saharan Africa in 1987 ($ millions)

France	$2,046
International Development Association	1,424
Italy	946
Federal Republic of Germany	761
United States	760
European Development Fund	712
Japan	509
Netherlands	426
Canada	332
United Kingdom	325
Sweden	323

Source: Organization for Economic Cooperation and Development, *Development Cooperation 1988 Report* (Paris: OECD, 1988).

Program (UNDP), U.N. Technical Assistance (UNTA), the U.N. Children's Fund (UNICEF), the World Food Program (WFP), and the Office of the U.N. High Commissioner for Refugees (UNHCR). That $712 million was 40 percent above the level of Japanese assistance. The only other non-European countries in the top ten donors in 1987 were Canada and the United States (Table 9.4).

Europe's loss of interest in Africa as a trading partner has not been reflected in the geographical distribution of aid by European member states: Africa's share of EEC member states' total aid programs has either remained fairly constant since 1973 or has increased substantially (as has been the case for Italy, the Netherlands, and West Germany) (Table 9.5). Although African states, like other potential beneficiaries, may have suffered from cutbacks in the overall size of the aid programs of some member states—most notably Great Britain—the data suggest that for the most part they have improved their position as recipients relative to the positions of other developing countries.

In recent years, many European countries have made the continuation of their aid to Africa conditional on African states having reached an agreement with the International Monetary Fund or the World Bank on a structural adjustment program. Coordination of the aid policies of major donors with those of the international financial institutions has ensured that African countries have no alternative but to implement structural adjustment agreements if they wish to continue to receive substantial program assistance. This coordination has considerably reduced African governments' (rather limited) capacity to shop around among the various donors.[6] In one way, it has also reduced the importance of European donors to Africa: The principal decision as to whether program aid will be extended will be made in Washington rather than in a European capital. European countries, however, often first play significant roles as champions of particular

TABLE 9.5 Sub-Saharan Africa's Percentage Share in Net Disbursements of ODA by European Community Countries, 1973–1987

	1973	*1976*	*1977*	*1981*	*1982*	*1983*	*1984*	*1985*	*1986*	*1987*
Belgium	69	66	68	67	67	57	63	67	70	64
Denmark	54	49	53	52	55	55	55	50	56	51
France	44	47	47	50	47	47	45	45	47	46
West Germany	20	21	26	31	29	29	30	30	29	30
Italy	19	14	34	61	49	49	59	57	64	61
Netherlands	18	21	28	31	28	28	33	33	39	37
United Kingdom	31	25	27	37	36	36	31	35	31	38

Source: Derived from data of the Organization for Economic Cooperation and Development contained in OECD, Development Assistance Committee, *Development Cooperation: Efforts and Policies of the Members of the Development Assistance Committee* (Paris: OECD, various years).

African governments in the board meetings of international financial institutions or in consultative group meetings; they may also assume the lead position as providers of finance once agreement has been reached in a consultative group meeting. Typically, France and the United Kingdom continue to be the major players and to champion the interests of some of their former colonies.

RELATIONS BETWEEN INDIVIDUAL EUROPEAN COUNTRIES AND AFRICA

Great Britain

Great Britain's loss of interest in Africa has been the most pronounced of the major former colonial powers. The strong Africa lobby of the 1950s and 1960s has largely disappeared from the British political scene. African events—except for crises and disasters—seldom receive detailed attention in the media. The economic problems Great Britain has experienced since the 1960s have led to a general turning inward and to an attempted redefinition of its role within Europe; as far as Africa is concerned, there has been much impatience and disappointment in political circles with Africa's economic and political evolution.[7] British politicians, particularly in the period of conservative government since 1979, have given the impression that the colonial legacy is something of an embarrassment, one in which they are unwilling to invest any significant political energies. The British Commonwealth continues as the principal institutional embodiment of the colonial legacy and is undoubtedly still valued by Great Britain as a lingering reminder of its former status as a great power. In recent years, however, the commonwealth heads of government meeting appears to have served primarily as a forum in which the former colonies voice their grievances about British policies, particularly those toward South Africa.

British capital—with the exception of rather maverick corporations such as Lonrho—has generally seen little advantage in attempting to increase ties with black Africa (Nigeria was an exception during the oil boom), given the region's poor economic performance and the capricious attitudes displayed toward foreign investment by several former British colonies in the 1970s. In contrast, British corporations have maintained their role as the single most important source of foreign investment in the Republic of South Africa, accounting for over 40 percent of the total.

The Thatcher government's preoccupation with cutting public expenditures produced cutbacks in the aid program that reduced its value by over 20 percent in the early 1980s. As Great Britain has traditionally given a major portion of its aid to Asian countries—India being the largest single recipient overall—the decline in the aid budget has reduced Great Britain to being a second-tier player in Africa. As Table 9.4 shows, in 1987 the overall value of the British aid program to Africa was only slightly more than that of Sweden and trailed not only its European Community colleagues of France, West Germany, Italy, and the Netherlands but also Canada, Japan, and the United States. Great Britain initially refused to support the World Bank's Special Facility for Africa but eventually made a contribution in 1985. Aid stagnated in real terms in the mid-1980s but increased in 1988–1989. The Thatcher government insisted that greater weight in the aid program be given to British commercial and political interests, which led to a rise in "mixed" credits;[8] the program was also criticized by the Foreign Affairs Committee of the House of Commons for moving away from agricultural projects to large construction projects intended to enhance British prestige abroad.[9]

In its last few years, however, the Thatcher government—under pressure from Great Britain's significant development assistance lobby—adopted a more progressive stance on the issue of African debt and structural adjustment. All outstanding loans to thirteen of the poorest African countries were turned into grants. The government supported the replenishment of the IDA and the trebling of the capital of the African Development Bank. Chancellor of the Exchequer Nigel Lawson deserves much of the credit for the plan for African debt relief devised at the 1988 Toronto economic summit. Great Britain pioneered the purchase of surplus food from African countries to be given as aid to their neighbors; it was subsequently successful in convincing its European Community colleagues of the merit of this idea for EC-financed food aid.

Although the Thatcher government was closely associated with the hard-line globalist posture on international affairs pursued by the Reagan administration,[10] this approach surprisingly did not spill over into its attitudes on a number of key African issues. The government ignored the calls of right-wing critics for a termination of aid to the government of Milton Obote and their protests over British assistance for Angola and Mozambique. The government's agreement to provide British training for Mozambique's army angered many within the Conservative party. Thatcher was insistent—despite pressure from various sporting bodies in Great Britain—on upholding the Gleneagles agreement on a commonwealth sports boycott against South Africa; in general, the government also observed the U.N. arms embargo against the republic. Again, somewhat surprisingly, Thatcher opposed the linkage made by the Reagan administration between a settlement of the Namibian issue and the withdrawal of Cuban troops from Angola.

The most controversial of the Thatcher government's African policies, however, was its stance on South Africa. Throughout most of the 1980s, the government encouraged an expansion of Great Britain's already strong economic ties with the republic. Initially it appeared that some British companies would seek to fill the gap left by U.S. disinvestment, although some larger British companies began to pull out by the end of the decade. The government permitted the state-owned Central Electricity Generating Board to continue to purchase uranium from South Africa (probably extracted in Namibia). Thatcher expressed a good deal of sympathy for the modest reform efforts undertaken by the South African government; her personal opposition to sanctions left Great Britain isolated in the commonwealth heads of government meetings through much of the 1980s. Thatcher's 1988 decision to attempt to take the lead in mediating a political settlement in South Africa did not bear fruit.

Thatcher's fascination with South Africa stood in significant contrast to the government's general lack of interest in the rest of the continent; indeed, the policies on South Africa did much to alienate other African leaders. More than thirty years after independence, Great Britain's political influence in most of its former African colonies appears negligible. An intervention by British troops to put down a military revolt, as happened in East Africa in 1964, is now unthinkable. The decline of British influence in Africa mirrors the country's loss of stature as a world power.

Federal Republic of Germany

In West Germany, Margaret Thatcher had a reliable ally in her efforts to oppose the imposition of sanctions against South Africa and to resist any significant restructuring of international economic regimes. Prior to unification, West Germany, like Japan, had tended to place business above politics in its relations with other countries; its objective had been to maintain good relations with its trading partners regardless of the type of regime in power. Africa (again with the exception of South Africa) is very low on the German political agenda; since the abandonment of the Hallstein doctrine, under which Germany broke diplomatic relations with countries that recognized East Germany, political developments on the continent have seldom been permitted to interrupt economic ties.

Germany sends a smaller percentage of its exports to black African markets than any of the other larger economies in the European Community. Germany, however—while not the most important trading partner for any African country—has been successful in establishing itself across the continent in both francophone and anglophone as well as lusophone countries. Rolf Hofmeier notes that Germany is consistently the second-, third-, or fourth-most-important business partner for African countries and thus has a wider geographical spread of trading and investment interests on the continent than the United States, Great Britain, or France.[11] And although Germany devotes a smaller proportion of its aid budget to Africa than any other European Community country, this share has risen from

20 percent in the mid-1970s to over 30 percent presently. Coupled with the increase in the size of its foreign aid program, this has raised Germany to the position of third-most-important bilateral donor to Africa, marginally above the United States. More than other major donors, German aid tends to be widely geographically dispersed throughout SSA.

Since 1960, Tanzania and the Sudan have been the most favored recipients of German aid, followed by Kenya, Ghana, Cameroon, Zaire, Togo, Mali, and Niger.[12] Tanzania's presence at the top of the list belies the normal German preference for countries with pro-Western sympathies that are pursuing market-oriented policies. With the 1982 installation of a conservative coalition government, however, responsibility for the Ministry for Economic Cooperation passed to the Bavarian-based Christian Social Union (CSU), which utilized its control of the ministry as a means of attacking the foreign policy pursued by its larger coalition partner, the Christian Democratic Union (CDU). A prolonged debate was initiated on the political suitability of some African aid recipients—notably Tanzania, Ethiopia, and Mozambique. Tanzania's economic reforms and willingness to comply with an IMF adjustment program quickly led, however, to its being restored as one of the more privileged recipients of German aid. To appease conservative interests, aid to Zaire was stepped up.

After 1982, in order to placate domestic constituencies, the conservative coalition placed a greater emphasis than its predecessor on the use of aid to serve the interests of German industry. An increase in the percentage of aid given as mixed credits occurred (which has the effect of automatically tying the aid to purchases from German suppliers). Since 1978, however, German aid to the least developed countries has been exclusively in the form of grants; the Federal Republic has also canceled all interest and repayment obligations from earlier credits for nineteen African countries.

The Bonn government has been among the most intransigent of the industrialized countries in North-South negotiations, insisting on the superiority of market mechanisms to interventionary schemes. Germany initially refused to support the World Bank's Special Facility for Africa when it was proposed in 1985. It has consistently opposed any significant improvement of the Lome Conventions, which link African as well as Caribbean and Pacific states to the European Community. In recent years, the Federal Republic placed a great deal of emphasis on policy dialogue and conditionality in its aid relations. Germany joined Great Britain on a number of occasions in criticizing the part of EC aid to Africa that had no strings attached.

West Germany has firmly resisted the imposition of economic sanctions against South Africa. Like Great Britain, it reluctantly went along with the limited sanctions imposed by the European Community in 1986 in order to preserve a facade of European unity, but it succeeded in preventing imports of South African coal from being added to the boycott. The Bonn government was also reluctant to cancel the cultural agreement that had existed with South Africa since 1962; this was eventually allowed to lapse in 1986. The CDU has, however, successfully resisted the urging of the CSU—in particular of its former leader Franz-Josef Strauss—to adopt an even more conservative stance on southern African issues. The CSU had voiced its support for the National Resistance Movement in Mozambique, while its political foundation—the Hans Seidel Foundation—provided support for the National Union for the Total Independence of Angola office in Munich.[13]

German industry remains one of the largest investors in the Republic of South Africa. In recent years, there have been a number of political scandals regarding illegal arms exports to South Africa, including the construction plans for an advanced submarine. Successive governments do not appear to have pursued those accused of illicit arms sales with any vigor.

France

France's determination not only to maintain but to expand its sphere of influence in Africa sets it apart from the other European former colonial powers. French policy toward Africa is one of the most important components of France's claim to middle-power or mini-superpower status (together with its independent nuclear arsenal and its efforts to play a leading role in promoting European integration) and of its determination to pursue an independent and active foreign policy.[14] Only in Africa does France enjoy the relative autonomy to pursue a dominant political (and often economic) role, unhindered in large part by either of the superpowers. The second crucial component of understanding French policy toward Africa is the determined promotion of French language and culture. Francophone Africa includes over half of the states worldwide in which French is an official language.[15]

French policy toward Africa, like its foreign policy in general, has been characterized by a striking continuity. Some would argue that this has been true over the centuries, but it is certainly apparent through the entire era of the Fifth Republic. Gaullism in foreign policy has long outlived de Gaulle. France's continuing quest for prestige and glory (*rayonnement*) stands at the heart of the policy. As Guy Martin points out, francophone African states have always been considered to be part of the French sphere of influence because of their historical links and geographical proximity: This has often been expressed in terms of a French preserve (*domaine reserve* or *pré carré*) from which other foreign powers are to be excluded.[16]

Regardless of the political complexion of the government of the day, there has also been a marked continuity in procedures for foreign policy decision-making. Ultimate responsibility for foreign policy lies in the hands of the presidency—a matter that was not seriously disputed even during the period of cohabitation between Mitterrand and Chirac. On African policy, successive presidents have always maintained their own advisers—for much of the Fifth Republic, this was the rather shadowy figure of Jacques Foccart.[17] Most recently, Mitterrand's principal African adviser has been his own son, Jean-Christophe Mitterrand. Although the elder Mitterrand came to office in 1981 with a pledge to "liberalize" policy toward Africa, the weight of entrenched economic and political interests has ensured that African policy during his presidency has been marked more by continuity than change.

The extent to which France's African policy has been successful has been a result of the significant resources—economic, diplomatic, and military—that have been devoted to it. It is no surprise to discover that France is the largest single aid donor to sub-Saharan Africa. Even if one disregards the approximate 50 percent of this sum that, as Martin points out,[18] supports the more than 10,000 French technical assistance personnel in Africa, the balance of French aid would still place France at the top of the list of bilateral aid donors to black Africa.[19]

Perhaps as significant as, and possibly more so than, the relatively generous French assistance program is the willingness of French governments to devote the diplomatic resources necessary not only to maintain political influence within the francophone states but to expand it to other African countries. The key to French success has been a willingness to spend the time and energy to convince African leaders that they enjoy a special relationship with Paris and that their views are taken seriously. This is reflected in data on state visits to African countries by French presidents, foreign ministers, and presidential advisers on African affairs and, similarly, on the number of visits by African heads of state to Paris. Martin reports that President Mitterrand made 13 state visits to Africa during his first presidency; former presidential adviser for African affairs Guy Penne undertook 81 missions in Africa and met privately with francophone heads of state on 205 occasions during his five-year tenure in office.[20] The contrast with the lack of interest in black Africa the British government has displayed is striking.

The focal point of French relations with Africa is the annual Franco-African summit inaugurated by President Pompidou in 1973. With rare exceptions, such as the 1984 summit following the French decision to terminate its military involvement in the Chadian imbroglio, these have been significant diplomatic successes for France. The number of African states attending has risen over the years to an average of thirty-eight during the Mitterrand presidency. In 1986, for example, besides the twenty-five full members (Benin, Burundi, Cape Verde, Central African Republic,

Chad, Comoros, Congo, Côte d'Ivoire, Djibouti, France, Gabon, Gambia, Guinea, Guinea-Bissau, Equatorial Guinea, Mali, Morocco, Mauritius, Mauritania, Niger, Rwanda, Senegal, Seychelles, Togo, and Zaire), fourteen other countries with observer status attended (Angola, Botswana, Egypt, Liberia, Mozambique, Nigeria, São Tomé, Sierra Leone, Somalia, Sudan, Tanzania, Tunisia, Zambia, and Zimbabwe).[21] The list of full members attests to French success in extending its sphere of influence beyond former French colonies: Besides the former Belgian colonies of Burundi, Rwanda, and Zaire, the list includes the former Portuguese colony Cape Verde, the former Spanish colony Equatorial Guinea, and Gambia, a former British colony.[22]

The success of French diplomacy in extending its influence beyond the francophone group has been a source of problems. The African francophone states have been quick to express their discontent at what they perceive to be the dilution of a privileged relationship with Paris. These feelings came to a head shortly after Mitterrand's election when the Ministry for Cooperation and Development was subordinated to the foreign office and its minister, Jean-Pierre Cot, attempted to fashion a broader role to include the supervision of development aid for all Third-World countries. Cot's resignation at the end of 1982 after eighteen months in office was widely perceived as a victory for the old guard. The 1983 Franco-African summit was preceded by a dinner in Paris for the heads of state of francophone countries; in 1985 the summit was preceded for the first time by a full-day meeting between Mitterrand and francophone delegations—a meeting dubbed *une réunion de famille*. African francophone states and conservative opposition parties within France had sought for special status to be given to the francophones. Finally, under the Chirac government, the Ministry for Cooperation was restored to a full-fledged ministry, with its responsibilities to be confined to francophone states.

The jealousies that emerged over the broadening of the francophone summit are indicative of the problems France faces in playing an interventionist role in Africa. French attempts to maintain good relations throughout the continent frequently necessitate an attempt to be all things to all states—ranging from the very conservative regimes of Felix Houphouet-Boigny in Côte d'Ivoire and Omar Bongo in Gabon to radicals such as the late Thomas Sankara in Burkina Faso. Inevitably, France becomes drawn into disputes between African states—for example, the decision to admit Morocco as a full member of the francophone group caused friction with Algeria, given the latter's support for the Polisario Front. At times, France's relations with its extended family have resembled a soap opera, with feuds over the activities of French-based exile groups, former emperors ensconced in French chateaux, and disclosures by French journalists of the extramarital affairs of the wives of African leaders. The usual solution to such squabbles has been the dispatch of the president's African adviser to soothe feelings in the appropriate African capital.

Another instrument of French influence in Africa is its considerable military presence. Excluding Chad, France maintains nearly eight thousand troops on a permanent basis in the Central African Republic, Côte d'Ivoire, Djibouti, Gabon, and Senegal. In addition, over twelve hundred French military advisers are stationed in twenty-six African countries. In some countries, French advisers retain control over military communications networks.[23] In addition to its personnel stationed in Africa, the Mitterrand government created a forty-seven-thousand–member rapid deployment force (Force d'Action Rapide), which can be quickly airlifted into African trouble spots. France has defense agreements with Cameroon, Central African Republic, Comoros, Côte d'Ivoire, Djibouti, Gabon, Senegal, and Togo; French troops frequently conduct joint exercises with local armed forces. France has military assistance agreements with these eight countries and twenty-five others in Africa including Benin, Burkina Faso, Burundi, Chad, Congo, Libya, Madagascar, Mali, Mauritius, Mauritania, Niger, Rwanda, and Zaire. Some of these agreements give France privileged access to strategic materials in African states.[24]

The record shows that Paris will not hesitate to intervene militarily if it believes French interests are threatened. Over the years since independence, it has deployed military forces in the Central African Republic, Chad on five occasions, Djibouti, Gabon, Mauritania, Zaire, and most recently, Togo, following an abortive coup in February 1986. Under Giscard in particular, France has happily assumed the mantle of defender of Western interests in Africa, most notably in the dispatch of troops in support of Mobutu following the Shaba invasions—an action that prompted *Le Nouvel Observateur* to dub Giscard the "gendarme of Africa." Within French political circles, there was a widespread perception that France was standing alone in Africa in defense of stability against externally induced unrest.[25] Through its intervention in Chad, the Mitterrand presidency showed it was no less willing than its predecessor to deploy French forces in Africa. Other Western powers, including the United States, appear happy to have France assume this role.

Two other sources of French influence in Africa should be mentioned. First is the continuing presence of French advisers in prominent political positions in some African countries—the Côte d'Ivoire is the most notable example. Some African leaders continue to feel more secure with expatriates rather than nationals as their principal advisers, presumably because the foreigners will be unable to develop power bases of their own. Second is the continued membership of fourteen former French colonies plus Equatorial Guinea in the franc zone.[26] The states that participate in the franc zone relinquish a great deal of control over their monetary policies. The value of the CFA is tied to that of the French franc; the central bank of each of the two monetary unions determines how much may be borrowed by individual countries; and reserves are held primarily in French francs. There is little doubt that the franc zone facilitates continued French influence in the economies of the member states and benefits French traders. Whether membership in the franc zone has had a positive or negative effect on the overall economic performance of the member states remains in contention.[27]

France has been particularly astute in portraying itself as a champion of Third-World interests in international negotiations. Paris has frequently voiced support for Third-World proposals, safe in the knowledge that another Western power—the United States, Great Britain, or West Germany—would veto any significant changes to international economic regimes.[28] France is the classic free rider on other states' conservatism; but in spite of what often appear as cynical French maneuvers, Paris still takes kudos as the West's Third-World champion.

To some extent, a similar statement can be made about French policy toward South Africa. France has been aggressive in voicing slogans and taking symbolic actions that have won it favor with black African states; it has been much more reticent in taking effective action—for example, in imposing trade and investment sanctions against South Africa—that might have a negative impact on its commercial interests. During the Giscard presidency, France supplied a nuclear reactor to South Africa's Koeberg station. Repeated accusations have been made of French corporations breaking the U.N. arms embargo toward the republic. And France remains one of South Africa's major economic partners. Certainly, the Mitterrand presidency has gone further than its European colleagues in pushing for stronger sanctions against South Africa, but again the government could rely on a West German or British veto on effective EC action. Mitterrand did prevent a South African tour by the French rugby team; he also withdrew the French ambassador from Pretoria. In July 1985, Paris imposed a ban on new investment in South Africa, but this has not been completely effective.

In no way can France's relations with its former colonies be said to have normalized. The key to continued French influence is the multidimensionality of the French presence in the countries and of French activities. If the concept of neocolonialism is justified anywhere, it is in French activities in Africa where the continued hegemony of the idea of *francophonie* has engendered African complicity in continued French domination.

Belgium, Portugal, and Spain

Lack of space precludes any detailed consideration of the other three major formal colonial powers. Belgium maintains its love-hate relationship with the Mobutu regime in Zaire; despite the repeated humiliations to which Belgian interests in its largest former colony have been subjected, successive governments in Brussels have not abandoned their *enfant terrible* and have resisted French attempts to muscle in on their preserve. Thus, despite its frustrations with Mobutu, Belgium continues to champion its interests in consultative group meetings. Most of Belgium's aid is directed to its former colonies in Africa.

Both Spain and Portugal were preoccupied in the 1980s, first with preparation for and then with adaptation to their entry into the European Community. Relations with Africa have generally had a low priority, and neither country has clearly articulated an African policy. Spain's Socialist government, in power since 1982, continues to be embarrassed by its only former colony in black Africa, Equatorial Guinea. Spain had broken diplomatic relations with the country's notorious dictator, Francisco Macias Nguema, before his overthrow in 1979 but propped up the country's bankrupt economy and the only slightly more enlightened successor regime until the mid-1980s. Madrid was greatly relieved by the admission of Equatorial Guinea to the Union Douanière et Economique de l'Afrique Centrale (UDEAC) in 1984 and to the franc zone in the following year and has given every indication that it is delighted that France wishes to include this unfortunate territory within its sphere of influence. Spanish aid to the former colony has been halved since the mid-1980s.

Spanish economic, diplomatic, and cultural ties elsewhere in black Africa are extremely limited. Until the mid-1980s, Spain had no foreign aid or technical assistance program outside of Equatorial Guinea; subsequently, very modest efforts have begun in Mauritania, Senegal, and Zimbabwe. Spain's primary commercial interests in black Africa are in oil exploration (Gabon and Nigeria) and in fishing. Spain has few interests in South Africa; its Socialist government has been prominent in calling for sanctions against Pretoria. Spain's primary interests in Africa are in the north of the continent, where its enclaves of Ceuta and Melilla have been claimed by Morocco. Although Spain provides military aid to Morocco, it views the Maghreb states and Libya as potential military threats.

Portugal has effected a remarkable reconciliation with its former African colonies in the years since its precipitous exit from Africa following the 1974 military coup in Lisbon.[29] The Lisbon government has occasionally been able to serve as an intermediary between South Africa and both Mozambique and Angola. Relations between Portugal and these two largest of its former African colonies have been complicated by the activities of exile groups in Lisbon and accusations that support has been given to the National Union for the Total Independence of Angola (UNITA) in Angola and the National Resistance Movement (MNR) in Mozambique. Due largely to suspicions on the part of Angola and Mozambique, Portugal has been excluded from the informal association that has sprung up between Africa's five lusophone states (Angola, Mozambique, Guinea-Bissau, São Tomé and Príncipe, and Cape Verde).

As the European Community's weakest economy, Portugal is not well placed to offer substantial assistance to African economies. Its small aid program is concentrated on its former territories, but Lisbon has also extended assistance to the Southern African Development Coordination Conference (SADCC). Attempts have been made to capitalize on its relations with Angola and Mozambique to extend trade ties with other frontline states. Portugal cannot readily take advantage of economic opportunities, however, and has steadily lost economic influence in its former colonies to other European countries. In particular, Guinea-Bissau and Cape Verde have grown much closer to France and may join the franc zone in the next few years.

Portugal's policy toward South Africa has been ambiguous. A principal reason for this is the size of the Portuguese settler community: Estimated at over 600,000, or approximately 14 percent of the white population, it is third behind the Afrikaners and the British. What is important is not just the numbers of Portuguese citizens concerned but the fact that their remittances are one of Portugal's major sources of foreign currency earnings. Portugal, accordingly, has been unwilling to take a strong stand on the sanctions issue.

MULTILATERALIZED RELATIONS BETWEEN EUROPE AND AFRICA: THE LOME CONVENTIONS

With successive enlargements of the European Community, Africa's trade relations with most of Western Europe have been increasingly regulated by Brussels rather than the individual European capitals. Africa's initial association with the European Community was effected by the Treaty of Rome at a time when France and Belgium maintained formal political control over their black African territories; with independence, the relationship was maintained with only minimal modification through the Yaounde Conventions. Finally, British accession to the EEC in 1973 led to the association with the EEC of former British colonies in Africa, the Caribbean, and the Pacific, accompanied by Ethiopia and Liberia, through the first Lome Convention, signed in 1975. Subsequently, the agreement has been extended to all independent countries in black Africa and currently links sixty-six African, Caribbean, and Pacific (ACP) states with the twelve members of the European Community.

As the EC is fond of reminding its ACP partners, the convention is the most comprehensive economic agreement offered by industrialized countries to a group of developing countries. In addition to a trade chapter, which grants free access to European markets on a nonreciprocal basis for most of the exports of the ACP countries, it includes a scheme to stabilize ACP earnings from the export of agricultural commodities (STABEX), a plan to encourage ACP mineral production for the European market (SYSMIN), arrangements for specific quantities of ACP sugar to be purchased by the EEC at prices close to those paid to European producers, the development of institutions to promote cooperation in the fields of agriculture and industry, and provisions for financial and technical assistance through the European Development Fund (EDF).

Negotiations were under way in mid-1989 for the fourth convention (each has run for a five-year period). As with previous renegotiations,[30] the expectation was that there would be modest, incremental improvements to the various chapters and an increase in the EDF provision to at least maintain its value in real terms but no significant innovations. After fourteen months of negotiations, twelve EC and sixty-eight ACP countries signed a ten-year agreement on December 15, 1989. Although EC aid was increased only modestly, STABEX scheme funds were increased significantly and the SYSMIN system was expanded to include uranium and gold. Seventeen years (1991) after its initial signature, the convention has disappointed those who held high hopes for what it might achieve. Launched with the heady rhetoric of interdependence and equality expressed by the Third World in its demands for a new international economic order, the convention has been routinized into what is primarily an aid relationship—albeit one that is of considerable value to Africa. As Table 9.4 shows, the EDF has become the sixth-largest donor to sub-Saharan Africa, contributing close to three-quarters of a billion dollars annually. And while the increase in the funding of the EDF over the years may have come at the expense of some of the member states' bilateral aid programs, the share of ACP countries in general and Africa in particular in the bilateral programs has not declined. This suggests that the ACP group probably receives more aid than would have been the case had the EDF not been established.

The intention of the ACP group in entering the Lome relationship was primarily defensive: first, to utilize the "special relationship" it enjoyed with its former colonial powers to safeguard its position in the European market; and second, to maintain its status as a privileged recipient of European aid—a strategy I characterize as "collective clientelism."[31] As suggested above, the ACP group has been largely successful in pursuit of its second objective.

It is in the trade sphere that the convention has been most disappointing. One reason is that the ACP group has not been able to persuade the European Community to maintain its margin of preference over excluded countries on a number of products of particular interest to the group. The

EC has gradually enlarged the Generalized System of Preferences (GSP) scheme it offers to other developing countries, often placing their market access on a par with that of the ACP group. The EC has argued that whereas the ACP group has the security of a "contractual" arrangement in its trade with the EC, other developing countries are dependent upon a unilaterally administered GSP scheme that changes from year to year. In reality, the contractual element of the convention is largely illusory: The agreement contains a number of escape clauses that enable the EC to take safeguard action should it perceive the ACP imports are damaging domestic producers. For example, while negotiations for the second convention were in progress, the EC threatened to take safeguard action against Mauritius unless it agreed to a voluntary export restraint on its sales of sweaters to the European market—despite the minuscule share of European imports Mauritius supplied. This action sent a clear signal to investors that exports of "sensitive" products from the ACP group would not be treated any differently than those from other European suppliers. Confidence in security of access was undermined. The EC has also taken a mean-spirited approach toward ACP agricultural products that compete with domestic production.

The enlargement of the EC to include Spain and Portugal brought additional problems to the relationship between the EC and the ACP in two dimensions. First, Spain and Portugal were producers of some of the agricultural products for which the ACP had been given limited off-season access (a problem far more severe for the Maghreb countries, which have a separate agreement with the EC). Second, both Spain and Portugal have long-standing ties with Latin America and insisted that both EC aid and trade preferences should be increased for countries of this region. A positive EC response to these demands was encouraged by the declining importance of Africa as an economic partner.

The Lome "partnership" has been largely reduced to an aid relationship. In itself, this has ensured that the equal partnership it was supposed to represent has not materialized. This trend has been reinforced by the EC's insistence on a greater element of policy dialogue in the aid relationship and on greater conditionality to be attached to those transfers, such as from the STABEX scheme, that were originally intended to be made automatically to ACP governments.

The conventions have offered the ACP group a forum through which it can maintain pressure on the EC as a whole to take stronger measures against South Africa. The ACP was successful in inserting a clause denouncing apartheid in the second convention. Although the Commission of the European Communities has been sympathetic toward an extension of sanctions, it has enjoyed little success in pushing member states forward on this issue given the resistance of two of the most important governments—

Great Britain and Germany. As with so many other of its activities, the EC's approach has been on the basis of the lowest common denominator. Its code of conduct for European firms operating in South Africa has been administered inconsistently on a national basis. Sanctions remain primarily symbolic.[32]

CONCLUSION

Enormous changes have occurred within a relatively brief period of time in Africa's relations with Europe. Africa's trade partners have become far more diversified: The importance of the former colonial metropole as an outlet for exports and a source of imports has declined dramatically. These changes to trade patterns are all the more remarkable given the persistence of traditional trading links, banking and currency arrangements, and similar factors.

The relationship between Great Britain and its former colonies in Africa was completely different at the end of the 1980s from that which existed twenty-five years ago. Anglophone countries no longer look to Great Britain for leadership; the prospect of British intervention in their internal affairs is remote. A similar change has occurred even more rapidly in the relations between Spain and Portugal and their former African colonies. France alone among the European powers has not only maintained its formidable presence in its former colonies but has extended it to some of those of Belgium, Portugal, and Spain.

As long as France perceives its African preserve as central to its claim to middle-power status, relations between Africa and Europe will not be normalized. In any event, there must be doubts as to what would constitute a "normal" relationship between the two continents. Geographical proximity and present economic complementarity ensure that Europe continues to be the dominant economic partner for Africa. And, with Africa's present economic woes, none of the other industrialized powers is likely to be willing to undertake the role of major aid donor that Europe currently plays.

NOTES

I am grateful to Lyn Fisher for research assistance for this chapter.

1. I. William Zartman, "Europe and Africa: Decolonization or Dependency?" *Foreign Affairs* 54, no. 2 (January 1976):325–343.

2. This section draws upon Joanna Moss and John Ravenhill, "Trade Diversification in Black Africa," *Journal of Modern African Studies* 27, no. 3 (September 1989): 521–545.

3. Data refer to the nine-member EC prior to its most recent expansion. Greece, Portugal, and Spain are excluded, as they were not members of the EC for most of the years covered by the Moss and Ravenhill study (see note 2).

4. See Joanna Moss, *The Lome Conventions and Their Implications for the United States* (Boulder, Colo.: Westview Press, 1982); and John Ravenhill, *Collective Clientelism: The Lome Conventions and North-South Relations* (New York: Columbia University Press, 1985).

5. See, among others, P. J. Lloyd, *International Trade Problems of Small States* (Durham, N.C.: Duke University Press, 1968); Albert O. Hirschman, *National Power and the Structure of Foreign Trade* (Berkeley: University of California Press, 1945); and John A. Conybeare, *Trade Wars* (New York: Columbia University Press, 1987).

6. Lenders are not completely united, however; some governments have been successful in exploiting differences between members of consultative groups.

7. See the useful surveys by Colin Legum that appeared annually in *Africa Contemporary Record* from 1971–1972 to 1985–1986.

8. "Mixed" credits typically combine grants or loans on concessional terms with export credits tied to purchases from the donor country.

9. According to the committee, finance for agricultural projects had fallen by a third in recent years. Foreign Affairs Committee of the House of Commons report, July 1985, cited in Colin Legum, "Britain's Year in Africa in 1985," in Colin Legum (ed.), *Africa Contemporary Record: Annual Survey and Documents 1985–1986* (New York: Africana Publishing Co., 1987), p. A189.

10. "Globalists" typically perceive local confrontations in terms of the overall East-West struggle. For a discussion of the globalist nature of the Reagan administration's African policies, see Donald Rothchild and John Ravenhill, "Subordinating African Issues to Global Logic: Reagan Confronts Political Complexity," in Kenneth A. Oye, Robert J. Lieber, and Donald Rothchild (eds.), *Eagle Resurgent? The Reagan Era in American Foreign Policy* (Boston: Little Brown, 1987), pp. 393–430.

11. Rolf Hofmeier, "Aid from the Federal Republic of Germany to Africa," *Journal of Modern African Studies* 24, no. 4 (December 1986):577.

12. For a more complete listing of the geographical distribution of German aid to Africa, see *ibid.*, pp. 588–589; and Brigitte Schulz and William Hansen, "Aid or Imperialism? West Germany in Sub-Saharan Africa," *Journal of Modern African Studies* 22, no. 2 (June 1984):304.

13. For further details, see the articles on West Germany and Africa by Rolf Hofmeier in successive issues of *Africa Contemporary Record*, 1984–1985, 1985–1986, and 1986–1987.

14. Stanley Hoffman, "La France face a son image," *Politique étrangere* 51 (1986): 25–53.

15. For further discussion of *francophonie*, see Robert Aldrich and John Connell, "Francophonie: Language, Culture or Politics?" in Robert Aldrich and John Connell (eds.), *France in World Politics* (London: Routledge, 1989), pp. 170–193.

16. Guy Martin, "France and Africa," in *ibid.*, p. 104.

17. Tamar Golan, "A Certain Mystery: How Can France Do Everything It Does in Africa—and Get Away with It?" *African Affairs* 80, no. 318 (January 1981):6–7.

18. Martin, "France and Africa," p. 108.

19. In recent years an increasing amount of French aid has been given as mixed credits in an attempt to utilize aid for export promotion purposes. The United States has been particularly critical of French subsidization of its exports to Third-World countries in this manner.

20. Martin, "France and Africa," fn. 47, p. 122.

21. Claude Wauthier, "France and Africa in 1986: Cohabitation and Its Ambiguous Consequences for French Policy," in Colin Legum (ed.), *Africa Contemporary Record: Annual Survey and Documents 1986–1987* (New York: Africana Publishing Co., 1988), p. A199.

22. There is no evidence that Spain resisted the growth of French influence in Equatorial Guinea, a country whose appalling economic, political, and human rights records have few parallels in Africa. Equatorial Guinea has moved so completely within the French sphere of influence that it has become a member of the franc zone.

23. Golan, "A Certain Mystery," p. 8. In Gabon, French pilots reportedly fly most of the air force planes. See Michael C. Reed, "Gabon: A Neo-Colonial Enclave of Enduring French Interest," *Journal of Modern African Studies* 25, no. 2 (June 1987):284.

24. Martin, "France and Africa," citing John Chipman, *French Military Policy and Africa Security*, Adelphi Paper no. 201 (London: International Institute for Strategic Studies, 1985).

25. Pierre Lellouche and D. Moisi, "French Policy in Africa: A Lonely Battle Against Destabilization," *International Security* 3, no. 1 (Spring 1979):108–133.

26. The monetary links between France and its former colonies again stand in marked contrast to anglophone Africa: By the middle of the 1980s, no African currency was linked to the pound sterling.

27. For a critical appraisal, see Guy Martin, "The Franc Zone: Underdevelopment and Dependency in Francophone Africa," *Third World Quarterly* 8, no. 1 (January 1986):205–235. Two recent quantitative studies have suggested that the economic performance of franc zone members is certainly no worse than that of other developing economies and is significantly better than the average for sub-Saharan Africa. Guillaumont, Guillaumont, and Plane attribute this to the relative commercial openness of franc zone countries and their relatively high levels of accumulation. Patrick Guillaumont, Sylviane Guillaumont, and Patrick Plane, "Participating in African Monetary Unions: An Alternative Evaluation," *World Development* 16, no. 5 (May 1988):569–576; see also Shantayanan Devarajan and Jaime De Melo, "Evaluating Participation in African Monetary Unions: A Statistical Analysis of the CFA Zones," *ibid.*, pp. 483–496.

28. International economic regimes are the institutions, norms, and rules that govern interaction in various economic issue areas.

29. Norman MacQueen, "Portugal and Africa: The Politics of Re-Engagement," *Journal of Modern African Studies* 23, no. 1 (April 1985):31–51.

30. John Ravenhill, "Renegotiating the Lome Conventions: A Little Is Preferable to Nothing," in I. William Zartman (ed.), *Positive Sum: Improving North-South Relations* (New Brunswick, N.J.: Transaction Publishers, 1987), pp. 213–258.

31. Ravenhill, *Collective Clientelism, passim.*

32. Martin Holland, *The European Community and South Africa* (London: Frances Pinter, 1988).

10

AFRICA AND THE MIDDLE EAST: PATTERNS OF CONVERGENCE AND DIVERGENCE

NAOMI CHAZAN AND VICTOR T. LEVINE

The Afro-Arab relationship has undergone considerable vacillation since the 1950s. On the one hand, contacts between black Africa and the Middle East, dormant throughout most of the colonial period, developed substantially both in scope and quantity during the postwar era. On the other, the quality of these links has varied dramatically. If during decolonization Arab states were little involved in the independence struggle south of the Sahara, in the 1960s the political emergence of Third-World states coupled with the growing Israeli presence in Africa accelerated Arab, and especially Egyptian, interest in the continent. The 1970s were marked by the forging of a short-lived, outward-oriented Afro-Arab alliance, which gradually unraveled during the 1980s. Clearly, beyond the unmistakable expansion of Afro-Arab links lies a history of both tension and durability. When do African and Middle Eastern concerns converge or diverge, and why? What accounts for the resilience of Afro-Arab ties, and what explains their fluctuations?

This chapter will explore first the constant and then the variable components of the association between Africa and the Middle East in an effort to identify areas of commonality and conflict and to illuminate ongoing trends. The starting point for this analysis is the assumption that the communities of Arab and African states simultaneously overlap *and* retain a historical and functional distinctiveness. Social, cultural, and religious ties have deep roots and have been sustained over time despite variations in range and strength. Functional interests, however, have dovetailed only occasionally: For most African states, relations with Europe, with the superpowers, and with countries beyond the Middle East have generally been far more significant economically and politically than have ties with Arab states (which in turn have usually viewed Africa as marginal to their own long-term preoccupations). Particular political and economic considerations, revolving primarily around the Arab-Israel conflict and certain economic exigencies, help to account for specific instances of Afro-Arab collaboration.

Peak periods of cooperation between African and Middle Eastern states (as in the mid-1970s) appear to have been associated with increased African unity and Arab solidarity, global economic recession, disenchantment with the West on the part of African and Middle Eastern countries, and heightened tensions between Arabs and Israelis. Differences have surfaced when intra-African and internal Arab discord has been apparent, superpower rivalry has been high, economic conditions have deteriorated substantially, or a lull has occurred on the Arab-Israel front. From the Arab perspective, therefore—the Islamic connection aside—instrumental political concerns closely linked to its conflict with Israel have usually guided the degree of its interest in the sub-Sahara, whereas for African states the coincidence of global closure and economic necessity has played an important role in the refinement of ties with the Arab world. These patterns suggest that in the 1990s, economic concerns will be secondary to cultural and religious bonds in Afro-Arab relations, while political considerations will continue to provide both opportunities and obstacles for ongoing interchange, mostly on the subregional level.

AFRO-ARAB RELATIONS: THE CONSTANTS

The African and Arab worlds interlock around four critical factors: geography, culture, history, and religion. Each of these elements, regardless of ephemeral variations, acts as an important adhesive in Afro-Arab relations and plays a role in determining the parameters of their interaction.

Historical and Social Links

Pre-Islamic contacts between the Middle East and Africa were centered on the Nile Delta and the Red Sea area. The Arabs of Muhammed's time were familiar with northeast Africa, and in 615 the prophet himself sent eighty of his persecuted followers to Abyssinia, where they received the protection of the Christian king.[1] During the middle of the seventh century, Muslim Arabs spread in force into North Africa; within a little over a hundred years, they conquered the entire Maghreb and reached Spain. At almost every step the Arab armies met fierce resistance, first from the remaining elements of the Christian Byzantine Empire and later (and much more formidably) from the indigenous Berber populations of what are today Tunisia, Algeria, and Morocco. Indeed, although converted to Islam and partly Arabized, to this day many Berbers continue to speak their own language and look upon Arabs as invaders and interlopers.

While Islamic armies drove westward across North Africa and south along the Nile River into the Sudan, Arab penetration overland across the Sahara and by sea along the East African coast followed the older, traditional patterns of trade, missionary activity, and settlement. When the Portuguese rounded the Cape at the beginning of the fifteenth century, they found a series of trading towns inhabited by peoples of Arab, African, and mixed African and Arab descent who owned large sailing fleets that conducted long-distance trade between East Africa and Arabia, India, and China. Some of these towns and nearby islands (such as Zanzibar and Pemba) gave rise to the Swahili culture (African in ethnic composition and Muslim and Arab in cultural orientation).

At the same time, commercial links were forged between North Africa and the central and western Sudan. The trans-Saharan trade was sustained by urban settlements (Timbuctoo, Gao, and Walata), which also became centers for the diffusion of Muslim-Arab culture and for the rise of the great precolonial empires of Ghana, Mali, and Songhai.[2] In these areas Islamic influences (language, customs, and religion) were introduced over a protracted period of time, gradually assuming an African character and striking deep roots in large portions of the Sahel and West Africa.

The Muslim penetration into Africa also provided a critical vehicle for the extensive Arab slave trade, which was conducted overland from West and central Africa along the trans-Saharan routes and from East Africa by sea to Arabia and the Persian Gulf area. Most African slaves were integrated into Arab society, although memories of the East African slave trade—which persisted well into the twentieth century—remained vivid in certain parts of the continent.[3]

The European intrusion into Africa had a twofold effect on African relations with the Middle East. On the one hand, the colonial conquest institutionalized political arrangements, formally separating the Maghreb from sub-Saharan Africa and virtually freezing opportunities for African contacts with the Arab world. Exchanges between Africa and the Middle East were conducted, if at all, within the framework of the imperial system. On the other hand, European rule facilitated Afro-Arab interactions (primarily in the Sahel regions of Mali, Mauritania, Chad, Niger, and Sudan) and contributed substantially to the spread of Islam on the continent. The rapid Islamization that took place under colonial auspices was partly a reaction to the Christianization efforts supported by the colonial powers and partly a natural outcome of the expansion of communication routes. By the middle of the twentieth century, therefore, "an important Arab socioreligious presence had become commonplace in much of Black Africa."[4]

The history of African relations with the Middle East and the Arab world highlights the themes of political ambiguity, cultural intermingling, and social separateness. Indeed, to speak of African–Middle East relations is already partly to deal in a geopolitical oxymoron: The five modern North African countries of the Maghreb (Morocco, Algeria, Tunisia, Libya, and Egypt) are considered an integral part of the Arab world. The Sahel states of Sudan, Mauritania, Somalia, and Djibouti are members of the Arab League. Together these countries, which constitute one-fifth of the states of the continent, encompass some 132,000,000 people—fully one-quarter of the total estimated population of the African continent.[5] On the basis of their religion, culture, and politics, they are part of both regions and are duly represented in both Arab and all-African institutions.

This geographic overlap, however, should not obscure demographic differences. The Arab residents of the Maghreb view themselves as distinct from the Africans south of the Sahara. In North Africa and the Middle East, the old notion of the *bilad as sudan* (the land of the blacks) survives as a psychological, if not an empirical, reality.[6] And along the coast of East Africa, descendants of Arab traders still see themselves as ethnoculturally separate from the African peoples originating in the hinterland. The contemporary physical contiguity of Arabs and Africans, a product of a long history of human interaction over time and space, has fostered both familiarity and ambivalence—attitudes that do not necessarily nurture mutual respect or induce cooperation.

Religious and Cultural Ties

In the past, Afro-Arab contacts generally accompanied the spread of Islam. Historically, the diffusion of Islam in Africa was accomplished through either conquest or peaceful conversion carried out by Muslim traders, preachers, or political leaders. Islam was initially propagated in sub-Saharan Africa by North African merchants who opened Koranic schools and built mosques in the trading cities of the west and central Sudan. They often succeeded in converting the ruling elites of these regions, who in turn helped to disseminate the faith farther to the south. The expansion and Africanization of Islam proceeded gradually in these regions between the eighth and eighteenth centuries, until the rise of militant states dedicated to Islamic reform pressed conversion through holy wars (*jihads*) against their neighbors. The Fulani states of Sokotoa and Macina, the Tukolor Empire established by El-Haj Omar, and the Manding state created by Samori Touré in the Guinea region all helped to implant Islam firmly in West and central Africa.

During the colonial period, Islamic institutions continued to flourish on the continent. Not only did the diffusion of Islam accelerate, but the religious leaders of the major Muslim brotherhoods (*turuq*)—such as the Qadiriyya, Tijaniyya, and (in Senegal) Muridiyya—became valuable allies of the European colonial rulers. Moreover, during this period, new Islamic orders—including the Wahhabiyya, the Ismailiyya, and the heterodox Ahmadiyya—gained adherents throughout the continent. By 1960 an estimated one out of every three residents of the continent was a Muslim.[7]

The period of independence also coincided with the rapid dissemination of Islam and the growth of Muslim institutions in Africa. However, in the 1950s and 1960s, efforts to propagate Islam were contained, not only because of the secular nature of African nationalism but also because of the paucity of direct contacts between newly independent African states and the central lands of Islam. These efforts revolved largely around Egypt, which under Gamal Abdel Nasser actively supported the creation of Islamic centers in the sub-Sahara and the training of Koranic teachers and Islamic leaders (either directly or through scholarships for African students to attend Al-Azhar University in Cairo).[8]

The pace of Islamization increased substantially in the 1970s. The activities of Libya following the rise of Muammar Qadhafi to power in 1969, coupled with growing Saudi Arabian involvement and ongoing Egyptian efforts at Islamization, contributed substantially to this process. The spread of Islam in the 1970s and 1980s was expedited by the demise of the first generation of African leaders who had espoused (at least initially) the separation of religion and politics, by rising anti-Western sentiment on the continent, by enhanced contacts between African and Arab leaders, and by the attraction of links with the Arab world in conditions of growing economic malaise.

A variety of means were used to promote the spread of Islam in this period.[9] First, generous grants were made by various Arab states to support the construction of mosques, schools, and Islamic centers throughout the continent. Second, Arab teachers were dispatched to African countries; subsidies for African scholars studying in Arab countries were augmented; plans were drawn up for the establishment of Muslim universities in Niger and Uganda; and endowments were made for chairs in Arabic and Islamic studies at major African universities. Third, Muslim communities in Africa were given direct financial support, mostly through the Islamic Development Bank established in 1974. Fourth, invitations were issued to African religious leaders to visit Arab countries, thus solidifying direct exchanges between Africa and the central countries of Islam. Fifth, monies were invested in radio broadcasts and publications aimed at African audiences. Finally, concerted efforts were made to convert African rulers to Islam, thereby increasing the opportunities for Islamic proselytization in their countries

(Omar Bongo of Gabon in 1973, Jean-Bedel Bokassa of the Central African Republic in 1976, and Mathieu Kerekou of Benin in 1980).

The results of these intensive actions have been to increase the number of African Muslims and to cement links between the Islamic world and Africa. By the end of the 1970s, the number of Muslims in Africa was well over 200 million and constantly growing.[10] With improved means of transportation, growing Islamic consciousness, and financial assistance provided by African governments, the number of African pilgrims performing the *hajj* to Mecca also increased, reaching over 250,000 annually by the beginning of the 1990s.

The strengthening of bonds between African and Arab Muslims has also been pursued by a variety of Arab agencies, including the Supreme Council for Islamic Affairs in Cairo, the Association for the Propagation of Islam (based in Tripoli), the Kuwaiti Office of Religious Trusts and Islamic Affairs, the Council for Islamic Coordination in Africa of the Arab League, and the Saudi-backed Muslim World League. African participation in pan-Islamic conferences has grown markedly, as has African membership in the Islamic Conference Organization (ICO) based in Jiddah, Saudi Arabia. Although only seven of fourteen invited black African states attended the first ICO summit in September 1969, by the fifth summit in 1986 the number had increased to eighteen (see Table 10.1 for 1990 estimates of percentages of Muslims in African countries).[11]

Clearly, the diffusion of Islam, and with it the Arabic language and Islamic culture, has magnified the importance of Middle East–African ties in recent years. Not only has Islam become an integral part of the contemporary African experience, but the significance of Islam as a political factor on the domestic level has also risen substantially.[12] Islamic assertiveness, to be sure, has also exacerbated tensions between Muslims and Christians in Africa (most recently in Nigeria, where an attempted Christian coup against the northern Muslim leadership was foiled in April 1990), given rise to fears of the Arabization of Islam in Africa, and accentuated the differences between countries with Muslim and Christian majorities on the continent (see Table 10.1). Nevertheless, Islam and its cultural legacy have provided an important and enduring bridge between the Arab world and Africa.

The historical, social, religious, and cultural experiences of Africa and the Middle East are simultaneously intertwined and distinct. Centuries of Arab penetration of the sub-Sahara and Arab condescension toward Africans, coupled with a lack of mutual knowledge, have cultivated distrust and even animosity.[13] At the same time, cultural and religious diffusion has made the Islamic dynamic an integral part of the African heritage. Both discord and potential cooperation have been most apparent when ambiguities have been especially salient: at the meeting point of Arab and African, Muslim

TABLE 10.1 Muslims in Africa: Estimated Percentage per Country, 1990

Arab Africa	
Algeria	99.9[a]
Egypt	91.5[a]
Morocco	98[a]
Sudan	73[a]
Libya	97[a]
Tunisia	99.9[a]

Sub-Saharan and Other Africa

Comoros	100[a]	Tanzania	35
Somalia	100[a]	Ethiopia	35
Mauritania	99[a]	Cameroon	25[a]
Djibouti	91[a]	Benin	20[a]
Senegal	91[a]	Ivory Coast	24
Niger	88[a]	Liberia	21
Mali	80[a]	Mauritius	18
Gambia	80[a]	Kenya	16
Guinea	70[a]	Ghana	16
Nigeria	45–50[a]	Mozambique	13
Chad	44[a]	Togo	10
Burkina Faso	43[a]	Rwanda	10
Sierra Leone	39[a]	Uganda	10[a]
Guinea-Bissau	38[a]		

Less than 5%: Angola, Botswana, Burundi, Cape Verde, Congo, Equatorial Guinea, Gabon[a], Lesotho, Madagascar, Malawi, Namibia, São Tomé and Príncipe, Seychelles, Swaziland, Zaire, Zambia, Zimbabwe

[a]Member of the Islamic Conference Organization.

Sources: Donald George Morrison et al., *Understanding Black Africa* (New York: Irvington Publishers–Paragon House, 1989), p. 80; Linda van Baren and Alan Rake (eds.), *New African Yearbook 1991–1992* (Edison, N.J.: IC Publications, 1991); Arye Oded, *Africa and the Middle East Conflict* (Boulder, Colo.: Lynne Rienner Publishers, 1987), p. 226; John Paxton (ed.), *The Statesman's Yearbook,* 125th ed. (New York: St. Martin's Press, 1990).

and Christian, the Maghreb and the Sahel. Interchanges at the geographic and human extremities of the continent have been more sporadic, reducing the relative intensity of the exchanges without mitigating their utility in given economic and political circumstances. The mixture of ambivalence and commonality therefore suggests that, variations in the frequency and substance of transactions notwithstanding, the Islamic impulse and the human and societal links forged over the centuries continue to bind Africa to the Middle East and to serve as lasting, long-term channels of ongoing communication between the two regions.

AFRO-ARAB RELATIONS IN THE POSTCOLONIAL PERIOD: THE VARIABLES

The more recent Afro-Arab connection has been most mutable in the political and economic spheres. These functional relations fall into three distinct phases: the first extending from 1957 to 1973, during which economic and political ties were elaborated slowly; the second from 1973 to 1978, when Afro-Arab solidarity peaked; and the third commencing with the signing of the Egyptian-Israeli peace accords in 1979, which has been accompanied by a fragmentation—although hardly a shattering—of the Afro-Arab alliance. These phases are visible in the nature and intensity of diplomatic and political, as well as aid and trade, relations between the two areas.

Political Links

Long-term Arab and African political interests have long revolved around their separate relationships with the industrialized world, which continues to be—protestations to the contrary notwithstanding—the principal focus of their respective international diplomacy. These broad preoccupations have converged in a shared concern for forging links with other Third-World states, used either as a mechanism for interacting with Europe and North America or as an alternative to such ties. Immediate political objectives have differed. For African states, issues related to decolonization were at the forefront of political initiatives until the 1990s. For Arab countries, the conflict with Israel has been paramount. Direct Afro-Arab political interactions have revolved around ongoing confrontations along the Sahel boundary (the eastern Horn, Sudan, Chad, and the western Sahara). The dynamic of the interplay surrounding each of these areas of contact has directly affected the cohesion and strength of the Afro-Arab alliance.

African Decolonization

The period of decolonization in North and sub-Saharan Africa, which commenced immediately after World War II, witnessed the emergence of anticolonial movements throughout the continent. The pursuit of independence in each of the regions, however, was conducted separately for the most part. Moroccan, Tunisian, and Algerian nationalists highlighted Arab and Islamic sentiments, while the emerging African leadership looked to the precolonial past and universal political tenets (such as self-determination) to buttress its claims for independence. Arab involvement in decolonization processes in black Africa was minimal in the 1950s, whereas

African troops were used by the French in Algeria, fomenting splits among African nationalists as well as divisions between them and their Arab counterparts. Regardless of rhetoric, contacts between Arabs and Africans during the first wave of independence were sporadic and not always mutually supportive.[14]

The role of Egypt in generating Afro-Arab ambivalence at this juncture was critical. Gamal Abdel Nasser viewed himself as a leader in the struggle against colonialism and imperialism in the Middle East and Africa. He pioneered the establishment of ties between Arab and African leaders and encouraged the creation of more formal frameworks for interaction (first through the Afro-Asian conference in Bandung in April 1955 and later through a series of pan-African and nonaligned conferences). He also provided sanctuary and assistance to a variety of African movements (often of a radical bent), thereby alienating other African groups. Most African leaders, although welcoming Nasser's overtures, disputed his claim to the leadership of the African struggle, questioned his revolutionary methods, and took umbrage at his condescension toward Africans.[15] In the early 1960s, the creation of the Casablanca bloc—which united Africa's progressive states of Ghana, Guinea, and Mali with Egypt, Morocco, and Algeria—underlined the split between sub-Saharan Africa's moderate camp (the Monrovia and Lagos groups) and the Afro-Arab radicals.

The first African Summit Conference held in Addis Ababa in 1963, at which the Organization of African Unity (OAU) was founded, had the dual effect of isolating Nasser and his militant ideas of Arab-led African unity and of incorporating the North African states into the new continental body.[16] The composition of the founding membership of the OAU thus formalized Arab participation in African institutions while rebuffing the Arab agenda for the continent. Pan-Arabism was thus separated from pan-Africanism, and the basis for their interaction was established. The incorporation of North African states into African agencies assured that they would back OAU decisions regarding African liberation movements in international forums and that they would lobby other Middle Eastern countries to follow suit. Indeed, throughout the second wave of African liberation struggles in the 1960s and 1970s, the Arab world—at least ostensibly—supported African positions on a wide range of issues.

The common verbal commitment to the struggle against colonialism was not always pursued in fact. Only in 1973 did Middle Eastern states respond to the OAU call to break diplomatic relations with South Africa and Rhodesia and impose economic sanctions on these countries. From the outset, it was clear that many Middle East states did not adhere to this boycott. In 1975, disclosures were made of Jordanian arms sales to Rhodesia; in the 1970s and 1980s, Somalia, Iraq, and Morocco entered into covert military deals with South Africa involving training as well as the purchase of South African weapons; Saudi Arabia and the United Arab Emirates provided key markets for South African gold; and, most significantly, almost all the oil-producing states in the Middle East continued to supply South Africa with much-needed petroleum products.[17] As evidence of Arab activities in South Africa mounted during the course of the 1980s, a rift began to develop between the OAU (including the Maghreb states) and some Middle Eastern countries on matters related to the ongoing struggle in South Africa. Although President Mubarak of Egypt (then chairman of the OAU) hosted Nelson Mandela in the spring of 1990, the activities of other Middle Eastern states vis-à-vis South Africa were increasingly called into question.

The checkered history of Arab support for the national liberation cause in Africa highlights the provisional nature of Arab involvement in critical African issues. Strong Middle Eastern support of African nationalist demands has been greatest either when these demands have not clashed with Arab aspirations or when they have coincided with Arab anti-Zionist or anti-imperial claims. In effect, insofar as the Arab effort to link Arab and African nationalist movements has been invoked as a matter of convenience[18] and insofar as African resolutions have not always been deemed binding on Middle East states, African confidence in Arab dependability on these subjects remains equivocal.

The Arab-Israel Conflict

If African political approaches to the Middle East countries have focused largely on decolonization, Arab interests have undoubtedly revolved primarily around the quest for African support in the Arab-Israel dispute. African attitudes toward Israel therefore furnish a key (albeit hardly the only) manifestation of convergence and divergence in Afro-Arab relations. The Arab-Israel conflict was introduced into Africa initially at Israel's insistence (1957–1973) and then as a result of Arab pressures (1967–1980). Only in the 1980s, with the crystallization of African support for the Palestinian cause, did the Arab-Israel conflict undergo a process of Africanization.[19]

In 1956, a year before Ghana became the first black African state to gain independence from colonial rule, Israel established a consulate in Accra, signaling the beginning of a decade of intense diplomatic, economic, and technical assistance activities on the continent.[20] By the middle of the 1960s, Israel had dispatched over two thousand Israeli experts to Africa (in the fields of agriculture, medicine, social work, community development, regional planning, education, and military training) and had hosted over ten thousand African trainees in these spheres in Israel. Several Israeli companies (Solel Boneh, Tahal, Zim Navigation, Teva Pharmaceuticals, Coor Industries, Meier Brothers, and Federman Construction) undertook projects in Africa, and trade relations commenced—albeit on a small scale. Within ten years Israeli diplomatic activity encompassed thirty-three newly independent African states, providing Israel with much-needed breathing space in international forums.

Until 1967, Arab states were unable to make substantial headway in confronting Israel in the African arena, as sub-Saharan countries prevented discussion of the issue at OAU gatherings. The 1967 war and the resulting occupation of Arab (and especially Egyptian) territories marked the beginning of a turning point in this regard.[21] In solidarity with the Arab position, Guinea ruptured diplomatic relations with Israel in 1967. Arab diplomatic efforts were stepped up, and appeals by Arab leaders (including the new Egyptian president, Anwar Sadat, and King Faisal of Saudi Arabia) to Third-World unity, Afro-Arab solidarity, and anti-Western feelings began to have an impact. In 1971, for the first time, the OAU summit voted to demand Israeli withdrawal from the occupied territories and sent a commission of four "wise men" to the Middle East to help mediate the conflict. Israeli disregard for the African mission coupled with growing African disaffection with the West combined to prod sub-Saharan states to identify more firmly with the united Arab position presented at that time.[22] In 1972 Uganda, Chad, Niger, and the Congo severed ties with Israel, and by the end of 1973—just before, during, and after the October 1973 war—all but four African states (Malawi, Lesotho, Swaziland, and Mauritius) had broken diplomatic relations with Israel.[23]

The reasons for Israel's diplomatic setback are varied. The immediate impetus for the massive African dissociation from Israel was African identification with Egypt, especially after Israeli troops crossed the Suez Canal into continental Africa during the October war. But substantial weight must also be given to African and Third-World unity at this juncture, to growing African reluctance to accept the continuing Israeli occupation of Arab territories, and to African disillusionment with Western aid. To be sure, the 1973 oil crisis and Arab financial inducements also played a role, especially in the decision by some of Israel's long-standing allies (such as Kenya, Côte d'Ivoire, Ethiopia, and Botswana) to sever ties. In all probability, however, at this point neither the Islamic factor nor Israel's relations with South Africa was of central importance.[24]

By the beginning of 1974, the transition from African avoidance of the Arab-Israel question to African support of the Arab position had been completed. This backing not only affirmed the consolidation of Third-World solidarity in the mid-1970s but also triggered the further diplomatic isolation of Israel in the international community, culminating in the acceptance by the United Nations General Assembly of the equation of Zionism with racism.[25] Arab diplomatic activity in Africa was stepped up, with Iraq, Saudi Arabia, Syria, Qatar, and South Yemen opening new missions in sub-Saharan states and African representation in the Arab world increasing proportionately. In 1977, the first Afro-Arab Summit Conference was held in Cairo in an effort to formalize the new alliance.[26]

Later in 1977, however, with Sadat's visit to Jerusalem and the commencement of the Israeli-Egyptian peace negotiations at Camp David, previous signs of unease about Afro-Arab relations rose to the surface.[27] The African response to the Israeli-Egyptian Accords was mixed, mirroring reactions in the Middle East. The debate between Egypt and Sudan on the one hand and between Egypt and other Arab states on the other was translated to OAU forums in 1979 and 1980. Rejectionist attempts to isolate Egypt and to expel it from the OAU and other Third-World bodies were blocked by African states, but many leaders voiced their reservations about Egyptian moves. Afro-Arab multilateral arrangements broke down, and African states were drawn into the uncertainties affecting Arab politics at this time.[28] The turn of the decade was characterized by increasing discord in the Arab world, the rise of Islamic fundamentalism in the wake of the Iranian revolution, the commencement of the Iran-Iraq war, and growing Libyan adventurism in sub-Saharan Africa.

Under these circumstances, it appeared that the African pendulum would once again shift in the Israeli direction. The Israeli-Egyptian rapprochement eliminated the declared reason for the severance of diplomatic ties in the early 1970s. Moreover, Israeli activities in Africa, which had never completely ceased after 1973, took on new momentum. Israeli trade and investment in black Africa grew in the late 1970s, along with the revival of aid operations. Military contacts between Israel and several African states were established; Israeli and African leaders began to meet on a regular basis; and Israeli-African diplomatic encounters in various forums improved. Israeli officials were encouraged about the prospects of a return to Africa, and the issue of the restoration of diplomatic relations with Israel began to be debated in African capitals.[29]

The optimism expressed in pro-Israeli circles at the beginning of the 1980s did not, however, take into account the substantial growth and heterogeneous character of Afro-Arab relations in the 1970s. These observers failed to attribute sufficient significance to Egyptian reluctance to assist Israel in its attempts to return to Africa and to note the fundamental shift that had occurred in African perceptions of the conflict. If in the past African positions toward the Arab-Israel dispute had been shaped by longstanding empathy for Egypt, by the time of the signing of the Camp David Accords independent African attitudes toward the conflict had coalesced around support for Palestinian self-determination and Israeli withdrawal from the territories occupied in 1967. Without casting doubts on Israel's right to exist, the Palestine Liberation Organization (PLO) was seen in many African capitals as the legitimate representative of the Palestinian people. Displeased with Israeli policies in the West Bank and Gaza and unhappy about the annexation of Jerusalem, African leaders had gradually formulated their own stance on the conflict—perhaps best articulated in the 1980 OAU resolution passed in Freetown: In their opinion, a lasting peace in the Middle East could be reached only through "the exercise of the Palestinian people of their inalienable rights, especially the right to return to their motherland and recover their national sovereignty [and] their self-determination without any foreign interference whatsoever and through the establishment of an independent state in their own territory."[30]

Assessments of the prospects for the renewal of African-Israeli ties also did not factor in changes in Israel's own positions and actions. From an African perspective, Israel had come to be increasingly associated with the West in general and the United States in particular. Moreover, Israeli foreign policymakers—by increasingly tying Israel's diplomatic fortunes closely to U.S. concerns—evinced little interest in Third-World and African affairs, made precious few preparations for a possible resumption of diplomatic and aid efforts, showed minimal understanding of Africa's growing economic predicament or of changes in global alignments, and proved insensitive to major African interests.[31] This was particularly true with respect to the Israeli–South African relationship, which flourished after the upgrading of Israel's diplomatic representation in Pretoria in 1974 and Prime Minister John Vorster's visit to Jerusalem in 1976. The growing economic, commercial, and military collaboration between Israel and South Africa was severely condemned by African leaders, who singled out Israel (as opposed to many other countries) for cynically pursuing its own goals without due regard for African aspirations. Israel's South African connection, an incidental factor at the outset of the 1970s, had by the close of the decade become a very real constraint on the revival of Afro-Israeli links.[32]

These developments in African relations with Israel and the Arab world set the stage for the launching of a new, more independent phase in African approaches to the Arab-Israel conflict, one in which pragmatism prevailed and neither side of the conflict could lay exclusive claim to African sympathies. In the 1980s, Israel—in search of international acceptance and respectability and an end to diplomatic isolation—embarked on a concerted drive to increase its representation on the continent. Spearheaded in 1981 by David Kimche, the newly appointed director-general of the Israeli Foreign Ministry, an all-out effort was made to woo African leaders. Although Israel's basic political, economic, and strategic motives for involvement in Africa did not change perceptibly, different methods were employed: Unlike the policies of the 1960s, military assistance as well as development aid became a key instrument of Israel's new African policy, although direct commitment of Israeli resources to African projects was reduced. What did remain in any case were extensive, unofficial relationships pragmatically fostered through Israelis and Israeli companies quietly operating throughout the continent. Despite several high-level visits of Israeli ministers to Africa, the restoration of diplomatic ties by several African states was delayed—first by the imposition of Israeli law on the Golan Heights, then by the Israeli invasion of Lebanon in June 1982, and later by the beginning of the Palestinian uprising (*intifada*) in December 1987. Nevertheless, by the end of the 1980s, eight African states (Zaire, Liberia, Côte d'Ivoire, Cameroon, Togo, Kenya, the Central African Republic, and Ethiopia) had reestablished full diplomatic relations with Israel.[33]

Most African states, although unwilling to denounce the actions of those who resumed ties with Israel, preferred not to follow suit. In part, they chose to keep any relationships with Israel on the informal level; in part, they did not share the internal security concerns of some of Israel's new partners;[34] and in part, they did not need to rely on Israel's good offices in Washington. Moreover, many sought to avoid alienating Arab states, whose economic assistance—however disappointing—they viewed as critical.[35] Nor could they reconcile themselves to Israel's ongoing relationship with South Africa, which—despite declared policy shifts in 1987—nevertheless continued apace.[36]

For the most part, however, African states—including those who had reentered a diplomatic partnership with Israel—rallied to the Palestinian cause. By 1990, thirty-four African states had recognized the November 1988 PLO declaration of Palestinian independence, and thirty-one had established full diplomatic relations with the PLO.[37] The fifty-second meeting of the OAU foreign ministers, held in Addis Ababa in July 1990, reiterated African support for an international peace conference and for negotiations with the PLO, denounced Israel's intransigence, and expressed concern over possible Israeli intentions to settle Soviet immigrants in the occupied territories.[38]

The Arab-Israel conflict, so central a pivot of Africa's relations with the Middle East, was exported by the main protagonists into the African environment. By 1990, the majority of African states had carved out a position that highlighted their own preoccupation with issues of self-determination, implicitly suggesting that they viewed other aspects of the conflict as marginal to sub-Saharan concerns. They thereby served notice that in subscribing to the Palestinian cause and questioning Israeli policy, they neither rejected contacts with Israel nor blindly accepted Arab dictates on these issues. In these circumstances, it is not unreasonable to assume that relations with Israel will continue to be an excellent indicator of the status of the Afro-Arab connection.[39]

AFRICAN-ARAB CONFRONTATIONS

Political Ties

The mutual political interests of Arabs and sub-Saharan African states have centered on the prolonged conflicts that have plagued the entire Sahel belt. Along the desert frontier, between Arab and black African civil wars, insurrections and interstate conflicts have festered since the early years of independence, periodically erupting into outright warfare.

The first round of these conflagrations, whose foundations were laid in the colonial demarcation of the continent, appeared in the 1960s—first in the Sudan, and then in the eastern Horn and the western Sahara. During the first decade of African independence, Moroccan irredentist claims to portions of the Spanish Sahara, Mauritania, Mali, and Algeria—together with the debilitating civil war in the Sudan and the emergence of the Eritrean liberation fronts—exacerbated tensions within the continent and unsettled efforts to consolidate continental unity.[40] By the beginning of the 1970s, the intensity of these confrontations had abated somewhat. Morocco had backed down from its Mauritanian escapade of the 1960s; the economic situation and internal fragmentation in Ethiopia had temporarily reduced the salience of the Eritrean question; and the 1972 Addis Ababa agreements between the southern Sudanese rebels and the central government had, at least for a while, stabilized the situation in that country.

In the first half of the 1970s, the rise of Muammar Qadhafi shifted the locus of conflict to the central Sahel, particularly to Chad. The Spanish withdrawal from the western Sahara in 1975, however, reignited the Moroccan–Mauritanian–Algerian conflict and introduced the Polisario as a new contestant in this arena. By the mid-1970s, the Ethiopian revolution had not only refueled the Eritrean struggle but provoked the Somali-Ethiopian Ogaden War of 1977–1978. And by the end of the decade, the bloody struggle between north and south in the Sudan had broken out anew. The mixture of poverty, instability, and external intervention combined to escalate Afro-Arab clashes, seriously affecting the cohesion of the OAU (first through the Moroccan-led boycott of eighteen African states in 1981 and then by the cancellation of the 1982 summit scheduled to take place in Tripoli).

The involvement of Middle East states on the side of the Eritreans and the Sudanese government has been fairly consistent. But in the Saharawi, Chad, and Somali disputes, Arab states have been divided among themselves. Algeria and Libya supported the Polisario against Morocco. Many members of the Arab League backed the Somali invasion of the Ogaden, but South Yemen, Iraq, and Libya denounced the move. And Libyan interventions in Chad, although not overtly challenged in the Arab world, were hardly welcomed by moderate Arab countries.[41] Throughout the 1980s, these wars persisted, constantly underscoring intra-African and Arab divisions and the difficulties they represented for the Afro-Arab relationship.

The vagaries of the political ties between African and Middle Eastern states reflect not only the heterogeneous interests of the parties involved but also their varying long-range and immediate priorities. Pragmatic considerations have alternately sown discord and permitted periods of solidarity and joint action. After more than three decades of African independence, however, it has become abundantly clear that neither the Arabs nor the Africans can take each other's support for granted and that both sides have raised the price of Afro-Arab solidarity considerably. Differences among Middle Eastern states and inequalities within Africa have highlighted the variability of pragmatic concerns and focused attention on the unresolved tensions in those regional flashpoints at which African and Arab objectives clash.

Economic Links

The Afro-Arab economic relationship evolved initially as a byproduct of political ties and tended to reflect specific political interests. The intense economic activities generated in the 1970s had stabilized by the beginning of the 1980s. The trends set in motion in the first three decades of independence, while fluctuating with shifting political purposes, nevertheless established the foundation for continuous—albeit still modest—economic relationships in the future. In this new equation, capital, raw materials, markets, resource mobility, and geographic proximity all play a potentially significant role.

African economic relations with the Arab states of the Middle East were sparse during the first decade of independence, although small amounts of trade and aid were provided by Egypt and, even more marginally, by Saudi Arabia. Toward the end of the 1960s, economic contacts were stepped up, and in the early 1970s, the petrodollar weapon was skillfully wielded by Libya, Algeria, and Saudi Arabia in their efforts to persuade African states to terminate their links with Israel. The year 1973 was a watershed in Arab-African economic relations: The oil crisis and the Arab use of financial aid to maintain the alliance with Africa yielded a dramatic rise in Arab assistance, investment, and trade in the sub-Sahara.[42]

Between 1973 and 1983, total bilateral and multilateral Arab aid to non-Arab African countries amounted to $8.3 billion, of which $5.3 billion was disbursed to assist projects and $2.9 billion constituted nonproject allocations (see Fig. 10.1).[43] Arab support was funneled through several multilateral institutions established for this purpose, the most important of which are the Arab Bank for the Economic Development of Africa, the Special Arab Fund for Africa (SAAFA), the Arab Fund for Technical Assistance to African and Arab Countries, and the OPEC Fund for International Development. The bulk of Arab aid to Africa, however, had been disbursed bilaterally, with Saudi Arabia, Kuwait, the United Arab Emirates, and Qatar (in that order) emerging as the key donors. Iraq, Algeria, Libya, and Egypt contributed smaller sums.[44] These flows accounted for nearly 25 percent of all development assistance to Africa in the 1970s.[45]

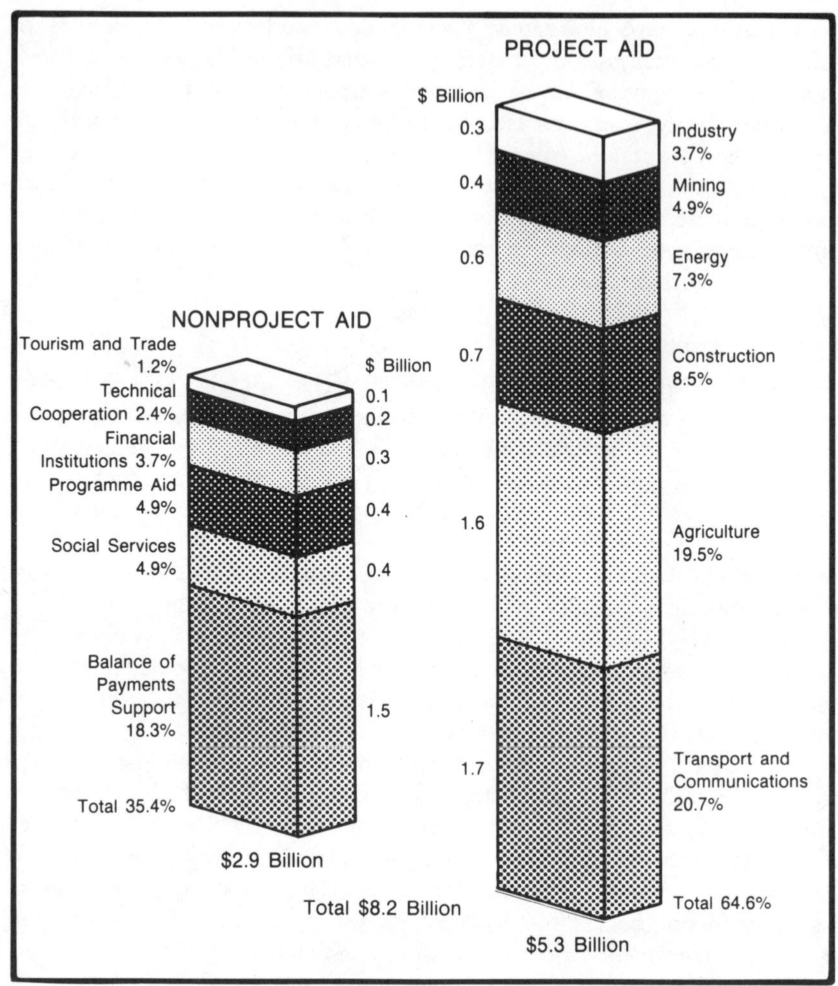

FIGURE 10.1 Breakdown of Arab financial transfers to Africa by sector and type of aid (1975–1983). *Source:* The Arab Bank for the Economic Development of Africa, *Annual Report 1984* (Khartoum: BADEA, 1987), p. 17.

Regardless of the considerable amounts involved, Arab aid to Africa nevertheless aroused controversy. In the first place, the allotment to African states represented only about 12 percent of all Arab assistance during the 1970s. Moreover, of Arab aid to sub-Saharan African states, two countries—Mauritania and Sudan (both members of the Arab League)—accounted for close to 50 percent, with almost all of the rest going to ten other countries (Guinea, Senegal, Zaire, Kenya, Uganda, Zambia, Mali, Niger, Chad, and Cameroon).[46] Second, it became apparent that most Arab aid was contingent on political support and religious considerations and therefore did not meet the nearly desperate needs of many of Africa's most impoverished countries. Third, investments in Africa as opposed to aid were limited to a few select and economically promising countries (Nigeria, Cameroon, Côte d'Ivoire, and Kenya) and, although reliable figures are unavailable, in all probability did not exceed $1.5 billion in the 1970s (only a fraction of Arab investments in the West). Finally, by the end of the decade, a gap had developed between Arab commitments and actual aid allocations, and the agreements negotiated at the Afro-Arab summit only partially dispelled rising discontent in African capitals.

In retrospect, however, the most serious repercussion of the Afro-Arab relationship was the impact of the high cost of oil imports on the floundering economies of most African states. Africa's non–oil producing developing countries paid about $700 million for oil in 1973. By 1976 that figure had spiraled to $6 billion, in 1980 to $11 billion, and in 1983 to $13 billion. The $350 million granted by SAAFA to help defray these new costs was laughable under the circumstances, as African countries borrowed heavily—often from Arab sources—to cover rising oil import bills. As the African economic crisis worsened, the economic trends set in motion by Arab policies had rendered African states not only more vulnerable to changes in the international environment but, ironically, also increasingly dependent on the West and less capable of fending for themselves. African demands for concessionary prices were left unanswered, and trade imbalances between African states and the Middle East intensified.

The spurt in Afro-Arab economic activity lessened in the 1980s with the reduction of oil revenues in Arab countries, the deterioration in African economic capacities, the decline in the importance of OPEC, and the decreasing Arab propensity to use economic leverage to lure or pressure African support. Although Arab financial assistance to Africa continued, it fell far below 1970s averages and constituted an even smaller percentage of total African receipts during this period. Trade relations also contracted. Between 1982 and 1988, Middle Eastern exports to Africa went down by over $1 billion (from $3.230 billion to $2.085 billion), and imports from Africa were stabilized (see Table 10.2).[47] Data on investments demonstrates that at the close of the 1980s, at least from the separate perspectives of the African and Arab states, their respective economic associations with the West far outweighed the significance attributed to nurturing their mutual relationship.

Nevertheless, economic ties between the African continent and the Middle East, the difficulties noted above notwithstanding, have expanded substantially since 1973. If in the 1970s the aid element was paramount, in the 1980s the importance of trade relations grew for certain African states. The opening of Middle East markets for African products became

TABLE 10.2 Middle East Exports to and Imports from Africa (millions of U.S. dollars)

		Exports							Imports						
		1982	1983	1984	1985	1986	1987	1988	1982	1983	1984	1985	1986	1987	1988
IFS World Total		176,161	137,065	121,972	113,697	87,580	100,697	—	140,354	134,311	121,773	102,892	94,053	94,965	—
DOTS World Total	001	167,968	138,314	127,314	112,518	80,661	97,173	100,508	139,641	132,558	119,568	102,324	91,350	95,909	110,632
Developing Countries	200	58,829	49,424	44,839	38,538	26,224	32,330	34,689	32,409	31,287	30,288	27,267	23,423	25,981	31,603
Africa	605	3,230	2,333	2,354	1,964	1,502	1,918	2,085	1,181	1,147	1,071	981	964	960	1,167
Algeria	612	58	41	44	34	26	51	77	14	68	55	3	56	1	2
Angola	614	17	15	15	14	12	14	16	—	—	—	—	—	1	—
Botswana	616	1	—	—	—	—	2	3	25	23	10	3	2	2	3
Burkina Faso	748	1	—	—	—	—	—	—	—	—	—	2	—	—	—
Burundi	618	27	24	29	27	20	23	20	—	—	—	—	—	—	—
Cameroon	622	8	—	1	1	3	4	5	3	2	—	1	1	—	—
Cape Verde	624	—	—	—	1	—	—	—	—	—	—	—	—	—	1
Central African Rep.	626	—	—	—	—	—	—	—	—	—	1	—	—	—	—
Chad	628	2	2	2	2	1	2	2	1	1	1	1	1	1	1
Comoros	632	—	—	4	—	—	—	—	—	—	—	—	—	—	—
Congo	634	—	—	—	5	1	1	1	—	—	—	—	6	7	7
Côte d'Ivoire	662	93	23	25	2	1	2	2	15	6	6	5	4	8	11
Djibouti	611	39	47	41	71	70	83	95	16	21	25	24	17	20	24
Ethiopia	644	13	28	29	25	32	38	60	75	66	52	51	26	37	42
Gabon	646	1	1	—	—	1	—	—	10	10	8	9	14	16	22
Gambia, The	648	—	—	—	—	1	—	—	—	—	—	—	—	—	—
Ghana	652	100	6	2	2	3	3	3	13	4	4	5	4	4	4
Guinea	656	2	1	—	—	—	1	1	10	9	11	11	11	14	16
Kenya	664	574	424	448	313	228	238	257	67	36	38	36	63	59	67

Lesotho	666	—	—	—	—	—	1	1	—	—	—	—	—	—	—
Liberia	668	55	1	—	2	4	1	2	8	1	4	4	8	1	2
Madagascar	674	89	52	68	48	14	32	34	—	1	—	—	1	—	—
Malawi	676	1	2	1	1	1	—	—	3	6	7	2	10	9	11
Mali	678	—	—	—	—	1	2	2	1	1	1	1	1	1	1
Mauritania	682	11	—	—	6	1	4	4	—	—	—	10	8	1	2
Mauritius	684	61	56	42	63	45	63	43	—	—	—	—	—	—	—
Morocco	686	825	701	753	473	332	490	494	69	90	111	120	110	134	178
Mozambique	688	49	47	38	37	62	64	67	11	30	11	5	4	8	3
Niger	692	1	—	—	—	—	—	—	—	—	—	—	—	—	—
Nigeria	694	62	45	28	18	27	38	43	2	5	4	3	4	3	5
Reunion	696	62	55	55	65	53	63	76	—	—	—	—	—	—	—
Rwanda	714	—	—	1	4	15	12	15	—	—	—	—	—	—	—
Senegal	722	1	8	—	—	8	2	2	3	3	1	—	—	—	—
Seychelles	718	11	14	6	5	9	14	13	—	—	—	—	—	—	—
Sierra Leone	724	—	1	—	2	—	2	2	—	—	—	—	—	—	—
Somalia	726	76	69	81	43	27	27	28	123	115	58	111	82	88	103
South Africa	199	78	83	106	63	66	79	102	168	170	173	175	203	214	207
Sudan	732	409	290	240	337	201	300	334	275	262	231	248	156	156	185
Swaziland	734	—	—	—	—	—	—	—	63	51	52	29	18	15	15
Tanzania	738	208	145	131	163	109	125	136	12	15	15	6	7	6	8
Tunisia	744	47	60	83	62	66	60	85	96	89	118	53	77	70	127
Uganda	746	13	9	9	6	5	6	6	11	8	7	8	7	8	9
Zaire	636	3	2	3	—	3	3	4	2	4	10	3	—	—	—
Zambia	754	199	61	9	21	11	4	6	6	1	1	4	8	26	30
Zimbabwe	698	—	—	7	—	3	1	1	68	20	41	22	28	23	46
Africa, not specified	789	35	21	51	47	40	65	42	13	32	15	25	28	28	36

IFS: International Financial Statistics; DOTS: Direction of Trade Statistics.

Source: International Monetary Fund, *Direction of Trade Statistics Yearbook, 1989* (Washington, D.C.: IMF, 1989), p. 38.

a significant component of the external commerce of countries such as Djibouti, Ethiopia, Kenya, Mozambique, Somalia, and Zimbabwe. This suggests that at least for those African states with easy access routes to Saudi Arabia and the Persian Gulf, contacts established during the 1970s paved the way for the elaboration of more enduring ties. Moreover, the Arab world had become a magnet for skilled and unskilled African labor, augmenting the movement of human resources between the two regions. Thus, although economic relations in the 1990s could not be expected to reach the unrealistic levels of the 1970s and the damage wreaked on African economies by Arab oil policies will take years to dispel, these activities did set the stage for the amplification of long-term economic relations between the two regions in the last decade of the century.

Political and economic relations between Africa and the Middle East have highlighted the tenuous nature of joint instrumental concerns. This connection has been affected not only by the intrusion of extraneous topics onto the Afro-Arab agenda but also by the resilience of other interests directed elsewhere. Africa's relations with the Middle East evolved in the first instance because of the political pressures applied by the participants in the Arab-Israel conflict. More than thirty years later, however, the relative importance of politics and economics has been reversed. The Arab states and Israel developed a growing recognition that their standing in Africa depended in no small measure on their ability to address Africa's pressing development needs. From an African perspective, the salience of economic concerns also suggested that they would increasingly assume center stage in the links of the African states to the Middle East. In the interim, it is reasonable to assume that political relations will continue to remain in a state of flux.

AFRICA AND THE MIDDLE EAST: TRENDS AND IMPLICATIONS

The Middle East–African association has been predicated on an unusual admixture of deep social, cultural, religious, and historical roots and very modern economic and political interactions. The fluctuating fortunes of these relations have depended less on the ongoing relevance of cultural connections and more on shifting global configurations, separate interests, and constraints or opportunities presented by changing relations within each of these regions. Despite the tumultuous features that have accompanied these contacts since 1960, it is nevertheless abundantly clear that for both sets of parties, exchanges with each other have come to assume a greater significance than ties with any other region beyond the Western world.

The future of the relations between African and Middle Eastern states in the 1990s will continue to be heavily influenced by the way international constellations shape up and especially by the structural changes that will accompany the reduction of superpower rivalry as well as the processes of liberalization in Eastern Europe and of unifications in Western Europe. Shifts in intra-Arab relations will also play an important role. The reincorporation of Egypt into the Arab League in the 1980s coincided with greater Egyptian involvement in continental affairs. But the precarious nature of relations between Arab states (most recently demonstrated by the Iraqi invasion and annexation of Kuwait) has lessened both their concern with Africa affairs and their capacity to design a unified African policy. And the lack of resolution in the Arab-Israel conflict has suggested that Africa will continue to be marginal to the central political concerns of the protagonists in this seemingly interminable dispute. From the African vantage point as well, the centrality of domestic preoccupations has signaled an unwillingness to enter into political commitments whose benefits are not immediately visible.

Under these circumstances, the course of African relations with the Middle East will be determined in the next few years primarily by economic and religious factors. This trend, unlike past processes, points in an inward-oriented direction. Both conflict and cooperation will be most evident in East Africa and where Islam meets Christianity on the continent. Thus, as subregional contacts gradually assume center stage, relations with other parts of the continent will probably become even more ambiguous and heterogeneous. By replicating existing patterns of overlap and separation, these relations will thereby add new dimensions to the complex and varied features that have marked African–Middle Eastern links in the recent past.

NOTES

1. For background information, see Joseph M. Cuoq, *Les Musulmans en Afrique* (Paris: G. P. Maisonneuve et Larose, 1975); James Kritzeck and William H. Lewis (eds.), *Islam in Africa* (New York: Van Nostrand, 1969); I. M. Lewis (ed.), *Islam in Tropical Africa*, 2nd ed. (London: Hutchinson, 1980); Vincent Monteil, *L'Islam Noir*, 3rd ed. (Paris: Seuil, 1980); and Mervyn Hiskett, *The Development of Islam in West Africa* (New York: Longman, 1984).

2. For details, see Nehemia Levtzion, *Ancient Ghana and Mali* (London: Methuen, 1973).

3. For more details, see Arye Oded, "Slaves and Oil: The Arab Image in Black Africa," *The Weiner Library Bulletin* 27 (new series), no. 332 (1974):34–47; and Bernard Lewis, *Race and Slavery in the Middle East* (New York: Oxford University Press, 1990).

4. Victor T. LeVine and Timothy W. Luke, *The Arab-African Connection: Political and Economic Realities* (Boulder, Colo.: Westview Press, 1979), p. 2.

5. These figures are calculated on the basis of information supplied by the World Bank, *Financing Adjustment with Growth in Sub-Saharan Africa, 1986–1990* (Washington, D.C.: World Bank, 1986).

6. In some parts of the Maghreb blacks are still referred to as *abdi* (slaves), and many poor villages in Morocco and Algeria are populated by the descendents of black slaves. The clashes between Senegal and Mauritania in 1989 and 1990 highlighted the ongoing distinction between "white" and "black" Moors and valley blacks in Mauritania (a country that only recently abolished slavery).

7. Ibrahim Abu-Lughod, "Africa and the Islamic World," in John N. Paden and Edward W. Soja (eds.), *The African Experience: Volume I: Essays* (Evanston: Northwestern University Press, 1970), p. 548.

8. See Jacques Baulin, *The Arab Role in Africa* (London: Penguin, 1962).

9. For details, see Arye Oded, *Africa and the Middle East Conflict* (Boulder, Colo.: Lynne Rienner Publishers, 1987), pp. 33–54.

10. Richard Weekes (ed.), *Muslim Peoples: A World Ethnographic Survey* (Westport, Conn.: Greenwood Press, 1978).

11. Arye Oded, "Islam in Afro-Arab Relations," *Middle East Review* 18, no. 3 (Spring 1986): 15–23. Also see Oded, *Africa and the Middle East Conflict*, pp. 47–49; and Umari Kokole, "The Islamic Factor in African-Arab Relations," *Third World Quarterly* 6, no. 3 (1984):687–702.

12. Nehemia Levtzion, "International Islamic Solidarity and Its Limitations," Jerusalem Papers on Peace Problems, no. 29 (Jerusalem: The Leonard Davis Institute for International Relations, 1979).

13. Dunstan M. Wai, "Afro-Arab Relations: Misplaced Optimism," in UNESCO, *Historical and Socio-Cultural Relations Between Black Africa and the Arab World from 1935 to the Present*, UNESCO General History of Africa, Studies and Documents no. 7 (Paris: UNESCO, 1984), pp. 68–69.

14. Abdul Aziz Jalloh, "The Policies of the Black African States Toward the Arab World: An Overview," in UNESCO, *Historical and Socio-Cultural Relations*, p. 19. Also see Olusola Ojo, "The Role of the Arab World in the Decolonization Process of Black Africa," *International Problems* 20, nos. 2–4 (1981):73–84.

15. Nasser, while reminding Arabs of their obligations toward Africans, also tended to phrase his remarks in patronizing terms: "We certainly cannot . . . relinquish our responsibility to help spread the light of knowledge and civilization up to the very depth of the virgin jungles of the Continent." See Gamal A. Nasser, *The Philosophy of the Revolution* (Cairo: National Publishing House, 1954), p. 69.

16. For details, see LeVine and Luke, *The Arab-African Connection*, pp. 2–7, and Tareq Ismael, *The U.A.R. and Africa* (Evanston: Northwestern University Press, 1971).

17. For details, see Oded, *Africa and the Middle East Conflict*, pp. 148–154; Layiwola Abegunrin, "The Arabs and the Southern African Problems," *International Affairs* 60, no. 1 (1983–1984):97–105; and Shipping Research Bureau, "How They Break the Oil Embargo: Oil Tankers to South Africa" (Amsterdam: Shipping Research Bureau, 1980–1983).

18. See Houari Boumedienne's statement at the OAU meeting in May 1973: "Africa cannot adopt one attitude towards colonialism in Southern Africa and a

completely different one towards Zionist colonization in North Africa." Quoted in Ali Mazrui, "Black Africa and the Arab-Israel Conflict," *Middle East International* 87 (1978):14.

19. This is a key theme in Joel Peters, *Israel and Africa: The Problematic Friendship* (London: Lester Crook, 1991, forthcoming). All references are to the unpublished manuscript, from which permission to quote was kindly granted by the author.

20. Israeli-African relations during this period have been covered in depth in several major studies. See Leopold Laufer, *Israel and the Developing Countries: New Approaches to Cooperation* (New York: Twentieth Century Fund, 1967); Z. Y. Hershlag (ed.), *Israel-Africa Cooperation Research Project: Progress Report* (Tel-Aviv: Tel-Aviv University, Department of Developing Countries, 1970); Shimon Amir, *Israel's Development Cooperation with Africa, Asia and Latin America* (New York: Praeger, 1974); Michael Curtis and Susan Aurelia Gitelson (eds.), *Israel and the Third World* (New Brunswick: Transaction Books, 1976); and Olusola Ojo, *Africa and Israel: Relations in Perspective* (Boulder, Colo.: Westview Press, 1988).

21. For an analysis of African positions immediately after the 1967 war, see Samuel Decalo, "Africa and the Mid-Eastern War," *Africa Report* 12, no. 8 (1967): 57–61.

22. The OAU mission is discussed in, among others, Ron Kochan, "An African Peace Mission to the Middle East: The One Man Initiative of President Senghor," *African Affairs* 72, no. 287 (1973):186–196; 'Sola Ojo, "The Arab-Israeli Conflict and Afro-Arab Relations," in Timothy M. Shaw and 'Sola Ojo (eds.), *Africa and the International Political System* (Washington, D.C.: University Press of America, 1982), pp. 139–167; and Yassin el-Ayouty, "OAU Mediation in the Arab-Israeli Conflict," *Genève-Afrique* 14, no. 1 (1975):5–29. For an excellent overview, see S.K.B. Asante, "Africa in World Politics: The Case of the Organization of African Unity and the Middle Eastern Conflict," *International Problems* 20, nos. 2–4 (1981):111–128.

23. Mauritius joined this group in 1976. For African statements connected with the rupture, see World Jewish Congress, African and Asian Media Survey, *African and Asian Attitudes on the Middle East Conflict* (New York: Department of Asian and African Studies, 1974).

24. There is still controversy over the exact combination of factors at work in the decision of African states. The most balanced evaluation may be found in Peters, *Israel and Africa*, pp. 57–82. For differing opinions, consult Susan Aurelia Gitelson, "Israel's African Setback in Perspective," in Curtis and Gitelson, *Israel and the Third World*, pp. 182–199; Arye Oded, "Africa Between the Arabs and Israel," *Hamizrah Hahadash* 25 (1975): 184–209; and Elliot P. Skinner, "African States and Israel: Uneasy Relations in a World of Crisis," *Journal of African Studies* 2, no. 1 (1975):1–23.

25. The roll call on the U.N. resolution is discussed in depth in Samuel Decalo, "Africa and the U.N. Anti-Zionism Resolution: Roots and Causes," *Cultures et Développement* 8, no. 1 (1976):89–117.

26. See Oded, *Africa and the Middle East Conflict*, pp. 7–31.

27. Some early indications of the transitional nature of the Afro-Arab coalition are discussed in World Jewish Congress, Department of African and Asian Affairs,

The Black African Connection: A New Era in the African-Arab Relationship (London: World Jewish Congress, February 1975).

28. For an excellent analysis, see Peters, *Israel and Africa,* pp. 113–125.

29. Naomi Chazan, "Israel in Africa," *Jerusalem Quarterly* 18 (1981):29–44; and Ethan Nadelmann, "Israel and Black Africa: A Rapprochement?" *Journal of Modern African Studies* 19, no. 2 (1981):183–219. For the African view, see T. A. Imobighe, "Israel-Egypt Treaty: The African Option," *Afriscope* 9, no. 6 (June 1979):10–12; Jimni Adisa, "Nigeria, Israel and Diplomatic Ties: The Conditional Thesis," *International Problems* 24, nos. 1–4 (1985):60–89; and "Commentary: Roundtable Discussion on the Establishment of Diplomatic Relations with Israel by Nigeria," *Nigerian Forum* 2, nos. 7–9 (1982):645–730.

30. OAU document, "On the Palestine Question: CM/Res. 787 (XXXV)" (Freetown: OAU, March 1980), as quoted in Peters, *Israel and Africa,* p. 141.

31. For a critique of the absence of adequate tools for the remolding of Israel's technical cooperation program, see Sisyphus, "Israel's Aid to the Third World: Lessons of the Past and Prospects for the Future," *Middle East Review* 10, no. 3 (1978):30–36.

32. The volume of literature on Israel and South Africa is immense. For basic works, consult Naomi Chazan, "The Fallacies of Pragmatism: Israeli Foreign Policy Towards South Africa," *African Affairs* 82, no. 327 (1983):169–199; James Adams, *Israel and South Africa: The Unnatural Alliance* (London: Quartet Books, 1984); Richard P. Stevens and Abdelwahab M. Elmesiri, *Israel and South Africa: The Progression of a Relationship,* rev. ed. (New Brunswick: North American Inc., 1977); Benjamin Beit-Hallahmi, *The Israeli Connection: Who Israel Arms and Why* (New York: Pergamon Press, 1987); and Kunirum Osia, *Israel, South Africa and Black Africa: A Study of the Primacy of Political Expediency* (Washington, D.C.: University Press of America, 1981).

33. For full details of this process, see Léon César Codo, "Israel et l'Afrique Noire (Aspects Récents): de l'Ère des Ruptures à l'Heure du Nouveau Réalisme Pro-Israelien," Première Partie, *Le Mois en Afrique* 233–234 (Juin-Juillet 1985):3–25; and Deuxième Partie, *Le Mois en Afrique* 235–236 (Aôut-Septembre 1985):36–51. Also see Léon César Codo, "Israel's Return to Sub-Saharan Africa," *Jerusalem Journal of International Relations* 11, no. 1 (1989):58–73; Naomi Chazan, "Israel and Africa in the 1980s: The Dilemmas of Complexity and Ambiguity," in Olajide Aluko (ed.), *Africa and the Great Powers in the 1980s* (Lanham, Md.: University Press of America, 1987), pp. 201–236; Lawrence P. Frank, "Israel and Africa: The Era of Tachlis," *Journal of Modern African Studies* 26, no. 1 (1988):151–155; and H. S. Aynor, "Black Africa's Rediscovery of Israel: Motivations and Expectations," *Jersualem Journal of International Relations* 12, no. 1 (1990):102–111.

34. For a description of Liberia's concerns, see Yekutiel Gershoni, "Liberia and Israel: The Evolution of a Relationship," *Liberian Studies Journal* 14, no. 1 (1989): 34–50.

35. It is important to note that Israeli trade with Africa, which had never been particularly high, dropped in the 1980s. Israeli exports to Africa (imports from Africa were minimal), which stood at $110 million in 1980, had fallen by nearly 50 percent by 1989. See *Statistical Abstract of Israel* (Jerusalem: Central Bureau of Statistics, 1989), pp. 245–246.

36. See Naomi Chazan, "Israeli Perspectives on the Israel–South African Relationship," *IJA Research Report* 9–10 (1987):12–19.

37. Full details of African-PLO relations (including economic and technical assistance programs) may be found in Arye Oded, *Africa, the PLO and Israel,* Policy Studies no. 37 (Jerusalem: Hebrew University of Jerusalem, The Leonard Davis Institute for International Relations, March 1990). For excellent background pieces, see Sulayman S. Nyang, "African Opinions and Attitudes to the Palestine Question," *The Search* 1, nos. 3–4 (1980):218–241; and Nzongola Ntalaja, "Africa and the Question of Palestine," *The Search* 5, no. 1 (1982):1–18.

38. *West Africa* 3804 (23–29 July 1990):2147.

39. There is currently a debate about the outlook for the renewal of diplomatic relations with Israel. Oded, *Africa and the Middle East Conflict,* suggests that prospects are meager, whereas Victor T. LeVine, "The African-Israeli Connection 40 Years Later," *Middle East Review* 21, no. 1 (1988):12–17, suggests that the possibilities for improved ties are quite good.

40. These conflicts are dealt with only schematically in these pages, as they are treated in depth by John Harbeson (Chapter 6) and Rene Lemarchand (Chapter 7) in this volume.

41. Oded, *Africa and the Middle East Conflict,* pp. 90–97 and 116–124, explicates Arab positions on these conflicts.

42. For background materials, see Hartmut Neitzel and Renate Notzel, *Africa and the Arab States: Documentation on the Development of Political and Economic Relations Since 1973* (Hamburg: Institute of African Studies, 1979); E. C. Chibwe, *Arab Dollars to Africa* (London: Croom Helm, 1976); and E. C. Chibwe, *Afro-Arab Relations in the New World Order* (London: Julian Freidman, 1976).

43. The Arab Bank for the Economic Development of Africa, *BADEA Annual Report, 1984* (Khartoum: BADEA, 1987), p. 17.

44. For excellent summaries of these transactions, see Robert Anton Mertz and Pamela MacDonald Mertz, *Arab Aid to Sub-Saharan Africa* (Munich: Kaiser, 1982 and Boulder, Colo.: Westview Press, 1983); and Oded, *Africa and the Middle East Conflict,* pp. 55–79.

45. Arye Oded, "Arab Aid to Africa (1973–1983)," *International Problems* 24, nos. 1–4 (1985):24–40.

46. See LeVine and Luke, *The Arab-African Connection,* pp. 18–29.

47. IMF, *Direction of Trade Statistics Yearbook, 1989* (Washington, D.C.: The International Monetary Fund, 1989), pp. 22–23 and 38–39.

11

THE SOVIET UNION AND AFRICA

MARINA OTTAWAY

Soviet policy toward Africa has gone through many changes since the early 1960s, when the process of decolonization first forced Moscow to turn its attention to a part of the world about which it had little previous knowledge. The Soviet Union initially considered Africa as fertile ground for Socialist transformation, and it provided support for radical leaders, whom it considered "revolutionary democrats." When a wave of coups d'état in the mid-1960s removed most of those radical leaders from power, the Soviets became much more cautious in their approach, downplaying the possibility of a quick transition to socialism on the continent and suggesting instead that African countries should follow a "noncapitalist road" to development. Soviet interest in radical transformation in Africa revived in the mid-1970s, when self-proclaimed Marxist-Leninist regimes rose to power in Ethiopia, Angola, and Mozambique. But these regimes also proved a disappointment as well as a heavy economic burden for Moscow, as they became mired in economic crises and civil wars.

In the late 1980s, Soviet attitudes and policies concerning Africa were again in a state of flux. The Soviets emphasized their "new thinking." However, an analysis of this new thinking revealed little more than a continuation of old debates. National reconciliation, the newest idea set forth by the Soviets as a solution to domestic and regional conflicts, was not defined clearly. Changes in policy were even less evident, and Soviet scholars and officials were admitting that inertia or outright opposition by more conservative elements in the military and the bureaucratic apparatus was slowing down policy changes in Africa, as elsewhere. The question thus remained open as to whether the so-called new thinking would translate into new policies or whether theoretical approaches and policies toward

Africa would remain as unrelated to each other in the Gorbachev years as they had been under Brezhnev. Indeed, the conclusion that the Soviets' African policy under Gorbachev had reached a turning point was partly a result of a new attitude on the part of the United States and partly a result of genuine new thinking in the Soviet Union.

The frequent shifts in Soviet views and policies on Africa can be explained by three major factors. First, the Soviet Union itself has undergone considerable change since it began to deal with independent African countries. The Khrushchev period was one of rapid reform—adventurism, critics would later say. The Brezhnev period was profoundly conservative. Gorbachev again launched a period of reform. All these changes inevitably influenced Soviet policy toward Africa. Second, Africa has limited importance for the Soviet Union. The vital interests of the USSR are affected by what happens within its borders, in Europe and Asia, and by its relations with the United States. In Africa, Moscow sought access to naval facilities that would allow its fleet to operate more easily in the Indian Ocean plus provide trade opportunities and fishing rights. It could forego these when conditions were not favorable. This made the Soviets' African policy both flexible and opportunistic. Third, the Soviets initially lacked direct knowledge of Africa. Even in the postcolonial period, few Soviets spent any time on the continent, with the exception of diplomats and journalists whose contacts were most often formal and official. Even in the late 1980s, it was not unusual to meet Soviet specialists on Africa who had never set foot on the continent. The Soviet perception of African countries, as a result, has been based on a mixture of limited information derived largely from Western sources and reinterpreted in Marxist-Leninist terms and of conclusions deductively derived from Marxist-Leninist theory.[1]

Due to the marginal position of Africa and the overwhelming importance of the United States in Soviet foreign policy, relations between Moscow and African countries are best understood as triangular—involving the Soviet Union, the country in question, and the United States. Moscow and Washington have been able to make a part of Africa strategic for each other simply by establishing a presence there. The rivalry between the United States and the Soviet Union has thus shaped their policies toward African countries, particularly those that are too small and too poor to become significant economic partners. As a result, events in some African countries have occasionally had significant repercussions on Soviet-U.S. relations.

Two major examples of such repercussions are the Angolan civil war in 1975 and the Ogaden War in 1977. Soviet-Cuban intervention on the side of the Popular Movement for the Liberation of Angola (MPLA) government in Angola at the time of independence and U.S. unwillingness to oppose the MPLA decisively were seen by Secretary of State Henry Kissinger as a major setback for the United States. "America's modest direct strategic and economic interests in Angola are not the central issue," he declared to the Senate Foreign Relations Committee. "The question is whether America maintains the resolve to act responsibly as a great power."[2] A few years later, National Security Adviser Zbigniew Brzezinski concluded that the U.S. failure to take a strong position against Soviet-Cuban intervention on behalf of Ethiopia in the Ogaden War triggered a process that eventually led to a serious deterioration in U.S.-Soviet relations. He argued that after underreacting initially, the United States felt at a disadvantage and eventually overreacted: "That derailed SALT, the momentum of SALT was lost, and the final nail in the coffin was the Soviet invasion of Afghanistan. . . . That is why I have used occasionally the phrase 'SALT lies buried in the sands of the Ogaden.' "[3]

THE SOVIET UNION AND THE REVOLUTIONARY DEMOCRATS

In the early 1960s, the combination of the rapid decolonization of Africa and the innovation-oriented leadership of Nikita Khrushchev in the Soviet Union led to a high level of Soviet involvement on the continent. In this period, Soviet thinking on Africa and policies toward it were quite consistent. But this phase was short-lived, and the close ties the Soviets established with many African countries proved ephemeral—failing to survive the overthrow of specific leaders.

Between 1957 and 1962, most African colonies became independent or at least entered the final period of transition to independence. Only Southern Rhodesia and the Portuguese colonies were still far from a settlement. In the euphoria of this period, the rhetoric of African leaders leaned heavily toward ideals of pan-Africanism and nonalignment between East and West. But pan-Africanism foundered on the reality of diverging political orientations, conflicting economic interests, and bitter border disputes, while nonalignment proved a position impossible to sustain for countries in need of economic and military aid. By the time of the creation of the Organization of African Unity in 1963, African countries were already divided into blocs.[4]

The Soviet Union had not played a significant role in the decolonization process—it was to become a significant provider of arms to the liberation movements only later, in the cases of Zimbabwe and the Portuguese colonies.[5] The Soviet position on the colonial question was clear in theory: Nationalist movements should be supported not only in words but in deed.[6] However, the Soviets also supported Communist parties in Africa, such as those in Algeria and Egypt, which recruited more members from the European than from the indigenous populations. As a result, these Communist parties often opposed the nationalist movement openly or at least took an ambiguous position.[7] So did some of the European Communist parties, particularly the French.

After independence, however, the more radical African leaders—seeking to distance themselves politically and economically from the former colonial powers—started looking at the Soviet Union as a possible supporter, although they sometimes continued to reject Marxism-Leninism as an ideology.[8] This rapprochement of radical African leaders with the Soviet Union was facilitated by Egyptian president Gamal Abdel Nasser. The Soviet Union had become the major supplier of arms to Egypt in 1955 and had further consolidated its position in the country by financing the construction of the Aswan High Dam after the United States and the World Bank withdrew from the deal.[9] In the early 1960s, Nasser—following his theory that Egypt belonged to the three circles represented by the Arab world, the Islamic world, and Africa—was an active and influential participant in African politics and a leading member of the radical group that included among its prominent members Ahmed Ben Bella of Algeria, Sekou Toure of Guinea-Conakry, Kwame Nkrumah of Ghana, and Modibo Keita of Mali.

All these leaders saw the Soviet Union as a counterweight to the dominant influence of the former colonial powers and to the political and economic ties binding the leaders to the West but not as a political or even an economic model to follow. African leaders at this time were greatly concerned with rediscovering their cultural roots and the African personality, and thus they were little inclined to look for foreign ideologies to embrace or foreign models to copy. Even the most Marxist among them, such as Toure and Nkrumah, felt the need to assert that their ideas were rooted in African traditions. Furthermore, most African leaders rejected the concept of class conflict that is central to Marxist theory, seeking instead a vision of a harmonious African society in which the interests of all social groups could be reconciled.[10]

Between 1959 and 1974, the Soviet Union extended $870 million in economic credit and $120 million in military aid to sub-Saharan Africa, and it sent thousands of advisers.[11] Several thousand African students went to the Soviet Union to study. To the radical leaders personally, the Soviet Union offered recognition of them as revolutionary democrats leading their countries through the phase of national democratic revolution that would open the way to socialism in the future.[12] But neither then nor later was the Soviet Union willing to accept the radical African regimes' claim that they were Socialist.

COUNTRIES ON THE NONCAPITALIST ROAD

The overthrow of President Ben Bella in Algeria in June 1965 marked the beginning of a series of coups that rapidly eliminated or left powerless the radical leaders of the immediate postindependence period. Nkrumah and Keita were also deposed. Nasser was paralyzed by Egypt's defeat in the 1967 war with Israel, the final blow to a country already weakened by a protracted and unsuccessful war in Yemen and mounting economic problems at home. Only Sekou Toure remained in power.

The downfall of these leaders left the Soviets with a greatly diminished presence on the continent and a deep mistrust of the fragility of African regimes. As a result, Moscow kept its distance from African countries. It continued to provide support for the liberation movements in the remaining colonies and gave some military and economic aid to other countries, but the enthusiasm of the early postindependence period was gone. The fact that the demise of the first generation of African radical leaders coincided with that of Khrushchev and the consolidation of the more conservative Brezhnev regime also contributed to the change in Soviet policy.

The lack of Soviet enthusiasm is reflected in the terminology used to discuss radical African countries in the late 1960s and the 1970s. Soviet writings of this period refer consistently to "countries on the noncapitalist road." The term had appeared before but in the late 1960s it permeated Soviet discussions of Africa.[13] In reviving the old debate as to whether Socialist transformation must be preceded by capitalist transformation, Soviet Africanists concluded that capitalist transformation was not necessary in African countries but that their backwardness made Socialist transformation impossible, at least immediately. African countries were thus relegated to an ideological limbo called the noncapitalist road.

Countries on the noncapitalist road should be governed by broad coalitions of progressive forces, including the military, rather than by tightly organized vanguard parties, the Soviets argued. These governments were expected to play a major role in promoting economic development, but they could not yet aspire to control the entire economy. Private enterprise and even investment and development assistance from Western countries were considered acceptable—indeed, essential—for countries on the noncapitalist road.[14]

African leaders and intellectuals never accepted the phrase "countries on the noncapitalist road." First, it had a negative rather than a positive connotation—the Soviets eventually responded to this issue by changing the terminology to "countries of Socialist orientation." Second, it did not make any concessions to African claims about historical and cultural uniqueness; implicitly, the concept was a rejection of African socialism. Finally, the idea was not satisfactory to the more radical African intellectuals, who themselves aspired to Marxism-Leninism and thus found the Soviet characterization of their countries as not ready for it demeaning. The model for African radicals in this period thus became China rather than the Soviet Union.[15]

The major exception to the generally distant Soviet attitude toward Africa in this period was its policy toward Somalia, suggesting that scholarly debates had little influence when they clashed with geopolitical considerations. A small, desperately poor country with a largely nomadic population, Somalia was a particularly unpromising candidate for Socialist transformation. Yet, it was singled out by the Soviet Union after 1969 for the first experiment in building Soviet-style political institutions in an African country.

Geopolitically, it is clear why the Soviet Union should have wanted a presence in Somalia. With its long coastline on the Red Sea and the Straits of Bab el Mandeb, Somalia has strategic importance in relation to the Middle East and the Suez Canal. Furthermore, in the 1970s the Soviet Union was actively seeking to expand its naval power, specifically its capacity to operate in the Indian Ocean. Access to Somali port facilities was thus attractive. For its part, Somalia looked to the Soviet Union for assistance in building up its army—an important goal for a military regime in a country that considered its decolonization incomplete and aspired to annex more territory, most notably the Ogaden.[16]

The Soviet Union also attempted to transform Somalia along Socialist lines, at least politically. The Soviets spent considerable effort helping the Somalis organize a Socialist party and training cadres. In 1976, the Somali Socialist Revolutionary Party was launched, in theory replacing the military council that had ruled the country since Mohammed Siad Barre's 1969 coup d'état. In reality, the military council simply became the new party's political bureau.[17]

The Soviets' effort to organize the new Somali party was not in keeping with their advice to African countries in this period—Moscow prescribed broad coalitions of progressive forces rather than vanguard parties. In practice, the Soviets had no experience with forging such broad coalitions, but they had much with organizing vanguard parties. Thus, they attempted to replicate the Soviet model in Somalia. The formation of the Somali Socialist Revolutionary Party was the harbinger of the policy that came to prevail in the late 1970s, when Soviet and East German advisers actively helped several African countries—most notably Angola, Mozambique, and Ethiopia—to set up Soviet-style political institutions.

Its relationship with Somalia represented the exception to the overall lack of Soviet interest in Africa, a lack that was clearly reflected in the levels of economic assistance. Although Soviet aid to the Third World increased rapidly between 1965 and 1974, the share to sub-Saharan Africa declined to 4 percent of the total, down from 13 percent in the preceding decade. North Africa's share declined from 34 to 9 percent.[18] Levels of trade remained low, in part because many African countries were dissatisfied with the terms offered by the Soviet Union. In their call for a new international economic order, many African and other Third-World countries made it clear that they considered the Soviet Union to be part of the industrialized North slowing down the development of the South.[19]

THE DILEMMA OF THE AFRO-MARXIST REGIMES

The revolution in Ethiopia in 1974 and the independence of the Portuguese colonies the following year opened up a new era in Soviet-African relations. Although the changes in these countries were not engineered by the Soviet Union, they did provide Moscow with unprecedented opportunities for establishing a strong presence in Africa. As it had done in Somalia, Moscow abandoned its caution and its doubts, making a considerable commitment to the new radical regimes. There are probably two major reasons for this turnaround in Soviet policy. One is simply that the opportunities were too tempting to disregard. The second is that in this period, the Soviet Union was seeking to strengthen its navy and to increase its ability to operate far from Soviet territory. Ethiopia, Angola, and Mozambique have long coastlines. However, Soviet theories about Africa did not change at all at this point; thus, the theoretical discussions and the policies became almost completely unrelated to each other.

The governments of Ethiopia, Angola, and Mozambique not only proclaimed themselves Socialist but also chose Marxism-Leninism, as interpreted in Moscow at the time, rather than African socialism as their ideology. Additionally, the three governments turned to the Soviet Union for urgently needed military assistance. Ethiopia was mired in an internal war in Eritrea and an external war against Somalia in the Ogaden. The MPLA regime in Angola was at war with UNITA, the rival liberation movement that had lost out in the struggle for power at independence and had turned to South Africa for help. Mozambique feared attacks from Rhodesia and South Africa and later faced its own internal war against Renamo. The need for weapons opened the way to a close relationship between these countries and the Soviet Union, just as a similar need had opened the way for a Soviet-Egyptian relationship in the 1950s and a Soviet-Somali relationship after 1969. In the cases of Ethiopia and Angola, Cuban troops also participated in the war efforts. Up to fifteen thousand Cubans fought in Ethiopia and fifty thousand in Angola.[20]

Geopolitical considerations encouraged the Soviet Union to make this commitment to the three radical regimes. As in Somalia earlier, however, Soviet aid went beyond what was strictly necessary to obtain access to facilities or was even justified by its theories concerning countries on the noncapitalist road. The Soviets preached broad political coalitions, but they encouraged and helped their new African allies to organize vanguard parties.

They prescribed mixed economies and cautioned against the dangers of rushing into collectivization and state ownership, but they financed large, mechanized, and ultimately nonprofitable state farms. The Soviet Union, it should be clear, did not impose this model on Ethiopia, Angola, or Mozambique; the three regimes sought to create it themselves. But the Soviets helped implement policies their theories considered to be very premature. As in the case of Somalia, we must conclude that the Soviets did not have a clear idea of how to implement their model of the noncapitalist road and thus fell back on a replica of their own system.

All these developments took place without any major change in Soviet thinking about African countries. Although some scholars argued that the self-defined Marxist-Leninist countries were at least somewhat closer to socialism than most, many others disagreed.[21] Ethiopia in particular inspired a few to nostalgic evocations of the Soviet revolution. Officially, however, the maximum concession the Soviets were willing to make was to drop the negative term "countries on the noncapitalist road" in favor of the slightly more positive "countries of Socialist orientation."

Ethiopia, Angola, and Mozambique proved to be burdensome allies for the Soviet Union. Beleaguered by civil war and on the brink of economic collapse, they were each given large amounts of military aid and lesser, but still considerable, levels of economic assistance. Ethiopia, which received an estimated $8.38 billion in arms between 1977 and 1987—almost all from the Soviet Union—was the most costly, particularly as its economic conditions made it a certainty that it would never be able to repay more than a minute percentage of what it had received.[22] Angola imported some $9.23 billion worth of arms in the same period, also overwhelmingly from the Soviet Union, but it could pay for a larger percentage out of its oil revenue.[23] Soviet military aid to Mozambique was never as significant, totaling about $2.03 billion between 1977 and 1987, but Mozambique was not in a position to pay.[24] The Soviet Union remained virtually Mozambique's only arms supplier, even when other countries—most notably Zimbabwe and Great Britain—started providing training for the Mozambican army.

The tangible benefits the Soviets derived from their relationship with the three countries appear modest in comparison with the costs, although it should be recognized that the real import of these benefits would only become obvious in case of conflict. Furthermore, the Soviet Union probably derived some less measurable political benefits from these relationships, such as confirmation of its superpower status and increased credibility as a patron of Third-World radical regimes. But the concrete benefits were limited. The Soviet Union developed naval facilities on the Dahlak Islands off the port of Massawa in Eritrea, but not on the mainland. It had access to Angolan airports and was thus able to fly surveillance over the southern Atlantic. Mozambique allowed the Soviet navy to call at its ports, but it did not provide permanent facilities. Economic benefits were even more limited. Neither Ethiopian coffee and hides nor Mozambican prawns could pay for the military aid provided. Angola, which paid for some military equipment and for the Cuban troops in hard currency, was oriented to the West economically. Oil companies in particular continued to invest in exploration and extraction despite the Angolan civil war. The fact that Mozambique joined the IMF and the World Bank in 1984 and Angola joined in 1983 confirmed the increasing Western orientation of these economies.

THE NEW THINKING

The general climate of renewal in the Soviet Union under Gorbachev and the different language emanating from Moscow led to much U.S. discussion about the new Soviet thinking concerning the Third World and Africa.[25] The Soviet Union appeared dissatisfied with the performance of its African allies, their endless conflicts, and their poor economic performance. Although there was no reason to doubt Soviet dissatisfaction, the extent of the new economic and, to a lesser extent, political thinking on Africa was greatly overestimated. Soviet writers simply reopened the old debates about socialism in the Third World, coming up with slightly different versions of the old answers with some new terminology. The economic thinking in particular did not appear to be at all new. The political new thinking—which emphasized the need for national reconciliation in Third-World conflicts rather than proclaiming the inevitability of the triumph of the oppressed classes—was at least to some extent a new version of the old idea that African regimes must be based on broad coalitions of all progressive forces in the country. The Soviets were undoubtedly pushing this concept much further, applying it to conflicts—such as those in Eritrea and Angola—to which they had never previously applied it. However, they did not specify what they meant by national reconciliation. Not only was the theory unclear, but there was no evidence as yet that Soviet policy under Gorbachev reflected the theory more accurately than it had under Brezhnev.[26]

The idea of a new economic thinking about Africa in the Gorbachev era was based on the fact that the Soviets were preaching moderation to their African allies, cautioning them about haste in nationalizing assets, suggesting that in no case should small businesses be absorbed by the public sector, and warning against collectivization of agriculture—at the very least until it could be accompanied by mechanization.[27] As we have seen, these were old, often-expressed ideas, although they were not observed in practice.

A study of Ethiopia prepared by Soviet advisers in 1985 received much attention as an indication of change in the Soviet position.[28] In reality, the document repeated what the Soviets had been saying for a long time in their writings, at international gatherings, and directly to African governments. In Ethiopia, for example, the Soviets had been cautioning the leadership against moving too far and too fast after the launching of the 1974 land reform, which they viewed as dangerously radical.

If the economic thinking was not new, were the economic policies followed by the Soviets in Africa different? Here, there were mixed signs. In Mozambique, for example, the Soviets did not oppose the government's decision to join the IMF and the World Bank and to implement the economic reforms they mandated in 1984. This suggested that Moscow was finally willing to live by its own advice that countries of Socialist orientation should develop mixed economies and accept assistance from all sources. By contrast, according to Mozambican president Joaquim Chissano, a few years earlier the Soviet Union had pushed its own model of socialism.[29] There were no examples of new policies being implemented by the Soviets through their own assistance projects. Money was still being channeled—as it always had been—toward large farms, industry, and infrastructure, while the peasant sector was totally ignored despite the theoretical assertions about its importance.[30]

In the political new thinking, the idea of national reconciliation had become the standard Soviet answer to the domestic conflicts plaguing many African countries and spilling over into regional conflicts. This was undoubtedly a departure, as in the 1970s the Soviet Union had tried to help its allies find military solutions to such conflicts, representing the opposing party as a reactionary force doomed to defeat. But national reconciliation was never defined. Thus, it remained unclear whether it meant the acceptance of many political parties, the absorption of existing ones into a new front, the integration of opposition parties and guerrilla movements into ruling parties and national armies, or simply amnesty for all political opponents. Whatever it meant in practice, the concept appeared to be based on the assumption that the differences between African governments and opposition parties were not unbridgeable, that they did not represent the choice of antithetical political and economic systems, and that the Soviet-supported side did not necessarily represent the inevitable march of history toward socialism. Gone were the days when the Soviets proclaimed the "invincibility of the liberation movement"—meaning the movement they backed.[31]

The idea of national reconciliation was undoubtedly a result of frustration with African conflicts that had proven impossible to solve militarily, despite the billions of dollars in arms provided by the Soviet Union since the mid-1970s. It also reflected the lack of vital Soviet interests in Africa—in the end, it makes little difference to the Soviet Union who is in power in Angola or Ethiopia or, for that matter, in South Africa. The stress on reconciliation was also a reflection of the triangular character of Soviet-African relations, which have always involved a consideration of U.S. reactions. In the late 1980s, the Soviets were especially interested in the continued improvement of East-West relations and were thus anxious to show their interest in the peaceful solution of regional conflicts.

Nevertheless, concrete signs of a new Soviet policy favoring national reconciliation were still difficult to find in 1990. Moscow was putting pressure on Ethiopian president Mengistu Haile Mariam to negotiate with Eritrean and other rebel movements, reportedly warning him that military assistance would be greatly curtailed once the current agreement expired. For the time being, however, arms deliveries were continuing at high levels, although scheduled to end by 1992. The number of Soviet military advisers was declining, but the number of Ethiopian military personnel trained in the Soviet Union had increased sharply.[32] Overall, the Soviets appeared to be trying to reduce their costs in the region while pushing for a negotiated solution, but they did not appear to be abandoning Ethiopia to its own devices.

The Soviet Union was also pushing Ethiopia to negotiate with the Sudan and Somalia in the late 1980s.[33] This could hardly be considered the result of new thinking, however, as the first Soviet-Cuban attempt to promote a negotiated solution to the Horn of Africa conflicts dated back to 1977 with the proposal for the creation of a Red Sea federation including Ethiopia, Somalia, Eritrea, and South Yemen.[34] But there was probably greater anxiety on the part of the Soviet Union to see negotiations get under way in the Horn in the late 1980s than in 1977 because of the obvious failure of the military solution. As a result, the Soviets were open to other parties' intervention, welcoming the September 1989 initiative by former President Jimmy Carter, who brought together representatives of the Ethiopian government and the Eritrean People's Liberation Front for preliminary talks.[35]

The case of Angola also does not provide clear evidence to support the idea that Soviet policy in Africa was guided by new thinking about regional conflicts and national reconciliation. Moscow did support the 1988 tripartite Angolan–Cuban–South African agreement brokered by the United States, which provided for Cuban withdrawal from Angola and independence for Namibia. But it also continued to provide military equipment for the Angolan government, just as the United States continued to support UNITA. In fact, intelligence reports suggested that Soviet military advisers had played a more central role in the battle for Mavinga in early 1990 than they had in any previous offensive. Even more important, the Soviet Union did not take concrete steps to encourage negotiations between the MPLA and UNITA to terminate the Angolan civil war. The initiative on this issue was still with the United States and, increasingly, with other African countries.

The only country in which there were unmistakable signs of Soviet disengagement was Mozambique, which increasingly received Western military and economic aid. Although arms deliveries were continuing, Soviet military advisers began to be withdrawn in 1989. However, the changes in Mozambique, where the Soviet Union had played a lesser role than in Ethiopia or Angola, started before the Gorbachev era and its new thinking. Furthermore, disengagement did not amount to the promotion of national reconciliation. Soviet policy toward Mozambique in the late 1980s, in conclusion, was certainly different from what it had been during the preceding decade. However, it was a policy that antedated Gorbachev's new thinking, and it did not appear to represent the implementation of basic concepts of the new thinking, such as national reconciliation.

At the theoretical level, there was also a dramatic change in the Soviet attitude toward South Africa. Although still opposing apartheid, in the late 1980s the Soviets were arguing that the situation in South Africa was not conducive to revolutionary change—which is positive in the Soviet thinking—and, thus, that violence would only lead to chaos.[36] As a result, black South Africans should seek a political, compromise solution to their grievances. Startling as these ideas sounded in relation to earlier Soviet positions, there was as yet no indication of how they would be translated in a new Soviet policy toward South Africa.

CONCLUSIONS

In concluding this brief overview of Soviet relations with Africa, two questions need to be addressed: (1) What have been the determinant forces in the relations, and (2) what impact has the Soviet Union had on Africa? The driving forces in Soviet-African relations have to be found, by and large, outside Africa itself, in the Soviet Union's own internal politics and in its relations with the United States. Events in Africa have provided opportunities or caused setbacks, but they have not been the main determinants of the relationships.

The three major concepts set forth by the Soviet Union in interpreting Africa—revolutionary democracy, countries on the noncapitalist road or of Socialist orientation, and finally the so-called new thinking—reflected changes in the Soviet Union itself. The hailing of the revolutionary democrats was a product of the freewheeling, less rigid, post-Stalinist mood of the Khrushchev era—of his adventurism, according to his Soviet critics. This mood also explained the policies enacted by the Soviet Union during this period.

The cautious, strictly constructed, orthodox theory of countries on the noncapitalist road reflected the narrow orthodoxy and caution of the Brezhnev years. Socialist transformation was not the result of enthusiasm and good will but of structural conditions, and these were not present in Africa. But the Brezhnev Soviet Union also saw the world divided into hostile camps and the Third World as a battleground in which the superpowers had to compete for influence. Opportunities to increase Soviet influence were not to be overlooked, no matter how little a country might be ready for socialism. Finally, the Brezhnev regime only knew one model of political and economic organization—the Soviet one—and thus tried to re-create that model in the African countries in which the Soviet presence was strong. Thus, although the thinking about Africa and policies toward Africa contradicted each other during this period, they had a common root.

Finally, the new thinking of the Gorbachev years was clearly related to the Soviet Union's disenchantment with its own brand of socialism, its efforts to launch different economic policies and to reorganize politically. Moscow's own uncertainty about how far to go and how to implement reforms was reflected in the vagueness of the concepts and the absence of concrete and coherent policy changes in the late 1980s.

Soviet policy toward Africa under Gorbachev also reflected the profound ambivalence of the U.S.-Soviet relationship. Both superpowers seemingly agreed on the necessity of negotiating political solutions to regional conflicts in Africa and elsewhere in the Third World. They both preached national reconciliation. Although it was not directly involved, the Soviet Union even cooperated with the United States in the negotiations that led to agreements on independence for Namibia and the withdrawal of Cuban troops from Angola. Nevertheless, Moscow and Washington were still arming their allies in all regional conflicts. Neither side quite believed that the other was ready to cooperate to solve conflicts in the Third World rather than trying to use them for its advantage.

The Soviet impact on Africa has been limited but not insignificant and more indirect than direct. No African country has turned to socialism because of the efforts of the Soviet Union. The embracing of socialism in any of its forms has invariably been the result of domestic factors. However, the Soviet Union has played an important role in enabling countries to follow the policies of their choice—there would be few state farms in Ethiopia if the Eastern bloc had not been willing to finance them, for example. Soviet military aid, furthermore, has enabled many African governments to pursue military solutions to their problems. Ethiopia and Angola offer clear examples of this.

The Soviet Union has had a significant indirect impact on many African countries by providing a blueprint for transformation. Paradoxically, this has been the case even when Moscow was arguing that the Soviet model was inappropriate for a country's stage of development. Many African leaders saw in the Soviet political and economic institutions a model that had worked in fostering political stability and economic growth—thus, that should be copied.

Finally, the vagaries of U.S.-Soviet relations also at times had an important and unexpected impact on the actions of African nations. The idea of détente between the superpowers has always been of great concern to African leaders, who are aware that the cold war gave their countries much greater importance in Soviet and U.S. eyes than they might have had otherwise. The fear of being forgotten in the mood of détente played a central part in the Egyptian decision to go to war with Israel in 1973, as the Egyptian government feared the Soviet Union would stop providing arms to Egypt in order to avoid antagonizing the United States.[37] In the late 1980s, the Somali government was trying desperately to revive Soviet-U.S. competition in the Horn—a concern because in the new climate of superpower cooperation, the United States was more inclined to look at human rights violations by the Somali government than at the Soviet threat in the Red Sea and had thus suspended its economic and military assistance to Somalia. Although Somalia's deliberate courting of the Soviet Union was an extreme manifestation of the problem, many other African governments feared they might be forgotten by the two superpowers.

The Soviet impact on Africa has not been inconsequential in the past. During the 1970s and 1980s in particular, the Soviet Union had a direct impact on African conflicts by providing large amounts of arms to the regimes it supported. But the USSR had an even more important indirect influence by offering a model of political and economic organization many African leaders found attractive, even when the Soviets cautioned that the model was inappropriate for Africa. The Soviet new thinking could also be important for the future of Africa, both directly and indirectly. If the new thinking becomes policy, it might lead in the short run to a decrease in Soviet arms deliveries to Africa and to an increase in efforts to promote negotiations in regional conflicts. In the long run, deescalation of the U.S.-Soviet rivalry might result in the marginalization of Africa in Soviet and U.S. policy. But the new thinking could also have a considerable indirect impact on Africa, even if it does not lead to fundamental alterations in Soviet policy. The Soviets' doubts about the validity of their own model are bound to raise questions in Africa as well. Some will undoubtedly respond by denouncing Soviet revisionism and proclaiming themselves the last true believers in socialism.[38] But many Socialist regimes will start their own searches for a new model.

NOTES

1. An interesting recent example of this is provided by G. A. Krylova, "The National Democratic Revolution in Light of the New Political Thinking (with Ethiopia as an Example)," *Narody Azii i Afriki* 1 (1989) (trans. by Paul Henze, Rand Corporation). The author is not a specialist on Ethiopia. The few sources cited include a number of Western authors, a few official Ethiopian documents, and works by Marx and Engels. Indeed, the article reveals more about the USSR than about Ethiopia.

2. The statement, made on January 29, 1976, is quoted in Robert M. Price, *U.S. Policy in Sub-Saharan Africa: National Interests and Global Strategy* (Berkeley: Institute of International Studies, 1978), p. 30.

3. Zbigniew Brzezinski, *Power and Principle* (New York: Farrar, Straus & Giroux, 1983), p. 189.

4. The most important of the blocs formed in this period were the Casablanca and Monrovia groups—the radical and the conservative group, respectively. The two groups were formed in 1961, with the Congo crisis acting as a catalyst. For a detailed analysis, see Immanuel Wallerstein, *Africa: The Politics of Unity* (New York: Random House, 1967), ch. 4.

5. Soviet military aid to African liberation movements has been defined as "small but undefinable" until 1970. Note that even military aid to independent African countries was fairly modest in the early period. See David E. Albright, *The USSR and Sub-Saharan Africa in the 1980s*, Center for Strategic and International Studies, Washington Paper no. 101 (New York: Praeger Publishers, 1983), p. 4.

6. Note, though, that the Communist International had initially dismissed the importance of nationalist movements in the colonies, taking the position that "the liberation of the colonies is only possible accompanied by that of the metropoles." See Jerry Hough, *The Struggle for the Third World* (Washington, D.C.: The Brookings Institution, 1986), p. 144. For an overview of the Soviet policy toward Africa before independence, see Edward T. Wilson, "Russia's Historic Stake in Black Africa," in David E. Albright (ed.), *Communism in Africa* (Bloomington: Indiana University Press, 1980), pp. 67–92.

7. One of the most dramatic examples is provided by Algeria. See Emmanuel Sivan, *Communisme et Nationalisme en Algerie, 1920–62* (Paris: Presse de la Fondation Nationale des Sciences Politiques, 1976).

8. The thinking of Sekou Toure and Kwame Nkrumah was somewhat influenced by Marxist ideas, but both sought to reconcile these ideas with African traditions or Islamic tenets. Marxist influences also appear in the *Charte d'Alger*, the ideological charter adopted by Algeria after independence. See David Ottaway and Marina Ottaway, *Afrocommunism* (New York: Africana, 1981), pp. 17–25.

9. In response to a Western embargo on arms sales to Arab countries, Nasser turned to Czechoslovakia in 1955, signing an agreement for some $200 million in Soviet arms. The agreement led the United States to withdraw its credit for the

project, resulting in the collapse of the deal with the World Bank, which was contingent on joint U.S. and British financing. For a short account, see John Waterbury, *The Egypt of Nasser and Sadat* (Princeton: Princeton University Press, 1978), pp. 67 ff.

10. For a discussion of African socialism, see William H. Friedland and Carl C. Rosberg, *African Socialism* (Berkeley: University of California Press, Institute of International Studies), especially Part I.

11. Albright, *The USSR and Sub-Saharan Africa,* p. 4. Note that the Soviet Union only became a major supplier of arms to Africa in the 1970s. Prior to 1971, it was in fourth place as a provider of arms, after France, Great Britain, and the United States. See Joachim Krause, "Soviet Arms Transfers to Sub-Saharan Africa," in R. Craig Nation and Mark Kauppi (eds.), *The Soviet Impact in Africa* (Lexington, Mass.: D. C. Heath, 1984), p. 127.

12. See David E. Albright, "Moscow's African Policy in the 1970s," in Albright, *Communism in Africa,* especially pp. 39 ff.

13. The idea of the noncapitalist road first arose in 1960 in response to the appearance of regimes in the Third World, such as that of Castro in Cuba, calling themselves Marxist-Leninist. Many debates took place over this concept, particularly concerning these countries' revolutionary potential and the extent to which national liberation movements were simply nationalist or protosocialist. Initially fairly optimistic on both points, Soviet writers became increasingly pessimistic in the late 1960s and the 1970s. See Hough, *The Struggle for the Third World,* pp. 156 ff.

14. Some of the studies of the noncapitalist road were translated and distributed in African countries during the 1970s. Among these were R. Ulianovsky, *Socialism and the Newly Independent Nations* (Moscow: Progress Publishers, 1974); and *Developing Countries on the Neo-Capitalist Road,* Proceedings of the Third International Conference of the Africanist Marxists of the Socialist Countries (Sofia: Publishing House of the Bulgarian Academy of Science, 1974).

15. See Marina Ottaway, "Soviet Marxism and African Socialism," *Journal of Modern African Studies* (September 1978):477–487.

16. Somalia had first turned to the Eastern bloc for military aid in 1963, rejecting as unsatisfactory an offer by the United States, Germany, and Italy to train a small army for internal security and border duty. The first Soviet military aid package amounted to $32 million. On the Somali army before 1963, see Richard Booth, *The Armed Forces of the African States, 1970,* Adelphi Paper no. 67 (London: Institute for Strategic Studies, 1970). After 1969, Soviet aid greatly increased and is believed to have reached $1 billion by 1977. This figure has received wide publicity, but I have never been able to find confirmation or even an original source for it.

17. For greater detail, see Marina Ottaway, *Soviet and American Influence on the Horn of Africa* (New York: Praeger, 1982), pp. 64 ff.

18. Albright, "Moscow's African Policy in the 1970s," p. 42.

19. The voting pattern on U.N. resolutions concerning economic issues usually shows African and other Third-World countries on one side, irrespective of their ideological leanings, with the Soviet Union either siding with Western industrial nations or abstaining. For more detail, see Ottaway and Ottaway, *Afrocommunism,* pp. 184 ff.

20. Cuban troops first arrived in Ethiopia in late 1977. They fought in the Ogaden but refused to participate in the war in Eritrea. By 1985, the Cuban government had withdrawn all but about 3,000 men on the ground that there was no longer a threat from Somalia, and in late 1989 it removed the remaining troops. The number of Cuban troops in Angola has fluctuated greatly, reaching 50,000 only in 1988 just before the tripartite accord between Angola, Cuba, and South Africa was signed. The accord provides for a phased Cuban withdrawal and independence for Namibia. Support for Angola has probably been less expensive for the Cuban government than support for Ethiopia, as the former country has been able to bear at least part of the costs because of its oil revenue. Ethiopia, on the other hand, is not in a position to pay.

21. Hough, *The Struggle for the Third World,* p. 167. See also R. A. Ulianovsky, "National and Revolutionary Democracy: Evolution Paths," in *Africa in Soviet Studies, 1986* (Moscow: Institute of African Studies of the USSR Academy of Sciences, 1986), pp. 13–24.

22. Arms Control and Disarmament Agency (ACDA), *World Military Expenditures and Arms Transfers, 1988* (Washington, D.C.: ACDA, 1989), p. 84. Total value of Ethiopian exports, which went mostly to the West, in the same period was $4.26 billion. In the 1983–1987 period, Ethiopia received $4.33 billion worth of arms, all but $130 million of which came from the Soviet Union (*ibid.*, p. 111). There is no reason to believe the situation was different between 1977 and 1982.

23. *Ibid.*, p. 74. Information concerning the value of Angolan exports is incomplete, but available data show that it ranged from a low of $1.4 billion in 1977 to a high of $2.1 billion in 1985. Oil revenue has declined thereafter because prices have been decreasing. In the 1983–1987 period, $5.8 billion of the $6.3 billion in arms imported by Angola came from the Soviet Union (*ibid.*, p. 111).

24. *Ibid.*, p. 96. In 1989, the Soviet Union started withdrawing its military advisers from Mozambique.

25. The term *new thinking* was used first by the Soviets and then adopted by Western scholars. The elements of the new thinking were not as systematically developed and organized as was the concept of countries on the noncapitalist road at an earlier period, and these elements must be gleaned from recent articles and papers. There is as yet no systematic codification of the new thinking. The ideas on which this section of the chapter is based are derived from the written sources cited and from a number of discussions by the author with Soviet scholars and diplomats during 1988 and 1989.

26. See Helen Desfosses, "The USSR and Africa," *Issues* 16, no. 1 (1987):3–10, for a discussion of Soviet thinking in the Brezhnev years. The old thinking bears a striking resemblance to the new. On this issue, see also Helen Kitchen, *Some Guidelines on Africa for the Next President* (Washington, D.C.: Center for Strategic and International Studies, 1988), pp. 1–6.

27. A good example is found in G. V. Smirnov, "Africa: Problem of Development of the Public Sector, in *Africa in Soviet Studies, 1985* (Moscow: Institute of African Studies of the USSR Academy of Sciences, 1985), pp. 44–51.

28. The text of the report, together with an analysis, is found in Paul B. Henze, *Ethiopia: Crisis of a Marxist Economy. Analysis and Text of a Soviet Report* (Santa Monica: The Rand Corporation, 1989).

29. Chissano's comment was made to the press during a visit to Washington, D.C., in 1987. He stated that the Soviet Union "no longer" opposed the Mozambique decision to join the international financial institutions and that it no longer tried to impose on Mozambique "its model of existence."

30. See, for example, the Soviet advisers' report on Ethiopia in Henze, *Ethiopia*, pp. A16 ff.

31. See Boris Ponomarev, "Invincibility of the Liberation Movement," *Kommunist* 1 (January 1980):11–27; translated in *Foreign Broadcast Information Service, Soviet Union* 3, no. 024, supp. 029, annex 004 (Feb. 4, 1980).

32. See Richard B. Remnek, "The Soviet Union and the Quest for Peace in the Horn of Africa," Paper presented at the conference "Peace and Stability in the Horn of Africa," Michigan State University, Lansing, April 1989, pp. 34 ff. See also ACDA, *World Military Expenditures and Arms Transfers, 1988*, p. 84.

33. For details see Remnek, "The Soviet Union."

34. Marina Ottaway and David Ottaway, *Ethiopia: Empire in Revolution* (New York: Africana, 1978), pp. 169 ff.

35. The talks accomplished little beyond the fact that the two parties met for several days rather than breaking off immediately as they had in the past, and they agreed to a framework for future talks.

36. For an analysis of recent Soviet writing on South Africa, see Winrich Kuehne, "A 1988 Update on Soviet Relations with Pretoria, the ANC, and the SACP," CSIS *Africa Notes* 89 (September 1, 1988). Examining the same literature, Colin Legum reached the conclusion that the new thinking still fits in with the old Soviet idea that South Africa would move toward socialism in stages, with the formation of a black regime being the first stage. See Colin Legum, "The USSR and Africa," in Dennis L. Bark (ed.), *The Red Orchestra* (Stanford: Hoover Institution Press, 1986), pp. 103–117.

37. See Ismail Fahmi, *Negotiating for Peace in the Middle East* (Baltimore: Johns Hopkins University Press, 1983).

38. A sign of this trend is the appearance in the late 1980s of "pro-Albanian" factions in some African organizations, including the Tigrean People's Liberation Front in Ethiopia and the Communist party in Tunisia.

PART FOUR

THE MANAGEMENT OF INTERSTATE CONFLICT IN AFRICA

12

THE LAGOS THREE: ECONOMIC REGIONALISM IN SUB-SAHARAN AFRICA

CAROL LANCASTER

Sub-Saharan Africa is currently engaged in the most extensive experimentation in regional economic cooperation of any region in the developing world. According to the World Bank, intergovernmental organizations in Africa, many of which have an economic focus, exceed two hundred.[1] These organizations include service, research, and professional organizations, such as the African Center for Monetary Studies or the West African Rice Development Association; the monetary unions, including the Union Monétaire Ouest Africaine; development finance and coordination organizations, such as the African Development Bank and the Southern African Development Cooperation Conference (SADCC); and eight regional integration experiments, the most prominent of which is the Economic Community of West African States (ECOWAS).

This chapter focuses on the three largest experiments in regional economic integration: ECOWAS, the Preferential Trade Area of East and Southern Africa (PTA), and the Economic Community of Central African States (ECCAS). These organizations, together with the Arab Maghreb Union of North African Countries, are intended as the first steps toward the creation of a continent-wide common market, which is called for in the Lagos Plan of Action. The Lagos Plan, signed by African heads of state at the Organization of African Unity meeting in 1980, sought to promote Africa's long-term industrialization and development through the creation, first, of larger, subregional markets and, by the year 2000, of a continent-wide market through merging the subregional markets.

The first section of this chapter explores the rationales as well as the politics behind the establishment of these three organizations and examines how the organizations have actually performed. The second section examines the lessons provided by the Lagos Three regarding economic regionalism in sub-Saharan Africa. The third section peers into the possible future of economic regionalism in sub-Saharan Africa.

ECONOMIC INTEGRATION IN SUB-SAHARAN AFRICA: HISTORY, RATIONALES, POLITICS, AND PERFORMANCE

Regional economic ties in Africa have a long history. Long-distance trade throughout Africa existed before the Europeans arrived. With the coming of European colonialism, economic activities of many kinds—trade, finance, monetary affairs, administrative responsibilities, transport, and communications networks—were organized on a regional basis during the colonial period. A number of those arrangements extended into the independence period, including the monetary unions between francophone countries and France, and the East African Common Services Organization among Kenya, Uganda, and Tanzania.

Africans gained independence at a time when regional economic cooperation was popular among developing countries in other parts of the world. The Latin Americans, supported by the Economic Commission for Latin America, were experimenting with their own schemes of regional cooperation, including the Central American Common Market and the Latin American Free Trade Area.[2] The Asians soon followed with the creation in 1967 of the Association of South East Asian Nations (ASEAN).[3] The European Economic Community (EEC), initiated with the signing of the Treaty of Rome in 1957, was already functioning and provided a model and source of encouragement for groups of developing countries wishing to create their own regional integration schemes.

In addition to a history of long-range economic contacts and regional economic organization during the colonial period, Africans brought to independence their own aspirations toward continental or regional unity. The most vocal advocate of pan-African unity was Kwame Nkrumah, the first president of Ghana. Other leaders of the new states affirmed their commitments to pan-Africanism, even if few supported Nkrumah's vision of immediate political union among themselves. Several groupings of states—Senegal and Mali and, later, Ghana, Guinea, and Mali—experimented with political unions. These soon proved unworkable and were abandoned.

Also in the early 1960s, African states began to organize themselves in loose political organizations, such as the Monrovia and Brazzaville groups, based primarily on the ideological orientations of member states. In 1963, the Organization of African Unity (OAU) was created to include all African countries. The OAU was, in part, an expression of the aspiration of unity among Africans, although it was not given the authority to make decisions that were binding on member states. It was also intended to head off the increasing division of Africa into ideological blocs, which threatened to introduce cold-war tensions into the continent. After the OAU was set up, the Monrovia and Brazzaville groups were dissolved, and no further formal subregional organizations based primarily on shared ideological orientations or political goals were established. Regional cooperation among African governments thereafter centered primarily on achieving common economic objectives.

There are at present eight experiments in regional economic integration among sub-Saharan African states.[4] The three largest and most ambitious are the Economic Community of West African States, with sixteen member countries; the Preferential Trade Area, with nineteen member states; and the Economic Community of Central African States, with ten member countries. The goal of these experiments is to create economic unions among member states. There are typically three stages in the process of creating such a union: the establishment of a preferential or free trade area through the reduction or elimination of barriers to trade among member states; the creation of a customs union or common market involving free or preferential trade among members plus the erection of a common external tariff on imports from nonmember states; and the initiation of a full economic union among members, involving the removal of barriers to the movement of goods, services, capital, and labor, the unification of customs regulations, the harmonization of macroeconomic policies, and the creation of a common currency and a common central bank.

Regional integration schemes may aim at achieving any one of the stages or at achieving all three, usually in successive steps. In addition, ECOWAS, the PTA, and the ECCAS each has a secretariat, and ECOWAS and the PTA have established development banks to finance regional projects and to compensate member states for losses resulting from membership in the organizations—for example, losses in government revenues from tariff reductions. The ECCAS plans to establish its own development bank in the future. ECOWAS and the PTA also have currency clearinghouses—organizations responsible for facilitating the settlement of trade payments among member states. The ECCAS plans eventually to establish its own clearinghouse. The objective of these houses is to encourage and facilitate the use of local currencies in trade financing among members and, thus, to encourage expanded intraregional trade.

What are the Lagos Three and other African regional integration experiments intended to accomplish? The answers to this question are of two kinds: economic and diplomatic. The existence and functioning of these organizations cannot be understood unless both are taken into account.

The basic rationale for regional economic integration has traditionally been the promotion of trade and economic welfare among member states. This rationale has evolved primarily with developed economies in mind.[5] The establishment of a free trade area or customs union among previously separate economies will result in the most efficient producers among them expanding their production and sales. Trade among member states will be created as less competitive producers are forced out of business. Economic resources in participating states will be employed more productively, and consumers will benefit through lower prices. This reasoning is drawn from international trade theory based on comparative advantage. Its main focus is on improving economic welfare through a more efficient use of resources. Its analysis is static. It is not focused on the dynamics of long-run growth or development, although a consequence of improved economic welfare may be stimulation of that growth.

However, economic development rather than resource efficiency has been the principal preoccupation of developing countries. The objectives for creating expanded markets among them have therefore focused mostly on promoting rapid growth through expanded investment. Although the links between economic integration and development have not always been clearly articulated by developed country economists, their reasoning has been based on the following assumptions: (1) Industrial development is a key element in overall economic development; (2) efficient industrial development typically requires producers to be large enough to achieve economies of scale;[6] (3) most industrial producers in the smaller, developing countries will require markets larger than their home markets to achieve economies of scale; (4) hence, it makes sense to merge smaller markets into larger markets that will encourage expanded investment, production, trade, national income, and growth; (5) however, the larger markets must be protected for a time from competitive imports from third countries while producers expand their investments to achieve scale efficiencies and benefit from the learning process associated with new or expanded investments.

This rationale is, in effect, a growth strategy based on import substitution within multicountry integration schemes. Efficiency is not its highest priority, and—indeed—at its initial stages, greater inefficiencies in resource use might occur as trade is diverted from more efficient producers within it. In theory at least, some of the less efficient producers in the scheme will, with sufficient market size and protection, eventually become both efficient and internationally competitive.

In contrast to economic integration among developed countries, the critical element in regional integration as a strategy for promoting industrial growth among developing countries is not its expansionary impact on trade. Indeed, most developing countries—particularly in Africa—have only limited potential for expanding trade with one another, given the similarities in what they produce—mainly, primary products. What is much more important to them is the stimulus integration can provide for expanded investment. Increased trade may be a consequence of greater capacity utilization by existing producers or of new investment, but it is not the ultimate end of regional integration schemes. This fact has too often been confused in discussions of regional integration among African countries.

A second rationale—more in the area of ideology than of economic reasoning—often used to justify regional integration in Africa has been the importance of achieving collective economic self-reliance among African states. A major symbol of the limitations on African self-reliance has been the heavy dependence of African countries on international trade, primarily with Western developed countries and—in southern Africa—with the Republic of South Africa. Most African countries produce and export a few types of primary products, such as groundnuts, copper, or cotton. They must import almost all of their manufactured goods. Their trade dependence on the rest of the world has heightened their sense of economic vulnerability and fed their desire to become economically self-reliant. However, most African countries are too small to become economically self-sufficient on their own. (There are at present twenty-one countries with a population of six million or less. Ten of these have a population of one million or less.[7]) They must rely on others. But Africans have often preferred to rely on other Africans in various forms of economic union, which they feel is less risky and more supportive of their dignity than relying on non-African powers.[8]

A further rationale behind regional integration schemes has been more strictly political in nature. It involves the bargaining power of African states vis-à-vis the rest of the world. Africans have long recognized that acting together in economic groupings enhances their bargaining power with foreign governments, international institutions, and multinational corporations. Together, they have more to offer or to deny others in terms of size, economic potential, and political weight. Alone, their small size, narrow range of exports, poverty, and reliance on external financing combine to make them weak and vulnerable to the pressures from external powers.

In addition to these general economic and political rationales, Africans have pursued specific diplomatic goals in joining regional integration schemes. A recounting of the circumstances leading to the creation of these schemes, the stated or apparent purposes of their members in joining them, and their functioning once established will illustrate this important point.

The Economic Community of West African States, established in 1975 among sixteen states of West Africa (see Table 12.1A for membership), is perhaps the most visible and certainly the most studied of the current experiments in regional integration in sub-Saharan Africa.[9] The creation of ECOWAS was in large measure a result of Nigerian diplomacy.[10] From the early years of independence, the Nigerian government had supported the idea of an African common market. This idea was inevitably put aside during the Biafra conflict. In the wake of that conflict, however, the Nigerian president, General Gowan, made economic integration a cornerstone of his regional diplomacy. In addition to believing in the economic importance of integration for the region, General Gowan wished to reduce his country's isolation from other West African countries, to regain and expand its influence, and to reduce the influence of France in the region. (The French had supported Biafra during the Nigerian civil war, while the Côte d'Ivoire had recognized Biafra. Both France and the Côte d'Ivoire were uneasy about the potential economic and political influence of Nigeria in West Africa and were hoping that a breakup of Nigeria would limit that influence.) Nigerian businessmen also supported the creation of ECOWAS, seeing it as providing them with opportunities for expanding their markets in West Africa. (A key provision of the ECOWAS treaty ensured that only products from businesses owned primarily by Africans would be eligible for preferential treatment within ECOWAS. This "rules of origin" provision effectively excluded the products from French-owned businesses in francophone countries from the benefits of intra-ECOWAS trade.[11])

Nigeria pursued a carefully planned strategy of persuading its often-reluctant neighbors to support the creation of ECOWAS. It recognized that agreement by the francophone countries was essential, and so it focused its efforts first on Togo, with which it had close relations. With Togo's support, Benin—which is sandwiched between Nigeria and Togo—would feel compelled to join to avoid being surrounded and isolated by pro-ECOWAS governments. It was expected that Niger (another neighbor with strong economic ties to Nigeria) would be unable to resist supporting ECOWAS if Benin and Togo agreed. These countries' support would begin to create a momentum among francophone states in support of ECOWAS and, Lagos hoped, would persuade the two key francophone states—Senegal and the Côte d'Ivoire—to join.[12]

In seeking the support of these and other countries, Nigeria used "spray" diplomacy, offering interest-free loans, grants, concessionally priced oil,[13] and equity investment in projects in neighboring countries. Nigerian efforts at persuasion, plus its effective leadership of the African, Caribbean, and Pacific (ACP) countries in their negotiations with the EEC on the first Lome Convention (associating the ACP countries economically with the EEC through special trade, investment, and aid arrangements), finally bore fruit when the francophone countries along with nine other West African governments signed the Lagos Treaty in 1975, which established ECOWAS. The Communauté Economique de l'Afrique de l'Ouest (CEAO)—an already-established integration experiment among francophone countries—would continue to exist, and its separate status was acknowledged in the Lagos Treaty.

Economic union among ECOWAS countries was planned to occur in three stages. In the first two-year period, members were to freeze their tariffs on primary products produced by other members and on manufactured goods eligible for preferential treatment in intra-ECOWAS trade. The second period, which was to last eight years, was to end with the elimination of import duties in intra-ECOWAS trade. The final stage would last five years and involve the erection of a common external tariff. The ECOWAS Treaty called for the free movement of labor as well as goods, services, and capital. However, at the request of the Nigerians, who feared a large influx of labor into their country, it was decided that free movement of labor would be implemented over a period of fifteen years.[14]

To provide compensation for the poorer members of ECOWAS for the costs of participation in the community, a Fund for Cooperation, Compensation, and Development was set up. ECOWAS members were to contribute to the fund on the basis of their relative income levels and gains from new investments in the community. The fund was also authorized to accept contributions from nonmember governments. Finally, a West African Clearing House was set up in association with ECOWAS to facilitate the use of local currencies in financing intra-ECOWAS trade.

ECOWAS has achieved few of its goals. The first stage of the integration scheme—involving the consolidation of customs procedures (including the freezing of tariffs)—has been approved by governments, but little action appears to have been taken to implement this stage. The *Annual Report* of ECOWAS in 1985 observed that "despite the impressive number of agreements reached and decisions taken regarding the harmonization of customs documents, the adoption of common procedures, and the program for deregulating non-manufactured crude goods, traditional handicrafts and industrial products, the Economic Community of West African States has not made tangible progress in practical terms."[15] The second and most critical stage of trade liberalization among member states was to have been completed by 1985 but has been postponed repeatedly; it was rescheduled to commence in 1990. It is not clear in early 1991 whether member states have begun to liberalize their trade with one another. The protocol on the free movement of labor was finally signed in 1986, but few states have actually ratified it and "systematic and flagrant violations" by member states continue. By 1989, member governments were $80 million in arrears in their contributions to the secretariat and the fund.[16] The record of the West African Clearing House was also regarded as disappointing, with member states financing a small and declining proportion of their intraregional trade through the institution.[17] Finally, the existence of ECOWAS has had no impact on the proportion of trade among ECOWAS states, which has remained at its 1980 level of just over 5 percent of their total trade.

Despite the continuing failure of member states to implement agreements reached at ECOWAS meetings or to pay in full their contributions to the community's institutions, most heads of state continue to attend the annual meetings, vociferously reaffirm their commitment to the goals of the organization, and frequently approve new and often ambitious schemes for ECOWAS to undertake. In 1987, the heads of state approved a three-year Economic Recovery Programme for the region, which was estimated to cost nearly $1 billion; they agreed to develop a common approach to debt negotiations; and they adopted a Monetary Cooperation Program aimed at creating a monetary union among member states.

The pattern of well-attended annual meetings, adoption of new initiatives, and inaction on past commitments has provoked criticism in the African media and among the heads of states. *West Africa* magazine commented on the 1989 ECOWAS summit in the following words:

> There is a pattern to ECOWAS summits which in some respects has become all too familiar, after 14 years of the organization's existence and 12 summits. There are the sterling calls to action, the urgent pleas for member states to carry out the protocols they have happily signed, and above all to pay the arrears in their membership subscriptions. . . . ECOWAS may be facing a make-or-break phase. Unless some sign of progress can be registered in sectors that matter, the imperatives that led to the Community's creation back in 1975 may be called into question.[18]

The failure of ECOWAS to achieve its goals of integration versus the continuing support (both in words and attendance at its annual meetings) among heads of member states and their tendency to approve new initiatives is puzzling. Why, on the one hand, do member governments fail to implement their commitments under the agreement and, at the same time, lament that failure, attend annual meetings, affirm the value and importance of ECOWAS, and adopt additional initiatives? ECOWAS, despite its failure to achieve its stated goals, is clearly viewed by heads of state as benefiting them and their governments; otherwise, they would stop attending its meetings.

Two benefits, both political, derive from ECOWAS's annual meetings. One is the exposure heads of state receive in their own media and in the media of other West African states from participating in a meeting with a large number of other heads of state. These annual ECOWAS meetings are a media event, even reported at times in the world press. But probably more important are the opportunities offered by these annual meetings for the political leadership of West Africa to deal with regional issues of importance to them that could not easily be dealt with in the much larger annual meetings of the Organization of African Unity or at the bilateral level. In several recent instances, the annual ECOWAS heads of state meeting has provided an opportunity for reducing tensions between member governments. In 1988, the attendance of the head of state of Ghana, Flight Lt. Jerry Rawlings, at the ECOWAS summit in Togo gave him and President Eyadema of Togo an opportunity to smooth the strained relations between them. In 1989, the presidents of Senegal and Mauritania met for the first time since the mutual expulsions of their citizens from the other country, and relations between them were reconciled. This increasingly important function was officially recognized at the 1990 ECOWAS heads of state meeting when a Nigerian proposal to create a Standing Mediation Committee was adopted.

The venue of a regional heads of state meeting, with participants attempting to mediate difficulties between member states, can play a useful role in African diplomacy, where personal relations between political leaders can greatly influence relations among their countries. ECOWAS is the only regional organization in West Africa that includes francophone, lusophone, and anglophone states and that can, therefore, mediate disputes among these countries. It also has the advantage of being smaller than the OAU, and so it can focus its efforts on regional issues without involving large numbers of governments outside the region.

ECOWAS appears to be becoming a regional diplomatic or political organization, and this evolution may sustain it even in the face of its failure to realize its formal goals of economic integration. There is, however, a serious danger to the future of ECOWAS as it becomes more active in mediating regional disputes, particularly where concerted action among member states is involved. An example is the ECOWAS intervention force in Liberia (Ecomog). Ecomog at one point nearly provoked a break with the ECOWAS states, with Burkina Faso and the Côte d'Ivoire openly opposing the intervention force, fearing it was a stalking horse for Nigerian policies supporting President Doe of Liberia. (The bulk of the Ecomog forces are Nigerian, along with several of the senior officers.) Should this or any other concerted ECOWAS action set member states against one another, the organization may break apart.

In 1981, the Preferential Trade Area of East and Southern Africa (PTA) was formed. It is the largest regional integration scheme, with nineteen members (see Table 12.1A for membership). The PTA treaty is modeled on that of ECOWAS, with an economic union among member states to be achieved in stages through the freezing and then progressive elimination of tariffs and nontariff barriers on eligible goods produced in member states. A regional common market was to be fully established by 1992, with the first reductions in tariffs to commence in 1984. There is a restrictive rules of origin provision in the PTA treaty, which requires that goods eligible for preferential trade among member states be produced by firms with majority African ownership. There is no compensation mechanism to offset the costs of membership in the PTA for poorer member states. All states are permitted to impose temporary tariffs or quotas on imports from other member states when they are suffering from persistent balance of payments problems or wish to protect their own infant industries. A Trade and Development Bank has been set up to finance development projects in members states, and a currency clearinghouse has been established that is run by the Central Bank of Zimbabwe.

The origins of the PTA have less to do with the regional diplomatic policies of member states than with the ideology of regional integration in Africa and the pressures from the Economic Commission for Africa (ECA) for the creation of integration schemes. The proposals in the Lagos Plan of Action were developed by the ECA, which, since its creation in 1958, had promoted the idea of regional economic integration in Africa. In approving the Lagos Plan, African heads of state implicitly approved the creation of the subregional integration schemes recommended in the plan. ECOWAS already existed in West Africa; what remained was to create the subregional market integration schemes in central and East Africa. The PTA was the designated scheme for East and southern Africa, and its midwife was the ECA.

Negotiations under ECA auspices on the creation of a regional integration scheme for East and southern Africa began in 1978 soon after the collapse of the East African Community. Nevertheless, a number of states had serious reservations about the new scheme based on its wide geographical spread, the poor transportation network shared by member states, and the lack of complementarity among member states' economies. Tanzania and Mozambique delayed signing the PTA treaty for several years. (Tanzania was also reluctant in the early 1980s to reopen its border with Kenya, as it would have to do as a member of the PTA. It had closed that border in the disputes with Kenya over sharing the assets of the failed East African Community.) The government of Zimbabwe needed to be persuaded to join by Kenya, Zambia, and its own business community.[19] Lesotho and Swaziland had to make sure the Republic of South Africa had no objections to their joining before they could sign the treaty.

It is not hard to understand why the more advanced states in the region supported the creation of the PTA. Both Kenyan and Zimbabwean businesses stood to benefit from improved export opportunities in the region. But it might well be asked what the poorer states hoped to gain, especially with the absence of any compensating mechanism to offset the costs of their membership in the PTA. The Somali government, according to one of its officials, joined primarily to avoid economic and political isolation. Siad Barre, the president of Somalia, decided to sign the PTA treaty (without consulting his staff) once it was clear that Somalia's neighbor, Ethiopia, was going to join.[20] Avoidance of isolation may have been a motivating factor for other of the smaller and poorer member states, such as Djibouti, Rwanda, Burundi, and Malawi.

The experience of the PTA has begun to echo the pattern of other African regional integration schemes.[21] Problems among member states have arisen on several issues. Objections were raised by Kenya and several other states over the rules of origin provision of the treaty; these states argued that the provision penalized their producers—many of which were more than 51 percent foreign-owned. The provision was ultimately eased. Poorer members have objected to the absence of any compensation mechanism; a study of the problem was undertaken, but no action was agreed upon. Meanwhile, it appears that although a degree of trade liberalization has occurred within the PTA, a number of member states delayed implementing agreed tariff reductions, forcing a postponement of the final date for achieving a common market until the year 2000. The currency clearing arrangement has yet to be fully utilized, although utilization is reported to have increased recently. Although the institutions of the PTA have suffered less than those of other integration schemes from the unwillingness of member states to provide agreed financing, there have been some shortfalls in the past. Trade among PTA member states remains at an average of 6 percent of their total trade worldwide. Meanwhile, PTA members have begun discussions of grandiose schemes that appear even less likely to be realized than their basic commitments under the PTA treaty, including the creation of a monetary union among themselves and the possibility of creating a PTA airline. Member states have agreed to impose economic sanctions against South Africa.

It is not yet clear whether the PTA will follow ECOWAS in the latter's failure to implement fully its economic integration policies and simply become something of a political umbrella under which member states conduct regional diplomacy. Although an increasing number of states have joined the PTA, members have thus far used it relatively little as a venue for regional diplomacy. The PTA may already be too large to serve such a purpose effectively, as its nineteen member states represent central, southern, and East Africa.

The most recently created integration scheme is the Economic Community of Central African States (ECCAS), with a total membership (see Table 12.1A) of ten.[22] The treaty of the ECCAS, like that of the PTA, was modeled on the ECOWAS treaty. A common market was to be completed in stages by the year 2000. With the commitment of African heads of state to the Lagos Plan and the pressures from the ECA to establish the third regional integration scheme envisaged by that plan, the creation of the ECCAS was probably inevitable. However, several potential member states strongly supported its creation. Zaire, for example, would now belong to a major integration scheme. (Its request to join the SADCC had been turned down, and it had not yet joined the PTA.) Chad and São Tomé and Príncipe would also end their isolation by joining such a scheme.

The ECCAS has gotten off to an exceedingly slow start. Only six of the ten heads of state attended the fifth summit in 1989, and their conclusion at that time was that "significant obstacles prevent an immediate and real economic integration of the countries."[23] No agreement was reached on the details of how a customs union and tariff liberalization should proceed, and members have not yet frozen existing tariff barriers on goods produced by member states. The free movement of labor also remains to be settled. Only four of ten member states have paid their contributions to ECCAS institutions. Thus far, the ECCAS has made little progress even in establishing its institutions and its plan for integration. It also does not appear to have given member states a venue for pursuing regional diplomacy.

ECONOMIC REGIONALISM: THEORY AND EXPERIENCE IN SUB-SAHARAN AFRICA

What methodology or theories can give us insights into the experience of the Lagos Three in sub-Saharan Africa? The most obvious place to look for relevant theories is in the political science literature on political and economic integration. Most of this literature is functionalist or neofunctionalist in orientation—that is, it focuses on the process by which "political actors in several distinct national settings are persuaded to shift their loyalties, expectations and political activities toward a new center, whose institutions possess or demand jurisdiction over the preexisting national states."[24] Functionalists have posited that successful cooperation among independent states on "technical" issues can spill over into areas that are more political, providing key elites with benefits or the expectation of benefits that derive from integration and a learning experience of effective international cooperation, which predisposes them to further cooperation.

Much of the functionalist and neofunctionalist literature of the 1960s is not very helpful in understanding economic integration efforts in the developing world.[25] Based primarily on the experience of the EC, this literature focuses on the process by which integration occurs. But although a certain amount of technical cooperation has taken place in Africa, it has not yet led to greater integration among African states. However, some of the later work in this area has begun to examine the experience of economic integration in developing countries and to emphasize the role of economic costs and benefits from integration in the success of integrative schemes.[26] The concept of costs and benefits deriving from integration schemes is the most helpful in explaining the experience of the Lagos Three. But, unlike much of the literature on integration among developing countries, the experience of these schemes tells us that we must consider diplomatic as well as economic costs and benefits.[27]

One of the basic problems of regional integrative schemes is that the economic costs of participation for member states can be immediate and concrete, while the economic benefits typically accrue only after a long period and are uncertain and often unevenly distributed among member states. The costs include, first, a decrease in government revenues when tariffs are reduced. For developing countries, many of which rely on tariffs for a substantial proportion of their revenues, this cost can be substantial. Another cost may be the collapse of local firms as they find themselves unable to compete with firms in other member countries, resulting in a loss in national income, production, and employment.

Benefits from integration may include immediate opportunities for expanding production and trade for eligible firms located in member countries. Most important, the major benefits sought from regional integration schemes among developing countries are the new investments stimulated by the larger markets and potential scale economies deriving from the schemes. But even when such investment occurs, it can bring costs as well as benefits. New investors will usually locate in better-off members of a union, where economies are more vibrant, transport and communications facilities more developed, and living conditions more pleasant. This is the polarization effect of economic integration. The poorer members of an economic union often perceive that they are losing opportunities for industrialization, and they demand compensation. This was the fundamental problem with the East African Community, in which Tanzania felt it was not being properly compensated when new investment located in Kenya—permitting Kenya to expand its income, employment, and trade. Poorer countries in an economic union typically fear that they will become and remain the "hewers of wood and drawers of water" for the more advanced member states and, in the end, be worse off in an integration scheme than they would have been without it.

Most integration schemes contain arrangements to compensate poorer states for losses from membership, including direct payment of compensation as in ECOWAS. However, new investment has not been stimulated by the Lagos Three, so these problems have yet to arise. Several added problems in Africa make the investment benefits of integration even less certain than in other parts of the world. The rules of origin restrictions in some of the schemes were intended to ensure that African-owned rather than foreign-owned firms reaped the benefits of integration. But there are few African-owned firms of any size in these schemes (except those owned by Nigerians), and there is relatively little capital owned by Africans who are willing to invest it in their own countries. The only alternative for new investments may be foreign-owned capital. Yet, the Africans have effectively discouraged that capital through the rules of origin requirements. A second factor discouraging foreign or domestic investment in sub-Saharan Africa is the economic malaise that has afflicted the region for over a decade, deriving from economic mismanagement by Africans themselves, a sharp deterioration in the terms of trade, a heavy debt burden, and a slowing of growth. Private investors are understandably reluctant to risk their capital under such circumstances. Moreover, political instabilities also undermine the confidence of potential investors. Coups, demonstrations, strikes, internal conflicts, and other uncertainties exist in Africa to a greater degree than in Europe, Asia, or even most of Latin America. Investors have many attractive opportunities elsewhere in the world.

One more peculiarity of African integration schemes has added to the challenges facing them. Within ECOWAS are two other regional integration schemes: the CEAO and the Mano River Union among Sierra Leone, Liberia, and Guinea. Within the ECCAS, there is the Union Douanière et Economique de l'Afrique Centrale (UDEAC), composed of six mainly francophone states of Central Africa, and the Communauté Economique des Pays de Grands Lacs (CEPGL) among Zaire, Rwanda, and Burundi. In West Africa in particular, something of an Alphonse and Gaston act has been going on between the CEAO and ECOWAS over which organization adjusts its trade preferences to fit the other first.[78] ECOWAS states that are nonmembers of the CEAO argue that they cannot reduce their tariffs on one another's products if another preferential trade area is within their membership. The CEAO members argue that they cannot reduce their tariffs on ECOWAS goods if other ECOWAS states are not prepared to do the same. The ECCAS has not yet reached the stage of conflict with the UDEAC, but this may come in the future. In fact, the dispute between ECOWAS and the CEAO, the latter now weakened by internal scandals and its progress toward trade liberalization stalemated, would not present a decisive barrier to progress toward integration within ECOWAS if key member states were prepared to move forward on trade liberalization.

The basic problem of regional economic integration schemes in Africa has been and remains that the economic costs of participation in such schemes are immediate, while the economic benefits are long-term and uncertain. Political leaders in Africa, like political leaders elsewhere in the world, are unwilling to sustain the immediate costs of integration for uncertain benefits available—if at all—only in the long run. This explains why member governments have mostly failed to implement trade liberalization and other agreements and why the schemes have failed to achieve their goals. However, it does not explain why Africans have continued to create such schemes, join them, attend their meetings, and repeatedly approve new initiatives for the faltering organizations.

Here, the answers are political and diplomatic. ECOWAS was a case where an aspiring regional hegemon—Nigeria—was willing and able, for diplomatic reasons, to sponsor (and pay for) the creation of ECOWAS. Nigeria, with its economic problems and absorption in its domestic political changes, is no longer willing or able to play the role of a regional hegemon in maintaining the momentum of integration in ECOWAS. In fact, there are no regional hegemons in black Africa today that are able and willing to sponsor effective economic integration schemes.

However, these schemes—even when they are ineffective in achieving their goals—have diplomatic value for member states. For some states, membership in and attendance at annual meetings of such schemes is a form of defensive diplomacy—the avoidance of isolation and an expression of regional solidarity. For others, such membership and attendance have become useful means of conducting quiet regional politicking under the guise of discussing economic matters. Since the creation of the OAU in 1963, Africans have been reluctant to set up regional political organizations that would challenge this symbol of continent-wide political unity. But they have been encouraged to set up regional economic cooperation schemes, and some of these, such as ECOWAS, have begun to become convenient venues for the conduct of regional diplomacy in cases where the OAU would be too large and too public a forum for such diplomacy. In order to provide these integration schemes with legitimacy and a raison d'être in the face of the obvious unwillingness of member governments to proceed with trade liberalization, however, heads of state repeatedly commit themselves to ambitious new initiatives.

THE FUTURE OF ECONOMIC REGIONALISM IN SUB-SAHARAN AFRICA

The prospects for effective economic cooperation among African states in the coming decade are not bright. Economic cooperation among sub-Saharan African states makes sense, as it ultimately promises them improved prospects for industrial development, enhancement of their bargaining power vis-à-vis the rest of the world, and greatly strengthened economic self-reliance. Africans will continue to believe in the value of regional cooperation. And if regional economic organizations provide diplomatic benefits to member states, these organizations may continue to be active, although repeated failure to follow through on old and new commitments may eventually destroy their credibility among African opinion-makers.

However, until the calculus of economic costs and benefits shifts in favor of the benefits, the organizations will fail to achieve their economic objectives. The economic costs and benefits appear unlikely to change dramatically in the coming decade. The costs will remain immediate and the benefits long-run and uncertain. It is possible that the World Bank and other aid-giving institutions and governments will attempt to push African governments toward economic integration through conditioning a proportion of their lending on progress in this area. The first experiment of this type may be with the UDEAC.[29] Foreign aid in sufficient quantities might be helpful in promoting trade liberalization in individual integration schemes, but unless the integrative process itself begins to generate economic benefits for member states, that aid will have been an ineffective palliative. In any case, it seems unlikely that sufficient foreign aid would be available—in addition to what is already being provided to African governments—to make a significant difference in the major integration schemes in sub-Saharan Africa.

Looking beyond the year 2000, the future of economic regionalism in sub-Saharan Africa may depend on the emergence of regional hegemons with the will and the resources to promote economic cooperation and integration. A postapartheid South Africa may eventually play that role in southern Africa. A politically stable and prosperous Nigeria could play that role in West Africa. Some day, a politically stable and prosperous Zaire could also claim that role in central Africa. But these are indeed long-term speculations, and their prospects are uncertain.

NOTES

1. World Bank, *Sub-Saharan Africa: From Crisis to Sustainable Growth* (Washington, D.C.: World Bank, 1989), p. 152.

2. There is a large body of literature on experiments in economic integration in Latin America. See, for example, the InterAmerican Development Bank (IADB), *Economic and Social Progress in Latin America: Economic Integration* (Washington, D.C.: IADB, 1984).

3. There is also ample literature on ASEAN. See, for example, the *ASEAN Economic Bulletin*, a monthly publication.

4. Other than the Lagos Three, there are the Communauté Economique de l'Afrique de l'Ouest among seven francophone countries, and the Mano River Union among Sierra Leone, Liberia, and Guinea. In central Africa, there is the Union Douanière et Economique de l'Afrique Centrale with six member states, mostly francophone; and the Communauté Economique des Pays de Grands Lacs among Zaire, Rwanda, and Burundi. In southern Africa, there is the South African Customs Union among the Republic of South Africa, Botswana, Lesotho, and Swaziland. SADCC is often thought of as a regional integration scheme. Although regional economic integration is among its major functions, it has never been a driving one.

SADCC has functioned much more as a regional development financing scheme, channeling aid to its member states.

5. For discussions of the economic rationales for establishing customs unions among developed economies, see, for example, Jacob Viner, *The Customs Union Issue* (New York: Carnegie Endowment for International Peace, 1950); and Bela Belassa, *The Theory of Economic Integration* (Homewood, Ill.: Richard D. Irwin Inc., 1961).

6. Economic integration is primarily an industrialization strategy, as agricultural production does not usually require large home markets to reach scale economies. For efforts to apply integration theory to the case of developing countries, see C. A. Cooper and B. F. Massell, "Towards a General Theory of Customs Unions for Developing Countries," *Journal of Political Economy* 73:461–476; and Peter Robson, *The Economics of International Integration* (London: Allen & Unwin, 1980).

7. See World Bank, *Sub-Saharan Africa: From Crisis to Sustainable Growth*, for population and other statistics.

8. This is a belief rather than an established fact. Neighboring countries can be as disruptive and destructive of economic progress as can distant countries. One has only to remember the number of African countries expelling foreign workers at one time or another or erecting trade barriers against one another.

9. There is a large body of literature on ECOWAS. A good introduction is Uka Ezenwe, *ECOWAS and the Economic Integration of West Africa* (St. Martin's: New York, 1983).

10. See Olatunde Ojo, "Nigeria and the Formation of ECOWAS," *International Organization* 34, no. 4 (Autumn 1980):571–604; and Daniel Bach, "The Politics of West African Economic Cooperation: CEAO and ECOWAS," *Journal of Modern African Studies* 21, no. 4 (Autumn 1983):605–623.

11. This provision was included in response to pressures from Nigerian businesses and to ensure their support of the organization. See Ojo, "Nigeria," pp. 585 ff. It is also in accord with the Nigerian policy of *indigenization*—that is, of requiring that between 40 and 60 percent of Nigerian firms be owned by Nigerians.

12. This strategy by Nigeria is recounted in detail in Ojo, *ibid.*, pp. 585 ff. Francophone states in West Africa had already created their own regional economic integration scheme—the Communauté Economique de l'Afrique de l'Ouest (CEAO).

13. See Olajide Aluko, "Oil at Concessionary Prices for Africa: A Case-Study in Nigerian Decision-Making," *African Affairs* 75 (October 1976):430.

14. For details on this issue of particular sensitivity to Nigeria, see Ralph Onwuka, "ECOWAS Protocol on Free Movement of Persons," *African Affairs* 81 (April 1982): 193–206.

15. Quoted in Makhtar Diouf, "Evaluation of West African Experiments in Economic Integration," in World Bank, *The Long-Term Perspective Study of Sub-Saharan Africa, Background Papers, Volume 4: Proceedings of a Workshop on Regional Integration and Cooperation* (Washington, D.C.: World Bank, 1990):22–23.

16. *Africa Research Bulletin*, Economic Series 26 (July 31, 1989):9593.

17. Bernadette Cole and Oudjoe Kpor, "A House in Need of Attention," *West Africa* (March 19, 1990):440 ff.

18. *West Africa* 3751 (July 10, 1989):1119.

19. Douglas Anglin, "Economic Liberation and Regional Cooperation in Southern Africa: SADCC and PTA," *International Organization* 37, no. 4 (Autumn 1983): 689. For more background on the PTA, see Ngila Mwase, "The African Preferential Trade Area," *Journal of World Trade Law* 19 (1985):622–636.

20. Interview with Somali permanent secretary for the PTA, Ministry of Commerce and Industries, Mogadishu, December 1986. Barre apparently did not ask the opinion of any of his economic officials before he signed the PTA treaty.

21. For a review of the history and experience of the PTA, see Guy Martin, "The Preferential Trade Area (PTA) for East and Southern Africa: Achievements, Problems, Prospects," *Afrika Spectrum* 2 (1989):157–171.

22. There is little written on the ECCAS. See Laurent Zang, "L'Integration Economique en Afrique Centrale: de Nouvelles Perspectives avec la CEEAC?" *Le Mois en Afrique* (February 1987):253–259, for one analysis.

23. "Fifth Summit (Bangui)," *Africa Research Bulletin*, Economic Series 26 (April 30, 1989):9491.

24. Ernst B. Haas, *The Uniting of Europe* (Stanford: Stanford University Press, 1958), p. 16.

25. There is a large body of literature on international integration, functionalism, and neofunctionalism. See, for example, Leon Lindberg and Stuart Scheingold (eds.), *Regional Integration: Theory and Research* (Cambridge: Harvard University Press, 1971); Ernst Haas, *Beyond the Nation State* (Stanford: Stanford University Press, 1964); Charles Pentland, *International Theory and European Integration* (London: Faber and Faber, 1973); and the set of articles in *International Organization* 24, no. 4 (1970). Most of this work focuses on the experience of integration in Europe.

26. See particularly Joseph Nye, "Comparing Common Markets: A Revised Neo-Functionalist Model," *International Organization* 24, no. 4 (Autumn 1970):796–834, for an effort to apply the theory to the experience of developing countries. See also Lynn Mytelka, "The Salience of Gains in Third World Integrative Systems," *World Politics* 25, no. 2 (January 1973):236–250.

27. Diplomatic factors also played a role in the creation of the EEC. Germany was willing to join because it saw membership as a means of restoring its international credibility; France and the rest of Europe (and the United States) wanted Germany in the EEC to constrain its future ability to pursue a militaristic foreign policy.

28. For more details, see Daniel Bach, "Francophone Regional Organizations and ECOWAS, or What Is Economic Co-operation About in West Africa," in S. Wright and J. Okolo (eds.), *West Africa Regional Cooperation and Development* (Boulder, Colo.: Westview Press, 1989), pp. 53–65.

29. For past experience in the use of aid to promote regional integration, see Lynn Mytelka, "Foreign Aid and Regional Integration: The UDEAC Case," *Journal of Common Market Studies* (December 1973):138–158; and Thomas Cox, "Northern Actors in a South-South Setting: External Aid and East African Integration," *Journal of Common Market Studies* 21, no. 3 (March 1983):284–312.

TABLE 12.1A The Lagos Three: Member States and Organizations

	Established	*Members*	*Major Institutions*
Economic Community of West African States (ECOWAS)	1975	Benin, Burkina Faso, Cape Verde, Gambia, Ghana, Guinea, Guinea-Bissau, Côte d'Ivoire, Liberia, Mali, Mauritania, Niger, Nigeria, Senegal, Sierra Leone, Togo	secretariat, ECOWAS fund, West Africa Clearing House
Preferential Trade Area of East and Southern Africa (PTA)	1981	Burundi, Kenya, Comoros, Djibouti, Ethiopia, Malawi, Lesotho, Mauritius, Rwanda, Somalia, Swaziland, Uganda, Tanzania, Zambia, Zimbabwe, Zaire, Sudan, Namibia, Mozambique	trade and development bank, clearinghouse, secretariat
Economic Community of Central African States (ECCAS)	1983	Gabon, Chad, Cameroon, Central African Republic, Congo, Zaire, Burundi, Rwanda, São Tomé and Príncipe, Equatorial Guinea	secretariat, development bank

13 INTER-AFRICAN NEGOTIATIONS

I. WILLIAM ZARTMAN

In inter-African relations, two makes a conflict, three is company, and fifty-one is a crowd of free riders. African negotiations over conflict and cooperation are a highly developed exercise with its own characteristics and patterns, strengths and limitations. In terms of outcomes, bilateral negotiations and broad multilateral negotiations tend to be ineffective in dealing with conflict; in between, mediation among the conflicting parties is frequently needed to bring negotiations to fruition. In cooperation, multilateral negotiations have a high record of success, although the impact of the product of such negotiations has its own limitations and characteristics. This chapter presents the characteristics of the negotiation process as practiced in Africa, giving examples, and seeks explanations for those characteristics.

In assessing results and analyzing the process by which they are achieved, it should be remembered that conflict is an inevitable—and sometimes a functional or even desirable—condition of interstate relations and that negotiation is a means of limiting it, whereas cooperation—although desirable and sometimes functional—is by no means inevitable and negotiation is the means of achieving it. As a result, the playing field has different slopes according to the subject, imparting different types of difficulties to the negotiation process. Across this distinction runs another, which is related to the size of the teams. At one end of a spectrum stand conflicts and cooperations that are highly personalized in the head of state, with little interest and involvement by society; at the other end are conflicts and cooperations that are national causes, affecting society deeply and arousing deep popular sentiments.[1] Although this dichotomy has an impact on negotiations, the distinction is not as sharp as might be expected. Personalist leaders speak in the name of their societies and mobilize societal interest behind their positions; states and societies do not negotiate—only people do.

BILATERAL CONFLICT NEGOTIATIONS

Direct bilateral negotiations are not an effective way of ending conflict in Africa. Nor are large-scale multilateral negotiations in regional or subregional organizations, although these organizations do play an important role in setting the norms and parameters for terminating conflicts—either by victory or by reconciliation. It is trilateral or mediated bilateral negotiations that are the most effective.[2] These characterizations call for an attempt at explanation.

Three reasons suggest themselves: First, because of the engrossing nature of African conflict and its often functional aspect, African states or leaders in conflict are so taken up with the unilateral pursuit of the dispute that they are unable to conceive of bi- or multilateral solutions on their own; they need help. Whether the conflict is a personal dispute between heads of state or the result of a societal feeling of personal right or of neighboring hostility, it becomes an emotional and political cause of high importance, leaving little leeway for creative thinking on alternative solutions. This characteristic is reinforced by the small size of foreign policy establishments, the absence of both a loyal opposition and public political debate, and the personal engagement of the head of state in foreign disputes.

Second, through the 1980s, African conflicts have been occasions for a competitive race for allies, first within the continent and then outside. Bilateral conflicts generally do not remain bilateral but engage, first, factions within the continent and then European powers and superpowers. This characteristic both prevents bilateral settlements and, paradoxically, facilitates mediation. The search for allies can be turned into an invitation to mediation when the level of assistance sought finds a foreign policy opportunity in reconciliation rather than reinforcement.

Third, in addition to the preceding reasons rendering bilateral negotiations unusually difficult, there is an additional reason supporting the exercise of mediation. Mediators have their own interests supporting their activities;[3] African mediators have an overriding interest in preserving the African state system and, hence, maintaining acceptance of the status quo. They therefore also have a framework within which to seek to place their mediated resolutions—reinforcing their efforts and facilitating their acceptance.[4]

Few unmediated bilateral negotiations have had any significant effect on conflict. An example illustrates the problems. The border dispute that has created troubled relations between Morocco and Algeria since their independence was initially and occasionally the subject of direct negotiations.

As early as the first three years of the 1960s, Moroccan kings met with the presidents of the Provisional Government of the Algerian Republic (GPRA) to discuss this problem, among others. When independence came to Algeria in 1962, the agreements to settle the problem between sovereign states were pushed aside, as they were unwitnessed and were considered nonbinding.[5] Instead, war broke out, and the dispute was taken up by the newly created Organization for African Unity (OAU). After further mediation, Morocco's King Hassan II and Algeria's President Ahmed Ben Bella met at Saidia in April 1965 and renewed the GPRA commitment. Ben Bella was overthrown by his army three months later, with the Saidia agreement cited as one of the specific grievances.[6]

Once again, the OAU provided the framework for a reconciliation between King Hassan and the new Algerian ruler, Col. Houari Boumedienne, in 1968—leading to bilateral summits in the following two years and then a final border treaty, again in the context of the OAU. The implementation of the Rabat border agreement of 1972 was interrupted by the eruption of the western Saharan issue, which destroyed all chances of an effective bilateral negotiation. As the war moved beyond initial expectations of duration and toward an apparent stalemate and division of the territory, preparations began for a bilateral summit at the end of 1978.[7] Boumedienne's death cancelled these plans, as Hassan expected the new Algerian president to be more flexible. Also, the new president, Col. Chadli Ben Jedid, had to consolidate his own position before any of his purported flexibility could be shown.

It took another five years and a new stalemate more favorable to Morocco—with many intervening failed mediations—to produce the bilateral summit in February 1983. Despite high hopes and an agreement, the mutual understanding fell apart almost immediately, specifically because there was no third party present to "hold the bets" and witness the agreement. Instead, each party soon felt betrayed by the other. Whatever agreements have followed have all benefited from this lesson and have been the result of active mediation. The lesson from this lengthy conflict, still unended, is not that mediated and trilateral negotiations are ipso facto assured of success but that bilateral negotiation is ipso facto assured of failure. As in other cases, the presence of one or more third parties to midwife and witness an agreement is the necessary—but not sufficient—condition of success.

There are many other negative examples. Conflicts between Angola and Zaire, Somalia and Ethiopia, Sudan and Ethiopia, Mali and Burkina Faso, and Senegal and Mauritania, among others, were not settled by bilateral summits; when settlement or progress toward settlement was made, it was in meetings that included parties other than the principals. As bilateral failure is so pervasive, we do not need to look for other necessary ingredients;

rather, we will turn to mediation to find out what else is necessary to make settlement occur.

MEDIATION

Africa does not lack mediators. Whether it is from a continental cultural tradition[8] or from a conscious interest in maintaining the African state system, African heads of state do more than stand ready to be of assistance—they rush in numbers, often competing to bring good and even better offices to the resolution of their colleagues' conflicts, to the point where there is a confusion of counselors trying to restore domestic tranquility in the African family. This profusion of mediators permits some conclusions on the characteristics of success—contextual, tactical, and personal.[9]

African mediators tend to come from neighboring states, from the same subregion, if not from contiguous states; indeed, contiguous states often have enough of their own problems with their immediate neighbor to be disqualified from or at least handicapped in mediation. There is one major exception: When the conflict is an internal dispute between a government and an insurgency in which a neighboring state serves as the insurgent's sanctuary, the neighbor can be a useful mediator if it delivers the agreement of the insurgent.[10] Mediators also tend to come from states of the same colonial background as the disputants when both of the conflicting parties are French- or English-speaking, illustrating the importance of both personal political ties and communication.

Mediation is a personal affair, conducted personally by African heads of state with other heads of state. It does not easily lend itself to practice by lesser officials—a point that is crucial in understanding the stillbirth of the OAU Commission for Mediation, Arbitration, and Conciliation, which mandated respected jurists and civil servants but not heads or former heads of state.[11] Of the three roles of the mediator—communicator, formulator, manipulator—African heads of state operate primarily in the first two, overcoming obstacles to communication between the conflicting parties and helping them to find and formulate mutually acceptable ways out of their conflict. As such, an adjunct function of the personal mediator is to reduce the aspects of risks and mistrust that impede the parties' agreement to reconciliation. As the conflict not only bears on the issue at hand but also colors the entire tone of relations between the disputants, they do not trust each other's word and do not know how much risk is involved in their agreement; thus, the mediator becomes the agent of trust and the assessor of risk.

The condition for effective mediation is the stalemate, which makes it possible for the mediator to be welcomed in his or her offer of a way out.[12] Both aspects are necessary; neither alone is sufficient: The stalemate makes the mediation possible; the mediation makes the stalemate fruitful. As a result of these characteristics, it can be seen that the African mediator's only weapon is persuasion, which reinforces the personal nature of the task. The mediator's only leverage is his or her ability to help his or her brothers out of the bind into which their conflict has led them. Unfortunately, there are not enough studies of the actual mediatory exchanges among heads of state to permit a detailed analysis, but all available evidence indicates that most such mediation is an exercise in pure persuasion.[13]

There are a few exceptions, none of them very clear. President Mobutu Sese Seko of Zaire, mediating (in the end, unsuccessfully) between president Eduardo Dos Santos of Angola and Jonas Savimbi of the National Union for the Total Independence of Angola (UNITA) at Gbadolite in June 1989, supposedly offered assistance to Angola's fishing industry in order to win Angola's agreement, and a French firm supposedly offered a large sum to acquire Savimbi's agreement to go into exile.[14] King Fahd, host of the 1987 summit between King Hassan and President Ben Jedid, was operating as Morocco's past funding source and Algeria's potential future funding source, whether or not specific financial arrangements were mentioned.[15] When the World Council of Churches moved the government of Sudan and the Southern Sudanese Liberation Movement (SSLM) toward Addis Ababa, where an agreement to end the southern Sudanese war was eventually signed, it threatened on occasion to withdraw from mediation and resume humanitarian supplies to the SSLM if its efforts were rejected.[16] There may be other examples. Taken together, they indicate that (rarely) promises of sidepayments and (more frequently) threats to withdraw from mediation are used, but that mediation in Africa is essentially conducted through persuasion.

Some such cases have been mentioned. The three successful moments of agreement between Algeria and Morocco—whatever the problems of renewed conflict new events would later bring—were the result of mediation, either third-party or institutional. The war of 1963 was ended through the good offices of Emperor Haile Selassie and Malian President Modibo Keita; the border treaty of 1972 was prepared by the mediation of Tunisian President Habib Bourguiba and then by the context of the OAU summit of 1968 when King Hassan made his first trip to Algiers; the agreement to set aside the Saharan conflict, proceed with Maghreb unity without a Saharan participant, and resolve the dispute by a referendum on terms favorable to Morocco came out of the border summit of 1987 chaired by King Fahd. When Mobutu's mediation at Gbadolite in 1989 fell apart because the host was more eager to call a meeting than to make sure he had an agreement to witness, other African heads of state shouldered Mobutu aside and took on the task of resolution themselves, with expectations of success after a new military stalemate had set in. Two years and U.S.-Soviet assistance have still not been sufficient to produce a conclusive result.

Mediators have also abounded in the Horn of Africa, making possible any of the incomplete progress toward ending conflicts that has been achieved to date. President Ibrahim Abboud of Sudan stepped into the 1963–1964 border war between Somalia and Ethiopia to bring about a ceasefire and other conflict management measures. President Julius Nyerere of Tanzania attempted the same in the "bandit" war between Somalia and Kenya the following year but was hindered by his approach and his own problems with Kenya. He was succeeded in his attempts by President Kenneth Kaunda of Zambia in 1967–1968, who was able to get the parties to talk as a new stalemate weighed on them. When the agreed-upon conflict management arrangements did not produce the next step, Somalia invaded Ethiopia. No one was able to mediate, although the United States did successfully press the Soviet Union to guarantee that Ethiopia would not cross the common border as it threw back the Somali invaders in 1978. Eight years later, Somalia offered a new round of conflict management measures; Djibouti, the host of the Inter-Governmental Agency on Drought and Development (IGADD), and the IGADD secretariat served as mediators to bring the two heads of state together and finally, in 1988, win Ethiopian agreement to the proposals.[17]

Elsewhere in the Horn, the war in southern Sudan was successfully ended in the 1972 Addis Ababa agreement by layers of mediation, beginning with the World Council of Churches and the All-African Council of Churches, backed by the Assistant Secretary-General of the OAU, Mohammed Sahnoun, with Emperor Haile Selassie acting as mediator of last resort at a crucial juncture.[18] When the Addis Ababa agreement was dismantled by its author—President Jaafar Numeiri, ten years later, and war broke out again, mediation became more difficult because of the active support of the new Marxist government of Ethiopia behind the Sudanese People's Liberation Movement/Army (SPLM/A). However, a former Sudanese foreign secretary from the South and a former Nigerian head of state devoted serious efforts to bringing the parties closer to an eventual agreement if the war should reach a point that the parties could agree to see as a stalemate.[19] In between these two theaters of war, the Eritrean rebellion that followed the dissolution of the Ethiopian-Eritrean Federation in 1962 invited a number of mediators from Africa, Europe, and the Soviet Union for over thirty years, culminating in the unsuccessful efforts of former U.S. president Jimmy Carter.[20]

Finally, from outside the Horn, an interesting set of mediations was conducted by the current OAU president as well as by the presidents of Togo and Nigeria and, later, a large number of African heads of state on the war in Chad, both during the period of General Felix Malloum leading to the establishment of the Transitional Government of National Unity (GUNT) under Goukouni Weddei, and then after the final takeover by Hissene Habre leading to the return of nearly all the former dissidents into the new government fold.[21] In a similar internal conflict in Liberia, first the Liberian Council of Churches and then leaders of fellow West African states within ECOWAS sought to mediate the civil war of 1990.

The cases of mediation are many, but it is difficult to sort out their reasons for failure over success. In general, failed attempts did not benefit from the conditions and tactics that caused success—effective perception of stalemate on the part of all parties, skillful persuasion by the mediator, and a convincing formula for a way out that is minimally satisfactory to all. At best, one can conclude that the mediator can pull an agreement on a salient solution out of a propitious context—accomplish a negotiation that overcommitment to the conflict prevents the parties from doing by themselves—but he or she cannot create a ripe moment and a winning solution out of thin air among peers in Africa anymore than anywhere else.

MULTILATERAL CONFLICT NEGOTIATION

The OAU has been the major multilateral African forum for conducting negotiations to deal with conflict,[22] although it has been joined on occasion by subregional organizations, such as IGADD, the Economic Community of West African States (ECOWAS), and the Economic Community of West Africa (CEAO). Often these other organizations were not created for conflict reduction but provided a forum where heads of state could meet for other reasons and work out differences; conflict reduction became a necessary precondition for carrying out their other business. Two different functions must be distinguished: One is the role of multilateral committees established to deal with specific conflicts; the other is the role of the plenary of summit meetings of the multilateral organizations themselves.

There is no need to spend time on the major African committee envisaged to reduce conflict among African states—the Commission for Mediation, Arbitration, and Conciliation. Indicated by the OAU Charter, it never came into existence, for it conflicted with the rapidly established characteristic of inter-African relations as being the domain of heads of state. Instead, the OAU appointed ad hoc committees to deal with conflicts as they arose on the summit agenda, with membership carefully apportioned to language, ideological, regional, experience, and other interest groups. The committees' record was not good—success in an average of one out of three cases in some two dozen instances in the first two decades of the organization.[23] In addition, many of the successes were only temporary, with the conflict breaking out in another form later on (and requiring a new committee).

On the other hand, batting .333 may not be a bad average when the circumstances are considered. Often conditions were not propitious, and, more frequently still, the purposes of the mother organization were not conflict resolution (as will be discussed below), and they therefore overrode the efforts of the committee. In a few more cases, conflict management—the reduction of the means of conflict rather than the settlement of basic issues—was the outcome of committee efforts. Unfortunately, it is impossible to calculate a similar batting average for private efforts at mediation in order to see whether OAU committees did better than individual heads of state.

Committee mediation has been a more important function of the OAU than its record might indicate, however. It overcame one major defect of private mediation, in that it provided coordination whereas private efforts often competed among themselves. This competition allowed the parties to the conflict to wait for better terms to be put forth by other private mediators. In OAU committees, many of the members were passive, overlooking and legitimizing the activities of a few members who did the active mediation. Furthermore, OAU committees were constrained by the guidelines of the organization and its summits; they could not seek just any terms for agreement, but at the same time they were the standard bearers of OAU principles. That dual role sometimes made it impossible to find terms of agreement to which both sides could subscribe. It is difficult to fault either the OAU committees or the private mediators in such conflicts as the Somali-Ethiopian dispute or the western Sahara; the contestants' positions were simply irreconcilable, and resolution had to await a change in the cost of holding out for one or both combatants that would soften their positions.

Thus, an OAU committee was named to mediate the Somali-Ethiopian border problem at the 1973 summit, and, when it failed, another was named at the 1976 summit. As they operated under the 1964 OAU resolution affirming the sanctity of colonial boundaries, they had little leeway to meet Somalia's grievances; instead, they reaffirmed the sanctity of boundaries principle. An OAU committee did extract a promise (false, as it turned out) from Ghana not to practice subversion against the Ivory Coast, Upper Volta, and Niger in 1965 in accordance with OAU charter principles, and another intervened to free Guineans held in Ghana on their way to the OAU summit the following year. In such cases, OAU committees—acting within charter principles—made it possible for transgressing states to return to behavioral norms without loss of face, a task for which multimembered OAU committees were even better suited than private mediators.

In these situations, risk, trust, persuasion, and stalemate are the common ingredients for success. The actual negotiations are accomplished by skillfully luring the erring party back from the limb onto which it has crawled while the mediator gives assurances concerning risk and trust and provides an atmosphere of unity and fraternity that prevents the other party from crowing. The conflicting parties have no dispute with the mediator; thus, it becomes difficult for them to refuse the mediator's assurances and reject his or her atmospherics.

The OAU itself is not a conflict resolution mechanism. It provides corridors and committees that operate as described above and principles that provide the guidelines for solutions, but a body with more than fifty members is not a mechanism for resolving disputes. If a point of decreeing a solution is reached, either the conflict on the ground or a great deal of negotiation has reached an intensity that makes that solution acceptable. Otherwise, the conflict will go on. This has been the fate of the major conflicts that have torn the OAU apart—the second Congo crisis, Biafra, dialogue with South Africa, the Sahara, and Chad.

Yet in handling each of these conflicts, the OAU has shown some important and even skillful negotiation. An example that shows the possibilities of negotiation within the organization versus the political stance of its summits is the Sahara. The OAU revived the 1964–1967 committee that investigated the causes of the Algero-Moroccan Saharan War as a committee of wisemen to resolve the western Saharan issue in 1978. The new committee was diligent and creative in trying to bridge the positions of Algeria and Morocco on the western Sahara. Then, at the 1981 summit—under pressure from the impending recognition of the Sahrawi Arab Democratic Republic (SADR)—Morocco agreed to a referendum, and the wisemen were transformed into an implementation committee of the OAU. It met three times and, through painstaking negotiation with the parties, essentially established guidelines for a referendum that were still in place as the parties moved toward a vote under U.N. auspices a decade later; at the same time, it held back the efforts of various parties at various times to undo previous aspects of the evolving agreement. However, at the close of the third meeting in February 1982, the OAU Council of Ministers disavowed its committee by admitting the SADR to membership. Curiously, the heads of state on the committee did not have the commitment to put their decisions into effect.

Other cases of OAU negotiations show similar characteristics. The work of the non-OAU committee on Chad, which met in Kano and Lagos in 1979 and set up GUNT, was followed by an OAU committee on Chad and then the 1981 summit in Nairobi; intense negotiations produced a plan for a multinational peacekeeping force and a timetable for negotiations between the Chadian factions, elections, and the withdrawal of the African troops.[24] Yet for all its coherence, the plan was unreal: Funding, mission, sanctions, and contingency plans were not provided. Some skillful negotiations that brought the conflicting parties close to agreement were undercut by the lack of political commitment within the OAU to carry the project to fruition.

Thus, the OAU summit—as distinguished from its committees—plays a number of roles in regard to conflict negotiations. It sets principles, appoints committees, and provides a forum and corridors; but, because of its own political divisions and the fear of offending other heads of state, it has been unable to take forthright positions of reconciliation in African disputes. The 1989 summit assiduously avoided the bitter dispute between Senegal and Mauritania; earlier summits were unable to follow through on their own conflict management and resolution mechanisms in the Saharan and Chadian conflicts.

NEGOTIATION FOR COOPERATION

Negotiation means overcoming conflict with agreement, but many negotiations lead to agreement on new cooperation rather than simply ending old conflict. All of the regional and subregional organizations in Africa, including the OAU, were established through negotiation, and a major multilateral set of cooperation agreements of the postwar world—the Yaounde series and then the Lome series between the European Community (EC) and the African and other states—also involved repeated negotiations within Africa. As in conflict negotiations, there is little that is specifically African in these experiences, but at the same time it is clear that African statesmen are negotiating and are developing a broad experience that, when successful, underscores some important universal lessons and characteristics of the process.

One characteristic stands out as a feature of African multilateral negotiations for cooperation that is similar to multilateral negotiations for handling conflict. In both arenas, the political purposes of the negotiating session override the technical commitments of the negotiated outcome. Indeed, cooperative negotiations can be divided into diplomatic and integrative cooperation; in the former, it is the declaration of the moment, attendance at the meeting, and the announcement of joining or not that matter, whereas in the latter, it is the long-term engagement that is important. In the first case, the substance of the negotiations is needed as an occasion or a cover for the diplomatic event of the moment, but its coherence, feasibility, and reality are less important. In the second, the substance is the event, and parties do not leave the table before they have agreed to something that will work.

In 1968, for example, Zaire negotiated for the establishment of an Economic Union of Central Africa (UEAC) to win the Central African Republic and Chad away from the Customs Union of the Central African States (UDEAC) of former French Equatorial Africa, which includes the rival state of the Congo. The goal was a diplomatic event in which the important matter was to see who would attend "Mobutu's party"; the substance of the economic "union" was secondary, and the negotiations did not waste time on its details. The Central African Republic soon left UEAC to return to UDEAC, leaving the remaining members of UEAC not even contiguous. Although this is a particularly striking example, it is typical of a large number of cooperative negotiations; momentary political effect is present as a consideration even in those cases where integrative cooperation is also present.[25]

Often the technical expertise comes from outside, as the technical resources of African states are sometimes limited. The Mano River Union of Liberia, Sierra Leone, and Guinea was based on a 1972–1973 United Nations Development Program mission report, and the subregional economic organizations—ECOWAS, the Preferential Trade Area of East and Southern Africa, and the Economic Community of Central African States—were based on studies of the Economic Commission for Africa.[26] The fact that the Mano River Union conflicted with provisions of ECOWAS, which were negotiated with the same members at about the same time, was an instance of a political decision bypassing the technical engagements. In the case of African negotiations with the EC, the external source of expertise has particularly difficult implications for Africa. European states are able to coordinate their political and technical diplomacy into an agreed proposal for aid and other aspects of their relationship with associated African states under the Yaounde Conventions and with the African, Caribbean, and Pacific states under the subsequent Lome Conventions that can be presented as a take-it-or-leave-it offer.[27] Only in 1975, in the negotiation of the first Lome Convention, did the African states develop enough solidarity among themselves under the political clout of Nigerian leadership and coordinate their own technical and political inputs to be able to make their own proposals as a basis for discussion and, finally, for agreement.[28]

At the same time, when the two inputs operate together, they play a crucial role in African negotiations for cooperation, and the fact that some states effectively integrate political and technical components of their diplomacy while others do not gives the former a clear edge in specific negotiations. A country that provides a proposed text has an advantage over the others, and African cooperative negotiations frequently proceed on the basis of a single negotiating text. The case of the Lome I negotiations and the examples of the external proposals for subregional economic communities are echoed on the intra-African level by a case such as the Maghreb Arab Union negotiated at Marrakech in 1989. Morocco and Algeria had minimalist and diplomatic notions of cooperation, and Libya and Mauritania were less precise in their expectations. But Tunisia came with a well-prepared draft that served as the basis of the agreement. (At an earlier time in bilateral cooperation, it was Libya that came to Jerba in 1974 with a political draft for a union, which Tunisia signed but then repudiated on closer examination.) The same characteristic marked the negotiation of the OAU itself in Addis Ababa in 1963, when Ethiopia proposed its own draft, elaborated by experts on the basis of the Rio Treaty of the Organization of American States in conjunction with the Monrovia-Lagos Group of African States; in this case, the similar Ethiopia and Monrovia-Lagos texts were confronted by a very different draft for a tighter union proposed by the Casablanca Group of African States, which provided an alternative that could be rejected as individual provisions were selected.[29]

Once the single negotiating text is in hand, African multilateral diplomacy generally proceeds in a classical fashion—by amendment and consolidation. Amendment involves the addition of proposals not contained on the main draft. An example is Tunisia's detailed proposal for the Commission for Mediation, Arbitration, and Conciliation added to the OAU Charter at Addis Ababa. The degree to which additional proposals are integrated into the main proposal is an indicator of the primacy of integrating over simply the diplomatic cooperation involved in the negotiations. Consolidation is often more characteristic, referring to a watering down of proposals to the lowest common denominator in order to achieve the necessary consensus. As consensus rather than coherence is required for diplomatic cooperation, consolidation is a frequent characteristic. It is also a common feature in the negotiation of OAU resolutions.

In multilateral cooperative negotiations, African state representatives behave as do other negotiating parties, but with some characteristics exhibited more strongly than others. The main emphasis in this analysis has been on the distinction between diplomatic and integrative cooperation, and the history of resulting regional and subregional organizations of cooperation bears out the distinction. Yet such organizations do exist, even if inefficacy is often the price paid for their continued existence. More strikingly, when they die they have to be reinvented, as the experiences of North, West, East, central, and southern Africa all show. Their creation, maintenance, and reinvention all require negotiation—of either the diplomatic or the integrative kind.

CONCLUSIONS

African states are becoming increasingly experienced in negotiation, and, if anything, their negotiating errs in overaccommodation rather than in overintransigence: They know how to make a deal more than they know how to keep one. Negotiations are more successful in dampening or managing current rounds of conflict or in providing frameworks for current rounds of cooperation than in devising lasting resolutions or durable integration. These, however, are no mean achievements, for they provide limits to conflict and experience in cooperation as well as reinforce the nature and rules of the ongoing African system of international relations.

Such behavior may be so pervasive because it finds its roots in cultural traditions, but such an explanation is more likely to be exaggerated cultural determinism. The tradition of blood money in some areas and the absence of any negotiating tradition in others may be just as characteristic.[30] More important has been the role negotiation has played in achieving independence.[31] All formerly colonial African states (with the possible exception of Guinea-Bissau) achieved independence through some degree of negotiation—in most cases after only minimal violence—and in those cases where violent struggle was prolonged—such as Algeria, Zimbabwe, Namibia, Angola, and Mozambique—negotiation was even more important.[32] Such experience and conditioning have been crucial to the establishment of contemporary political cultures and behaviors. In that sense, Africa can be said to have a culture of negotiation—contrasted, for example, with the culture of violence some observers have noted growing within Latin American countries.[33]

Such a culture faces important challenges for the future. It is promising for the outcome of the major conflict over sociopolitical integration in South Africa, where the experiences of neighboring states may be used to overcome the absence of a negotiating tradition within South Africa itself. In a situation that by many counts is prerevolutionary, the specter of a bloodbath for both sides brought about a change from a conciliating to a winning mentality at the beginning of the 1990s and opened up the long process of negotiating a new constitutional regime in South Africa.[34] A negotiated solution would be a major achievement in the avoidance of violence and the peaceful achievement of African goals. Colonial training in negotiation is also absent in Ethiopia, where a negotiated solution with Somalia and Eritrea to the problems of empire also poses a challenge to African practices of peaceful change. Yet, limited negotiations have taken place in the conflicts in the Horn of Africa, with some results for conflict management if not for full resolution—providing partial lessons for the region.

The challenge is ongoing; thus, it is more important than ever to end with the traditional call for more research. Little has been done on the actual practice of negotiation in Africa, as has been noted at several points above, and yet the field of examples is rich. The challenge of finding out "who said what to whom with what effect," so necessary to a deep understanding of negotiating behavior, is probably no greater in Africa than elsewhere and may actually be lessened by the value given to the practice. The few studies that exist have shown that the challenge can be overcome. A better understanding of the African negotiation process can expand an understanding of the methods and potentialities of the process itself and also reinforce the culture of negotiation in Africa.

NOTES

1. On state-society relations in Africa, see Jean-François Bayard, *L'Etat en Afrique* (Paris: Fayard, 1989); and Donald Rothchild and Naomi Chazan, *The Precarious Balance* (Boulder, Colo: Westview Press, 1989).

2. I. William Zartman, "Conflict Prevention, Reduction and Resolution," in Francis Deng (ed.), *Conflict Resolution in Africa* (Washington, D.C.: Brookings Institution, 1991).

3. See Saadia Touval and I. William Zartman (eds.), *International Mediation in Theory and Practice* (Boulder, Colo.: Westview Press, 1985), pp. 8–10 and 251–254.

4. See I. William Zartman, "Africa as a Subordinate State System," *International Organization* 21, no. 3 (1967):545–564; and Yassin el-Ayouty and I. William Zartman (eds.), *The OAU After Twenty Years* (New York: Praeger, 1984), especially Chapters 2 and 7.

5. I. William Zartman, *International Relations in the New Africa* (Englewood Cliffs: Prentice-Hall, 1966), p. 110; and Nicole Grimaud, *La politique extérieure de l'Algerie* (Paris: Karthala, 1984), Chapter 6.

6. I. William Zartman, *Ripe for Resolution: Conflict and Intervention in Africa*, 2nd ed. (New York: Oxford, 1989), p. 31.

7. *Ibid.*, p. 52.

8. Robert G. Armstrong et al., *Socio-Political Aspects of the Palaver in Some African Countries* (Paris: UNESCO, 1979); see also Sally Engle Merry, "Mediation in Non-Industrial Societies," in Kenneth Kressel and Dean Pruitt (eds.), *Mediation Research* (San Francisco: Jossey Bass, 1989); but cf. Laura Nader and Harry Todd (eds.), *The Disputing Process—Law in Ten Societies* (New York: Columbia University Press, 1978), where mediation appears only in non-African cases.

9. For some recent studies—both conceptual and applied—on mediation, see Kressel and Pruitt, *Mediation Research;* Touval and Zartman, *International Mediation;* and Christopher Mitchell and Keith Webb (eds.), *New Approaches to International Mediation* (Westport, Conn.: Greenwood Press, 1988).

10. See Touval and Zartman, *International Mediation*, pp. 257 ff.; I. William Zartman, "Negotiations and Prenegotiations in Ethnic Conflict: The Beginning, the Middle and the Ends," in Joseph Montville (ed.), *Conflict and Peacemaking in Multiethnic Societies* (Lexington, Mass.: D. C. Heath, 1990), especially pp. 520–524 and 530–532.

11. C.O.C. Amate, *Inside the OAU* (New York: St. Martin's, 1986), Chapter 5.

12. See Zartman, *Ripe for Resolution*, Chapter 6.

13. For two exceptional accounts, see John Stremlau, *The International Politics of the Nigerian Civil War* (Princeton: Princeton University Press, 1977), Chapters 6 and 7; and Saadia Touval, *The Boundary Politics of Independent Africa* (Cambridge: Harvard University Press, 1972), Chapter 9.

14. *Angola News Briefs*, 2, no. 1 (15 June 1989); *Washington Times*, 22 June 1989.

15. Zartman, *Ripe for Resolution*, p. 68.

16. Hizkias Assefa, *Mediation of Civil Wars* (Boulder, Colo.: Westview Press, 1987), pp. 128 ff.

17. On the earlier rounds, see Touval, *Boundary Politics*, Chapter 9; on the later rounds, see Zartman, *Ripe for Resolution*, Chapter 3.

18. Assefa, *Mediation;* and Dunstan Wai, *The African-Arab Conflict in the Sudan* (New York: Africana, 1981).

19. Francis Deng, Olusegun Obasanjo, and I. William Zartman, *Quest for Peace in Sudan* (Washington, D.C.: Brookings Institution, 1990).

20. A good study is needed on the diplomacy of the Eritrean conflict. The 1980–1981 period is covered in I. William Zartman, *African Insurgencies: Negotiations and Mediation* (Washington, D.C.: State Department, 1989), IRR 206, pp. 8–10.

21. On the earlier period, see Virginia Thompson and Richard Adloff, *Conflict in Chad* (Berkeley: University of California Institute of International Studies, 1981); I. William Zartman, "Conflict in Chad," in Arthur Day and Michael Doyle (eds.), *Escalation and Intervention* (Boulder, Colo.: Westview Press, 1986); and Dean Pittman, "The OAU and Chad," in el-Ayouty and Zartman, *OAU After Twenty Years.* On the later period, see Zartman, *African Insurgencies*, pp. 13–14.

22. On the OAU role in general, see Yassin el-Ayouty (ed.), *The OAU After Ten Years* (New York: Praeger, 1975); Michael Wolfers, *Politics in the Organization of African Unity* (New York: Barnes & Noble, 1976); el-Ayouty and Zartman, *OAU After Twenty Years;* R. A. Akindele, *The Organization of African Unity 1963–1988*, special issue of *Nigerian Journal of International Affairs* 14, no. 1 (1988).

23. Figured from annex 6, mediation efforts, in el-Ayouty and Zartman, *OAU After Twenty Years.*

24. On the Chadian peacekeeping force, see chapters by Dean Pittman and Henry Wiseman in el-Ayouty and Zartman, *OAU After Twenty Years;* and Nathan Pelkovits, "Peacekeeping: The African Experience," in Henry Wiseman (ed.), *Peace-keeping: Appraisals and Proposals* (New York: Pergamon Press, 1983).

25. Cf. I. William Zartman, *International Relations in the New Africa* (Lanham, Md.: University Press of America reprint, 1987), especially pp. 147 ff.

26. Peter Robson, *Integration, Development and Equity* (London: Allen & Unwin, 1983).

27. I. William Zartman, *The Politics of Trade Negotiations Between Africa and the European Communities* (Princeton: Princeton University Press, 1971), p. 225 and *passim;* and I. William Zartman, "Lome III: Relic of the 1970s or Model for the 1990s?" in C. Cosgrove and J. Jamar (eds.), *The European Community's Development Policy: The Strategies Ahead* (Bruges, Belgium: College d'Europe, de Tempel, 1986).

28. John Ravenhill, *Collective Clientelism* (New York: Columbia University Press, 1984); Joanna Moss, *The Lome Conventions and Their Implications for the United States* (Boulder, Colo.: Westview Press, 1982); and I. William Zartman, "An American Point of View," in Frans Alting von Geusau (ed.), *The Lome Convention and a New International Economic Order* (Leyden: Sijtoff, 1977), especially pp. 141 ff.

29. Boutros Boutros Ghali, *The Addis Ababa Charter*, International Conciliation Series no. 546 (New York: Carnegie Endowment for International Peace, 1964); T. O. Elias, "The Charter of the OAU," *American Journal of International Law* 59,

no. 2 (1965):243–276; and Lawrence Marinelli, *The New Liberia* (New York: Praeger, 1964), pp. 138–140.

30. See the discussion of various subregional attitudes toward negotiation in Zartman, *Ripe for Resolution*, pp. 49 ff., 109 ff., and 156 ff.

31. See Donald Rothchild, "Racial Stratification and Bargaining: The Kenya Experience," in I. William Zartman (ed.), *The 50% Solution* (New Haven: Yale University Press, 1987). Unfortunately, similar studies or even purely historical accounts do not exist for most other African countries.

32. Jeffrey Davidow, *A Peace in Southern Africa: The Lancaster House Conference* (Boulder, Colo.: Westview Press, 1984); Stephen Stedman, *Peace Making in a Revolutionary Civil War: Zimbabwe* (Boulder, Colo.: Lynne Rienner Publishers, 1990); and Zartman, *Ripe for Resolution*, Chapter 5 (Namibia). Unfortunately, there are no similar studies of a number of other cases.

33. Daniel Garcia, "Negotiating with the Rebellion in Colombia," in Zartman, *Negotiating Internal Conflicts.*

34. See I. William Zartman, "Negotiations in South Africa," *Washington Quarterly* 11, no. 4 (1988):141–158; and Zartman, "Negotiating in South Africa," in Zartman, *Negotiating Internal Conflicts.*

14

REGIONAL PEACEMAKING IN AFRICA: THE ROLE OF THE GREAT POWERS AS FACILITATORS

DONALD ROTHCHILD

The late 1980s saw the emergence of opportunities in U.S.-Soviet relations for mutual accommodation on a variety of specific issues. The "new thinking" evident in the Soviet Union represents, in some areas at least, a change in approach from totalist to pragmatic perceptions of foreign policy questions. Past priorities of arms reductions, military spending, and the settlement of regional conflicts have undergone revision along lines that are more compatible with U.S. national interests and values.[1] This shift from adversarial to cautiously cooperative relations is significant for contemporary Africa, particularly with respect to conflict management. In a number of regional confrontations, globalist and regionalist politics have become intertwined, creating new possibilities for easing tensions.[2] Problems previously regarded as intractable now seem open to new efforts at creative statecraft, and the West has every reason to encourage these trends.

The new thinking, with its emphasis on tacit cooperation at the international level, has the effect of challenging traditional views in both countries on how best to manage the U.S.-Soviet rivalry. Tacit cooperation is one of the alternatives to formal agreement and normally assumes the form of parallel (or concerted diplomatic) action in Africa. For two Soviet observers, Andrei Kozyrev and Andrei Shumikhin, ideology played a major role in the rivalry that took place between the superpowers in the Third World. The two powers became entrapped in what Kozyrev and Shumikhin described as a "zero-option game," in which each side assessed its actions in terms of the degree to which they "impinge[d] upon the interests or made inroads into the positions of the ideological enemy," not of the benefits it would derive for itself.[3] Rather than being drawn further into conflicts that might involve "growing material and manpower losses and the danger of a direct clash between American and Soviet armed forces," these authors urged a return to the notion of peaceful coexistence.[4] In place of a costly ideological and military-political rivalry, the superpowers would "minimize their involvement while maximizing their contribution to the search [for] political solutions" by paying greater attention to national, religious, and ideological disparities, national reconciliations, and political coalitions.[5]

Those in the Soviet Union who were engaged in the new thinking were clearly coming closer to positions long held in the United States. If more and more leaders in both countries accept the premises of new thinking and move from adversarial to mixed competitive-cooperative relations in their dealings with the Third World, widely held priorities and commitments will have to be reexamined. Such a review will possibly lead to new emphases upon Africa's economic development, infrastructural improvement, debt relief, human rights improvements, ecological rehabilitation, and disease prevention. But is great-power support for Africa's social and economic reconstruction likely to accompany the strategic and military disengagement of these countries from the continent? An easing of superpower tensions could free up resources for developmental purposes, but one must take care not to overstate the positive effects of military disengagement in a period of mounting U.S. and Soviet debts and a burgeoning Soviet need for domestic economic modernization.[6] Furthermore, U.S.-Soviet parallel action—even if unstable and limited to certain issue-areas—is likely to weaken the thrust of nonalignment, as such a stance cannot be expected to have the same payoffs as it did during the period of cold-war tensions.[7] Expressing Third-World uncertainties on these issues, an editorial in *Africa and the World* commented: "Gone are the days of *non-alignment* which was predicated on East-West cold war, especially among the superpowers. Gone are those moments when one could win America by turning against the Soviets or vice versa. . . . Therefore *Glasnost* implies that Africans must open up and articulate policies bereft of wrong-headed assumptions of permanent American/Soviet antagonism."[8]

The new thinking, then, brings complexities and uncertainties into play for all the world's political actors. As power becomes more and more diffused and the superpowers exercise less control over the smaller countries of the Third World, it is not surprising that U.S. and Soviet priorities have shifted and that they have tended increasingly to look inward in an effort to cope with their domestic problems. Interventions in Vietnam and Afghanistan proved politically and economically expensive for both countries, and their rivalries in Africa and elsewhere often seemed to entail significant risks with limited payoffs. In cases where, as in Africa, vital interests are not at stake, a move toward "normal" state competition seems less than surprising.[9] This can mean greater autonomy and self-determination for the African states but at a possible cost in terms of the economic support that comes with great-power involvement. In brief, the current opportunity for great-power cooperation entails unanticipated consequences for all players.

Despite the indications of U.S.-Soviet accommodation in the late 1980s, old suspicions and reservations have by no means disappeared.[10] All too often, a fear of communism or capitalism gives continuity and purpose to U.S. and Soviet foreign policies; it structures and simplifies an otherwise complex world. Hence, making more informed and realistic appraisals of each other's intentions in such regional conflicts as southern Africa and the Horn represents a necessary start toward clarifying old suspicions. But beyond this is the central problem of creating new opportunities for choice. How have the two superpowers, with limited but divergent interests in southern and northeastern Africa, utilized the present-day window of opportunity to facilitate the search for peace, and what further possibilities in these and other areas are open to them in the future? How can they learn to compete without seeking to prevail, and how can they move in separate but related ways so as to avoid destructive conflicts and achieve mutual objectives?

With respect to such issues and questions, both the southern and northeastern regions of Africa represent good tests of the possibilities and prospects for parallel actions in the years ahead. Southern Africa, as Donald McHenry remarks, is different from the Middle East in that "neither of the superpowers nor their closest allies is directly involved [there] or, for that matter, places a high priority on the southern African region."[11] Similarly, the Horn remains relatively low in superpower priorities at this time. Certainly, both global powers are involved, but in a limited way—making these propitious regions for the parallel pursuit of similar objectives.

DIVERGENT SUPERPOWER INTERESTS

As might be expected in relationships between powerful states, the United States and the Soviet Union have separate and distinct interests—in southern and northeastern Africa as elsewhere. Their needs are different, and their motives for engagement vary significantly. Moreover, each is characterized by internal differences in perceptions of the national interest that may prove as important as the cleavages between them. In the Soviet Union, the so-called generalists may be more prepared than their regionalist counterparts to compromise on certain political issues in order to assure the arms accords and domestic developmental objectives they value so strongly. And in the United States, the globalists diverge from the regionalists in their emphasis on the sources of tensions (regional or international) in the African context.[12]

Both of the superpowers have real but limited interests in Africa. At the top of the U.S. list is the determination to counter the perceived threat of enhanced Soviet influence in Africa; as George Bush put it during the 1988 election campaign, "Domination of Africa by a power hostile to the West would represent a serious danger to our collective security."[13] Also high on the list of U.S. objectives are the promotion of trade and investment, the procurement of minerals and raw materials, and the encouragement of Africa's economic development. Additional U.S. interests include gaining and maintaining African diplomatic support at the United Nations and in other multilateral bodies (reflecting a competition between the superpowers for allies) and furthering human rights and racial justice (reflecting political values as well as domestic pressures).[14]

By contrast, Soviet interests in Africa tend to concentrate upon political, geostrategic, and ideological rather than economic factors.[15] In the process of gaining recognition as a global power, the Soviets took on a series of political and strategic obligations to the beleaguered Afro-Marxist regimes of the continent. They made extensive commitments; thus, their credibility in Marxist-Leninist circles was deemed to be at stake, requiring that they stand by their allies—at least, in the case of Angola, until the threat of South African destabilization was removed.[16] But in the late 1980s, whenever its guarantees to the Afro-Marxist regimes were not at risk, the Soviet regime gave clear indications of seeking to avoid new, far-reaching commitments. Winrich Kuhne, during a visit to Moscow in late 1986, found Soviet diplomats reluctant to respond to Zimbabwe's appeal for closer military cooperation and anxious to avoid any further escalation of violence in South Africa.[17] Such tendencies became more apparent to Kuhne in 1988, when he observed a shift of emphasis among Soviet African specialists away from armed struggle and toward a political solution of the South African question. Not only were the Soviets concerned over such matters as their capabilities and the effects of increased violence on the South African economy, but also they were troubled over the possibility that an escalation of violence would interfere with other priorities on arms control and economic development—matters that involved Washington's cooperation.[18] Thus, the USSR's increased emphasis upon reduced strategic and military expenditures abroad and its concern over its own domestic economic growth run counter to an expansion of its commitments in the Third World, leading to a tempering of its obligation to spread revolutionary change. Indicative of this more pragmatic orientation on East-West issues was General-Secretary Mikhail Gorbachev's 1988 speech at the United Nations in which he commented on the need to "de-ideologiz[e] relations among states."[19]

In line with a strong emphasis upon political rather than revolutionary change in southern Africa, the current Soviet leadership espouses preferences that largely converge with those held by many in the United States,[20] creating a situation conducive to parallel actions on regional conflicts. The national interests of the two superpowers continue to diverge in terms of strategic interests and commitments, but not to the extent of establishing an insurmountable barrier to tacit collaboration on specific issues. Moreover, both countries share a number of interests in southern Africa: most prominently, a joint determination to end white minority dominance and apartheid, a mutual interest in ensuring that developments in the region do not interfere with other critical objectives (in particular, the growth and development of their domestic economies and their relations with one another), and a common concern that their local allies do not drag them into a costly, drawn-out regional conflict or—worse yet—into a wider global conflict. With the emergence of the new realism of perestroika, it should be more possible than before to build on a recognized mutuality of interests between the two parties so that neither country will be placed in a position in which it appears that it has "lost" to the other (or to its allies) or that its evidences of goodwill on regional conflict issues will be exploited by the other.

THE COSTLY CONFRONTATIONS OF THE MID-1970S

The mid-1970s represented a low point in U.S.-Soviet relations in Africa. On the Horn of Africa, the Ogaden crisis and the heavy involvement of the Soviets and Cubans in turning the tide of the Somali-Ethiopian War in favor of the Addis Ababa regime shocked the liberal internationalists in the Carter administration. U.S. concern over the situation on the Horn deepened in early 1977, as the Soviets cemented close relations with the new Afro-Marxist regime in Ethiopia and proceeded to launch a major air and sea lift of over $1 billion in military assistance—with much more to follow. For a time it seemed possible that the Soviets, closely following Fidel Castro's initiatives, might have been able to bring about a reduction in tensions and even the formation of a federation between the Socialist regimes of Ethiopia and Somalia, but Somalia's president Siad Barre's determination to expand his territory to include all ethnic Somalis proved to be at cross-purposes with Mengistu Haile Mariam's insistence on holding a shaky Ethiopia together against all challengers (Somali, Eritrean, and other nationality groups).[21]

Inevitably the Soviet reconciliation effort failed, and Somali army "volunteers" joined the Western Somali Liberation Front forces and advanced deep into the Ogaden. In November 1977, Somalia announced the abrogation of its Treaty of Friendship with the USSR, and Soviet officials and military advisers withdrew from that country. To stop the Somali march, the Soviets sent some one thousand military personnel, eleven thousand Cuban combat troops, and extensive military supplies to support the Ethiopians, halting the Somali forces at Jigiga; they then launched a major Ethiopian-Cuban counteroffensive that successfully regained the Ethiopian territory. The fact that the Ethiopian-Cuban forces stopped their forward movement at the border is, in part at least, attributable to diplomacy at the highest levels. By March 1978, President Carter had received direct assurances from the Soviets that the Ethiopian-Cuban counteroffensive would not cross the Somali border. Carter, who was sensitive to OAU principles about respecting existing boundaries as well as responsive to Soviet representations, thereupon reaffirmed his pledge to limit U.S. military assistance to the Somalis and pressured Barre to withdraw his forces from the Ogaden.[22] This withdrawal was completed on March 15. The quiet diplomacy conducted between the superpowers on the Ethiopian-Somali disengagement question represented an important superpower achievement in the area of crisis management at that time. In avoiding a potentially dangerous confrontation between the superpowers, this episode pointed to the need for improved communication between policymakers in Moscow and Washington regarding regional conflict issues and, in terms of joint problem solving on the part of the great powers, proved a precursor of events to follow during the 1980s.

In southern Africa, following the collapse of the Portuguese hold on its overseas territories, a series of intense conflicts surfaced between rival groups intent upon gaining control of the states and their institutions. Although the African populations in these countries clearly paid by far the heaviest price for these struggles, they also came to entail substantial costs for the superpowers. The financial costs, particularly for the Soviets, have been significant but bearable (in Angola, an estimated debt of $2.6 billion had been incurred to the Soviet Union by early 1988, a figure that rose dramatically in the next year).[23] More burdensome, however, have been the political costs in superpowers relations, for the continuing crisis in Angola gravely complicated U.S.-Soviet cooperation on other issues, deepening mutual perceptions of threatening behavior and creating grave suspicions regarding the implications of any conciliatory gestures. Although the backlash of the 1980–1982 period in the United States was "emotionally spent," remarked Daniel Yankelovich and Richard Smoke, "détente" remained "a pejorative word in the American lexicon. . . . The public attitude is: 'once burnt, twice shy.' "[24] In the public's mind, Soviet "expansionist" behavior in the Third World was indicative of its intentions elsewhere—a perception that proved costly, for even after Gorbachev came to power and proclaimed his new realism, it slowed efforts to create a political framework for stable relations.

If Soviet and U.S. interests and objectives diverged in the Rhodesian (now Zimbabwean) and Mozambican struggles, it was the wide-ranging regional conflict over Angola (and with it, Namibia and South Africa) that posed a critical test for Soviet-U.S. relations. As in Afghanistan, Cambodia, and Nicaragua, Angola involved adversarial politics that could have escalated dangerously. Moreover, for many Americans Angola symbolized the dangers of détente, for they linked an easing of tensions in the European theater with a greater opportunity for Soviet military expansionism in the Third World. President Ford, expressing concern over the lack of effective Western assistance to the insurgent movements in Angola, argued that such support was necessary "to reverse the tide and block the Soviet-backed effort to take over the country by force."[25] Moreover, two neoconservative writers observed soon after these initial events, "When détente was invoked—belatedly, as if to show that Kissinger feared putting it to the test—it proved to be what some had always suspected it was: not a name for eased tensions, let alone for peace, but a cover for the tactical retreat by one deeply troubled power in the face of the growing might and brazenness of the other."[26] The appeal of Reagan realism in the United States can only be fully understood when looked at against this backdrop of perceived Soviet "adventurism" and the liberals' lack of resoluteness in mounting an effective response.[27]

From the standpoint of Soviet policymakers in the 1970s, the projection of Eastern bloc support for an Afro-Marxist regime in Angola following the collapse of Portuguese colonialism reflected the responsibilities of bloc leadership. Soviet leaders emphasized the importance of gaining world recognition of its superpower status, demonstrating its capabilities (by projecting its power abroad), reestablishing its revolutionary credentials, and—in contrast with U.S. indecisiveness following Vietnam—showing its determination to stand by its African friends (especially in light of South Africa's incursions). But in sending support teams of military technicians and advisers and an estimated $200 million in military equipment, and in ferrying some 11,000 Cuban combat troops to Angola, they fueled latent U.S. suspicions about Soviet intentions at that time. As the Soviet-backed Popular Movement for the Liberation of Angola (MPLA) quickly consolidated its position in most of the country, two basic schools of thought emerged in the United States as to how the government should respond to the changed situation. Secretary Kissinger, refusing to "accept the proposition that the use of extracontinental military force supported by one of the superpowers is the only way of achieving the aspirations of the black African countries," urged strong measures to restore a balance in the area.[28] The Senate liberals, pulling back from such a confrontationist stance, played down the global dimensions of the crisis and argued instead that the time for a costly military engagement had passed. By 1976, the Senate liberals had carried the day. They voted the Clark Amendment into effect, thereby forbidding further strategic assistance to the National Liberation Front of Angola (FNLA) or to the National Union for the Total Independence of Angola (UNITA) forces. Partly as a consequence, the FNLA became gravely weakened, and UNITA became isolated (and largely dependent on South African military backing).

With covert support to the insurgent movements forbidden, Kissinger—the realist—turned from an ineffective policy of confrontation to one that sought to cooperate with black Africa's demands for independence and self-determination. But U.S. misgivings over the continuing Soviet military role in Angola never completely disappeared. Subsequently, President Carter—although determined to shun mechanical cold-war responses to African issues—expressed increasing concern over Soviet intentions in the latter half of his term. "The Soviet Union," he declared at Annapolis, "can choose either confrontation or cooperation. The United States is adequately prepared to meet either choice."[29] In brief, then, the USSR's military role in Angola kept latent U.S. suspicions of Soviet intentions alive, even under the liberal internationalist administration of Jimmy Carter. With Ronald Reagan's election to the presidency, these suspicions solidified and became the basis for the new administration's ideological stance on foreign policy issues.

With Reagan in power, the long-delayed reaction to Soviet adventurism surfaced prominently. A series of linked moves—Assistant Secretary of State for African Affairs Chester A. Crocker's introduction of the linkage issue (insisting on a parallel withdrawal of Cuban troops from Angola at the same time that South African forces left Namibia); the continuing refusal to recognize the legitimacy of the MPLA regime; Congress's decision to repeal the Clark Amendment; and the application of the Reagan Doctrine to Angola and, with it, the provision of military weapons to Jonas Savimbi's UNITA—represented determined administration responses to Soviet initiatives in the region. The cumulative effect was to involve high costs in terms of heightened tensions between the superpowers. With the Angolan confrontation dragging on and seemingly unwinnable on the ground, it became apparent by 1987 that the stalemate could only be overcome through new approaches. Thus, the stage was set for a move from confrontation to parallel actions.

THE NEW PRAGMATISM OF THE MID-1980S

By their nature, stalemates are always difficult to overcome. Adversaries become frozen into opposing positions, unable to surmount the negative remembrances of past struggles or to reverse their commitments to constituents, coalition supporters, or international alliance partners. These problems are even more pronounced when the two superpowers become locked into an antagonistic encounter involving competing world views and visions of the future. However, with Gorbachev's rise to the pinnacle of power in the Soviet Union, a unique event occurred—the emergence of a new leadership prepared to move from adversarial to pragmatic relations with the West. Such a shift in strategy and perceptions had positive implications, for it opened up new possibilities for tacit cooperation on ending Third-World regional conflicts.

By the mid-1980s, Soviet policymakers had come to speak openly of the danger regional conflicts in the Third World posed to world peace. In an important statement, academician Yevgeni Primakov addressed this issue directly: "Most important . . . is that under persisting international tension regional conflicts could upset the military-political stability in the world and pose a real threat to universal security. . . . In the new Soviet foreign-policy philosophy, settlement of regional conflicts and solution of humanitarian problems, including general observance of human rights, are seen as major ways of stabilizing the international situation."[30]

Even though U.S. spokesmen generally exhibited what presidential candidate George Bush described as "a prudent skepticism," it nonetheless seems reasonable to characterize the informed public as moving cautiously by 1988 toward a redefinition of national security policy that took changing Soviet priorities into account.[31] "Turning to regional issues," President Ronald Reagan declared in Moscow, "Mr. Gorbachev and I agreed that there must be peaceful solutions to these conflicts. Our goal is to advance independence, security and freedom."[32] And the Democratic nominee for the presidency, Michael S. Dukakis, although emphasizing the need for a strong defense posture, also urged the United States to "seize the initiative" and test the limits of the new thinking in the Soviet Union.[33] Hence, considerable common ground began to appear at that time between the leadership of the two superpowers regarding the desirability of new initiatives, including efforts to end regional conflicts. But could these countries go beyond their new thinking and agree upon the terms and conditions for disengagement in the Third World? Would they, in fact, exert the necessary influence on local combatants in southern and northeastern Africa to induce a change of preferences? Unless their parallel actions were tested and led to substantive results, the new thinking was likely to be regarded by future generations as a lost opportunity.

It should be kept in mind that tacit cooperations between the United States and the Soviet Union are by no means limited to the post-Gorbachev period. As already noted, experiences with tacit collaboration go back many years. One analyst noted in 1988 that parallel actions on the part of the superpowers at the United Nations were a factor in ending all five of the Arab-Israeli wars over the previous forty years: "While the five wars produced eventual American-Soviet cooperation in halting their dangerous escalation, in no case did the two powers act jointly to prevent their outbreak, let alone promote a durable peaceful settlement of the conflict."[34] Tacit cooperation (as opposed to engaging in problem solving by means of formal agreement) has also been apparent to some observers in the so-called Kalahari Incident of 1977 (when Soviet intelligence informed its U.S. counterpart about possible South African preparations for a nuclear weapons test), in pressures exerted by the superpowers to limit the extent of the Ethiopian-Cuban advance in the Ogaden in 1977–1978, and in the distribution of food during the drought and famine in Ethiopia in 1985–1986.[35]

In the post-Gorbachev period, the process of tacit cooperation has picked up and has become a regular feature of the international landscape. Less and less able to influence the Third-World countries in a directly military manner, the superpowers have moved cautiously toward common positions in a number of regional conflict situations. In 1986, in opposition to the preferences of the African National Congress, the United States and the Soviets took a common position by voting to block a motion to expel South Africa from the International Atomic Energy Agency.[36] And following the Reagan-Gorbachev summit meetings in 1987 and 1988, more concerted efforts at settling long-standing conflicts became unmistakable—in the Iran-Iraq War, Afghanistan, Cambodia, and Nicaragua.[37] To the extent that the superpowers have cooperated (albeit tacitly and informally) to promote the peacemaking process, they have enabled the United Nations to step in and perform an indispensable mediatory role in these regional conflicts. Yet as necessary as U.S.-Soviet parallel action is to managing such conflicts, it is important to stress that even this factor may not be sufficient to deal with the confrontations at hand. Not only must other powerful international actors be taken into account (such as China in the Cambodian conflict), but the superpowers may not be able to bring sufficient pressure to bear on local actors to induce a change of preferences. The United States and the Soviet Union can threaten trade sanctions or withhold military arms from their "allies," but it is by no means clear that such pressures would have a decisive impact on the courses of action chosen by the MPLA or UNITA—or South Africa. The "weak," then, have greater leverage than a straightforward assessment of their capabilities might suggest. The two great powers—working together—can facilitate the process of reaching agreement on regional conflict issues, but given the limited extent of the commitments they are currently prepared to make to these areas, they cannot force agreements as such.

A major test case for parallel cooperation and its ability to resolve long-standing regional conflicts has been the civil war in Angola. Although the possibility of some form of diplomatic cooperation with the Soviets was favored in some circles of the State Department from the time of Angola's early years of independence, serious initiatives to overcome the impasse were only made in earnest when the costs of internal warfare became severe and the new thinking gained credibility.[38] The attack by Angolan government forces upon UNITA and South African units at the village of Mavinga in late 1987 led to bitter fighting and a subsequent retreat to the support base at Cuito Cuanavale. The fight for Cuito Cuanavale proved intense. Guerrilla forces—backed by elements of the South African army—shelled government positions over a six-month period; however, government troops—reinforced by Cuban ground and air units—stood up to this pounding and, at heavy cost to all parties, eventually broke the siege.[39] The general military stalemate that ensued (combined with a change in Soviet priorities on regional conflicts) gave an impetus to the ongoing diplomatic effort to bring peace to the region.

Certainly, regional political actors have been at center stage in this diplomatic effort. The Angolan government, worn down by the heavy costs of protracted war, made conciliatory moves on such thorny issues as possible future contacts with representatives of UNITA (other than guerrilla leader Jonas Savimbi and his chief lieutenants), a comprehensive arrangement for the withdrawal of all Cuban troops from Angola, and a commitment to redeploy Cuban forces in the north during the transition period—all intended to keep the negotiations on track.[40] Savimbi was not represented at the series of talks in 1988, but he always loomed large in the regional peace equation. He made proposals of his own, calling for negotiations, a ceasefire, an interim national government (in which he would not necessarily be included), and subsequent elections. Similarly, the South West African People's Organization (SWAPO) was not a direct participant in the talks; yet it made its presence felt in a variety of important ways, including—significantly—some timely gestures regarding its willingness to comply with a ceasefire and assurances on private ownership and continued white employment in the civil service in an independent Namibia.[41] And the Cubans and South Africans—slightly bruised but determined to fight on if necessary after the sharp military encounters at the Calueque Dam area in June and July 1988—continued to thrust and parry during the late summer and fall of 1988 on the issues of a ceasefire, parallel withdrawal, and the timetable for redeployment and disengagement.[42] In the end, the superpowers did manage to influence the political preferences and perceptions of the contending parties, but the relative autonomy of the forces on the ground must not be underestimated.

Although we must keep the impact of the superpowers on the negotiating process in perspective, it is still appropriate to comment here on the facilitative role they did play in Angola and Namibia. On the U.S. side, Assistant Secretary of State for African Affairs Crocker, determined from the time he took office to find an internationally acceptable solution to the Namibian question, relentlessly pursued every possible opening in an effort to move the regional actors toward a peaceful outcome. At times, as with his initial suggestion of the idea of linkage, he may have complicated his task for some years (prior to the stalemate, although the diplomatic process remained fluid, linkage may well have made a peace settlement more difficult; once the stalemate was recognized, however, linkage became a means for face-saving and for addressing the differences).[43] In any event, Crocker's meeting with Angolan government, South African, UNITA, SWAPO, and frontline state leaders and with various non-African representatives were an effort to advance a process that was frustrating in its inconclusiveness. Then, as the events of 1987–1988 revealed a new seriousness in the region about the peace process, Crocker showed himself to be ready to assume the mantle of mediator—a role that received official recognition from the negotiating parties in the statement of principles they issued in July 1988.[44]

But Crocker was by no means a disinterested mediator. At the same time the Soviets were pressuring their Angolan and Cuban allies to make concessions at the bargaining table, the Americans were exerting a similar influence on the South Africans. Determined to bring about a settlement in Angola and Namibia before leaving office, Crocker increasingly exerted leverage on the South Africans. The pressure took various forms, both positive and negative: implementing the sanctions legislation mandated by Congress, bypassing the South African government to give support to antiapartheid groups in the country, warning the Botha regime of the consequences of continued destabilization, and failing to protest the significant increase in the size of Cuban forces in 1987–1988.[45] In addition, Crocker "repackaged" the linkage proposal so that Namibia would gain its independence *before* the full withdrawal of Cuban troops from Angola.[46] Paradoxically, when the implications of linkage as newly formulated became clear, the South Africans attempted to reverse their position on this issue, but to no avail.[47]

Less evident, however, was the facilitative role the Soviet Union played in these various deliberations. As Angola's major ideological supporter and supplier of military equipment, the Soviets were particularly well placed to encourage Luanda's leaders to negotiate in earnest and to adopt a more conciliatory stance on such issues as the timing of the Cuban troop redeployment and withdrawal and the continuance of external assistance to the various insurgent groups. When the new thinking—with its evident pragmatism about settling regional conflict issues—gained prominence in 1987, it became apparent to various observers in the region that the Soviets were using their influence to encourage Luanda to resume talks with the South Africans. As the series of negotiations unfolded in the following year, it became even clearer that the Soviets were an important behind-the-scenes factor—pressing the Angolans to continue the deliberations and helping to clarify critical points of contention.[48] At the Moscow summit meeting in June 1988, the U.S. and Soviet representatives set September 29—the tenth anniversary of U.N. Security Council Resolution 45, which provided for the withdrawal of South Africa's illegal administration from Namibia, a ceasefire, and British-administered elections—as a target date for the settlement of outstanding differences on the Angolan conflict. Following the summit, Deputy Foreign Minister Anatoly L. Adamishin—seeking to keep the process of reciprocal concessions on track—declared that the Soviet Union was willing to play a more active role in the peace process, including acting as "a co-guarantor of a peace settlement and becoming a direct participant in the negotiations 'if others want it.' "[49]

The Soviets were now publicly committed to the southern African peace process. They were active in contributing to the pace of the ongoing exchanges, in the critical caucusing process between meetings, and in inducing reasonable concessions on such issues as redeployment of the Cuban troops and the disengagement of South African and Cuban forces. There were also indications that this facilitative role extended to the delicate question of direct negotiations between the Luanda government and UNITA, a matter that became the subject of subsequent Zairian- and Portuguese-led mediation efforts following acceptance of the Namibian and Angolan Accords.[50] In the important negotiations at Geneva in August 1988, where a ceasefire and a sequence of steps leading up to a disengagement of forces were agreed upon, Soviet officials were very helpful to the U.S. mediatory effort; not only did they meet with the Americans before and after the negotiating sessions, but they placed pressure on the Angolan government and Cuban delegations to be flexible on key points at issue.[51] Following the signing of the accords, Soviet diplomats worked behind the scenes at the emergency meeting of the joint commission to supervise the implementation process in April 1989, when they pressed the Cubans to adopt a conciliatory stance on redeploying SWAPO guerrilla forces north of the 16th parallel. Although Cuban leaders had been determined to pursue such a course in order to avoid the costs of a further military engagement, Soviet pressures to avoid another confrontation with South African troops doubtless encouraged this stance.[52] Not surprisingly, at the time the tripartite agreement was signed, Crocker publicly recognized the "important and constructive role" played by the Soviets in the negotiating process. It had been "a test in practical cooperation between the superpowers," he declared.[53]

OTHER OPPORTUNITIES FOR SUPERPOWER COOPERATION

As shown thus far, parallel actions have contributed to reducing tensions in a number of regional conflicts—Angola, the Ethiopian-Somali confrontation, Afghanistan, Cambodia, the Arab-Israeli wars, and Central America. In what other venues might tacit cooperation among the superpowers prove significant in advancing the peace process? A number of regional struggles come to mind, but for the purposes of this chapter I will limit myself to the continuing conflicts in northeastern and southern Africa.

In northeastern Africa, the two superpowers have made some important initial efforts toward peace negotiations in the Sudan and Ethiopia. In the mid-1980s, the United States was cautiously supportive of Sadiq al-Mahdi's regime in the Sudan, partly because it was democratically elected and partly out of irritation with Colonel John Garang's (the Sudanese People's Liberation Army [SPLA] leader) refusal to negotiate in earnest with either the Transitional Military Council or the al-Mahdi regime on an end to the civil war.[54] By February 1989, the State Department had undergone a significant mood change, and the United States declared its "central objective" in that country to be the ending of the civil war.[55] To promote that goal, it offered to mediate the war between the Sudan government and the SPLA insurgents and approached Moscow for its help in bringing this conflict to a halt. According to a State Department spokesman, the Soviets "have an important potential role to play in light of their position in Ethiopia."[56] Nothing came of this initiative, as Sudan's Constituent Assembly turned down the proposal as an unnecessary involvement in the Sudan's internal affairs.

A second important conflict in the region, which holds possibilities for superpower cooperation in delivering food aid to isolated regions and in the peace process, is that of Ethiopia—particularly its conflict with Eritrea. Here the Soviets, who have developed close relations with the Mengistu government, are in an advantageous position to push for an easing of tensions. Anxious to reduce their role in what has come to seem a quagmire, by 1988 the Soviets were sending signals to the Ethiopians of a desire to move ahead with some kind of political solution to the Eritrean war. On the whole, Soviet military assistance to Ethiopia to help that country deal with insurgent movements has diminished since 1984, although a big shipment of arms to the area was reported in August–September 1988.[57] (This unusual spurt in Soviet arms assistance was probably explained by the Soviet perceived need to show its continuing commitment to the Mengistu regime at that time.) In addition, the number of Socialist country advisers sent to Ethiopia has been declining. The Soviets, moreover, appear to have fixed a ceiling on their military assistance to Ethiopia, a constraint Mengistu was reminded of during his trip to Moscow in 1988.[58]

Subsequently, the Soviets proposed that either France or Italy take on the role of mediator, an idea Mengistu resisted at first and then—recognizing the limits of his capacity to solve the Eritrean challenge by means of force—began to take more seriously. By September 1989, the Ethiopian government, indicating its preparedness to make significant concessions (possibly including regional autonomy and a federal solution) in order to achieve a negotiated peace, sent a delegation to Atlanta for talks with the Eritrean People's Liberation Front (but not the other insurgent movements) under former President Carter's aegis.[59] Although well placed as a private mediator to facilitate talks between an independent state and an insurgent movement, Carter proved unable to gain agreement on anything but procedural issues. In the face of a deteriorating military situation in Eritrea and Tigre, the Soviets reportedly put Mengistu on notice that they planned to cut military assistance to his regime substantially in 1991. In part, this warning appeared to be intended as a means of pressuring Mengistu to cooperate with U.S.-led peace talks between the Ethiopian government and the Eritrean People's Liberation Front in early 1991. At this time, the parties to the conflict still seem far apart; yet Moscow's willingness to cooperate with its superpower rival in reducing tensions in the area raises hopes for future progress on settling this war.

In southern Africa, Mozambique's desperate situation would seem to require a joint response from the world community, particularly from the two great powers. No country in the region has suffered more from South African destabilization and the ravages of continuing war. In 1987 a Canadian fact-finding team found some four million civilians "in imminent danger of starvation" and "more than 42 percent of the population on the move, forced to abandon fields and homes by the massive bandit activities throughout the rural areas."[60] An April 1988 report issued by the U.S. State Department reconfirmed the dimensions of the crisis, estimating that the Mozambican National Resistance had been the cause of some one hundred thousand civilian deaths as well as of hundreds of thousands of people leaving the country.[61] As a consequence, the Mozambican government has had little opportunity to focus on developmental problems. It has been forced to deplete its resources on security and survival, striking embarrassing accords with the South African government in a desperate effort to reduce the pressures on itself.

This would seem to be an important entry point for future parallel action between the superpowers. Although still relying heavily on the Soviet Union for military assistance, the Afro-Marxist regime in Mozambique turned to the West in 1983 and came to depend increasingly upon the countries of Western Europe and the United States for food and economic aid, the rescheduling of debts, and (British) military training.[62] Recognizing Mozambique's vulnerability and not wishing to be drawn alone into a costly confrontation with South African forces, the Soviets have not stood in the way of these increasing contacts with the West.[63] Thus, by the late 1980s, Mozambique had diversified its dependence across ideological blocs, looking to both sides for support against a highly destructive Mozambican National Resistance banditry. In such a circumstance, where both superpowers support the Mozambican government and the efforts of the Catholic church and the Italian Foreign Ministry to mediate the way, this highly exposed African country would seem a propitious place for some well-calculated parallel actions. The Italian mediators, working directly or indirectly with their great-power and African supporters, may find it necessary to increasingly use various inducements to provide the impetus needed for a settlement.

Facilitating a transition from white minority dominance to democratic rule in South Africa is another entry point for tacit cooperation between the superpowers. Both the U.S. and Soviet leadership have stated their firm opposition to white dominance and apartheid in all their manifestations. Both powers are involved at least minimally in the process of change, which they seek to facilitate without a breakdown in the South African economy (something deemed harmful to the interests of all communities in the country).[64] And committed to the objective of regional stability, both are prepared to expand contacts with all groups within South Africa, refusing—for the moment, at least—to exclude any of them from future negotiations. Clearly, they share a common sense of urgency about avoiding a possible "racial conflagration with [its] frightening implications" for the entire southern African subsystem.[65] The regime of President F. W. de Klerk has raised some hopes that a peaceful transition to nonracial democracy can be negotiated, thus averting a worst-case scenario.[66] Yet the forces aligned against negotiations on the right remain stubbornly determined, requiring effort on the part of the international community to provide confidence-building mechanisms and to give support to moderate elements in all communities seeking evolutionary change. The opportunity exists here, as one Soviet analyst put it, "for further superpower cooperation in reducing tension in the region."[67]

Without overstating the leverage the two great powers possess in this situation, it is important to note that they have sought to encourage South African officials to reconsider their choices by pursuing two tracks simultaneously: first, pressing for full black participation in every aspect of the country's life, and second, helping to build confidence by clarifying the nature of political and constitutional options, as discussed below. The first (or hard) track has involved a package of diplomatic, economic, educational, and military initiatives intended to strengthen both the frontline states and the African opposition within South Africa. This has certainly taken a toll. International pressures have limited South African political and economic options, denying the country political legitimacy as well as access to world markets for certain goods, technology, and services. Real growth fell from 5.8 percent a year during the 1960s to below 2 percent a year in the 1980s (accounted for in part by falling gold prices), and average incomes are estimated to be 15 percent lower than they would have been without sanctions and disinvestment.[68]

To be fully effective, this hard track has been interlinked with the second (or soft) track of diplomacy and mediation. External facilitators can play an indispensable role in helping to manage conflict by initiating a dialogue, communicating among possible parties, clarifying the points of contention, proposing agendas, and outlining principles of possible agreement. In this, both U.S. and Soviet officials have made cautious exploratory efforts to push the process of political exchange forward. For example, George Shultz's September 1987 address in New York was an important attempt to set out principles for a possible constitutional solution that would link majority rule and equal political, economic, and social rights for all citizens with effective constitutional guarantees for minority rights. In addition, Shultz urged South Africans to address basic ideas on a constitutional allocation of powers between the national government and the regional and local units and on the establishment of an economic system that would be free and fair and that would allow South Africans to acquire and own property.[69] Interestingly, some Soviet officials—expressing a kind of new pragmatism—have shown themselves to be open to similar confidence-building measures on parliamentary government, white minority rights, and federalism. Although supporting the ANC (as does the United States), Soviet analysts warn against violence and a thoroughgoing nationalization of white-held properties.[70] Thus, in government circles in the United States and the Soviet Union, many top officials share some similarities in viewpoint on the need for a negotiated political settlement in South Africa at this time, making a joint initiative more feasible.

CONCLUSION: THE GREAT POWERS AS CONFLICT MANAGERS

African governments and insurgent movements are relatively autonomous actors, capable—in part, at least—of determining their own agendas; thus, it is necessary to look at the local and regional sources of African conflicts in order to understand the interactional processes at work. In the struggle between Eritrea and Ethiopia, for example, four Eritrean factions are locked into a complex relationship with each other as well as with the Ethiopian regime; to make matters more complex, the Eritreans rely upon the Sudan and—to some extent—upon sympathetic governments in the Middle East for assistance (as well as upon captured Ethiopian military equipment), while the Mengistu government has received backing from the Soviet Union and other Eastern bloc countries. In Angola, UNITA has built a base of support for itself in southeastern Angola, an enclave that boasts a kind of de facto autonomy known as *Terras Libres de Angola*. It counts for the most part on its exports of timber and diamonds for economic survival and uses some of these revenues to provide for its own schools and health services.[71] Savimbi does look outward for diplomatic and military backing from South Africa, Zaire, and, recently, the United States. The MPLA regime in Luanda receives critically important help from the frontline states in the region and, in addition, from the Soviets and Cubans. Similarly, in the Sudan, South Africa, and elsewhere, relatively autonomous local actors have complex ties and relationships within their own country and region as well as with the great and other external powers. Often these actors are the critical participants in the conflicts around them—a point that must be kept in mind, for it gives perspective on the extent of the roles the superpowers can play.

But a comprehensive view of the conflict management process in Africa requires a global as well as a regional perspective. In certain cases in which the superpowers have come to ally themselves with local states and movements, they have become entangled in the conflict and gained an element of indirect influence over governments or movements that share their preferences. Again, the degree of superpower influence must not be overstated, but it has surfaced at times and has enabled the great powers to move local actors toward constructive (as well as destructive) ends.

In the Gorbachev era, as the ideological differences between the superpowers declined in importance and as the two countries assessed their budgetary constraints and the possible dangers to them arising from regional conflicts in the Third World, the United States and the USSR underwent a change in perceptions and attitudes toward one another that opened up new possibilities for cooperation. Old disputes in Third-World settings lost some of their relevance, allowing a shift from sponsors of conflict to facilitators of peace negotiations. In adopting this new stance, the superpowers moved cautiously toward parallel actions to promote regional stability in northeastern and southern Africa. In the circumstances of the late 1980s, such actions were the most appropriate means available to long-standing rivals who had come to reassess their former strategies and, for reasons of national interest, had decided to pursue common objectives on certain selected issues. It was a largely uncoordinated process of collaboration; yet, it created new options in a number of regional conflict situations.

However, the joint action of the superpowers as currently constituted lacks institutionalization; thus, its application is likely to remain limited and irregular. Over the long term, what is needed is what Henry Kissinger has described as "a *political* framework for dealing with the consequences of foreseeable change."[72] To create such a political framework, it is necessary to go from today's selective pragmatism to learned patterns of relationships. In this regard, the achievements in Angola and the parallel actions elsewhere in Africa are a significant beginning. They represent an important learning process for the superpowers (and local combatants) on the management of conflict and hold out the prospect of enhanced peace in Africa as an immediate beneficial outcome.

NOTES

I wish to express my appreciation to I. William Zartman, Miroslav Nincic, Bruce Jentelson, Richard Remnek, John Ravenhill, Alexander Groth, John Harbeson, and Caroline Hartzell for comments on the first draft of this chapter.

1. Richard H. Ullman, "Ending the Cold War," *Foreign Policy* 72 (Fall 1988):130.
2. Chester A. Crocker, "Summing Up . . . and Looking Ahead," CSIS *Africa Notes* 96 (March 16, 1989):1. Whereas a globalist perspective tends to be extremely ideological and to view African issues in terms of an all-encompassing East-West struggle, a regionalist perspective emphasizes Africa's uniqueness and the local sources of its conflicts. See Donald Rothchild and John Ravenhill, "Subordinating African Issues to Global Logic: Reagan Confronts Political Complexity," in Kenneth Oye, Robert Lieber, and Donald Rothchild (eds.), *Eagle Resurgent? The Reagan Era in American Foreign Policy* (Boston: Little, Brown, 1987), p. 394.
3. Andrei Kozyrev and Andrei Shumikhin, "East and West in the Third World," *International Affairs* (Moscow) 3 (March 1989):66.
4. *Ibid.*, p. 69.
5. *Ibid.*, p. 71.
6. Martin Lowenkopf, "If the Cold War Is over in Africa, Will the United States Still Care?" *CSIS Africa Notes* 98 (May 30, 1989):5.
7. Robert Axelrod, *The Evolution of Cooperation* (New York: Basic Books, 1984), p. 126.
8. *Africa and the World* 1, no. 2 (January 1988):iv.
9. Particularly noteworthy in this regard is the statement by Politburo member Vadim A. Medvedev to the effect that the current regime rejects the notion of world struggle against the West. Bill Keller, "New Soviet Ideologist Rejects Idea of World Struggle Against West," *New York Times*, October 6, 1988, p. 1.
10. For evidence of deep-seated U.S. feelings of mistrust of Soviet leaders and their motives, see Daniel Yankelovich and Richard Smoke, "America's 'New Thinking,'" *Foreign Affairs* 67, no. 1 (Fall 1988):7.
11. "South Africa and the Western Alliance," in Gregory F. Treverton (ed.), *Europe, America, and South Africa* (New York: Council on Foreign Relations, 1988), p. 120.
12. See Rothchild and Ravenhill, "Subordinating African Issues," p. 394.
13. George Bush, "The U.S. and Africa: The Republican Platform," *Africa Report* 33, no. 4 (July-August 1988):13.
14. Rothchild and Ravenhill, "Subordinating African Issues," p. 394.
15. Ullman, "Ending the Cold War," p. 143.
16. On the historical and structural "necessity" of these relations, see L. Adele Jinadu, "Soviet Influence on Afro-Marxist Regimes: Ethiopia and Mozambique," in

Edmond J. Keller and Donald Rothchild (eds.), *Afro-Marxist Regimes: Ideology and Public Policy* (Boulder, Colo.: Lynne Rienner Publishers, 1987), pp. 226–230.

17. Winrich Kuhne, "Moscow Scorns the 'Comrades' in S. Africa's Black Townships," *Africa Analysis* (December 12, 1986):1.

18. Winrich Kuhne, "A 1988 Update on Soviet Relations with Pretoria, the ANC, and the SACP," CSIS *Africa Notes* 89 (September 1, 1988):4.

19. *New York Times*, December 8, 1988, p. A6.

20. Boris A. Asoyan, the deputy chief of the Department of African Countries in the Foreign Ministry, summed up current Soviet thinking on this issue: "We support the A.N.C. and South Africa. But we also believe that there is really no alternative to a peaceful solution." *New York Times*, March 16, 1989, pp. A1, A6. Also see Leonid L. Fituni, "A New Era: Soviet Policy in Southern Africa," *Africa Report* 34, no. 4 (July-August 1989):64.

21. See Edmond J. Keller, "United States Foreign Policy on the Horn of Africa: Policymaking with Blinders On," in Gerald J. Bender, James S. Coleman, and Richard L. Sklar (eds.), *African Crisis Areas and U.S. Foreign Policy* (Berkeley: University of California Press, 1985), p. 186; Richard B. Remnek, "Soviet Policy in the Horn of Africa: The Decision to Intervene," in Robert H. Donaldson (ed.), *The Soviet Union in the Third World: Successes and Failures* (Boulder, Colo.: Westview Press, 1981), Chapter 6; and Harry Brind, "Soviet Policy in the Horn of Africa," *International Affairs* 60, no. 1 (Winter 1983–1984):75–95.

22. Larry C. Napper, "The Ogaden War: Some Implications for Crisis Prevention," in Alexander L. George (ed.), *Managing U.S.-Soviet Rivalry: Problems of Crisis Prevention* (Boulder, Colo.: Westview Press, 1983), pp. 237–238.

23. See Gillian Gunn, "A Guide to the Intricacies of the Angola-Namibia Negotiations," CSIS *African Notes* 90 (September 8, 1988):5.

24. Yankelovich and Smoke, "America's 'New Thinking,' " p. 7.

25. Letter from President Ford to Speaker of the House Carl Albert, reprinted in *Department of State Bulletin* 74, no. 1912 (February 16, 1976):183.

26. Bayard Rustin and Carl Gersham, "Africa, Soviet Imperialism & the Retreat of American Power," *Commentary* 64, no. 4 (October 1977):35.

27. This point is not lost on current Soviet analysts. See, for example, Kozyrev and Shumikhin, "East and West in the Third World," p. 68.

28. Henry A. Kissinger, press conference, Washington, D.C., April 22, 1976. Also see Henry A. Kissinger, *Implications of Angola for Future U.S. Foreign Policy, a Statement Before the Senate Subcommittee on African Affairs of the Foreign Relations Committee*, January 29, 1976. (Washington, D.C.: Department of State, Bureau of Public Affairs, 1976), P.R. 40, p. 2.

29. The Annapolis address is quoted in *New York Times*, June 8, 1978, p. A22. For a discussion of the behind-the-scenes differences within the Carter team on responding to Soviet initiatives in Africa, see David B. Ottaway, "Administration Split on Africa Policy," *Manchester Guardian Weekly* 118, no. 5 (February 26, 1978):15.

30. Yevgeni Primakov, "USSR Policy on Regional Conflicts," *International Affairs* 6 (1988):3.

31. *New York Times,* August 19, 1988, p. A8. Also see Walter S. Mossberg and John Walcott, "Strategic Shift: U.S. Redefines Policy on Security to Place Less Stress on Soviets," *New York Times,* August 11, 1988, p. A1.

32. Quoted in *New York Times,* June 2, 1988, p. A6.

33. Quoted in *New York Times,* September 14, 1988, p. A18. Also see the article by Graham T. Allison, Jr., a Dukakis foreign policy adviser, "Testing Gorbachev," *Foreign Affairs* 67, no. 1 (Fall 1988):18–32.

34. Gideon Rafael, "Five Wars, One Peace. What Next?" *Middle East Review* 20, no. 4 (Summer 1988):9.

35. See Napper, "The Ogaden War," p. 237; and Robert S. Jaster, "Pretoria's Nuclear Diplomacy," CSIS *Africa Notes* 81 (January 22, 1988):2.

36. Kuhne, "A 1988 Update," p. 6.

37. On the successful efforts by the great powers to facilitate a peaceful settlement in Central America, see Michael Kramer, "Anger, Bluff—and Cooperation," *Time* 135, no. 23 (June 4, 1990):38–45.

38. Nathaniel Davis, a former assistant secretary of state for African affairs, writes that an interagency National Security Council Task Force on Angola, which he chaired in 1975, "urged that the U.S. government privately approach the U.S.S.R. or build public pressure to induce the U.S.S.R. to reduce its support of the M.P.L.A. or, ultimately, to support or promote a U.N. or OAU mediation effort." "The Angola Decision of 1975: A Personal Memoir," *Foreign Affairs* 57, no. 1 (Fall 1978):112.

39. For a description of the military clashes at Cuito Cuanavale, see Karl Maier, "Angola: The Military Stalemate," *Africa Report* 33, no. 3 (May-June 1988):34–35.

40. For an excellent play-by-play description of these ongoing negotiations, see Gunn, "A Guide to the Intricacies of the Angola-Namibia Negotiations."

41. John D. Battersby, "With Peace Near, Namibian Rebel Leader Softens His Stand," *New York Times,* August 19, 1988, p. A6.

42. Significantly the Cubans, described as "the most enthusiastic protagonist[s] of the fighting," showed some flexibility following the Cairo talks. Jorge Risquet Valdez, the chief Cuban negotiator, declared at that time, "We are not seeking a military victory over South Africa but a just and honourable solution that will bring independence to Namibia, security to Angola, and peace to the region." Alan Rake, "End Game for South Africa," *New African* 251 (August 1988):9.

43. For one participant in the mediation process, linkage was the "only available framework for a settlement." Chas. W. Freeman, Jr., "The Angola/Namibia Accord," *Foreign Affairs* 68, no. 3 (Summer 1989):133. Also see Colin Legum, "Southern Africa: Analysis of the Peace Process," *Third World Reports* L. B/1. (January 11, 1989):6; and G. R. Berridge, "Diplomacy and the Angola/Namibia Accords," *International Affairs* (London) 65, no. 3 (Summer 1989):471.

44. In African eyes, this U.S. mediatory role was a positive one indeed. See the interview with Nigeria's General Olusegun Obasanjo in *Africa Report* 33, no. 3 (May-June 1988):39.

45. Michael Clough, "Beyond Constructive Engagement," *Foreign Policy* 61 (Winter 1985–1986):9; and Pauline Baker, "The American Challenge in Southern Africa," *Current History* 88, no. 538 (May 1989):245–246.

46. Baker, "The American Challenge," p. 245.

47. Legum, "Southern Africa," p. 5.

48. Gunn, "A Guide to the Intricacies of the Angola-Namibia Negotiations," pp. 9–10; and Berridge, "Diplomacy and the Angola/Namibia Accords," p. 469, fn. 25.

49. Bill Keller, "Moscow Wants to Expedite a Settlement of Angola War," *New York Times*, June 6, 1988, p. 4.

50. See Donald Rothchild and Caroline Hartzell, "The Road to Gbadolite: Great Power and African Mediations in Angola," in I. William Zartman (ed.), *Negotiating Internal Conflicts*, forthcoming.

51. Robert Pear, "Southern Africa Accord Set," *New York Times*, August 9, 1988, p. A4; and Robert Pear, "Panel to Monitor Truces in Africa," *ibid.*, November 16, 1988, p. A5.

52. Gillian Gunn, "Keeping Namibian Independence on Track: The Cuban Factor," CSIS *Africa Notes* 103 (October 23, 1989):4.

53. Quoted in Hella Pick, "Namibia Independence Pact Signed," *Manchester Guardian Weekly* 140, no. 1 (January 1, 1989):8.

54. Donald Rothchild, "Africa's Ethnic Conflicts and Their Implication for United States Policy," in Robert I. Rotberg (ed.), *Africa in the 1990s and Beyond* (Algonac, Mich.: Reference Publications, 1988), pp. 273–274.

55. U.S. Department of State, *The U.S. and Sudan: Peace and Relief* (Washington, D.C.: U.S. Department of State, Bureau of Public Affairs, February 1989), p. 1.

56. Colin Legum, "Horn of Africa: Super-Powers' Cautious New Initiative," *Third World Reports* L. F/2 (February 8, 1989):2.

57. Comment by Colin Legum at a panel of the African Studies Association, Atlanta, November 5, 1989.

58. *Indian Ocean Newsletter* 347 (September 10, 1988):1.

59. *Ibid.*, 396 (September 9, 1989):1.

60. Quoted in John S. Saul, "Development and Counterdevelopment Strategies in Mozambique," in Keller and Rothchild, *Afro-Marxist Regimes*, pp. 138–139.

61. Robert Pear, "U.S. Asserts Mozambicans Fled from Rebels' Brutality," *New York Times*, April 21, 1988, p. A4.

62. Starting in mid-1989, the Soviets began to pull out a number of their military advisers and to reduce their military assistance to Mozambique. See Colleen Lowe Morna, "Mozambique: Hopes and Fears," *New African* 271 (April 1990):18.

63. See Winrich Kuhne, "What Does the Case of Mozambique Tell Us About Soviet Ambivalence Toward Africa?" CSIS *Africa Notes* 46 (August 30, 1985):1–5.

64. Kuhne, "A 1988 Update," p. 2; and George Shultz, "The Democratic Future of South Africa," Current Policy no. 1007 (Washington, D.C.: Department of State, Bureau of Public Affairs, 1987), p. 5.

65. Commonwealth Group of Eminent Persons, *Mission to South Africa: The Commonwealth Report* (Harmondsworth: Penguin Books, 1986), pp. 138–139. For an analysis of this effort to mediate the conflict, see Donald Rothchild, "From Exhortation to Incentive Strategies: Mediation Efforts in South Africa in the Mid-1980s," in Edmond J. Keller and Louis A. Picard (eds.), *South Africa in Southern Africa* (Boulder, Colo.: Lynne Rienner Publishers, 1989).

66. De Klerk told the country at the time of being sworn into office that "history, I believe, offers us a unique opportunity for peaceful solutions." See Christopher

S. Wren, "South Africans Put Rising Faith in Negotiations," *New York Times,* September 4, 1989, A6.

67. Fituni, "A New Era," p. 65.

68. *The Economist,* October 14, 1989, pp. 45–46.

69. Shultz, "The Democratic Future," p. 4.

70. Kuhne, "A 1988 Update," pp. 1–8.

71. Linda M. Heywood, "Unita and Ethnic Nationalism in Angola," *Journal of Modern African Studies* 27, no. 1 (March 1989):60.

72. "A Memo to the Next President," *Newsweek* 112, no. 12 (September 19, 1988):34.

15

GREAT POWERS AND SOUTHERN AFRICA: RIVALRY OR COOPERATION?

VITALEY VASILKOV

One of the important foreign policy fields in which perestroika should help to overcome previously created ideological stereotypes is the collective search for ways to overcome Third-World conflict situations, including those in southern Africa, on the basis of "comprehensive security"—that is, "security for all."[1] The problem of regional conflict resolution has two main dimensions. The first is the origin of regional conflicts and the second is the role of foreign—mainly great—powers with respect to such conflicts. The first dimension arises from the specific development stage at which the majority of Third-World nations find themselves. This exists objectively regardless of external influence. But to a certain degree, this problem is also connected to external influence; it is dependent on the prevailing trends in world politics, which may serve to encourage or discourage—directly or indirectly—the violent resolution of regional issues. The second dimension depends mainly upon the approach of the great powers, who pursue their own policies in the Third World. Insofar as this dimension is concerned, the problem of regional conflict has little in common with objective local realities. But to a certain degree, great-power reaction is also determined by local factors through the mechanism of treaty commitments, speculations about ideology or the self-interests of the great powers, and the rivalry between them.

On the one hand, regional conflicts may be seen as an inevitable repetition by the developing countries of the historic path trod by the old world nations, a path accompanied by great violence. Unfortunately, the growing conflict in the developing states, with which the outside world has little to do, remains a prospect to be reckoned with. This conflict is linked to the objective processes of nation building, economic and political development, and struggles for power in these countries. In fact, these circumstances are causing the regional conflicts to become a global problem.

On the other hand, no less objective and rather encompassing is the purposeful influence foreign powers may exert on these conflicts. Regional conflicts are taking place in an interdependent and indivisible world in which countries with a wide diversity of cultural, historical, and economic levels coexist. Such influence may change considerably the scale and nature of the conflicts in one direction or another and, under certain conditions, allow for external control of the conflicts. Great-power policies do not amount to unilateral manipulation of local forces but instead necessarily include the local actors' influence on these powers. The combination of great-power and local-power influence widens further the sphere within which purposeful influence may affect these regional conflicts, and such influence can be directed either to escalation or deterrence. Thus, if the experience of human civilization has any practical importance, one may be optimistic that direct or indirect external influence may, within reasonable limits, shift East-West confrontation in the Third World toward cooperation and minimize the level of conflict.

Military force has long been the only real means of regional conflict resolution. Its use has grown considerably, in both qualitative and quantitative terms, during recent decades. However, following the nuclear stalemate, certain limits have also emerged on the use of conventional forces in regional conflicts; this complicates the achievement of any long-term political goals with the help of military force. The most dangerous conflicts, those in which the great powers have participated directly, have shown that military force is becoming less and less functional as each side finds itself trapped in a military deadlock. Vietnam and Afghanistan are the best examples of this.

Such a deadlock may be interpreted as a spontaneously emerging mechanism, serving to restrict the use of military force in regional conflicts. Perhaps this mechanism's sphere of action will objectively widen, embracing regional conflicts with indirect great-power participation or without any such participation. The cessation of the Iraq-Iran War may be a good example. It appears that this beneficial mechanism can be enhanced (thus allowing the powers involved to avoid large-scale loss of human and material resources) by the deliberate use of preventive or preemptive consultations between the great powers before the actual use of force occurs or before decisions leading to the use of force are made. As Donald Rothchild notes in this volume, the fact that ad hoc tacit cooperation between the USSR and the United States has taken place and has produced positive results in the past gives one grounds to believe that cooperation at higher levels may be possible.

The possibility exists for effecting a transition from ad hoc consultations to a permanent negotiation mechanism for the prevention of regional conflicts. At this juncture, Mikhail Gorbachev's ideas, expressed in his 1988 U.N. address, seem to be topical. He spoke of "the binding nature of international law for all nations" and of the USSR's wish "to see the supremacy of legal norms in the process of problem-solving," which requires "some agreements under U.N. auspices on the uniform understanding of international legal norms and principles, their codification under new conditions, and the elaboration of legal norms for new fields of cooperation." "The effectiveness of international law," he concluded, "must rest not on coercion, but on norms, reflecting the balance of interests of all states."[2] Another idea is to establish an international nongovernmental scientific center, which, through offering recommendations on potential conflict situations, could play an influential role in the decision-making processes of governments.

The existence of the above-mentioned sphere of deliberate Third-World conflict resolution makes cooperation physically possible. The declining effectiveness of the use of military force in regional conflicts, predetermined by its ineffectiveness at the nuclear level, as well as the long-term interest of all states in constructive rather than destructive developments in the Third World may serve as incentives for such cooperation. There is also an urgent need to shift from huge military expenditures to spending on development and to remove the destabilizing effect of regional conflicts on international affairs as a whole. Finally, the internationally recognized obsolescence of the traditional approach to formulating states' interests only as selfish ones (an approach that implies a single—military—outcome to any conflict situation and demands only "victory") creates a political base for such cooperation. Zero-sum games, in which any question is decided by force—principally military force—are inappropriate in the nuclear age.

The conflict in southern Africa, where the USSR and the United States have a stored experience of confrontation and missed opportunities, deserves a new approach such as the one discussed here. As one of the greatest postdétente regional conflicts, southern Africa is in many ways indicative of the imperfect détente of the 1970s as well as of the fruitful search for more long-standing and effective principles of Soviet-U.S. regional relations in the 1980s. It also uniquely exemplifies the interplay of complicated domestic and international factors, which at the initial stages sharpened the conflict but in the final stages are helping to settle it. Finally, this is the last subregion of colonial conflict in Africa and worldwide; it is characterized by emerging norms of North-South relations for the 1990s and beyond that will, we hope, no longer include the notorious notion of neocolonialism.

CONFRONTATION IN SOUTHERN AFRICA

On January 15, 1975, in the Portuguese city of Alvor, three Angolan groups—the Popular Movement for the Liberation of Angola (MPLA), the National Front for the Liberation of Angola (FNLA), and the National Union for the Total Independence of Angola (UNITA)—reached an agreement with the government of Portugal on the date and conditions of granting independence to Angola. They also agreed among themselves on the division of power and on carrying out elections right after independence. This solution—known as the Alvor Agreement—seemed satisfactory to everybody, although one could foresee the rivalry for power among the three organizations.

On January 31, the transitional government came to power in Angola. On February 21, the chairman of the USSR Council of Ministers, Alexey Kosygin, sent a cable to the Angolan government, welcoming this event as "a great victory achieved by Angolan people."[3] But as early as January 22, the National Security Council's 40 Committee—the Washington interagency group responsible for Central Intelligence Agency (CIA) covert operations—had authorized a covert grant of $300,000 to the FNLA. This decision shows how even small moves provoked the civil war in Angola, particularly as this action was reminiscent of the scenario prompted by Kissinger in Mozambique a year earlier. In Mozambique, Kissinger had placed his main hopes for "containing communism" on the right-wing Portuguese settlers in Maputo, headed by Jorge Jardin—a millionaire of Portuguese origin—and his supporters in Lisbon. There were also several weak black African groups, the most well known of which was headed by Paolo Gumane. Gumane later admitted that he had had contacts with the CIA since the 1960s and had received covert CIA financing in the spring of 1974 to initiate anti–Front for the Liberation of Mozambique activities. Angola therefore became the second, not the first, act in the southern African drama. This pattern of interventions seriously affected the decisions of all the participants in Angola, including the Soviet Union.

UNITA did not get covert U.S. aid until July 1975 because, at that time, U.S. analysts believed that the FNLA and UNITA could find common ground and form a united front against the MPLA.[4] The 40 Committee decision in January, according to John A. Marcum, was based on "past connections" the United States had with the FNLA and on "an irrepressible habit of thinking in terms of 'our team' and 'theirs,' which entices the Administration into choosing sides."[5] Moreover, in September 1975 the CIA directly rebuffed UNITA leader Jonas Savimbi's appeal to explore the possibility of reaching a negotiated settlement with the MPLA. "We didn't need soft allies," explained John Stockwell, the former head of the CIA Angolan Operational Task Force.[6] Thus, one cannot help but agree with Wayne S. Smith's conclusions: "The United States, then, was responsible for setting in motion actions that destroyed the Alvor Agreement and that touched off a bloody civil war that was to rage in Angola well into 1976. It was not a move that served U.S. interests. To the contrary, it proved unnecessary and foolish."[7]

At the same time, such action on the part of the United States was natural. As Nathaniel Davis has observed, "Both during the final weeks of the Vietnam War and during the Angolan crises of 1975, the Secretary and the President seem to have believed that it was better to roll the dice against the longest of odds than to abandon the competition against our great adversary. The Secretary would freely acknowledge, I believe, that he saw Angola as part of the U.S.-Soviet relationship, and not as an African problem."[8]

In such a situation the USSR and Cuba had no choice except to take appropriate countermeasures, which helped to ensure the MPLA's victory in early 1976. However, political momentum is a dangerous thing. In retrospect, it is fair to say that following the MPLA victory, the Soviet Union missed the opportunity to make use of a more far-sighted, wise, and courageous—although more difficult—policy option than the one adopted. An attempt to encourage conciliation between the MPLA and UNITA would likely have been the proper tactic. Had such an approach been successful, meeting the needs of the Angolan people might have been ensured through the realization of a more representative government and conditions for the peaceful development of the country. Moreover, the Luanda government, which had been weakened by UNITA's activities in southern Angola, would have been strengthened by the prestige it would have gained. Finally, in this scenario any speculations about East-West "victories" or "defeats" would have been preempted, and a basis would have been established for subsequent constructive U.S.-Soviet cooperation, such as on working toward an independent Zimbabwe.

These opportunities for U.S.-Soviet cooperation were missed. Instead, at the twenty-fifth Communist Party of the Soviet Union Congress held in February 1976, General-Secretary Leonid Brezhnev explained the MPLA victory in terms of "the current state of world class forces." The Soviet-Mozambican communiqué, adopted in May 1976, read, "The present epoch is characterized by the mounting peoples' fight for national and social liberation." The Soviet-Angolan statement, issued on October 14, 1976, noted "the loss by imperialism of its positions in Southern Africa."[9] Thus, events in southern Africa were interpreted as a "victory" for the East and a "defeat" for the West—outcomes that were the result of a global power equilibrium favorable to socialism—and simultaneously as a factor strengthening and ensuring further "intensification of the fight" against imperialism.

U.S. activities at this juncture also did not encourage superpower cooperation. U.S. actions in 1975–1976 in Mozambique, Angola, and Rhodesia—undertaken in full collaboration with South Africa—were a blunt effort to install client regimes in southern Africa and to inflict "defeat" on the Soviet Union. The United States had completely lost Moscow's confidence following its encouragement of the bloody coup in Chile in 1973, the barriers to Soviet-U.S. trade it erected in 1974, and its failure to initiate discussions on southern African issues with the Soviet Union. All these facts notwithstanding, it is still doubtful that Soviet policy in Angola in 1975–1976 (best explained as a mere adoption of a Washington-imposed zero-sum game) was the best course to follow.

There is no documentary confirmation that the USSR made any effort to discuss the Angolan case with the United States or to promote a rapprochement between the MPLA and UNITA. The only evidence of any such effort was a short note: "After consultations between President Ford and Soviet Ambassador Anatoly Dobrynin, the Soviet Union halted its airlift to Angola" on December 4, 1975, but "resumed" it on December 25.[10] The exact circumstances surrounding this incident are still unclear. One may speculate that the flow of covert U.S. aid to the FNLA and UNITA, disclosed in the U.S. press only in December, led to a feeling of betrayal on the part of the USSR. In 1976 and 1979, Cuba—perhaps on the advice of the Soviets—made unilateral cuts in the number of forces it had stationed in Angola, thus taking steps toward reconciliation in the region. But the United States chose "not to understand" these actions as hints of cooperative intent and did not show reciprocal restraint. According to John Marcum, as the first Cuban withdrawal (which began as early as April 1976) proceeded, "the Carter Administration missed an opportunity in early 1977 to accord relatively noncontroversial recognition to the [MPLA] government. Soon after, the exodus of Cuban troops was ended and reversed because of overflights of South African aircraft and mounting antigovernmental insurgency."[11] In fact, in retrospect it is clear that this tense situation required not just "a diplomacy of hints" but more fundamental and explicit agreements between the USSR and the United States.

The Soviet government did not take seriously the change in U.S. policy declared by Kissinger at Dallas on March 22, 1976, at which time he outlined "two equally important principles: . . . support for majority rule in Africa and firm opposition to military intervention."[12] True, this change in policy included strong elements of what even friendly observers called "an attempt to save by diplomacy something which failed to be saved by force."[13] However, an underestimation of the opportunities (such as those contained in the concept of a negotiated settlement for Rhodesia) and a failure to consider possible Soviet-U.S. cooperation in solving African problems, at least during the next administration, proved to be serious miscalculations.

Nothing changed during the Carter years. His initial program did contain a number of constructive ideas beyond the inherited Republican concept of negotiated settlement. For instance, Secretary of State Cyrus Vance noted that "the basis of our position in Africa is the African perception that we see them and their problems in their own terms, and not as an arena for East-West differences. . . . We would welcome Soviet help—which we regret we do not have—in achieving a peaceful transition to majority rule in Rhodesia, Namibia and elsewhere in Africa."[14] Under the circumstances, the USSR certainly had grounds to doubt the sincerity of such assertions but not to reject others categorically for ideological reasons.

Nevertheless, the chairman of the Presidium of the Supreme Soviet of the USSR, Nickolay Podgorny—during a visit to Africa in March–April 1977—stated in Maputo on March 29 that Angola and Mozambique formed "the crest of a powerful anticolonial, antiracist wave," their boundaries with Rhodesia and South Africa "being not just interstate but class frontiers." With respect to a possible peaceful solution in Rhodesia, Namibia, and South Africa, he said, "Just one thing: Transfer, gentlemen, the power to the majority of the population, that is, to the Africans in the person of their genuine representatives, eliminate the apartheid policies, and the problem will be removed."[15]

Soviet-U.S. relations under the Carter administration were troubled from the beginning. But Carter's approach to problems in southern Africa stood out against the background of general U.S. policy as one of realism and of readiness to make necessary compromises. This approach might have been explained in part by purely pragmatic estimates of the situation in Rhodesia. Moscow's willingness to hold a constructive dialogue on the Rhodesian issue would probably have provided an impetus for favorable changes in the overall atmosphere of the Soviet-U.S. relationship and could have helped to weaken or even to eliminate the outbreaks of confrontation between the two powers that followed in 1977–1978 with the uprisings in the Zairian province of Shaba and the conflict on the Horn of Africa. Nor can the possibility be excluded that given such U.S.-Soviet dialogues, the situation in Afghanistan would have developed in a different direction.

Both sides ran the risk of having détente tested to the utmost, although it had not been structured to withstand such stress. The series of Soviet-U.S. agreements of the early 1970s did not contain any direct arrangements regarding regional conflicts. The extension of the agreed-upon general principles of relationship to the sphere of regional conflicts allowed for a very general understanding, which each side could interpret in its own favor: The Soviet Union could interpret the general principles as having meant that the United States agreed to consider peaceful coexistence as a form of class struggle, and the United States could interpret the principles as a Soviet obligation to keep itself aloof from the support of national liberation movements and to give the United States carte blanche in the Third World in return for détente. Each of these misinterpretations was unacceptable to the other party. But instead of searching for more profound agreements during the period of the conflict, both sides preferred to intensify confrontation.

The two nations took different paths to confrontation. The USSR had always insisted that neither side should gain any unilateral advantages in the Third World. The United States, to the contrary, had openly tried to keep its supremacy there, describing Soviet ideology as aggressive and its own as defensive. This is why—even following the lines of international law—in the U.S. view, the Soviet Union was taking intolerable actions. This ideology of U.S. manifest destiny left no outcome except confrontation.

As a result, despite certain informal U.S.-Soviet understandings that helped to bring about the declaration of Zimbabwean independence in 1980, the late 1970s and early 1980s became a period of a renaissance of conflicts. In many ways, this was provoked by superpower behavior: by the Reagan Doctrine, which was directed toward the escalation of the East-West contest in the Third World rather than the settlement of disputes; and by the ministerial reshuffle in the USSR, during which the Soviet Union could at best keep inertially afloat its previous policy of reaction to imperialist intrigues. All this served to paralyze political will on both sides, turning the occasional U.S.-USSR discussions on regional issues into conversations of the deaf. Attempts to build a mechanism for such negotiations were also precluded, which undermined U.N. capabilities in this respect. In the end, a Namibian settlement was blocked, the process of reform in South Africa was stopped, the scale of Pretoria's destabilizing efforts against the frontline states rose sharply, and the internal conflicts in Angola and Mozambique assumed an irretrievable character.

These ongoing conflicts inflicted considerable human and material losses on the nations of southern Africa. Moreover, entire generations in these countries have known nothing but armed struggle, a situation that may have unforeseeable consequences in the future. These conflicts have destabilized international relations and have not brought success to either superpower. The USSR failed to ensure the stable and peaceful development of friendly regimes in Angola and Mozambique. The United States did not manage to overthrow those regimes or obtain a solution in Namibia. And the implementation of limited sanctions against the Republic of South Africa in 1985–1986 signaled the abandonment of the failed constructive engagement policy.

New political thinking was necessary in order to give impetus to the political settlement of these conflicts. However cautiously the West still regards it, one must admit that it was the new thinking that allowed both Soviet and U.S. policies in southern Africa to get past the deadlock. In his December 7, 1988, U.N. address, Gorbachev observed: "The year 1988 has brought a ray of hope in this sphere of our common concerns. It touched upon almost all the regional crises and somewhere there are shifts for the better. We welcome them and have encouraged them within [the] reasonable limits of our capabilities."[16] Undoubtedly, the agreements on the southwest Africa region signed in New York on December 22, 1988, are among these shifts.

In order to transform these shifts into enduring patterns of cooperation, it is important to learn the right lessons from the previous period of confrontation. In the United States and the Soviet Union, there are those who are convinced that it was the Reagan administration's confrontational stance and military buildup that persuaded the USSR to abandon its goals and make unilateral concessions to an allegedly superior force in the Third World and elsewhere. The U.S. proponents of this view conclude that because this policy has proved to be effective, its continuation will produce further concessions—particularly as the USSR is now facing serious internal problems. Like-minded people in the Soviet Union may believe it is only necessary to wait until this troublesome period is over, to accumulate power, and to strike a retaliatory blow at the proper moment. Such thinking unites all of perestroika's opponents, who consider the search for foreign enemies to be a means of compensating for internal problems.

The experience of the U.S. post-Vietnam debates, when the same arguments helped to lead to a rise in military expenditures and the sharpening of global confrontation, demonstrates that such speculations only further escalate global tensions. Obviously, the U.S. proponents of the cold-war approach feel indebted to their Soviet counterparts, who contributed to the victory of the U.S. hard-liners. The latter, who now in effect propose to reciprocate by strengthening the hard-liners in the Soviet Union—rendering these groups' positions in both countries self-confirming. Application of these mutually reinforcing hard-line positions is the path of least resistance, for destabilization is always simpler and cheaper than stabilization—particularly in Africa, whose weak national and state institutions make it vulnerable to even limited outside interference.

Meanwhile, during the period under consideration, the Soviet Union found itself in the role of stabilizing force for the regimes in Angola, Mozambique, and Ethiopia, which came to power with its help. The United States, on the other hand, attempted to prevent the Soviet Union from playing this role—a role that represented a reversal of their roles during the Vietnam War. The superpowers' failure to "win" in the face of the other side's counteraction is best explained not by their weakness but rather by the logic of confrontation in an era of nuclear parity and their comparable military-economic capabilities. In turn, the nature of counteraction, which was given shape by the atmosphere of confrontation between the two powers, gained its own momentum. The perceived responsibility of either side to intervene arose from any real or perceived actions by the other rather than from the actual national interests or local realities of either side. The paradox inherent in such a situation speaks for itself.

Justified by ideological motives, the USSR and the United States gave opposite answers to the question of whether the new structures they were trying to create in some Third-World countries were good or bad. But the problem was that in reality, the logic of confrontation had turned this question (usually looked at as a principal incentive for their actions) into a secondary one. The real merits of these structures could be discerned mainly in peacetime; the more democratic the given structure was, the more difficult its survival became in times of war. Military victory demands different characteristics of the state (or the ability to acquire such characteristics in the course of the conflict) than does the prosperity of the nation in times of peace. Hence, not only the prestige and interests of the great powers but also the democratization of the Third World, as well as the direct human and material losses of the developing nations, were made victims of global confrontation.

If the experience of superpower confrontation has produced any positive outcomes, it is the evidence that no serious regional conflict can be solved without the cooperation of the great powers. Interference and counter-interference by the great powers is usually enough to drag out crises indefinitely. The real national interests, ideological and pragmatic, of the great powers and those of the developing nations coincide in the case of cooperation and dictate the establishment of mechanisms for permanent political settlement of regional conflicts. What can be suggested in this regard for southern Africa?

FOUR GUARANTEES FOR SOUTH AFRICA'S FUTURE

Conflict in southern Africa, although consisting of several conflict situations—dismantling of apartheid in South Africa, Namibian independence, cessation of destabilization against a number of frontline states (FLS)—also forms a single whole. A settlement in South Africa seems to be the central issue in the region, while the others are derivative or peripheral. But the processes of settling these peripheral issues should include at least some preliminary arrangements for solving the central problem of South African apartheid; otherwise, any settlement will necessarily be temporary.

In the early 1980s, the South African government apparently came to the conclusion that its cooperation in resolving the region's problems would not produce a breakthrough in its own political isolation in Africa and worldwide but, on the contrary, would worsen its position. As a result, it adopted a total strategy of destabilizing neighboring regimes.

For the South African government, this strategy involved (1) ensuring its state security by exporting to the region the struggle of the apartheid regime for survival by attempting to destabilize its neighbors; (2) keeping order domestically by appearing to inch toward the reform of apartheid according to its own timetable and by exporting to the region the "reforms-with-repression" package it had already adopted at home; (3) overcoming international sanctions by using the neighboring states, which are economically dependent on the Republic of South Africa, both as hostages and as potential trading partners to enable it to circumvent the sanctions; and (4) preserving a framework of regional cooperation by contemplating the creation of a constellation of southern African states, which would accomplish regional economic and political integration on the basis of South African hegemony. If South Africa were to be convinced that in a multifaceted political settlement in the region its interests would be taken into account, it might then agree to a solution acceptable to the opposition, to itself, and to the entire world. In the absence of such guarantees, South Africa has no option but to try to secure these interests on its own. In the latter case, it will strive for a solution that will far exceed the terms of any reasonable political settlement.

A South African unilateral strategy would amount either to creating puppet regimes in Namibia, Angola, and Mozambique or to perpetuating a regional crisis that would inevitably lead to dragging out reforms within the country itself. South African military, financial, and economic capabilities have seemingly enabled it to pursue both strategies simultaneously for some time, although at high cost. No country or constellation of forces has been capable of dissuading South Africa from this course. This is not the best option for the Republic of South Africa, but it has recognized no viable alternative strategy.

What would guarantees for South Africa entail? What guarantees would it be possible to demand from South Africa in return? And what is the most promising alternative in the long run: to get a political decision on this basis or to face the prospect of a protracted conflict in the region?

First, if Namibia, Angola, Mozambique, and similar countries are seen by Pretoria as its forward defense lines, then it will most likely require firm guarantees from these sources regarding the renewal of any armed attacks. This means the abandonment of the armed struggle by SWAPO and the ANC, a pledge by the frontline states that their territories will not be used for transporting guerrillas or supplying armaments for the military wing of the African National Congress, and the complete withdrawal of Cuban forces from Angola. In return, South Africa would be obliged to legalize the ANC, the South African Communist Party (SACP), SWAPO, and other African political organizations; guarantee Africans freedom of political activity; release all political prisoners; stop all military support for UNITA and the Mozambican National Resistance; cease armed attacks against the frontline states after withdrawing its forces from Angola and Namibia; and contribute administratively, diplomatically, and financially to the implementation of U.N. Security Council Resolution no. 435.

Such suggestions may at first glance appear unacceptable to those fighting apartheid; however, some of these suggestions were included in the New York Accord on Namibia, which was signed in 1988. Furthermore, the armed struggle against apartheid is important only as a means of stirring up mass support; it is the single real means of action for black South Africans, who have been driven into desperate circumstances by apartheid's denial of all political rights and of the legal means of striving for such rights. But on the whole, armed conflict has never played the principal role in the antiapartheid struggle. Demonstrations, strikes, and boycott campaigns have appeared to be more effective measures. The more armed struggle has been captured by extremists, the more it has provoked the authorities to tighten repression. Thus, discontinuance of the armed struggle can in no way be considered a tactical dismantling of the African National Congress, provided the ANC is given the ability to participate through voting. By legalizing African political movements, Pretoria in turn would contribute greatly to channeling political struggle in a more civilized and constructive direction. The very fact that South Africa has agreed to negotiate with parties previously treated as deadly enemies may prove that diplomacy is not a weak tool in dealing with Pretoria, even with respect to domestic issues.

Second, if South Africa believes that it needs to secure time for reforming apartheid, then the outside world should recognize the usefulness of the reforms that have already been made, although these have been insufficient up to now. It will be necessary to reach a certain level of understanding between South Africa and the world community on the terms of further progress along the path of reform and on beginning a dialogue among all of South Africa's political forces.

Third, if South Africa is led to see implementation of these reforms as a way of overcoming sanctions, then new sanctions would not be applied. Those already introduced would be lifted if the conditions set out under the first two guarantees were met.

Fourth, it seems necessary to recognize that South Africa, as the most industrialized country in the region, has a natural economic role to play there. It would be counterproductive to obstruct its legitimate efforts to widen its financial, technical, and other assistance to neighboring states.

CAN THE UNITED STATES AND THE SOVIET UNION COOPERATE?

We now face several difficult questions. What are the real Soviet and U.S. national interests in southern Africa? Can the two superpowers develop a common platform for securing these four guarantees for the Republic of South Africa? Are there any alternatives?

To begin at the end, the Soviet Union and the United States face a similar dilemma: They must either strive for an internationally recognized, widely acceptable, stable, peaceful compromise that is both in their interests and in the interests of the nations on the scene, or they must support their traditional, historical allies to the utmost to ensure "victory" for their respective sides. In other words, the alternative is either joint (parallel) action or confrontation. The latter is only a theoretical possibility if one takes into account the following interpretation of great-power interests.

U.S. interests in southern Africa have, on many occasions, been officially formulated in detail. Among the most successful attempts to do so was Secretary of State George Shultz's statement that "apartheid is not only morally indefensible, it's in the long run unsustainable."[17] It follows that the United States is sincerely interested in changing the apartheid regime and that it proceeds from the assumptions that apartheid politically discredits the capitalist system; hinders South African economic progress; negatively affects the profits of transnational corporations; radicalizes the regional situation; threatens a social outburst that may result in the protracted ruin of South Africa's economy, thus denying the West reliable access to the region's raw materials; complicates relations with U.S. allies; provokes public indignation throughout the world; and contributes to sharpening ethnic differences and human rights problems in the Western countries. Concern that the USSR might use a crisis situation to gain unilateral benefits also plays a role in the formulation of U.S. interests.

Soviet interests in southern Africa, as in other Third-World regions, have not been officially set forth, aside from constant condemnation of the apartheid regime since the early 1950s. The total repugnance and complete nonacceptance of apartheid by all successive Soviet governments and by public opinion in the Soviet Union have a long history. Soviet Africanists have also traditionally limited themselves to declaring the single interest of the USSR to be "assistance to the liberation of the South of the continent," reducing real actions to "non-recognition and resolute condemnation of the racist regime [and] participation in all kinds of boycotts and sanctions against it."[18]

Not all Soviet interests are mentioned here, and the described real policy is interpreted as that of a passive observer. In this context, Gorbachev's assertion that "the Soviet Union does not have any special interests in the South of Africa" seems untrue.[19] The term "special" may refer to the long-known Soviet refusal to draw unjust benefits from the situation there.[20] Alternatively, it may also be understood as a negation of any interests worthy of note. This would be misleading, as it would make it appear as though the USSR is spending billions of rubles (which are badly needed at home) for purely philanthropic reasons. Frankly, no one believes this. In practice, the USSR has not been a passive observer in southern Africa. It has been actively engaged in the conflict there, rendering help to the frontline states and to national liberation movements at considerable material and political cost. If such a policy exists when interests are officially nonexistent, then the situation provokes at best bewilderment both at home and abroad and at worst a wish to interpret it in the worst light for the USSR. The long-delayed official and positive declaration of these interests would easily eliminate all doubts.

The USSR remains committed to support for the peoples who struggle for independence and sovereignty. Such an interest may not always be as diametrically opposed to the interests of the West as it has often been considered to be. This is even more true now that the anticolonial (although not the antiapartheid) struggle is over.

New Soviet political thinking—although not ignoring the differences that may occur among states in the international arena, as distinct from ideological differences—suggests the possibility of a more enlightened vision of the Third World. It is time to recognize, for instance, that nationalism may well be the principal ideology in the majority of developing nations, thus making a contest for gaining Eastern and Western ideological allies counterproductive. It is also true that the development of capitalist relations may often be more historically justified and, thus, progressive in these countries than artificially and prematurely imposed pseudo-Socialist models, which only discredit real socialism. This way of thinking, instead of combating capitalism, focuses the task of encouraging its development in more civilized, democratic, and moral forms rather than reactionary forms, such as apartheid.

It is this policy that will best serve the real national interests of the Soviet Union. Such a policy will encompass the tasks of preserving and developing its positions in southern Africa. First, it will be a means of participating in regional settlements in order to achieve for the region as democratic a form of government as is possible. Second, it will ensure the USSR's diplomatic influence in the world and protect its regional economic interests, including the billions of rubles it has already invested.

But the main national interest of the USSR now seems to be a nonapartheid regime in the Republic of South Africa—a democratic, nonracial, and stable government with which the Soviet Union will be able to establish mutually advantageous diplomatic and economic relations without harming the rest of its foreign policy interests. This embraces a sensible view of the white community's legitimate interests in and real contributions to South Africa's development. It also embraces the need for securing a fair place in the country's future for the black majority and all political forces, including the ANC and SACP.

Continued unilateral actions by the two superpowers along previous lines will only be counterproductive to the achievement of the ends they may share. Soviet concentration only on support of the ANC ignores the role of other political forces in the region. U.S. concentration on the survival of the Pretoria regime prevents its accommodation of other interests. Furthermore, the monopoly of Soviet support for the ANC could lead the movement to orient itself toward complete and uncompromising victory. Such a goal might give rise to dogmatism and scare away both white and black citizens. Meanwhile, the USSR has taken a passive position toward the rest of the country's opposition forces and toward the government itself. This paradox should be overcome (and is presently being overcome), for it delays the resolution of conflict.

Given the coincidence of some Soviet and U.S. interests in the region and the fact that unilateral moves would be too risky and would be beyond the capacity of each side, the USSR and the United States may be expected to find a common ground to jointly guarantee South Africa the four points outlined previously. This line of action seems to be the optimum way of securing their own interests as well as the most favorable settlement possible in southern Africa. It does not preclude unilateral diplomacy by each power with respect to the Republic of South Africa. Such cooperation would also help the two countries overcome the diplomatic failure their previous unilateral actions helped to produce.

It may well be that the situation in South Africa has not evolved enough for negotiations to occur. Estimates in 1986–1987 by leaders of the ANC and SACP, as well as some Western observers (the Commonwealth Eminent Persons Group, for example), indicated that the South African government was not yet ready to negotiate the future of apartheid in a serious manner.[21] Although right-wing resistance is a powerful reason for this stance, feelings of uncertainty and insecurity in the white minority are also important reasons. The suggested four-points program is aimed at dispelling this feeling. Simultaneously, the ANC also sees the negotiated solution as unreliable, for it doubts whether Pretoria will be sincere and whether its own influence in the country is strong enough to compel change. The four points may also prove helpful in dissipating these doubts, as the international guarantees would also help the opposition.

It should also be noted that negotiations have been held on South Africa since 1985. These have been informal talks, but they have been a necessary preliminary stage in such a delicate situation. As far as practical results are concerned, one sees not only burgeoning informal contacts but also a real change of positions. For instance, the declaration of principles for negotiations by the OAU and ANC, dated August 21, 1989, reads: "We believe that a conjuncture of circumstances exists which, if there is a demonstrable readiness on the part of the Pretoria regime to engage in negotiations genuinely and seriously, could create the possibility to end apartheid through negotiations."[22] This is a sharp contrast to the ANC position of 1987 and provides a real platform for discussion with the de Klerk government.

However, even if commonsense arguments do not prevail and any real negotiations on apartheid are doomed to be preceded by a bloody probe of forces, Soviet-U.S. cooperation will at least encourage all sides to move to the negotiating table, limit the contest, and save the USSR, the United States, and the southern African peoples from becoming involved in a senseless but dangerous rivalry in the region. Such cooperation should allow all parties to rid themselves of extremist views on which it is impossible to build anything worthwhile.

NOTES

1. *Materialy XXVII s'ezda KPSS* [Materials of the 27th Communist Party of the Soviet Union Congress] (Moscow: Politizdat, 1988), p. 64; Mikhail Gorbachev, *Perestroika and New Thinking for Our Country and for the Whole World* (Moscow: Politizdat, 1987), p. 145.
2. *Pravda*, December 8, 1988.
3. *SSSR i strany Afriki: Dokumenty i Materialy* [The USSR and African Countries: Documents and Materials, 1971–1976, Part 2] (Moscow: Politizdat, 1985), p. 8.
4. Rene Lemarchand (ed.), *American Policy in Southern Africa: The Stakes and the Stance* (Washington, D.C.: University Press of America, 1978), pp. 75, 79.
5. John A. Marcum, "Lessons of Angola," *Foreign Affairs* 54, no. 3 (April 1976):414.
6. John Stockwell, *In Search of Enemies: A CIA Story* (New York: W. W. Norton and Co., 1978), p. 193.
7. Wayne S. Smith, "A Trap in Angola," *Foreign Policy* 62 (Spring 1986):68.
8. Nathaniel Davis, "The Angola Decision of 1975: A Personal Memoir," *Foreign Affairs* 57, no. 1 (Fall 1978):123–124. See also Stockwell, *In Search of Enemies*, p. 43; William Colby and P. Forbath, *Honorable Men: My Life in the CIA* (New York: Simon and Schuster, 1978), pp. 439–440; Aaron Latham, "The Pike Papers," *Village Voice* 21, 7 (February 16, 1976):85; Roger Morris, "The Proxy War in Angola:

Pathology of a Blunder," *The New Republic* (January 1976):21; Marcum, "Lessons of Angola," p. 414.

9. *Materialy XXV s'ezda KPSS* [Materials of the 25th CPSU Congress] (Moscow: Politizdat, 1977), p. 13; *SSSR i strany Afriki*, pp. 149, 228.

10. "The United States and Angola: A Chronology," *Department of State Bulletin* 89 (February 1989):17.

11. John A. Marcum, "Africa: A Continent Adrift," *Foreign Affairs* 68, no. 1 (1988–1989):161.

12. "Foreign Policy and National Security," Address by Henry Kissinger, Dallas, Texas, March 22, 1976, *Department of State Bulletin* 74 (April 12, 1976):464.

13. *NATO's Fifteen Nations* 23, no. 3 (1978):35.

14. Statement of Cyrus Vance, June 19, 1978. Subcommittee on International Relations (Washington, D.C.: Department of State Press, June 19, 1978), p. 5.

15. *Pravda*, March 31, 1977.

16. *Pravda*, December 8, 1988.

17. "Southern Africa: Toward an American Consensus," Address by George Shultz before the National Press Club, April 16, 1985, *Department of State Bulletin* 85 (June 1985):22.

18. See, for example, *Aktualnye Problemy otnosheniy SSSR so stranami Afriki* [Urgent Problems of the Relationship Between the USSR and African Countries] (Moscow: Mezhdunarodniye Otnosheniya Publisheres, 1985), p. 6.

19. Gorbachev, *Perestroika and New Thinking*, p. 196.

20. At the 25th Congress and on many other occasions, it was stated: "Our party supports and will support the peoples fighting for their freedom. By doing so the Soviet Union does not seek any advantages for itself, does not hunt for concessions, does not try to gain political domination, does not solicit military bases. We are acting as our revolutionary conscience, our communist convictions, demand." *Materialy XXV s'ezda KPSS*, p. 12. This sounded right, but, as opposed to the issue of what the USSR does not want, it left open the question of what it does want.

21. See "Statement of the National Executive Committee of the African National Congress on the Question of Negotiations." (Lusaka: African National Congress, October 9, 1987).

22. "Declaration of the OAU Ad-Hoc Committee on Southern Africa on the Question of South Africa." (Harare, Zimbabwe: Organization of African Unity, August 21, 1989), p. 2.

ABOUT THE BOOK AND EDITORS

African states have been on the periphery of world politics since independence; they will likely continue to be marginalized as cold-war tensions abate and economic and political ties to the industrialized world weaken. At the same time, however, international attention has been increasingly focused on issues that are vital to Africa—economic reform, human rights, environmental degradation, refugees, AIDS, and democratization—and major powers and multilateral agencies such as the World Bank and the IMF have been insistent that African countries address them effectively.

Africa in World Politics explores the region's changing position in international relations. In the first section contributors address the colonial heritage and other economic, historical, and cultural factors that have shaped the continent's position in international affairs and the world economy. The second section examines several of the region's most intense conflicts, including those in southern Africa and the Horn. Next, contributors focus on the evolution of African relations with other regions and powers: Europe, the Middle East, the United States, and the Soviet Union. A concluding section explores patterns of intra-Africa conflict and cooperation, including prospects for regional integration and the role of the superpowers in mediating conflict.

John W. Harbeson is professor of political science in the Graduate School and at City College of the City University of New York. **Donald Rothchild** is professor of political science at the University of California–Davis.

ABOUT THE CONTRIBUTORS

Thomas M. Callaghy is associate professor of political science at the University of Pennsylvania. He has written *The State-Society Struggle: Zaire in Comparative Perspective* (1984). His current work centers on the politics of economic reform in the Third World. As part of a six-person team he has contributed to *Fragile Coalitions: The Politics of Economic Adjustment* (1989) and *Economic Crisis and Policy Choice: The Politics of Development in the Third World* (1990), both edited by Joan Nelson. He is a contributor to and coeditor with John Ravenhill of *Hemmed In: Responses to Africa's Economic Decline* (forthcoming).

Naomi Chazan heads the Harry S Truman Institute and is professor of political science and African studies at the Hebrew University of Jerusalem. She is coeditor with Donald Rothchild of *The Precarious Balance: State and Society in Africa* (Westview, 1988). She has coauthored *Politics and Society in Contemporary Africa* (1988) and has written *An Anatomy of Ghanaian Politics: Coping with Uncertainty* (1983).

Kenneth W. Grundy is Marcus A. Hanna Professor of Political Science at Case Western Reserve University. His books include *Confrontation and Accommodation in Southern Africa* (1973), *Soldiers Without Politics* (1983), *The Militarization of South African Politics* (1986, 1988), and *South Africa: Domestic Conflict and International Crisis* (Westview, 1991).

John W. Harbeson is professor of political science in the Graduate School and at City College of the City University of New York. His books include *The Ethiopian Transformation: The Quest for the Post-Imperial State* (Westview, 1988), *The Military in African Politics* (1987) (editor), and *Nation Building in Kenya: The Role of Land Reform* (1973).

Jeffrey Herbst is assistant professor of politics in the Woodrow Wilson School at Princeton. He has written *State Politics in Zimbabwe* (1989) and *Politics in Ghana* (forthcoming).

Carol Lancaster is assistant professor of political science in the School of Foreign Service at Georgetown University and visiting fellow at the Institute of International Economics. She is in the process of writing *Foreign Aid, Development, and Africa* (forthcoming).

René Lemarchand is professor of political science at the University of Florida. He is the editor of *The Greens and the Blacks: Qadhafi's Policies in Africa* (1988).

His *Rwanda and Burundi* (1970) received the African Studies Association's Melville Herskovits award in 1971.

Victor T. LeVine is professor of political science at Washington University in St. Louis. His recent works include *Political Corruption*, coauthored with A. Heidenheimer and C. Johnston (1989), and *The Arab-African Connection* (1983).

Ali A. Mazrui is Albert Schweitzer Professor in the Humanities and director of the Institute of Global Cultural Studies at the State University of New York at Binghampton. He has written *Towards a Pax Africana* (1967), *Africa's International Relations* (1977), *Nationalism and New States in Africa* (1984), and *Cultural Forces in World Politics* (1990).

Marina Ottaway is associate professor in the School of International Service at the American University in Washington, D.C. Her books include *Afrocommunism* (1981), coauthored with David Ottaway, and *Soviet and American Influence in the Horn of Africa* (1982).

John Ravenhill is Senior Fellow in the Department of International Politics in the Research School of Pacific Studies at the Australian National University. He is the author of *Collective Clientelism* (1985) and editor of *Africa in Economic Crisis* (1986).

Donald Rothchild is professor of political science at the University of California at Davis. His books include *Racial Bargaining in Independent Kenya* (1973) and *Scarcity, Choice, and Public Policy in Middle Africa* (1978). He is coauthor of *Politics and Society in Contemporary Africa* (1988) and coeditor of *Eagle in a New World: American Grand Strategy in the Post–Cold War Era* (1991).

Vitaley Vasilkov is a researcher at the Institute of the USA and Canada of the Soviet Academy of Sciences, where he works on U.S. policy in the Third World, especially southern Africa. His publications include *U.S. Foreign Policy Strategy in South Africa* (1989) and *Typology of U.S. Treaty Relationships with Developing Countries* (1989).

Crawford Young is Rupert Emerson Professor of Political Science at the University of Wisconsin at Madison. His books include *Ideology and Development in Africa* (1982); *The Politics of Cultural Pluralism* (1976), which won the African Studies Association's Melville Herskovits award in 1977; *Politics in the Congo* (1965); and *The Rise and Decline of the Zairian State* (1985), coauthored with Thomas Turner.

I. William Zartman is professor and director of African studies at the Nitze School of Advanced International Studies of Johns Hopkins University. His several works on negotiations and on African international relations include *International Relations of the New Africa* (1986) and *Ripe for Resolution: Conflict and Intervention in Africa* (1985, 1989).

INDEX